ALGORITHMS FOR
GRAPHICS AND
IMAGE PROCESSING

BOOKS OF INTEREST

Ahmad and Fung
Introduction to Computer Design and Implementation

Andrews
Principles of Firmware Engineering in Microprogram Control

Arsenault and Roberts
Reliability and Maintainability of Electronic Systems

Baer
Computer Systems Architecture

Breuer (ed)
Digital System Design Automation: Languages, Simulation, and Data Base

Breuer and Friedman
Diagnosis and Reliable Design of Digital Systems

Calingaert
Assemblers, Compilers, and Program Translation

Even
Graph Algorithms

Horowitz and Sahni
Fundamentals of Computer Algorithms

Horowitz and Sahni
Fundamentals of Data Structures

Pohl and Shaw
The Nature of Computation: An Introduction to Computer Science

Roth
Computer Logic, Testing, and Verification

Tomek
Introduction to Computer Organization

Ullman
Principles of Database Systems

ALGORITHMS FOR GRAPHICS AND IMAGE PROCESSING

THEO PAVLIDIS
Bell Laboratories

COMPUTER SCIENCE PRESS

Computer Science Press
11 Taft Court
Rockville, MD 20850 U.S.A.

2 3 4 5 6   87 86 85 84 83

Library of Congress Cataloging in Publication Data
Pavlidis, Theodosios.
  Algorithms for Graphics and Image Processing

  Includes bibliographical references and index.
  1. Computer Graphics.   2. Image processing.
3. pattern recognition systems.   4. algorithms.
I. Title.
T385.P38   001.55   81-9832
ISBN 0-914894-65-X   AACR2

PREFACE

The technological developments of the last ten years have made computer graphics and image processing by computer popular. Pictorial pattern recognition has also shown significant progress. Clearly, there exist overlapping interests among the three areas of research. Graphic displays are of concern to anyone involved in image processing or pictorial pattern recognition and many problems in graphics require methodologies from image processing for their solutions. The data structures used in all three areas are similar. It seems that there is a common body of knowledge underlying all three areas, *pictorial information processing by computer*.

The novelty of these fields makes it difficult to design a course or to a write a book covering their basic concepts. Some of the treatises on graphics focus on the hardware and methods of current interest while treatises on image processing often emphasize applications and classical signal processing. The fast evolution of technology causes such material to lose its relevance. For example, the development of optical fibers has reduced the importance of bandwidth compression. Similarly, the reduction in price of raster graphics devices has caused a major shift in emphasis in the graphics field. It is important for an introductory course to concentrate on the material that is expected to be relevant in the long run. The mathematical tools used in pictorial information processing seem to be of a more permanent nature and therefore I chose to emphasize those. By the same token I have de-emphasized topics where the analytical tools must be supplemented with heuristics or perceptual considerations. For example, shape analysis is treated in only two sections, even though the subject is of great interest to me and has been my major research area. On the other hand, thinning algorithms have a well defined objective and they can be the "workhorse" for many pattern recognition schemes. I hope that the reader is not left with the impression that thinning is in the core of shape analysis. Similarly, the emphasis on the mathematical tools does not imply that this is all that one needs for designing a good pictorial information system. Familiarity with computer engineering, the fundamentals of human visual perception, and some understanding of the visual arts are also essential.

Most of the material of this book has been used twice in a course I taught at Princeton University, in 1978 and in 1980. The audience consisted primarily of seniors or juniors in computer science. In addition, some sophomores and graduate students, as well as students in engineering and the mathematical and physical sciences, took the course. On the whole, they had a strong background in computers and all were experienced programmers. Therefore no effort was made to introduce simple computer science concepts. The course was supplemented by a laboratory, lectures by guest lecturers, and field trips, in order to bring the current state of the art to the students' attention. Within the text, I have tried to keep specific applications and heuristics to a minimum.

A special challenge facing the developer of such a course is the dependence of pictorial information processing on a broad mathematical and computational background. Calculus, elementary statistics, elementary graph theory, geometry, signal processing, data structures, analysis of algorithms, and programming are all required. It is unfortunate that early specialization by students makes acquiring such background difficult. This not only introduces difficulties in the design of a course but also has been a real impediment to the progress of research in the field. For example, image segmentation requires some expertise in both stochastic signal processing and data structures and algorithms. Today's curricula rarely provide the opportunity for a student to acquire both.

The text is organized as follows: Chapter 1 is the introduction describing the forms of pictorial data. Four such forms are identified, roughly corresponding to gray scale (class 1), bilevel or binary (class 2), curves (class 3), and points or polygons (class 4). Chapters 2 to 4 deal with gray scale images and emphasize transforms and statistical techniques. Chapter 5 is an introduction to the reconstruction techniques used in computerized tomography. A first course on signal processing is a prerequisite for understanding these four chapters, all dealing with class 1 images. The rest of the text does not depend on that background. Chapter 6 discusses data structures for pictorial data, while the subject of Chapters 7 to 9 is processing bilevel images and topics such as contour tracing, contour filling, and thinning. All the algorithms presented in these three chapters are in essence graph traversal algorithms. Familiarity with graph terminology is assumed. Chapters 10 to 13 are on curve and surface fitting. Although formally they depend only on a knowledge of simple calculus, some mathematical maturity is helpful. Chapters 14 to 17 are on the generation of graphic displays and the underlying methods are those of linear algebra. They deal primarily with class 4 images.

Some of the chapters include more material than that needed for a basic course. This is particularly true for Chapters 8, 9, 10, 11, and 15 where I have included additional basic algorithms that are useful to practitioners of the art. For a one semester course it is best to stay with one algorithm for each of contour filling, thinning, or polygon clipping. In particular, one may select the simplest algorithms, 8.4, 9.4, and 15.2. For such a course it is probably enough to cover only Bezier polynomials, or only splines, or only splines with uniform knot distribution. (A minimal introduction to curve fitting could cover only Sections 10.1, 10.2, 11.1 to 11.3, 11.6 and 11.7, and 10.8, in that order.)

If the scope of the course is more limited than the scope of the text, then some chapters could be ignored altogether. A course with emphasis in graphics could cover only Chapters 1, 6 to 8, 10, 11, and 13 to 17. A course emphasizing image processing could cover only Chapters 1 to 7 and 9. Chapters 4, 9, and 12 are particularly relevant for pictorial pattern recognition.

The writing of this text was completed over a period of three and a half years starting in late 1977 and was carried out in three places: Princeton University, University of California at Berkeley, and since June 1980 at Bell Telephone Laboratories in Murray Hill, New Jersey. A first draft was completed early in 1980 and was used as a text for the course during the spring semester at Princeton. An extensive revision was completed during the winter of 1980-81.

I was fortunate to receive the help of many individuals who were kind enough to take the time to read carefully various versions of the manuscript. Doug McIlroy contributed many comments on both the technical content and the form of the manuscript. His suggestions included more elegant proofs for a number of the propositions and theorems. Carolyn M. Bjorklund, Lorinda L. Cherry, Chris Van Wyk, and Li-de Wu made many constructive suggestions on the whole text. The parts dealing with curve fitting were improved as a result of suggestions by Carl de Boor. Larry Shepp provided me with comments on the parts dealing with reconstruction techniques. The following also helped by finding errors and making a number of constructive suggestions: Larry S. Davis, Kenneth Fasman, Stein Grinaker, R. Hilbert, Christopher Larson, and Murray Loew. It was a pleasant surprise to have the copy editor Carolyn Ormes catch my mistakes not only in the language, but also in the mathematical formulas.

The matrices of Figure 3.8 were computed by P. C. Chen. Most of the pictures used in the examples of Chapters 1 to 5 were given to me by John F. Jarvis and he also provided me with laboratory facilities for producing hard copies of the computer displays. I am grateful for the originals provided to me by Dr. Stanley S. Siegelman for Figure 5.1, Ken Knowlton for Figure 6.8, Turner Whitted for Figure 17.1, and David M. Weimer for Figure 17.2.

The manuscript and the final text were prepared using the various software facilities of the the UNIX† operating system at Princeton and at Bell Laboratories. The text was checked for errors using the programs *spell, diction*, and *style* by Lorinda L. Cherry. The final copy was produced by using the formatting programs *tbl, eqn*, and *troff*. Figures 10.8, 11.4, 11.9, 12.1, 12.7, 12.8, and the front cover were produced by using the *pic* language by Brian W. Kernighan. (The smooth curves on the cover figure were formed using B-splines of the type described in Section 11.7.) Figures 15.1 and 17.7 were produced using the *ideal* language by Chris van Wyk. Figure 10.1 was produced by a general purpose plotting routine running on the phototypesetter.

Last, but not least, I want to thank my wife Marion and my children Paul, Karen, and Harry for their patience and understanding while I was pre-occupied with the writing of the book. Very often their help was more direct: Marion entered in UNIX a large part of the text which was originally written in longhand and Paul pointed out the shading rules used by artists (Section 13.10).

Theo Pavlidis

Murray Hill, New Jersey
September 30, 1981

---

† UNIX is a Trademark of Bell Laboratories.

TABLE OF CONTENTS

For Paul, Karen, and Harry

Chapter 1

INTRODUCTION

1.1 GRAPHICS, IMAGE PROCESSING, AND PATTERN RECOGNITION

Processing of pictorial data by computer takes different forms in a variety of applications. It has been customary to classify such work into three areas: *graphics, image processing,* and *pictorial pattern recognition.*

Graphics deals with the generation of images from nonpictorial information and covers diverse applications. The complexity of the programs as well as the computational effort required to produce displays varies significantly, depending on the task.† Examples of displays, in order of increasing complexity, include production of plots of functions or of experimental data, composition of displays for the increasingly common computer games, and production of the scenes used in flight simulators. Note that while the plots are static with time, the game displays change with time, and the simulator scenes not only change with time, but must also create the illusion of depth. Computer art and animation are two applications of graphics that require not only technical expertise but also other talents. Currently, these seem to be the areas of fastest growth. The term *interactive graphics* refers to devices and systems that accept input from the user expressed in terms of

---

† The reader should not confuse the complexity of the program with what is often called computational complexity, the computational effort required for its execution. See Section 1.12 for more on the subject.

the display they create: for example asking to draw a line between two points on the screen that the user points to.

Image processing deals with problems in which both input and output are pictures. Image transmission systems, where one is concerned with noise removal and data compaction, is one example. Overexposed or underexposed or blurred pictures can be improved with contrast enhancement techniques. Sometimes it is desirable to apply more drastic transformations. An image with a wide range of illumination may be reduced into an image where one sees only two levels of illumination. The resulting silhouettes may be reduced further into stick type figures. Other times we may even create a new image from a set of others, such as constructing images of cross-sections of the human body from lateral x-ray pictures.

Pictorial pattern recognition deals with methods for producing either a description of the input picture or an assignment of the picture to a particular class. In a sense, pattern recognition is the inverse problem of computer graphics. It starts with a picture and transforms it into an abstract description: a set of numbers, a string of symbols, or a graph. Further processing of these forms results in assigning the original picture to one of several classes. An automatic mail sorter that examines the postal code written on an envelope and identifies the digits is a typical example of an application. Automated medical diagnosis requires the detection of certain anomalies on radiographs or other medical images.

Figure 1.1 summarizes the differences and the similarities among the three fields. While each of them has at least a twenty year history, it is only recently that the similarities among them have been emphasized. The connection between pattern recognition and image processing was realized first because it is possible to transform an image in such a way that the classification problem becomes easier. The realization of the connection between these two areas and computer graphics is more recent. One class of problems of obvious common interest is the internal representation of pictures in a computer: data structures, storage and retrieval, compaction, etc. The common ground is less obvious in some other problems. For example, image processing deals often with *contour tracing* while an equally common problem in graphics is *contour filling*. Since one operation is the inverse of the other, it is not surprising that certain theoretical questions are common to both areas.

The following example describes an application where the integration among the three areas is complete.

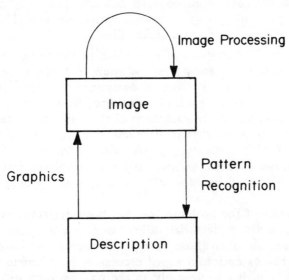

Figure 1.1   Diagram illustrating the relation between graphics, image processing, and pattern recognition

Example 1.1:   A problem of practical interest is the transmission of images of documents over communication links. In order to have a good reproduction of the form of an alphanumeric character, one must digitize each such symbol in a matrix of at least 20 rows and 15 columns (this includes some of the surrounding blank space). Faithful reproduction of font (e.g., italic, bold, etc.) requires much higher resolution. The matrix can be binary, so that one must send at least 300 bits per character. Image processing is concerned with transformations that will map this matrix into fewer than 300 bits while the application of the inverse transformation at the receiver will produce the original image, or at least a good approximation of it. Such known transformations can reduce the number of required bits by a factor of six at most. Suppose, on the other hand, that one performs pattern recognition and for each character identifies its name, which is then sent to the receiver. Eight bits are usually enough for the description of the name; therefore, the amount of data to be transmitted has been reduced by a factor of almost 40. Of course, the receiver must reconstruct the images of the characters, which is a simple problem in graphics. We may also point out that a character can be displayed by a smaller matrix: ten rows and seven columns are usually enough. In this way one can achieve a "permanent" data compaction. The problem becomes more challenging if the text is mixed with pictures. Then one must switch between different modes of encoding. Reference [1.PC] describes in detail a system based on this principle. □

Example 1.1 illustrates a case in which image processing, graphics, and pattern recognition are necessary. Such applications become more and more numerous as the cost of computing and that of peripheral devices keeps decreasing. Each of these three fields is broad enough so that it is not possible to cover all three of them in a single text. Instead, we shall concentrate on shared problems and those questions that are fundamental to the processing of pictorial information. We will not deal with hardware questions, not only because of the fast changes in technology, but also because of our emphasis on algorithms and methods.

One aspect of the problem that has been neglected in the past is the peculiar nature of pictorial information, which requires different methods of analysis than those used for acoustical and electrical signal processing. The extension of signal processing from one to two dimensions is nontrivial. It also depends on the physical interpretation of the dimensions. Thus a signal depending on time and a space variable requires different processing than a signal depending on two space variables. The mathematical similarity between the forms can be misleading.

1.2 FORMS OF PICTORIAL DATA

It is convenient to distinguish four classes of images when we talk about their processing by computer. The classification has less to do with the real visual perception of the images than with the way they are represented and processed.

1.2.1 Class 1: Full Gray Scale and Color Pictures

Class 1 is the form of usual television pictures. Such images present a close representation of "reality." The pictures are represented as matrices with integer elements for which the terms *picture element, pixel,* or *pel,* are commonly used. In most applications these matrices tend to be quite large: 512×512 is a fairly common size. For this reason they are not always stored as simple matrices, and more elaborate data structures are frequently used. We shall discuss those in Chapter 6. Color pictures can be represented either as three matrices (for red, green, and blue), or as one matrix where different bits of each element correspond to different colors. Usually, the human eye cannot distinguish levels of illumination that differ by less than one percent, so that a byte per color per pixel is enough. However, one can obtain reasonable results using three bits for two of the colors and two for the third, so that the image may be stored using only one byte per pixel. We shall discuss this point in more detail in Section 2.5. Sometimes it is mathematically convenient to think of color pictures as matrices of three-dimensional vectors.

1.2.2 Class 2: Bilevel or "Few Color" pictures

A display of a page of text is a typical class 2 or bilevel† (black and white) picture. Such pictures can be represented as matrices with one bit per element but also as "maps," since they contain well defined regions of uniform color. This is the reason that we group pictures of "few colors" and bilevel together, even though the bit matrix representation is good only for the latter. One problem with using one bit per pixel is that there is no standard way among the various computers and display devices for packing bits into a byte and bytes into a word. Thus, the leftmost pixel may be packed into the least significant bit of a byte or into the most significant. Therefore, users must always check the form valid for the devices they use. We shall describe later how maps can be represented in a computer. Notice that the distinction between many and few color pictures is not clear and becomes relevant only in terms of the form we are using to represent the images.

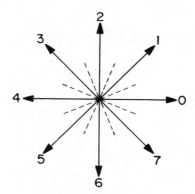

Figure 1.2 Definition of the basic chain code. The broken lines delineate the set of directions which are assigned to a particular element of the code.

---

† We prefer the term "bilevel" to "binary" although both are used in the literature. The word "binary" has an association with computers and digital devices and some people are puzzled when they see it used for analog signals.

1.2.3 Class 3: Continuous Curves and Lines

Contours of regions and waveforms or charts (graphs) are examples of class 3 images. The data are *sequences of points* that can be represented by their x-y coordinates. However, this method is rather inefficient and the same is true for a representation using the differences $\Delta x, \Delta y$ in the coordinates between successive points. More efficient representations are offered by *chain codes* in which the vector joining two successive points is assigned one symbol from among a finite set. Figure 1.2 shows a common chain code using eight directions. If the points are sufficiently close to each other, then the error introduced by the quantization can be acceptable. If the points were chosen from among adjacent elements of an image matrix (along rows, columns, or diagonals), then representing them by their differences in their matrix indices will require four bits per point (to represent the values −1, 0, and +1 for each coordinate) while the chain code requires only three bits per point.

An even more efficient form is offered by the *differential chain code* where each point is represented by the difference between two successive absolute codes. We still have eight values (0, ±1, ±2, ±3, and 4), but their occurrence is not equally likely. For smooth curves we expect the values 0 and ±1 to occur more frequently than all the others, while the value 4 will be extremely rare. Then we can use a *variable length code* to represent each direction. Table 1.1 shows one possible assignment.

Table 1.1: Variable Length Encoding for Differential Chain Code

Direction	Code
0	0
+1	01
−1	011
+2	0111
−2	01111
+3	011111
−3	0111111
4	01111111

Such an encoding usually requires no more than two bits per point on the average. Tests by the author on a variety of data showed average values of 1.8 to 1.9 bits for alphanumeric characters and 1.5 to 1.9 bits for outlines of objects such as a stemmed drinking glass or a bolt. A small circle, which represents an unfavorable case, required 2.3 bits per pixel. Whether a chain code representation is desirable for curve manipulation depends on the application, but the conversion to x-y coordinates and vice versa is simple (see Problem 1.4).

1.2.4 Class 4: Points or Polygons

Class 4 images consist of sets of discrete points which are spaced far apart so that they cannot be represented by a chain code. Instead, one must use an array of their x-y coordinates. The points may be joined by straight lines or other simple curves using the display hardware. Again, the distinction between this class and the previous class is not clear and becomes meaningful only when we consider the form of representation. One may still use chain codes of more than one element for points far apart, and the choice between the two forms of representation must be made on the basis of the statistical distribution of the distance between points. Indeed, let l be the average, and L the maximum length between points. Then a variable length chain code will require about $2l$ bits per point. A $\Delta x, \Delta y$ form will require $2\log_2(L)$. If the variations in length between points are small, then L will not be much larger than l, and the description by coordinate differences will be more efficient.

Images of this type are the ones most often used in graphics applications. Although the display may be a class 2, or even a class 1 image, the internal representation of the image is class 4. This is particularly true when we examine the descriptions of three-dimensional objects that are projected on the screen plane in order to form the display image. Most applications use one of the following forms:

(a) Polyhedral approximations of the surface. The faces are usually triangles. When projected, the image consists of polygons. (b) Curvilinear approximations of the surface. A set of curves is drawn on the surface of the solid, and their descriptions are then used for the projections, which appear as class 3 images. (c) Higher order surface patches. These are similar to the first type, but instead of plane polygons, the elements forming the surface of the object are patches from a higher order surface.

In all cases there is a small number of points which specify the position of the object so that class 4 images are indeed of central interest in graphics.

1.3 PICTORIAL INPUT

An analog image must be converted into an array of numbers before it can be processed by a computer. The process is called *digitization* and involves two other processes: *sampling* and *quantization*. The first deals with the selection of a set of points over the field of observation. The characteristics of the image at each such point are measured and then used for all later processing. Since all computers have finite memory, one must describe these measurements by a finite number of digits in a process called quantization. One often talks about *spatial resolution* to refer to the density of the sample points, and *gray level* (or *color*) *resolution* to refer to the accuracy of the measurement representation. The selection of proper resolutions is discussed in Chapter 2, while here we give only a brief review of the hardware used and the basic software tools.

A television camera is used in many digitizers since it already performs the transformation from optical to electric signal. The signal can then be sampled and quantized by an *analog-to-digital* (A/D) converter. The only problem is the huge rate of data coming out of a standard camera. Commercial television transmits 30 frames a second, each of about 500 raster lines. If we want to use similar vertical and horizontal resolutions, then we must deal with about $30 \times 500 \times 500$ samples per second. A/D converters with capacities of 10 million samples per second are available, so that the problem is not so much one of technology as one of cost. Also, the large flow of data may overwhelm the supporting computer system. If real time processing is not necessary, then one can either modify the camera to a slower rate or use a bandwidth compressor. The simplest way to achieve this compression is to sample along vertical lines. One waits for a full raster scan (or more) before proceeding to the next line. The position of the vertical line is controlled by the computer, which moves the line after emptying the buffer into permanent storage. In this way a rate reduction around 500 to 1 can be obtained.

Special purpose digitizers use carefully controlled light beams that scan the image in a predetermined fashion. For *drum scanners* the image is mounted on a rotating drum, while the light beam moves in a direction parallel to the drum axis. Such digitizers are usually slower than those based on television cameras, but provide much better quality output. Both of these types produce class 1 images, although sometimes it is possible to produce class 2 images by using a coarse quantization. Another type of digitizer is the *flying spot scanner* which can scan the image row by row, or may be programmed to follow the contour between two areas of different intensity or color so that the output is a class 3 image. Finally, *tablet digitizers* provide a facility where one can trace a line drawing and obtain a digitized sequence of the coordinates of points traced. This result is achieved by placing the drawing over a magnetized surface and identifying points by an electric stylus or a cursor. The result is again a class 3 image.

Direct object digitization is necessary for certain graphics applications. It is usually done by special purpose devices with a pointer that follows the surface of an object while its coordinates are sampled. Another method uses two projections of the object which are digitized simultaneously using a tablet digitizer. Then the description of the three-dimensional object can be reconstructed from the two plane drawings, because a point in space is completely defined by its projections on two planes. A promising area for the interaction between pattern recognition/image processing and graphics is the automation of these processes. One could take different views of an object with a camera and then process the resulting images to obtain the object description. The process could be facilitated if one used, instead of light intensity images, *range* data. The latter are obtained when a laser, radio, or ultrasound beam is aimed at the object and the reflections received at various points are used to form an image. The reconstruction techniques discussed in Chapter 5 could also be used for this purpose.

The software needed for digitization of pictorial data is relatively simple and not particularly different from that used for any other digitization. Usually, a *read(device,buffer)* type of command will transfer data from the sampling device into the buffer array. The digitization program contains a loop with such a command and sampling is terminated either when a special interrupt signal occurs, or when a given number of data points have been collected (see Problem 1.1).

On the other hand, it is often convenient to have the input system incorporated into an *editor,* a program that allows the user to modify the entered data. For example, one may wish to select a subimage of the input or modify the location of a point of a digitized curve. Editors require an interactive graphic system and their complexity varies widely, depending on the options desired by the user. A simple editor can be written in a couple of days while some of the more elaborate packages represent many man-years of work. We shall discuss various aspects of editors in the appropriate parts of the text, starting with Section 1.9.

1.4 DISPLAY DEVICES

While digitizing is a rather straightforward process, the conversion of the data into pictorial form is far more complex, and a wide variety of devices is available. The reason for the complexity is that the input to the device need not be in the exact form of the display so that the device must do not only the digital to analog (D/A) conversion but also a certain amount of data processing. First, one must distinguish between *hard copy* and *cathode ray tube (CRT)* devices. For hard copy usually only one pass is made and therefore the input must be sorted to generate the appropriate commands in the proper order for the motion of the writing instrument. CRT displays do not have to follow a strict order of display but on the other hand there is a need to repeat the process so that the displayed image can be viewed for any length of time. *Phototypesetters* often combine the two processes in the sense that the image is created on a CRT and then photographed to create the hard copy.

Modern CRT devices contain a microprocessor and a memory buffer. The host computer loads the pictorial information into the buffer, and then the microprocessor scans the buffer and displays the data as often as is necessary to create a visual impression. If the device is not connected to another computer (i.e., if it "stands alone"), then the buffer is filled by whatever input means are available. In either case, the contents of the buffer are instructions to the microprocessor. The most primitive form of instruction is $write(x,y,z)$ which positions the electron beam at point (x,y) of the screen to produce a bright spot with intensity or color proportional to z. For a monochrome display one needs at least three D/A converters: one for each of the x, y, and z values. For color displays the minimum number of D/A converters is five: two for the coordinates, and three for each of the colors (z is now a vector). The term *display file* is often used for referring to the contents of this buffer. This file is a program of the following general form:

> start:
>> $\cdots$
>>
>> instructions of the type $write(x,y,z)$.
>> $\cdots$
>>
>> if no interrupt has occurred, then go to start.
>
> end;

Usually the microprocessor performs certain transformations on the contents of the buffer so that the host computer (or the user in stand alone systems) does not have to be concerned with the details of the display and can prepare a display file with "higher level" commands. Hard copy devices may also contain a certain amount of computing power, but it is usually much less than that of CRTs.

Important as the difference between CRT and hard copy might be to the user, it is not very significant in terms of the conversion process, or the form of the display file. The major distinction is between *vector* and *raster graphics*. (Sometimes vector graphics are called "calligraphic".) As a matter of fact, some of the special preprocessing associated with hard copy devices has to do with the conversion from vector to raster representations and can be discussed best in this context. We review here the major characteristics of each type.

1.5 VECTOR GRAPHICS

Vector graphic devices produce class 3 (or 4) images. The primitive instructions are usually of the following type:

$p(x,y)$ position electron beam at point (x,y)
$s(z)$ set beam intensity to the value z.

To display an object, one must create a sequence of such instructions giving its form. The available device may have higher level instructions, each equivalent to a group of primitives needed for the creation of some common forms. This is typically the case with instructions for the display of alphanumeric characters. Now let S_1, S_2, $\cdots S_n$ be the sequences corresponding to each one of n objects forming a particular display. Then the program executed by the processor controlling the display is of the form:

```
start:
          S₁
          S₂
          . . .
          Sₙ
          if no interrupt, then go to start
end;
```

To modify the appearance of the ith object, one must modify only the corresponding sequence S_i. This can be the case, for example, when one object is moving in front of others. There is no need to tamper with any other sequence. There are many ways for implementing the updating; the simplest is to detect interrupts from the host processor or an input device.

```
start:
          S₁
          S₂
          ....
          Sₙ
          if an interrupt has occurred, then skip the next instruction
          go to start
          process input
          go to start
end;
```

Each time the loop is executed we say that the screen is *refreshed*. The *rate of refresh* is inversely proportional to the length of the loop. If the time between refreshings is long compared to the decay of the fluorescence of the material of the screen, then one will observe flickering or dimmer displays. Therefore, there is an upper bound on the length of the loop (and hence on the complexity of the display).

1.6 RASTER GRAPHICS

Raster graphics devices produce class 1 or 2 images, but they may also possess hardware which enables the user to simulate vector graphics. We shall use the term "raster graphics" for devices with this option and we shall call devices without vector display capacity "image displays." The major feature of raster graphics is a large memory with one location for each addressable screen location. The values of all pixels of an image are computed and stored in that memory, and then the display is generated by reading the memory and displaying the value of each location at the appropriate part of the screen. The names *frame buffer* or *refresh memory* (or combinations thereof) are used for this memory. The basic instruction of such a device is of the following form:

read (I, x, y, z) read memory location I and determine z from the contents of I. (x and y are determined from the address of I.) Then execute a *write* (x, y, z) instruction.

Then the major display loop will be:

```
start:
            For all memory locations I do:
                    begin
                    read (I,x,y,z)
                    write (x,y,z)
                    end
        go to start
end;
```

If N is the refresh memory size, then the display controller always executes N pairs of instructions. Most raster graphics devices use television monitors for output and it is necessary to execute the loop at least thirty times a second in order to produce an image without too much flicker. All devices contain more than one processor: the set of instructions doing the the display refreshing is performed by dedicated hardware and another processor handles the loading of the memory with the descriptions supplied by the host computer or the user. Thus, the length of the loop is fixed, and the quality of the display does not depend on its complexity. However, descriptions of objects intermingle. In vector graphics, in order to eliminate an object, all that one has to do is remove the corresponding sequence from the display loop. Things are not as simple in raster graphics. In particular, one cannot set the intensity of all pixels of an object to zero because this will also erase other objects overlapping with it. The solution to this problem is to introduce *partitions* of the memory and display each object on a separate partition.

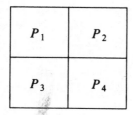

Figure 1.3 Partition of the memory of a display device. Each quarter maps onto the same screen.

There are two possible implementations. The first uses more than one copy of the screen on the memory. For the arrangement of Figure 1.3, parts P_1, P_2, P_3, and P_4 all address the same screen coordinates. Thus, the user may load the description of each one of four objects into a different part. The second uses *word partition*. For each memory location a certain number of bits are reserved for the description of a particular object. If the contents of the location determined uniquely the brightness and color of the respective screen location, then such a partition would force the color and intensity of each object. However, many raster graphic devices have an additional feature that removes this difficulty. The contents of location I are used to address a table whose contents then determine the color and brightness. The contents of such a *video lookup tables* are defined by the user and may change between displays. Thus, all objects may use the same color and intensity range.

Example 1.2: A device has 12 bits per word, a lookup table and three D/A converters, one for each basic color. The four lower bits out of the lookup table go to blue, the next four to green, and the last four to red. A simple form of the contents of the table is the *identity*: if the value of a location is n, the output of the table is also n. In this case if a memory location contains octal 17, the respective spot on the screen will be bright blue. Octal 360 will produce bright green, octal 7400 bright red, etc. We wish to display a scene as a background which is available with three bits per color plus two moving objects, whose descriptions are available with two bits per color. To create independent displays we must reserve certain bits from each word for the background and the objects and then we need $9 + 6 + 6 = 21$ bits, more than the available storage. One could display all of them together, but then, when an object moves, it will be necessary to restore the background image into the refresh memory. Or we could sacrifice some of the color range to achieve independent objects and background as follows: bits 0-5 of each location are reserved for the background (two bits per color). Bits 6-8 are used for the first object (one per color) and bits 9-11 for the second object. Now octal 1000 corresponds to the lowest bit of the second object that we may display pixels with that value in blue. Then the respective value of the lookup table may be octal 10. Octal 100 corresponds to the lowest bit of the first object and we map that also to octal 10, and so forth. The whole arrangement is shown in Figure 1.4. Note that we are not limited to bit by bit correspondence: the lookup table maps values might have chosen, for example, to map octal 100 and octal 1000 to octal 17, etc. This solution presumes that we can address selectively certain bits of each word in the refresh memory. This is indeed the case for most raster graphics devices (see Instruction 13 in Table 1.2). □

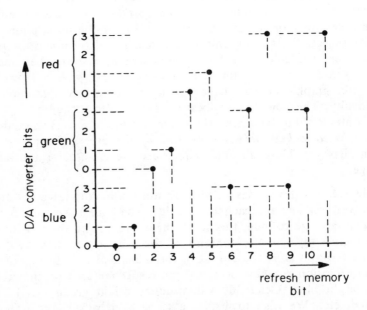

Figure 1.4 Map determining the relation between color and intensity and bits of a word of the refresh memory for Example 1.2

Table 1.2: Common Graphics Primitives

	Name	Function
1	$setp(x,y)$	Set the current point at coordinates (x,y).
2	$vec(x,y)$	Draw a vector from the current point to a point with coordinates (x,y), thus producing a class 3 or 4 picture.
3	$char(a)$	Display alphanumeric symbol "a" at current point.
4	$win(x,y,X,Y)$	Define a rectangular window area on the display device with upper left corner at (x,y) and lower right at (X,Y).
5	$fore(b)$	Set intensity or color for drawing vectors (foreground) to b.
6	$back(b)$	Set background intensity to b.
7	$wpic(buff)$	Display the contents of the buffer $buff$ at the defined window. Each element of the buffer generates a picture element, so that a class 1 picture is generated.
8	$wrast(buff)$	Same as the previous instruction, but each picture element corresponds to a bit of the buffer so that a class 2 picture is generated.
9	$rpic(buff)$	Read the image displayed on the window into the buffer $buff$.
10	$erase$	Set the area of the window to the background intensity.
11	$readp(x,y)$	Place into (x,y) the coordinates of the point of the display pointed to by the user.
12	$enable(u)$	Examine word u, and from now on allow all other instructions to modify only those bits in the refresh memory words which correspond to bits set to one in u.
13	$color(u,v)$	From now on when a word has the bit pattern of u display the color determined by v.

1.7 COMMON PRIMITIVE GRAPHIC INSTRUCTIONS

We mentioned above that the microprocessor controlling a display can do a certain amount of processing so that it is not necessary for the user to prepare display files in their most primitive form. Usually there is a wide repertory of instructions that are available. Because the emphasis of this text is on algorithms rather than devices, we shall use the term *primitive instructions* for them, and we shall ignore in the sequel any lower level instructions of the type discussed in the previous two sections. Table 1.2 contains a list of some primitive commands used in both types of devices with the abbreviations that will be used for them in this text. We use the term *current point* to denote the last point addressed on the display. The concept is useful for defining relative distances.

The arguments of instructions *setp* (1), *vec* (2), and *win* (4) can be either *absolute addresses* or *relative addresses* with respect to some preset values. Often these values are the coordinates of the current point. The exact form or name of an instruction depends on the particular device, but the ones given in the list are typical. Instructions *setp* (1) and *vec* (2) exist in all vector graphics devices, and many of them also contain instructions *char* (3) and *fore* (5). All are common in raster graphics. Instruction *readp* (11) is used in interactive graphics. It allows the user to point out a position on the display surface, either with a light-pen or a cursor which is controlled by a joystick, trackball, or other similar device.† The last two instructions are useful for establishing word partition in the memory of raster graphics, and for enabling the assignment of colors and intensities to bit patterns (recall Example 1.2).

Modern graphic displays often include other options, such as rotating an image, operating on pairs of images, etc. Strictly speaking, these are not display commands since they involve operations in memory. Although the technological trend is to assign more and more operations to the display devices, we shall assume here that only the primitive operations listed above are available and that operations that involve nontrivial algorithms must be supplied by the user. Since this text is addressed to engineers rather than to routine users of graphics equipment, such methods will be covered in detail.

1.8 COMPARISON OF VECTOR AND RASTER GRAPHICS

The major advantage of vector graphics is the separation between the object description and the screen. Therefore the resolution of such a system (i.e. the minimum distance between two points on the screen) is determined by the electronics of the hardware that is used to

---

† Since we decided not to describe hardware in detail we do not describe such devices here. There is a variety of them in the market and any graphics facility has one or more of them. It is possible that the development of touch-sensitive screens will make most such devices obsolete.

write on the screen. Thus 4096×4096 screen matrices are common.† In addition one may use the motion of the beam to draw a straight line between two points in an *analog* rather than digital mode.

On the other hand, raster graphics require one-to-one correspondence between screen pixels and refresh memory locations. Thus any increase in the resolution requires an increase in the memory size and currently, the maximum screen matrix available is 1024×1024. Straight lines can be displayed only in digital form and this, together with the limited resolution, results in a "staircase" like appearance.

Another disadvantage of raster graphics is that whether memory is partitioned along addresses or within words, the number of possible partitions is small, and therefore the number of objects that can be handled independently is small.

Raster graphics display class 1 or class 2 images without any difficulty. One need only place the appropriate values in the refresh memory. Is is impossible to display class 1 images in a vector graphics system without converting it in effect into a raster graphics system. Class 2 images may be displayed with some effort by drawing closely spaced parallel lines over the area of each region of a given color. (This method has been used to produce this text on a photo-typesetter.)

1.9 PICTORIAL EDITOR

Our discussion of pictorial input and output in the last two sections dealt only with the more primitive aspects of these operations. In most practical situations it is desirable to have more than a system that simply digitizes pictorial data. As we mentioned in Section 1.3 one would like to integrate the input operations into a *picture editor*. We use this term to denote a program which can be used to input and modify pictorial data in the same way that a *text editor* is used to input and modify text.* Such an editor also provides a convenient environment for implementing and testing various algorithms for pictorial information processing. In turn, the results of such efforts can be added to the editor to increase the options it offers to the user.†† From a practical

---

† The phototypesetter used to produce this text is a vector graphics device with an address range of about 0-8000.

* It is best to avoid the term *graphics editor* because it can have two meanings: One as an editor to input pictorial data, and another as a text editor using a graphics display.

†† For this reason such an editor is ideal as an ongoing laboratory project. Laboratory assignments are essential for the study of graphics and image processing and considerable work can be done with simple means. For example, Chapter 5 describes a fairly complex project using only a lineprinter as an output device. A great part of the effort goes into input and output procedures and integrating such projects into an editor makes sense.

viewpoint it is probably necessary to create two editors, an *image editor* for handling class 1 and 2 data and a *point editor* for handling class 3 and 4 data. We shall discuss point editors at the end of Chapter 10, while here we outline image editors. Essential parts of such a system are a digitizer; a display device; and a device for pointing to pixels, i.e., one implementing the instruction *readp*(x,y) of Table 1.2. It is probably best to do the selection of subimages by digital rather than analog means. Thus, the digitizer may output the data directly on the refresh memory of the display device. Then the user selects a window on the screen and uses a *rpic*(*buff*) (read image into buffer) instruction to save the appropriate subimage.

The basic structure of any editor consists of a loop which is executed repeatedly. The first step of the loop usually produces a prompt sign for the user who is then expected to supply a character string describing the desired operation. Then the program examines the string† and calls an appropriate subroutine. Sometimes, it is convenient to use a *menu* in a graphic display in order to identify the command. The user points to an area of the screen instead of typing a command. Figure 1.5 shows how the display for a simple editor might look. The left part of the screen is reserved for image display, while the right part lists the menu commands. We assume that the user has the means of moving two cursors over the screen, and a way of signaling the system to read the cursor position. (The *readp*(x,y) instruction.) The bottom part of the display lists a set of file names.

The following mode of operation is typical. The user brings the first cursor to the menu area and signals the system to execute a *readp*(x,y) instruction. Then the program checks the (x,y) values against a list in order to choose the required action. The commands "READ TAPE" and "DIGITIZE" cause the program either to read a file from a tape or to collect data through its digitizer. In both cases the resulting image is displayed on the screen. If actions "TL CORNER" or "BR CORNER" are pointed to, then the program executes the *readp*(x,y) instruction for the second cursor, to obtain values for the coordinates of the top left or bottom right corner. The "SAVE" command causes the program to read the position of the second cursor to determine a file name for the saved image. The image saved is the one bounded by a rectangle defined by its top left and bottom right corners. The "SHRINK" command replaces the image defined by the rectangle with one of (approximately) one quarter the size, while "EXPAND"

---

† Thus the main loop consists of a series of "**if** ... **then**" statements (or a **switch** in C, **case** in Pascal, computed **GOTO** in FORTRAN, etc.)

has the opposite effect.† We shall discuss ways of implementing the last commands, as well as additional commands, in Chapters 2 to 4.

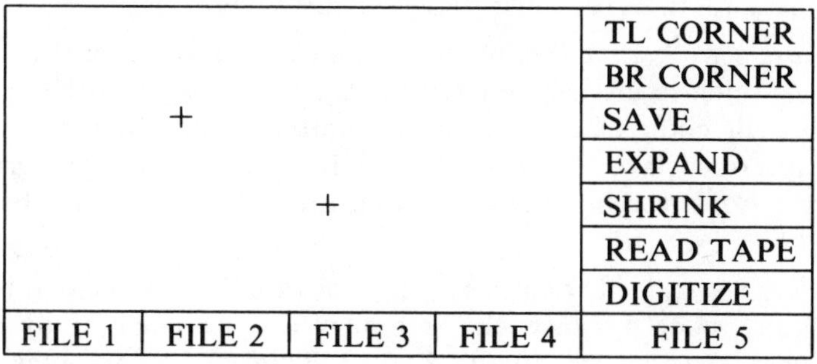

				TL CORNER
				BR CORNER
+				SAVE
				EXPAND
	+			SHRINK
				READ TAPE
				DIGITIZE
FILE 1	FILE 2	FILE 3	FILE 4	FILE 5

Figure 1.5 Display used for a simple image editor. The two cross signs denote the cursors used to address points on the screen.

1.10 PICTORIAL TRANSFORMATIONS

Many of the problems discussed in the literature can be expressed as transformations between classes of images and a few of them as transformations within classes. We review them briefly here.

Class 1 to 2: This process is called *segmentation* and it identifies regions where the color and/or brightness are approximately uniform. The term often refers to a process where one looks for uniformity in terms of some more complex property, like texture. However in this text we shall deal only with the more elementary segmentation schemes, which we shall present in Chapter 4.

Class 2 to 3: One possible transformation is *contour tracing* while another is *thinning*. In the former (discussed in Chapter 7) the region is mapped into a closed curve, while in the latter (discussed in Chapter 9) it is mapped into a graph, called the *skeleton* of the region.

Class 3 to 4: Sometimes called *curve segmentation,* this process attempts to find *critical points* along the contour. In the cases of polygons these points are the corners. Such transformations are usually the subject of the pattern recognition literature and may involve sophisticated mathematical methods. Some of the simpler schemes for finding critical points are discussed in Chapter 12.

Class 4 to 3: This includes the processes of *interpolation* (discussed

---

† We could have chosen some other fraction besides one quarter, or have allowed the user to select from a list of reduction or expansion rates.

in Chapters 10 and 11), in which a smooth curve is drawn to pass through a set of points, and *approximation* (discussed in Chapter 12), in which the smooth curve must pass near the points.

Class 3 to 2: If the input is a contour, then we have the problem of *filling,* which is often expressed as that of *shading.* In the latter the brightness or color of a region is not uniform but varies according to some prescribed law. Methods for solving this problem are presented in Chapter 8. If the input is a skeleton, then the region must be reconstructed by *expansion.*

Class 2 to 1: The display of a picture in few colors is often aesthetically poor because the contours are detected easily by the human eye (see Figures 2.9 and 2.10 on Plate 3). A smoother appearance can be achieved by the use of *low pass filters* or the addition of *dither noise.* These techniques are discussed in Chapters 2 and 3.

Roughly speaking, the transformations from a lower class to a higher class are of interest to pattern recognition, while the transformations from a higher class to a lower are of interest to graphics. Image processing deals with both, but also with *within-class* transformations. For example, *enhancement* is a within-class transformation, while *compaction* is often between classes 1 and 2.

An important class of problems deals with transformations between two-dimensional images and three-dimensional objects. The term *projection* is used to denote an operation which transforms a three-dimensional object to a two-dimensional picture, or in a special case the two-dimensional cross-section of an object into a one-dimensional array. The term *backprojection* denotes the reconstruction of a solid object (or its cross-section) from its projections. There exist two major applications in which these problems are important.

In cross-axial tomography a cross-section of a solid body is reconstructed from a series of x-ray projections. The term *reconstruction algorithms* refers to procedures for solving this problem. These are discussed at the end of Chapter 5.

In computer graphics it is often desired to display a certain view of a three-dimensional description of a solid. It is easy to perform a geometrical transformation and find the projections of all points of the object onto the plane of the display. However, such an image will not be that of a view since all points of the object are shown, even though in reality some of them are behind others, and therefore not visible. Thus, it is necessary to have algorithms for *hidden line* or *hidden surface* removal. Chapters 16 and 17 deal with such topics. The two problems are sometimes combined as the following example illustrates.

Example 1.3: A physician wishes to have different views of the heart of a patient. Cross-axial tomography may be used to find a sequence of cross-section images which are then assembled to form a description of the heart. A graphics system can then be used to display different views of the organ. □

Transformations within image classes tend to be relatively simple. The following are some examples.

Within Class 1 or 2: Filtering. This includes contrast enhancement, removal of high frequency noise, etc.

Within Class 3 or 4: Change of coordinate system. This includes rotations and translations.

Within any Class: Series expansions. The Fourier transform is the most common among them. They are often used for data compaction.

1.11 ALGORITHM NOTATION

The algorithms of this text are given in an Algol-type notation using the following conventions: Keywords are shown in **bold face**, variables in *italics*, and everything else in roman type. Parentheses are used to enclose array indices, as well as function and procedure arguments. Braces ({}) are used to enclose comments. The notation $f(*,l)$ means all the elements of the lth column of the two-dimensional array f. The implementation of the algorithms in Algol, PL/I, C, Pascal, Ratfor, etc. should be straightforward. Implementation in FORTRAN may be more difficult, but we hope that in the 1980s most people are familiar with one of the other languages or know how to translate structured algorithms into FORTRAN.

We illustrate our notation by giving as an example an algorithm for producing a class 1 image by overprinting. This was a useful research tool before the advance of raster graphics and is now a popular hobby. It can also be convenient for instructional purposes, since line-printers are still far more common than raster graphic displays. We assume that a matrix C exists which contains the overprinting code. All the letters in the jth column of the matrix are overprinted to encode gray level j. A good choice for C is given in Table 1.3. In the listing of the algorithm M denotes the number of rows of C.

Algorithm 1.1 Production of gray scale images by overprinting.

1.   **For** each row $f(*)$ of the image **do**: {We do not bother with the details about how f is found since these depend on the particular implementation.}
         Begin.
2.   **For** i from 1 to M **do**:
             Begin.
3.   **For** k from 1 to n **do**: {n is the number of elements in an image row.}
                Begin.
4.   Set $p(k)$ equal to $C(i, f(k))$.
                End.
5.   Print array p without a line feed.
             End.
6.   Line feed.
         End.
7.   **End of Algorithm.**

Statement 1 can be implemented either as a **for/do** loop if the number of rows is known, or by a **while** loop checking an end-of-file condition. Statement 2 is straightforward, and statement 3 can be implemented either as a **for/do** loop or as a **while** loop if the end of the row is marked by a null character. In most languages, statement 4 will be $p(l) = C(i, f(l))$, although it may have to be executed in two steps in FORTRAN. Finally, statement 5 requires a knowledge of the carriage control characters. In PL/I the SKIP command should be omitted, while in formatted FORTRAN, the first character should be a '+'. The algorithm assumes that C has as many columns as possible gray scales. If this is not the case, then one must make appropriate subscript checks. We will never list such checks as part of algorithms in this text since we assume them to be part of good programming practice (see for example [1.KP]). In the present case, one may want to use a more sophisticated mapping g between gray levels and columns of C, so that in step 4 we should write $C(i, g(f(l)))$. For the choice of such a map, see Section 3.2. A more efficient implementation is to expand the original C to match the number of available gray levels. However, the description of the algorithms in this text will not be concerned with such questions, because they are matters of good programming practice and style.

People interested in implementing Algorithm 1.1 may wish to use the following table of values for the matrix C. It has been proposed by Henderson and Tanimoto [1.HT]. Their paper contains some interesting information for those motivated enough to try to implement the algorithm in assembly language.

Table 1.3: Matrix of Characters for Producing Gray Scale by Overprinting

```
MMMMMMMMMHHHHHHXHXOZWMNHOOS=I*++=:-.-'
WWWWWWWW###*++----        =   -   -
######OO+-
OOOOO
OO+
+
```

1.12 A FEW WORDS ON COMPLEXITY

Any discussion of algorithms must cover the subject of computational complexity, and whenever we present an algorithm in this text we shall make an effort to give some idea about the time and space required for its execution. Here we would like to point out a common error that many students make: confusing computational and programming complexity. In general, the length of the program implementing an algorithm has little to do with the speed of execution, or even the memory requirements. If there is any relation it tends to be in the opposite direction. "Complicated" algorithms are usually faster than "simple" algorithms. For example, a (nonrecursive) program for the fast Fourier transform is both longer and logically more complex than a program implementing the summation formula for the transform. However, it runs much faster. Similar examples are offered by sorting algorithms.

It is often tempting to use the recursive form of algorithm because it is much shorter than the nonrecursive and the number of operations of the two forms is the same. In such cases one must keep in mind the high cost of recursive calls, the need for the machine to save register values, etc. If the number of such calls is small compared to the number of the other operations, then this cost may be well worth the resulting simplicity in the program. Otherwise the nonrecursive form yields more efficient programs.

While programming simplicity may seem attractive to a student who has to meet a deadline and plans to run his or her program on limited data, it is detrimental in any applications environment where a program is run over large volumes of data.

1.13 BIBLIOGRAPHICAL NOTES

A number of texts on image processing and graphics discuss the hardware design of displays, digitizers, etc. [1.NS] and [1.BO] are good places to start. The state of the art in this field changes rapidly and a close watch on what the manufacturers offer is advisable. Publications of professional societies and meetings are a good source. In the United States the ACM Special Interest Group on Graphics (SIGGRAPH) publishes a quarterly *Computer Graphics* and holds an annual meeting (usually during the summer) which includes a major equipment fair. One can find details about this meeting by consulting the calendar of the *Communications of the ACM*. The IEEE publications *Spectrum, IEEE Computer Graphics,* and *Computer* always contain sections with advertisements and announcements for hardware and these often include image processing and graphics equipment.

Research papers in the general field of pictorial information processing appear also in the following journals. *Computer Graphics and Image Processing* (abbreviated *CGIP*), *IEEE Transactions and Pattern Analysis and Machine Intelligence,* the newly announced *ACM Transactions on Graphics,* etc.

1.14 RELEVANT LITERATURE

[1.BO]   Booth, K. S. *Tutorial: Computer Graphics,* New York: IEEE, 1979.

[1.HT]   Henderson, P. and Tanimoto, S. "Considerations for Efficient Picture Output via Lineprinter," *CGIP,* **4** (1974), pp. 327-335.

[1.KP]   Kernighan, B. W. and Plauger, P. J. *Software Tools,* Reading, Mass: Addison-Wesley, 1976.

[1.NS]   Newman, W. F. and Sproull, R. F. *Principles of Interactive Computer Graphics,* 2nd ed. New York: McGraw-Hill, 1979.

[1.PC]   Pratt, W. K.; Capitant, P. J.; Chen, W. H.; Hamilton, E. R.; and Wallis, R. H. "Combined Symbol Matching Facsimile Data Compression System," *IEEE Proceedings, 68* (1980), pp. 786-796.

1.15 PROBLEMS

1.1.   Write a digitization program for one of the devices available in your installation.

1.2.   *Bit packing:* A gray scale image contains only two distinct values of gray levels, so it may be encoded as a bilevel image. Assume that all pixels have now a value 0 or 1. Write a program to store the image with eight pixels per byte.

1.3.   *Bit unpacking:* In order to display the previous image we must have one byte per pixel. Write a program to "unpack" it.

1.4. *Chain code:* Write a program for finding the x-y coordinates of a pixel whose chain code direction from another pixel is known. Also implement the reverse operation, finding the chain code from the x-y coordinates.

1.5. Implement the simple editor described in Section 1.9, except for the EXPAND and SHRINK commands. You should try to make the program as device independent as possible. For example, you may create a procedure that takes the cursor coordinates and identifies the command from them. Instead of calling the procedure to execute the appropriate action there, the input procedure should return a string with the command name to the main program. In this way the main editor does not need to know the details of the graphics commands.

1.6. *Gray scale by overprinting:* Implement Algorithm 1.1. If you like, you may use the code given in Table 1.3.

Chapter 2

DIGITIZATION OF GRAY SCALE IMAGES

2.1 INTRODUCTION

When a picture is to be processed by computer, it is often described as a matrix, or some other discrete data structure. But a picture is primarily a signal that conveys information to an observer, and there are many applications where this consideration is particularly important. We shall devote this and the next chapter to the discussion of such problems, especially for gray scale (class 1) images. The first problem is the conversion of a continuous picture into a discrete form, and this involves two processes: *sampling,* which is the selection of a discrete grid to represent an image, and *quantization,* which is the mapping of the brightness and color values into integers. In graphics one is concerned with similar problems: specifically the choice of the display resolution and number of gray levels or colors. These processes are also relevant in one-dimensional data and have been studied thoroughly in that case, but two-dimensional data present new problems. We shall devote the first part of this chapter to a review of transform techniques and then we shall discuss sampling for the one-dimensional case, followed by sampling for pictures. Quantization will be treated in the last section.

2.2 A REVIEW OF FOURIER AND OTHER TRANSFORMS

Fourier transforms are a common tool in signal processing and are defined both for one- and two-dimensional functions. The following two formulas are valid for the continuous case: If $f(t)$ is a function defined over an interval $[0,\infty)$, then its Fourier transform is

$$F(w) = \int_{t=0}^{\infty} f(t)\exp(-jwt)dt \qquad\qquad 0 \le w < \infty \qquad (2.1)$$

If $f(x,y)$ is a function of two variables defined over the infinite plane, then the two-dimensional transform of $f(x,y)$ is:

$$F(u,v) = \int_{-\infty}^{\infty} \int_{-\infty}^{\infty} f(x,y)\exp(-j(xu+yv))dxdy \qquad 0 \le u,v < \infty \qquad (2.2)$$

The term *spectrum* is often used as a synonym for the Fourier transform. The transform can also be defined for functions whose argument is an integer ranging from 0 to $N-1$. Such functions can be thought of as consisting of N samples from a continuous signal, but this need not always be the case. Formally, we have for the one-dimensional case

$$F(u) = \sum_{k=0}^{N-1} f(k)\exp(-j\frac{2\pi}{N}uk) \qquad\qquad 0 \le u \le N-1 \qquad (2.3)$$

and for the two-dimensional

$$F(u,v) = \sum_{k=0}^{N-1} \sum_{l=0}^{N-1} f(k,l)\exp(-j\frac{2\pi}{N}(ku+lv)) \qquad 0 \le u,v \le N-1 \quad (2.4)$$

The above equations are usually referred to as the *discrete Fourier transform (DFT)*. It is possible to make the limits of the two sums different and define the *DFT* over a rectangular domain. However, there is no way to define the two-dimensional Fourier transform over a region of arbitrary form. If we restrict the limits of integration in Equation (2.2), or the limits of summation in Equation (2.4), then the result will depend not only on the values of f, but also on the shape of the domain of summation/integration.† The *discrete inverse Fourier transform (DIFT)* is defined as

$$f(k) = \frac{1}{N}\sum_{u=0}^{N-1} F(u)\exp(j\frac{2\pi}{N}uk) \qquad\qquad 0 \le k \le N-1 \qquad (2.5)$$

---

† It can be shown that the resulting integral equals the complex convolution of the Fourier transform of f with the Fourier transform of the characteristic function of the domain of integration.

and

$$f(k,l) = \frac{1}{N^2} \sum_{u=0}^{N-1} \sum_{v=0}^{N-1} F(u,v) \exp(j \frac{2\pi}{N}(uk+vl)) \quad 0 \le k,l \le N-1 \quad (2.6)$$

The transform equations can be written in many ways, some of which are helpful in motivating other transforms as well as efficient ways for computation. Let us denote the exponential $\exp(-j\frac{2\pi}{N})$ by z and let us define the matrix Z as follows:

$$Z = \begin{bmatrix} 1 & 1 & 1 & . & 1 \\ 1 & z & z^2 & . & z^{N-1} \\ 1 & z^2 & z^4 & . & z^{2(N-1)} \\ . & . & . & . & . \\ 1 & z^{N-1} & z^{2(N-1)} & . & z^{(N-1)(N-1)} \end{bmatrix}. \quad (2.7)$$

In other words, $Z_{uk} = z^{uk}$. For most applications N is not only even but also a power of 2. The matrix Z can be simplified by observing that $z^N = 1$, $z^{N/2} = -1$, $z^{N/4} = -j$, and $z^{3N/4} = j$. We also note that it is a symmetric matrix and that the scalar product of any one of its columns (or rows) with another column (or row) is zero. The scalar product of a column (or row) with itself is N. Thus Z has the important property that its inverse equals its conjugate transpose times $1/N$. A matrix such as $1/\sqrt{N}Z$, where the inverse equals the conjugate transpose, is said to be a *unitary* matrix. Let now f denote a column vector whose elements are the values $f(k)$ and F a column vector with elements $F(u)$. Then Equation (2.3) can be written in matrix form as

$$F = Zf . \quad (2.8)$$

For the two-dimensional case we observe that the transform is equivalent to multiplying first all the columns of $f(k,l)$ by Z, and then all its rows by Z' (transpose of Z) from the right. Then Equation (2.4) becomes

$$F = ZfZ' . \quad (2.9)$$

The expressions f and F denote the image matrix and the transform matrix. Similar expressions can be found for the inverse transform, if Z is replaced by $1/N$ times its complex conjugate transpose Z^*.

One can now define additional transformations by using Equations (2.8) and (2.9) and changing the definition of Z as long as $1/\sqrt{N}Z$ is a unitary matrix. One such choice yields the *Hadamard transform*. The matrices for that transform can be defined recursively as follows:

$$Z_2 = \begin{bmatrix} 1 & 1 \\ 1 & -1 \end{bmatrix} \qquad\qquad (2.10a)$$

$$Z_{2N} = \begin{bmatrix} Z_N & Z_N \\ Z_N & -Z_N \end{bmatrix} \qquad\qquad (2.10b)$$

Thus, the Hadamard transform corresponds to expansions along square waves rather than the sine and cosine waves of the Fourier transform. Furthermore, the Z matrix could be put in a form similar to Equation (2.7) with $z = -1$ but with a different rule for changing the exponents. The major advantage of the Hadamard transform is that complex multiplications are replaced by sign changes, an important consideration in the early years of computing, where floating point arithmetic units were hard to come by. Otherwise it produces results that are similar to those obtained by the Fourier transform.

The major application of transforms is in the design of filters for image enhancement and also in certain data compaction techniques. They also provide the foundations for image reconstruction from projections, techniques which we discuss in Chapter 5. Their use for data compaction is justified in cases where most of the $F(u)$'s are zero. Then Equation (2.5) or (2.6) can be used for recovering the values of $f(k)$ from fewer than N values of the transform. However, the user should be aware that each of the transform elements may require more bits for its description than the values of the original function. Therefore, the compaction ratio may not be as high as one would expect.

The use of the defining equations for the computation of a transform given by Equation (2.8) requires N^2 calculations for the one-dimensional case and N^4 for the two-dimensional. It is possible to rearrange the terms of the sum in Equation (2.3) and use the fact that the product uk takes the same values for different values of u and k to arrive at a more efficient algorithm, the *fast Fourier transform (FFT)*. This is described in Appendix 2.A, where it is shown that only $N\log_2 N$ operations are required for the one-dimensional case. The fast Fourier transform algorithm can be used to evaluate the two-dimensional transform by finding first the transform of each row of the image, and then the transform of all the columns. This is shown in Algorithm 2.1, where $FFT(N,x)$ is a procedure that replaces the N element array x by its discrete Fourier transform.

Algorithm 2.1 Two-dimensional FFT

1.   **For** $l=0$ to $N-1$ **do**:
         Begin.
2.   Copy $f(*,l)$ into the array x.
3.   Call $FFT(N,x)$.
4.   Replace $f(*,l)$ by x.
         End.
5.   **For** $k=0$ to $N-1$ **do**:
         Begin.
6.   Copy $f(k,*)$ into the array x.
7.   Call $FFT(N,x)$.
8.   Replace $f(k,*)$ by x.
         End.
9.   **End of Algorithm.**

Each call to $FFT(N,x)$ entails a computational cost proportional to $N\log_2 N$. Since there are $2N$ such calls, the total cost will be of order $N^2\log_2(N^2)$.

2.3 SAMPLING

In order to process a picture or any other signal by computer, we must convert it into a finite set of numbers. Sampling is the selection of a set of discrete points in the continuum of time or space. Only the values of the signal at those points will be used in further processing.

2.3.1 One-dimensional Sampling

In the one-dimensional case the fundamental mathematical result is Shannon's sampling theorem, which is expressed in terms of the spectrum of the signal. Let $d(t)$ be the digital representation of $f(t)$, consisting of unquantized pulses at intervals of T units, so that

$$d(kT) = f(kT) \qquad k = 0, 1, \cdots \infty \qquad (2.11a)$$

$$d(t) = 0 \qquad \text{if } t \neq kT \qquad (2.11b)$$

Then it can be shown that the Fourier transform $D(w)$ of $d(t)$ is related to $F(w)$ by the equation

$$D(w) = \sum_{n=-\infty}^{\infty} F\left(w - \frac{2\pi n}{T}\right) \qquad (2.12)$$

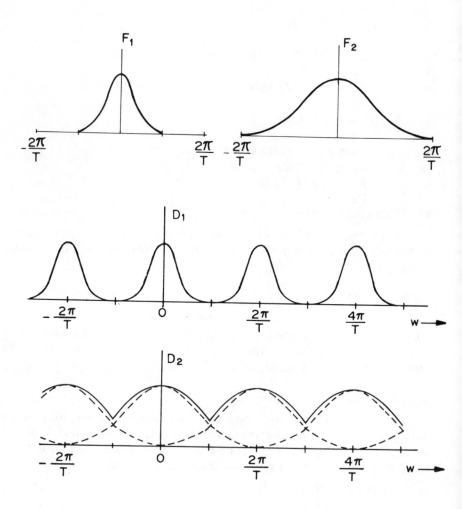

Figure 2.1 Fourier transform of sampled signals. The top row shows the spectra $F_1(w)$ and $F_2(w)$ of two unsampled signals: $f_1(t)$ and $f_2(t)$. The middle diagram shows the spectrum $D_1(w)$ of the sampled signal $d_1(t)$, while the bottom diagram shows $D_2(w)$. $F_1(w)$ is zero outside a frequency band, but this is not the case with $F_2(w)$. The broken lines in the bottom diagram show the shape of the transform of the continuous signal repeated every $2\pi/T$ frequency units.

In other words, the Fourier transform of $d(t)$ consists of a summation of shifts of the Fourier transform of $f(t)$. Note that Equation (2.12) does not refer to the discrete Fourier transform of $d(t)$, but to the continuous transform of a function that happens to be nonzero at certain discrete times only. The difference between the transforms of the functions d and f can be seen from the examples of Figure 2.1. In the top left diagram, $F(w)$ is zero for $w > \pi/T$, while this is not the case in the top right diagram. The plots of $D(w)$ for these two cases are shown in the middle and bottom diagrams respectively. In the first case, given $D(w)$, we can find $F(w)$ exactly and can therefore reconstruct $f(t)$ from $d(t)$. This is not possible in the second case because of the overlap of the terms of Equation (2.12). This leads to the following formulation of the sampling theorem:

Theorem 2.1: *(Shannon's Sampling Theorem)* Let w_{max} be the largest value of w for which $F(w)$ is nonzero. Then $f(t)$ can be reconstructed exactly from the samples if the time between samples is less than

$$\frac{\pi}{w_{max}}$$

i.e., the sampling frequency is at least twice the size of w_{max}.

Note that this theorem does not suggest a way for reconstructing the continuous signal from its discrete samples. It only says that it is possible. As a matter of fact, it is necessary to use fairly sophisticated techniques to reconstruct a signal when it is sampled at the minimum frequency. If one is confined to a particular form of reconstruction, then the sampling frequency may have to be well above the minimum suggested by the sampling theorem.

Example 2.1: Suppose that the reconstruction consists of a constant, equal to the sample value as shown in Figure 2.2. Let $f(t) = E \sin(\omega t)$ for some ω. If we want a maximum error between the reconstructed signal and the original of not more than a given quantity e, then Figure 2.2 shows that the following equation should hold

$$|f(kT \pm \frac{T}{2}) - f(kT)| < e \qquad (2.13)$$

where k is a sampling instant and T is the sampling interval. The mean value theorem of calculus can then be used to show that this inequality will hold if the maximum of the absolute value of the derivative of $f(t)$, $f'(t)$, is less than $2e/T$. For the particular choice of $f(t)$ we may also compute the maximum of the difference in Equation (2.13) by a trigonometric formula and find that this equation is equivalent to

$$E\left|\sin\left(\frac{\omega T}{2}\right)\right| < e \ .$$

If we approximate the sine of a small angle by the angle itself we find that the above inequality becomes

$$T < \frac{2e}{E\omega} \ , \tag{2.14}$$

giving a bound well below the Shannon limit. The same answer is found if we use the mean value theorem. $\square$

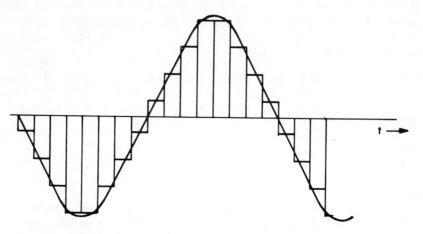

Figure 2.2   Reconstruction of signal by a piecewise constant approximation

2.3.2 Two-dimensional Sampling

The choice of the form of reconstruction is usually limited in picture processing, and this fact should be kept in mind whenever a generalization of the sampling theorem in two dimensions is used. Even though Shannon's theorem can be extended trivially to two dimensions, it is not particularly relevant because of the limitations of the available reconstruction algorithms. Therefore, pictorial data must usually be sampled at a much higher rate than what one might expect from a spectral analysis. In particular, one may want to use an upper bound of the form of Equation (2.14). The resulting sampling interval will be $2e/(E\pi)$ times the value required by the sampling theorem. If e/E is 1%, then one must sample about 157 times as often as what is required by the Shannon limit!

Figures 2.3 to 2.5 (Plates 1 and 2) illustrate the problem. The first is an image at a high resolution (256x256) which for most observers is indistinguishable from an analog image. The other two have been obtained from the former by skipping samples, so that Figure 2.4 consists of 64x64 samples and Figure 2.5 of 32x32. They are displayed on a bigger screen by repeating the value of each sample 16 and 64 times respectively. They are certainly of low quality, but this is not due only to undersampling. The reader may try to look at them from a distance or by squinting his or her eyes. The quality of the pictures improves because most of the information is there. It is the piecewise constant reconstruction that introduces the apparent distortions. It is possible to develop algorithms that interpolate linearly between samples (see Problem 2.3), so that if a low resolution image is displayed on a high resolution screen, the additional pixels have intermediate values between those of the given samples. However, the interpolation process can be quite slow so that its use with a conventional display is not practical. Only when graphic displays that will do this interpolation locally (by special purpose hardware) are developed will it be feasible to sample images closer to the rate predicted by Shannon's theorem. (In digital filter terminology these devices will be equivalent to *high order hold* elements.)

The need for oversampling is often an obstacle to the development of a complete digital pictorial information processing system. One possible compromise is to mix analog and digital output by using television technology. A monitor receives signals from two sources: a raster graphics controller and a television camera or analog video tape. It is possible to mix the two and create an overlay of, say, statistical information (produced digitally) over the (analog) map of a city.†

The definition of sampling points is straightforward for one-dimensional signals, but serious problems occur in two dimensions. We define formally some of the terms which we will be using frequently.

Definition 2.1: Let P be the plane containing an analog image. A *digitizing cell* is defined as a compact and convex subset of P over which the value of a sample of the digitized picture is calculated. The union of all such cells is defined as the *(sampling) grid*. A single sample is called a *picture element,* or *pixel,* or *pel.* If D is the display plane, then pixels are mapped onto *display cells* that result in the reconstructed analog picture. □

---

† This arrangement was described to me by Dr. Jean-Paul Jacob of IBM Research Laboratories.

We should point out that we do not assume that the digitizing cells are disjoint. In most digitizing devices they actually overlap, although display cells are usually nonoverlapping. Figure 2.6 shows a typical sampling grid and the corresponding display. Although it is theoretically possible, and sometimes practically inevitable, to use different grids for sampling and display, this is not advisable because of the resulting distortions. Most digitization procedures are characterized by a *point spread function, g*(r), which reflects how different points contribute to the value of a sample depending on their distance r from it. The function $g(r)$ is a decreasing function of r and it is zero outside the digitizing cell. If $g(r)$ decreases fast enough, then one can assume nonoverlapping cells and as a first approximation use the term "cell" to refer to both digitizing and display cells.

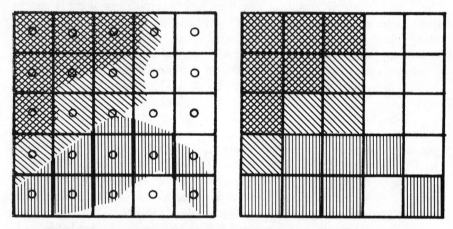

Figure 2.6 Two-dimensional sampling and corresponding display. Note the introduction of sharp edges in the latter. These correspond to the high frequencies introduced by the sampling as shown in Figure 2.1. This figure also offers a detailed explanation of the reasons for the poor appearance of Figures 2.4 and 2.5.

The most common grid used in picture processing is the *square grid* consisting of square cells arranged as a chessboard. The *hexagonal grid* (Figure 2.7) is often discussed in the literature but is rarely implemented. While the one-dimensional sampling theorem deals only with the size of the sampling interval, any result about the size of the cells of the grid will also depend on their shape and the exact form of the point spread function. In the sequel we deal primarily with square grids and refer to other types only occasionally.

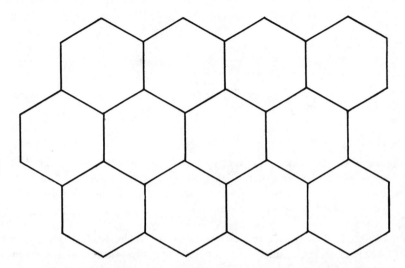

Figure 2.7 Hexagonal grid. It has the advantage that all neighbors of a cell C have the same form of contact with C, while in a square grid we must distinguish between neighbors touching on sides or corners. It also has the disadvantage that the distance between cell centers is different in the vertical and horizontal directions.

2.4 ALIASING

If the sampling interval does not satisfy the conditions of Theorem 2.1, then a distortion of the spectrum occurs as shown in the bottom diagram of Figure 2.1. High frequencies are folded onto lower frequencies, producing a phenomenon called *aliasing*. Figure 2.8 shows its generation in the one-dimensional case: a high frequency signal appears as a low frequency signal after sampling at too low a rate. A typical example in the case of pictorial data is the sampling of an image with text. If the samples are too sparse the result will be a random looking pattern of dark and light areas, rather than the shapes of the letters. Another example is the digitizing of an image where the appearance of gray level is produced by varying the density of black and white dots. If the sampling rate is comparable to the spacing of the dots, then the sampled values will correspond to black or white but with a different distribution than the original dots. The resulting appearance can be very poor.

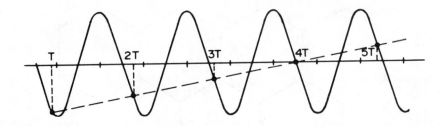

Figure 2.8 Illustration of aliasing: the solid line is the signal which is sampled at intervals slightly shorter than its period. The solid circles are the samples which are interpreted as representing a very low frequency signal (broken line).

In the case of text, the remedy is to increase the sampling rate. A different remedy is required in the second case: the values of the original dots must be averaged. In other words, it is necessary to pass the signals through a low pass filter before sampling.

Example 2.2:   Suppose that we are interested in frequencies only below 1000 cps but the signal contains an "uninteresting" component at 1800 cps. Sampling at 2000 cps will result in a 200 cps component which is an alias of the 1800 cps component. In order to eliminate it, the original signal must be processed by a *analog low pass filter* before sampling to suppress all frequencies above 1000 cps. □

Aliasing presents major problems in picture processing because of the difficulty of designing analog filters for preprocessing the signal. Defocusing the optical system of the digitizer is equivalent to passing the image through a simple low pass filter and this may be sufficient in some cases.

In the computer graphics literature the term aliasing is often used to describe the distortion introduced by piecewise reconstructions such as those shown in Figures 2.4 and 2.5. Strictly speaking, the problem there is not the mapping of a high frequency onto a low frequency, but the introduction of additional high frequencies because of the reconstruction method. The confusion has occurred because one of the remedies for this problem is to increase the sampling rate (Example 2.1), and the same remedy is also used to eliminate aliasing. The distinction between the two phenomena becomes clear when we notice that the appearance of Figures 2.4 and 2.5 is improved by defocusing, a low pass filter applied on the *digital image*. Such a filter could not correct aliasing unless it were applied on the *analog image*.

2.5 QUANTIZATION

When an analog signal is sampled, the values obtained must be represented by a finite number of bits, the one available in the computer used. This process, called *quantization,* can be considered to be a mapping from the real numbers into a range of integers. The choice of the number of gray levels to represent a black and white picture must take into account the properties of human vision, but a treatment of this subject is beyond the scope of this text. It is certainly true that eight bits (256 levels) are enough for most images, and that one can often achieve good displays with only six bits. For good quality color pictures one may have to go as high as six bits (64 levels) for each of the three basic colors (total of eighteen bits), or even more. However, four bits (16 levels) per color may be enough in many applications. Using a byte per pixel and allocating three bits for two of the colors and two bits for the third gives marginal results. Figures 2.9 and 2.10 (Plate 3) show examples of black and white images quantized at different levels. A comparison of both images to the eight-bit original of Figure 2.3 (Plate 1) shows a deterioration in appearance, mainly because of the visible contours between gray levels. However, there is considerable gray level information present, even in the two-bit image. The quality of a sixteen level image (four-bit) is so good that it is impossible to distinguish it from the original when both images are printed on paper. (It is possible to tell the difference, though, when the images are viewed side by side on a television monitor.)

It is possible to improve appearance of the coarsely quantized images by the addition of *dither.* If the value of the image at some point (x,y) is $f(x,y)$ we add to it a dither $d(x,y)$ before quantization. The dither $d(x,y)$ can be generated by a random process, or can be determined from the location of the point (x,y). In either case its value is not related in any systematic way to $f(x,y)$. This process tends to break up the contours, and even though we add noise to the picture the overall appearance is improved. Figures 2.11 and 2.12 (Plate 4) are dithered versions of Figures 2.9 and 2.10 (Plate 3) respectively and were produced as follows. The value of $d(x,y)$ was taken with uniform probability from the set of the five numbers

$$-2^{(6-b)}, \; -2^{(5-b)}, \; 0, \; 2^{(5-b)}, \text{ and } 2^{(6-b)} \, ,$$

where b is the number of bits to be displayed. Then the b most significant bits of the sum were used as the pixel value. (If the sum was negative, it was set to zero before the bit masking.)

A problem that has received little attention is the tradeoff between sampling rate and quantization levels. If we have a fixed number of bits available for storing a given picture, what is the best allocation of bits for each process? For example, 8192 bits can be used to store a 64×64 grid (4096 pixels), with 4 grey levels (2 bits), or a 32x32 grid (1024 pixels) with 256 grey levels (8 bits). It is obvious that the answer depends on the type of picture, but also that for a given picture one may want to use variable sampling and quantization for different parts. Section 3.2 describes some related problems. Another consideration is the amount of computation needed. In most problems the cost of computing is a function of the number of samples (pixels) but is not affected by the number of bits per pixel, as long as they do not exceed the word size for the computer used. Thus the time for processing a picture of 4096 one bit pixels may be four times the amount for a picture of 1024 pixels occupying four bits each.

Most studies in the published literature are experimental and the Bibliographical Notes give some related references. The following example illustrates some of the specific problems involved.

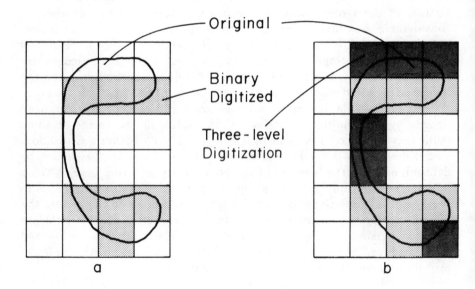

Figure 2.13 (a) Creation of a gap because of insufficient resolution. (b) The increase in the number of gray levels allows the detection of the proper topology of the character.

Example 2.3: Our task is to digitize two-level images such as pages of printed text. However, because of the nature of the spread function of the digitizing device a wide range of values is observed. (We may assume that the value of a sample is the average value of the input over a sampling cell.) Thus we must deal with a class 1 image while the input was a class 2 image. We may attempt to return to a class 2 image by using only one bit per pixel and giving it the value zero if the input is below some threshold and the value one otherwise. Clearly, pixels which correspond to sampling cells near the region boundaries of the original will be assigned zero or one in a more or less arbitrary fashion, and this may result in creating or bridging gaps, as shown in Figure 2.13a. For this reason one may choose sampling cells of sufficiently small size so that, even at the narrowest parts of a region, a whole cell is contained entirely in a single color area. (See Chapter 7 for more on this topic.) Alternatively, one may choose to quantize at four levels (two bits per pixel) at a lower resolution, as shown in Figure 2.13b. □

2.6 BIBLIOGRAPHICAL NOTES

Most books on image processing discuss in detail the use of transforms and linear filtering operations. The book by Pratt [2.PR] is a good source for more advanced reading on the topics covered in this and the next chapter. It emphasizes signal processing and has a good discussion of optics. The book by Castleman [2.CA] is more concise but also of more limited scope. Hall [2.HA] and Rosenfeld and Kak [2.RK] cover many of these topics and they also discuss segmentation and pattern recognition related subjects. There are many papers dealing with the practical aspects of quantization and sampling in discrete images. Knowlton and Harmon [2.KH] offer an interesting review of the early work. The perception of "grossly" sampled images similar to Figure 2.5 has been discussed by Harmon and Julesz [2.HJ].† [2.JJN] discusses some of the uses of dither. A recent review of image coding that covers the questions of sampling and quantization can be found in [2.NL]. A more extensive theoretical treatment of coding is given in [2.PR2]. [2.SA] is of particular interest because of the discussion of the human visual system. The applications of sampling theory for the proper display of images is a topic that has been gaining popularity in

---

† Dali has painted a picture using these concepts and seemingly motivated by their work. It consists of blocks where the color is close to, but not exactly, uniform. When people view it from a distance they see only the blocks and perceive a "grossly" sampled image of Lincoln. When viewers approaches the image, then they can detect the details within each block and the image of a woman in front of a window appears.

the literature on computer graphics. (The reader is reminded that what is called aliasing in that literature is not always aliasing as understood in the image processing literature. The informal expression "elimination of the jaggies" is a more accurate term.) [2.GS] and [2.KU] are two recent papers that contain interesting theoretical results.

2.7 RELEVANT LITERATURE

[2.CA]   Castleman, K. R. *Digital Image Processing,* Englewood Cliffs, New Jersey: Prentice-Hall, 1979, 428 pp.

[2.GS]   Gupta, S. and Sproull, R. F. "Filtering Edges for Gray-Scale Displays," *SIGGRAPH'81*, Dallas, Texas (August 1981), pp. 1-5.

[2.HA]   Hall, E. L. *Computer Image Processing and Recognition,* New York: Academic Press, 1979, 584pp.

[2.HJ]   Harmon, L. and Julesz, B. "Masking in Visual Recognition: Effects of Two-Dimensional Filtered Noise," *Science,* **180** (1973), pp. 1194-1197.

[2.JJN]   Jarvis, J. F.; Judice, C. N.; and Ninke, W. H. "A Survey of Techniques for the Display of Continuous Tone Pictures on Bilevel Displays", *CGIP,* **5** (1976), pp. 13-40.

[2.KH]   Knowlton, K. and Harmon, L. "Computer-Produced Grey Scales," *CGIP,* **1** (1972), pp. 1-20.

[2.KU]   Kajiya, J. and Ullner, M. "Filtering High Quality Text for Display on Raster Scan Devices," *SIGGRAPH'81*, Dallas, Texas (August 1981), pp. 7-15.

[2.NL]   Netravali, A. N. and Limb, J. O. "Picture Coding: A Review," *IEEE Proceedings,* **68** (1980), pp. 366-406.

[2.PR]   Pratt, W. K. *Digital Image Processing,* New York: J. Wiley, 1978, 750 pp.

[2.PR2]   Pratt, W. K. (ed.) *Image Transmission Techniques,* New York: Academic Press, 1979, 281pp.

[2.RK]   Rosenfeld, A. and Kak, A. C. *Digital Picture Processing,* New York: Academic Press, 1976, 457 pp.

[2.SA]   Sakrison, D. J. "Image Coding Application of Vision Models," *in* [2.PR2], pp. 23-71.

2.8 PROBLEMS

2.1.   Implement Algorithm 2.1 assuming that there is sufficient space to store the image in fast memory.

2.2.   Repeat Problem 2.1 assuming that the image does not fit in fast memory. This will require writing a procedure to find the transpose of a matrix without ever having the whole matrix stored as an array.

2.3.   Write a program to implement a piecewise linear reconstruction (*first order hold*) of a sampled image. You may want to use the following formalism. If a, b, c, and d are the values of four pixels forming a square,

$$
\begin{array}{cc}
a & b \\
c & d
\end{array}
$$

x and y denote the coordinates relative to the top left corner, and h the size of the side of the square, then we can define the value z of the intermediate points as

$$z = \frac{y \cdot (c-a)+x \cdot (b-a)}{h} + a \qquad x < h - y$$

$$z = \frac{y \cdot (d-b)+x \cdot (d-c)}{h} + c + b - d \qquad x \geq h - y$$

(These equations can be derived from elementary geometry or from Equation (16.2).)

2.4.   Use the above program to study tradeoffs between sampling and quantization. (You may wish to write these programs as part of an image editor. See next problem.)

2.5.   Enrich the image editor of Problem 1.5 by adding features which allow you to study variations in the sampling rate or the number of quantization levels, as well as tradeoffs between the two.
Hints. You may implement the command EXPAND and study variations in the sampling rate by taking a subset of the pixels of the original image to create a new one and then display it on the same size through expansion. You may choose to add two new commands to the menu: SAMPLE and LEVEL. Each time the first one is executed it takes every other pixel in the vertical and horizontal directions (one out of four) and then uses expansion to display the result. LEVEL blanks bits starting from the end. Or you may choose commands which accept numerical arguments specifying precisely the sampling rate and the number of quantization levels.

2.6.   Analyze the dithering scheme discussed in Section 2.5.

APPENDIX 2.A: FAST FOURIER TRANSFORM

We provide here a brief review of the fast Fourier transform. The reader can consult a text on signal processing or algorithms for a more detailed analysis. Our starting point is Equation (2.3) replacing the exponential by z as defined in Section 2.2.

$$F(u) = \sum_{k=0}^{N-1} f(k)z^{uk} \quad 0 \leq u \leq N-1 \tag{2.A.1}$$

We introduce a new index of summation, m, which varies from 0 to $(N/2)-1$ and which is related to k by the following equations.

$$k = 2m \qquad \text{for } k \text{ even} \tag{2.A.2a}$$
$$k = 2m+1 \qquad \text{for } k \text{ odd} \tag{2.A.2b}$$

Then Equation (2.A.1) can be rewritten as

$$F(u) = \sum_{m=0}^{(N/2)-1} [f(2m)z^{2mu} + f(2m+1)z^{(2m+1)u}] . \tag{2.A.3}$$

Let us now define $M = N/2$ and

$$g = \exp(-j\frac{2\pi}{M})$$

and observe that $z^2 = g$. Then Equation (2.A.3) can be written as

$$F(u) = \sum_{m=0}^{M-1} f_e(m)g^{um} + z^u \sum_{m=0}^{M-1} f_o(m)g^{um} \tag{2.A.4}$$

where f_e and f_o are two new functions obtained by considering separately the points for even and odd values of the argument. The two sums in Equation (2.A.4) look very much like Fourier transforms of functions with M points except that u varies from 0 to $N-1$. However, we notice that

$$F(u+N) = F(u) \tag{2.A.5}$$

since $\exp(-jN\frac{2\pi}{N}) = 1$. Thus, the M values of the Fourier transform of f_e (or f_o) can be used to find N values trivially. Therefore we have the following *recursive* equation for the Fourier transform.

$$F(u) = F_e(u) + \exp(-j\frac{2\pi u}{N})F_o(u) \tag{2.A.6}$$

Equation (2.A.6) is the foundation of the fast Fourier transform. First, it provides an easily programmable method for the computation.

This is given as Algorithm 2.A.1.

Algorithm 2.A.1 Fast Fourier Transform
Procedure FFT(N,f)

1. **If** N equals 2, **then do:**
    Begin.
2. Replace $f(0)$ by $f(0) + f(1)$ and $f(1)$ by $f(0) - f(1)$.
3. **Return.**
    End.
4. **Else do:**
    Begin.
5. Define g as consisting of all points of f which have an even index and h as consisting of the remaining points.
6. **Call procedure** *FFT(N/2,g)*.
7. **Call procedure** *FFT(N/2,h)*.
8. Replace $f(i)$ by $g(i) + \exp(-j2\pi i/N)h(i)$ **for** $i = 0$ to $N-1$.
    End.
9. **End of Procedure**

The procedure calls itself if N exceeds 2, while for $N = 2$ it uses the formula

$$F(0) = f(0) + f(1) \qquad (2.A.7a)$$

$$F(1) = f(0) - f(1) \qquad (2.A.7b)$$

Clearly, the successive halving of N can proceed smoothly only if N is a power of 2 and it is only for such values that there is a simple algorithm for the fast Fourier transform. Second, Equation (2.A.6) can be used to calculate the cost of the computation. Let $C(N)$ be the cost for N points. After the evaluation of the two transforms in the righthand side, Equation (2.A.6) requires effort proportional to N because of the multiplication of the terms by the exponential and the subsequent addition. If c is a constant reflecting the cost of such operations, then we have the following equation for $C(N)$.

$$C(N) = 2C\left(\frac{N}{2}\right) + cN \qquad (2.A.8)$$

Similarly we find that

$$C\left(\frac{N}{2}\right) = 2C\left(\frac{N}{4}\right) + c\frac{N}{2} \qquad (2.A.9)$$

and so forth. Because of Equations (2.A.7) we know that $C(2)$ equals the cost of two additions, which we denote by c'. If we write equations similar to Equation (2.A.9) for $C(\dfrac{N}{L})$, where $L = 4, \cdots, N/4$, multiply each one of them by L, add them to Equation (2.A.8), and add Equation (2.A.9) multiplied by two, we find that

$$C(N) = \frac{N}{2}c' + cNn \qquad\qquad (2.A.10)$$

where n is the number of such equations. In particular n equals the number of terms in the series $1, 2, 4, \cdots, N/4$ which is equal to the base 2 logarithm of N, $\log_2 N$, minus 1. Then Equation (2.A.10) becomes

$$C(N) = cN\log_2 N + O(N) \qquad\qquad (2.A.11)$$

where the last expression denotes terms linearly proportional to N.

Chapter 3

PROCESSING OF
GRAY SCALE IMAGES

3.1 INTRODUCTION

There are two major types of gray scale image processing: within class transformations, such as *filtering* and *image enhancement,* and class 1 image to class 2 image transforms, such as *segmentation.* Most methods for performing such processing use, directly or indirectly, statistics computed on images. We shall discuss two of them, the *histogram* of distribution of gray levels (in Section 3.2), and the *co-occurrence matrix* of pairs of gray levels at pixel pairs (in Section 3.3). Their applications in filtering are discussed in Sections 3.4 and 3.5, while their use for segmentation is presented in the next chapter.

If we treat an image as a random process, then we must define the *first order* probability density function $p_1(P,Z)$ that a pixel P (specified by its location) has brightness level, or color Z. For monochrome pictures we shall always assume that Z varies between 0 (very dark) and some value $L>0$ (very bright). The dependence of this probability on the location of a pixel allows the use of the model to generate meaningful images.

Example 3.1: Consider an image that contains a dark character on a light background. Let C_0 be the set of pixels that belong to an ideal form of the character and have value D. Background pixels have value

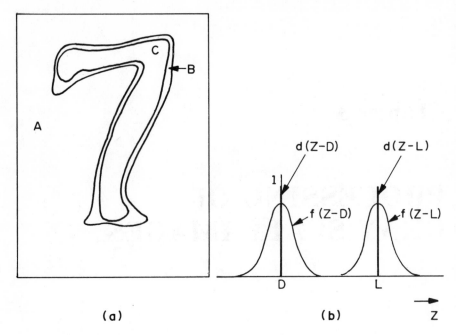

Figure 3.1 (a) Definition of regions A, B, and C for Example 3.1. (b) Definition of the functions $f(x)$ and $d(x)$ for Example 3.1. The integral of $f(x)$ over all the values of x should be one.

L. Because of noise, each time we make an observation of the character we see a different set of dark pixels, C_i. Let C be the intersection of all possible C_i's and B the difference between the union of the C_i's and C. For moderate amounts of noise we expect C to be a subset of C_0 and the union of B and C to include C_0. Clearly, B is a zone of pixels around the boundary of C_0. Let A be the remainder of the image outside B and C. (Figure 3.1a shows one particular configuration.) If there were no noise, then $C = C_0$ and B is empty. Then the picture is produced by the following probability law:

$p_1(P,Z) = d(Z-D)$ if P is in C.

$p_1(P,Z) = d(Z-L)$ if P is in A.

where $d(x)$ is a function that equals one when its argument is zero, and is zero otherwise. If there were noise present, then the image could be produced by the following probability law:

$$p_1(P,Z) = f(Z-D) \text{ if } P \text{ is in } C.$$

$$p_1(P,Z) = f(Z-L) \text{ if } P \text{ is in } A.$$

$$p_1(P,Z) = \frac{f(Z-D)+f(Z-L)}{2} \text{ if } P \text{ is in } B.$$

where $f(x)$ is the function shown in Figure 3.1b. $\square$

This example also shows some limitations of the model. The region B will have a random dot appearance, even though one would expect pixels near C to be dark, and pixels near A to be white. A more realistic model should also use the *second order* probability density function $p_2(P,Q,Z,Y)$, that pixel P has value Z and pixel Q has value Y.

Example 3.2: An image with alternating vertical dark and light stripes can be generated by the following specification of $p_2(P,Q,Z,Y)$:

$p_2(P,Q,Z,Y) = f(Z-Y)$ if P and Q line up vertically, or if they line up horizontally and their distance is an even multiple of the stripe width.

$p_2(P,Q,Z,Y) = 1 - f(Z-Y)$ if P and Q line up horizontally, and their distance is an odd multiple of the stripe width.

These specifications are not complete because they do not specify $p_2(P,Q,Z,Y)$ for other relative positions of P and Q, except when the two are in the same vertical or horizontal line. A complete specification of p_2 would require considerably more space. $\square$

These examples point out one difficulty in the use of probability densities, especially of second order: the large size of the respective arrays, if the functions are given in a tabular form, or the need for complex specifications, if they are given in closed form. One common simplification is to ignore the dependence on P for the first order probability density, and consider only the relative position of P and Q for the second order density. Furthermore, a single image may be used to estimate these functions. Readers familiar with the theory of random processes will recognize that this approach is justified only under the assumption of ergodicity, which does not hold for most nontrivial picture generating processes. Therefore, the resulting estimates must be used with caution.

3.2 HISTOGRAM AND HISTOGRAM EQUALIZATION

Algorithm 3.1 shows how to compute an estimate of $p_1(P,Z)$ from a single image under the assumption that it is independent of P. The result is known as the *histogram* $H(Z)$ of the image. If $f(P)$ denotes the brightness level at pixel P, then Algorithm 3.1 can be used to evaluate $H(Z)$. The histogram of Figure 2.3 is shown in Figure 3.2.

Algorithm 3.1 Histogram Evaluation

Notation: $f(P)$ is value of pixel P with range $[0,L]$. H is histogram array.

1.   Initialize the array $H(Z)$ $(0 \leq Z \leq L)$ to zero.
2.   **For** all pixels P of the image **do**:
          Begin.
3.   Increment $H(f(P))$ by 1.
          End.
4.   **End of Algorithm.**

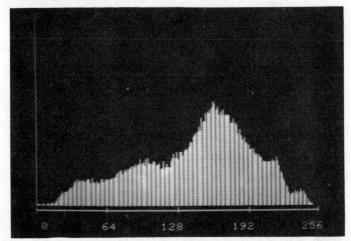

Figure 3.2   Gray level histogram for Figure 2.3. Note that some levels are missing. These are also missing from the original image due to a problem in the A/D converter during digitization. One of the bits was never set and therefore some gray levels have not been realized.

The histogram can be used for image enhancement or encoding in the following manner. It is possible that $H(Z)$ is zero for many values of Z, and this means that the available levels of quantization are not used efficiently. It would be desirable then to reassign them so that the dynamic range of the image increases. Figure 3.3 (see Plate 5) shows an underexposed photograph and the corresponding histogram. There exist few pixels with values between 180 and 255. One could try to scale the values in order to occupy the full range, but this is not always feasible, and certainly not for the current example. A better way of using the available display range is to reassign values so that the resulting histogram is as flat as possible.

Let A be the image area and N the number of available brightness levels. For a perfectly flat histogram one must have A/N pixels at each level. If the brightness value of some level Z is k times that average, then that level must be mapped into k different levels from, say, Z_1 to Z_k. Thus we must introduce a rule for doing this one-to-many mapping. There is no general policy that works well in all applications, but the following are three possibilities.

Rule 1 Always map Z onto the midlevel $(Z_1+Z_k)/2$. (This does not result in a flat histogram, but one where brightness levels are spaced apart.)

Rule 2 Assign at random one of the levels in the interval $[Z_1,Z_k]$. (This can result in loss of contrast if the original histogram had two distinct peaks that were far apart.)

Rule 3 Examine the neighborhood of the pixel, and assign to it a level from $[Z_1,Z_k]$ which is closest to the neighborhood average. (This can cause edge smearing, and requires considerably more computation than the other two rules.)

The first rule is purely heuristic. It does not produce truly equalized histograms, but it achieves full utilization of the dynamic range with less effort than the other rules. (In one particular implementation the second rule required about four times as much time as the first because of the need for randomization.) The motivation for the second rule is a desire to avoid any systematic error: when an arbitrary choice must be made, do so in a random fashion. The third rule attempts to enforce some coherence among pixel levels. It assumes that the closer two pixels are on the plane, the more likely it is that they have similar values. (See Section 3.4 for more on this point.)

Algorithm 3.2 Histogram Equalization

Notation: H is the histogram array. H_{int} is an integral of the histogram. *Z* denotes the old levels and *R* the new ones. Each *Z* is mapped onto an interval $[left(Z), right(Z)]$.

0.   Read an image, evaluate its histogram and store it in the array *H*. Let H_{avg} be its average value.

1.   Set $R = 0$ and $H_{int} = 0$.

2.   **For** $Z = 0$ to *L* **do**:
     Begin.

4.   Set $left(Z) = R$ and add $H(Z)$ to H_{int}.

5.   **While** H_{int} is greater than H_{avg} **do**:
          Begin.

6.   Subtract H_{avg} from H_{int} and increment *R*.
          End.

7.   Set $right(Z) = R$ and define the value of *new* (*Z*) according to the rule used. For Rule 1 set *new* (*Z*) to the average of *left* (*Z*) and *right* (*Z*). For Rule 2 set *new*(*Z*) to the difference $right(Z) - left(Z)$. (For Rule 3 *new*(*Z*) is left undefined.)
     End.

8.   **For** all pixels *P* of the image **do**:
     Begin.

9.   **If** *left* ($f(P)$) equals *right* ($f(P)$), **then** set the new value of the pixel *P* to *left* ($f(P)$).

10.   **Else**:
          If Rule 1 is used, set the value to *new* ($f(P)$).
          If Rule 2 is used, choose a point at random from the interval $[0, new(f(P))]$, add its value to *left* ($f(P)$), and use the result for the new value of *P*.
          If Rule 3 is used, compute the average of the neighborhood of *P*. If it exceeds *right* (*Z*) use *right* (*Z*) as the new value. If it is below *left* (*Z*) use *left* (*Z*) as the new value. Otherwise use the average as the new value.
     End.

11. **End of Algorithm.**

Algorithm 3.2 implements histogram equalization for any of these rules. Step 0 prepares the histogram according to Algorithm 3.1. Steps 1 to 7 do the equalization by mapping the old brightness levels onto the new levels. Steps 8 to 10 compute the new image. Figure 3.4 (Plate 6) shows the results of its application to the image of Figure 3.3.

This kind of processing cannot be applied to images indiscriminately because equalization can often cause a deterioration in appearance. Figure 3.5 (Plate 7) shows an image and its histogram, while Figure 3.6 (Plate 8) shows the results of equalization. Because the bimodal histogram has spread, the equalized image has a "dirty" appearance.

Histogram equalization can also be used to produce a coarser quantization of an image. For example, an image may have been digitized with many gray levels (e.g., 256), but it must be displayed on a device with only eight levels available. Algorithm 3.2 can be used with L equal to the new maximum brightness (7 in this case). The same value should also be used to find the average of the histogram H_{avg}. Note that in this case it is unlikely that a single level has to be mapped into many, so that steps 7 and 10 of the algorithm can be simplified. Figure 3.7 (Plate 9) shows the results of such quantization for the image of Figure 2.3. A comparison between Figure 3.7 (Plate 9) and Figures 2.9 and 2.10 (Plate 3) shows clearly that considering only the most significant bits is not the optimal solution. In particular, there may be applications where the cost of a preprocessor for histogram equalization may be less than the cost of additional refresh memory required for displays with more bits. If the limiting factor is not the memory cost but the optical characteristics of the display medium, then a function of the type *color*(u,v) described in Section 1.7 (Table 1.2) can be used to implement the equalization.

A related problem occurs in the use of *pseudocolor*. In some applications the detection of important information requires the discrimination between gray levels that are near each other. It is possible to use histogram equalization to expand the range of intensities used in the region of interest. Alternatively, we may map such levels not on a gray scale but on *color*. Because the number of distinct colors available may be small we must use histogram equalization for that purpose also.

Example 3.3: In many medical diagnosis or industrial quality control problems one is interested in detecting dark spots in a radiographic image. The form of such spots is important for the diagnosis so that they must be picked up from the background carefully. If one looks at the original image such "pathological" spots may be confused with "shadows." One form of image enhancement is to increase the brightness resolution for the darker parts of the image. If the range of the original data is [0,255], then such an enhancement can be done by mapping the range [0,31] onto [0,254] (using Algorithm 3.2 with Rule 1) and the range [32,255] onto the value 255. Brightness values now should differ from each other by about ten percent or more. An alternative arrangement is to consider the histogram in the range [0,31] only, map it onto eight values, and then assign each one of them to one of eight colors through a *color* (u, v) instruction (see Table 1.2). □

3.3 CO-OCCURRENCE MATRICES

A *co-occurrence matrix* is an estimate of $p_2(P, Q, Z, Y)$ over a single image under the assumption that p_2 depends only on the relative position of P and Q. We denote such a matrix by $C_r(Z, Y)$ where r stands for the relation between P and Q. The number of such matrices can be quite large, and some further simplifications are in order. First, one may consider only the immediate neighbors of a pixel: one above it, or one to the right of it. Second, one may ignore the orientation completely, and average the matrices obtained for various orientations. Algorithm 3.3 is a modification of Algorithm 3.1 and calculates such matrices. If averaging of the matrices is desired, then the initialization to zero should be done outside the first loop, and the final result divided by the number of relations used.

Algorithm 3.3 Evaluation of Co-occurrence Matrices.

1.   **For** all relations r between pairs of pixels **do**:
         Begin.
2.   Initialize the array $C_r(Z, Y)$ $(0 \leq Z \leq L, 0 \leq Y \leq L)$ to zero.
3.   **For** all pixels P of the image **do**:
               Begin.
4.   Let Q denote the neighbor of P according to relation r. Increment $C_r(f(P), f(Q))$ by 1.
               End.
         End.
5.   **End of Algorithm.**

It is possible that if P is a pixel near the image frame, the pixel Q defined by the relation r does not exist. In this case we may replace $f(Q)$ by a zero or by some other special value. In the sequel we shall assume that pixels P and Q are always adjacent. Also, in the examples of this section we shall consider only two relations: when Q is to the right of P (relation 1), and when Q is above P (relation 2). Many properties of the matrix C_r are obvious from the way it is constructed. First, its diagonal elements are approximately equal to the areas of regions, with the $C_r(k, k)$ element equal to the area of regions whose pixels have value k. Second, the off diagonal elements have values approximately equal to the length of the boundaries between regions, with the $C_r(k,j)$ element equal to the contour length between regions whose pixels have values k and j. For pictures with low contrast, elements far from the diagonal should be zero or very small, while the opposite will be true for high contrast images. A major difficulty in using co-occurrence matrices is their large dimension ($L \times L$). It is possible to overcome this problem by introducing a coarser quantization while estimating the matrix. The technique based on histogram equalization, described in the previous section, may be used for this purpose.

Example 3.4: Suppose that in the image of Example 3.2 each stripe is five pixels wide, the image is bilevel, and has dimension $N \times N$. Then the two co-occurrence matrices will be (approximately)

$$C_1 = \begin{bmatrix} 4N/10 & N/10 \\ N/10 & 4N/10 \end{bmatrix} \tag{3.1a}$$

$$C_2 = \begin{bmatrix} N/2 & 0 \\ 0 & N/2 \end{bmatrix} \tag{3.1b}$$

Note that these equations would remain the same if the picture were changed as long as the number of stripes and their average width were unchanged. $\square$

Three additional examples of co-occurrence matrices, calculated over parts of Figure 2.3, are shown in Figure 3.8. In order to reduce the matrix size an eight level quantization was used. The levels were found by histogram equalization over the whole image so that the result was the same as Figure 3.7b (Plate 9). Matrix (a) was evaluated over a 128×128 square on the curtain, matrix (b) over a 90×90 square on the hair, and matrix (c) over a 80×80 square on the shirt. Each matrix is the average for four relations: above, below, left, and right. Clearly, these matrices provide information about the *texture,* as well as the average brightness of the image. Although texture is a term people easily understand, its formal definition is much harder. One can assume that if two areas of an image have the same set of co-occurrence matrices, then they will also appear to have the same texture (see Bibliographical Notes).

	1	2	3	4	5	6	7	8
1	0	0	0	0	0	0	0	0
2	0	0	0	0	0	0	0	0
3	0	0	353	444	17	0	0	0
4	0	0	444	5791	1902	595	17	0
5	0	0	17	1902	2452	2077	138	0
6	0	0	0	595	2077	5970	1812	5
7	0	0	0	17	138	1812	3676	51
8	0	0	0	0	0	5	51	17

(a)

	1	2	3	4	5	6	7	8
1	483	422	9	8	0	0	0	0
2	422	7350	1450	71	0	0	0	0
3	9	1450	3068	413	1	0	0	0
4	8	71	413	267	4	0	0	0
5	0	0	1	4	0	0	0	0
6	0	0	0	0	0	0	0	0
7	0	0	0	0	0	0	0	0
8	0	0	0	0	0	0	0	0

(b)

	1	2	3	4	5	6	7	8
1	650	127	31	32	21	29	28	91
2	127	535	124	55	18	21	41	48
3	31	124	435	142	33	39	51	110
4	32	55	142	667	113	88	85	172
5	21	18	33	113	253	179	55	108
6	29	21	39	88	179	317	111	201
7	28	41	51	85	55	111	109	338
8	91	48	110	172	108	201	338	4589

(c)

Figure 3.8 Three co-occurrence matrices

3.4 LINEAR IMAGE FILTERING

A significant amount of image processing can be performed without repeating the statistical analysis of the previous section for each new image. Only some limited *a priori* knowledge is enough. For example, suppose that the form of the co-occurrence matrix of an ideal image is known and that we want to improve a noisy copy of the original. If the matrix has its largest elements along or near the main diagonal, then we know that most pixels should have the color of their neighbors. If we wanted to equalize the histogram of such an image, then we would be justified in using Rule 3, as discussed in Section 3.2. If we want to eliminate noise, then the replacement of each pixel of the noisy image by a weighted sum of its neighbors will reduce the variability among adjacent pixels, and we will obtain a picture that is closer to the original (see Example 3.5 below). In this way, we are led to an equation that describes the relation between the original image $f(x,y)$ and the *filtered* image $g(x,y)$:

$$g(x,y) = \sum_{i=-M}^{M} \sum_{j=-M}^{M} h(x,y,i,j)f(x+i,y+j) \tag{3.2}$$

The process that carries out this operation is said to be a *linear filter,* and in particular a *moving average* filter because at each pixel we replace its value with some type of an average of the value of its neighbors. If the weighting function h is the same throughout the picture, and does not depend on (x,y), then Equation (3.2) can be written as

$$g(x,y) = \sum_{i=-M}^{M} \sum_{j=-M}^{M} h(i,j)f(x+i,y+j) \tag{3.3}$$

This is called a *space invariant* filter. Such filters are common in the processing of time signals, but their relevance to picture processing is questionable. Equation (3.3) takes a simpler form when written in terms of Fourier transforms. It can be shown (see Bibliographical Notes) that

$$G(u,v) = H(u,v) \cdot F(u,v) \tag{3.4}$$

The effect of the filter is to attenuate certain frequencies and amplify others, depending on the magnitude of $H(u,v)$.

Example 3.5: If it is desired to remove high frequency noise from a picture, then such a smoothing can be accomplished by using, among others, the following form of $h(i,j)$:

$$h(0,0) = \frac{1}{4} \tag{3.5a}$$

$$h(1,0) = h(0,1) = h(0,-1) = h(-1,0) = \frac{1}{8} \qquad (3.5b)$$

$$h(1,1) = h(1,-1) = h(-1,1) = h(-1,-1) = \frac{1}{16} \qquad (3.5c)$$

The effect of the filter can be seen by comparing the difference in the values of neighboring pixels before and after its application. In particular, a simple calculation shows that

$$g(x,y)-g(x+1,y) = \frac{1}{8}[f(x,y)-f(x+1,y)] +$$

$$\frac{1}{8}[f(x-1,y)-f(x+1,y)] +$$

$$\frac{1}{16}[f(x,y-1)+f(x,y+1)-f(x+1,y-1)-f(x+1,y+1)+$$

$$f(x-1,y-1)+f(x-1,y+1)-f(x+2,y-1)-f(x+2,y+1)] \qquad (3.6)$$

If D_f denotes the maximum absolute difference between adjacent pixels in $f(x,y)$ and D_g the corresponding difference in $g(x,y)$, then the above equation implies that

$$D_g \leq \frac{1}{8}D_f + \frac{3}{8}D_f + \frac{1}{16}4 \cdot 2 \cdot D_f = D_f \qquad (3.7)$$

i.e., that difference cannot increase. Equality occurs only when the maximum difference between n pixels is n times the difference between a pair, i.e., when $f(x,y)$ is a linear function of its arguments. If this is not true, then the difference will decrease and regions will become more uniform. Usually, because such a simple filter is not sufficient for the removal of the noise, one must use a higher order filter. One possible implementation of higher order filters is to use a simple filter and apply it repeatedly to the image. Figure 3.10 (Plate 11) shows the results of such processing: (a) is the original image that was obtained from Figure 3.9 (Plate 10) by adding *Gaussian white noise*, and (b) is the result obtained after eight applications of the filter of Equation (3.5). One can see, immediately, that this process removes not only high frequency noise, but also smears out the edges. Indeed, if we apply Equation (3.6) to a perfect edge

$$f(x,y) = 1 \quad \text{for} \ x \leq X$$

$$f(x,y) = 0 \quad \text{for} \ x > X$$

we find

$$g(X,y)-g(X+1,y) = \frac{1}{8}+\frac{1}{8}+\frac{4}{16} = \frac{1}{2}$$

In other words the difference between the values of adjacent pixels has been halved and this clearly resulted in the loss of contrast.

We can also study the effects of the filter in terms of the Fourier transform of $h(i,j)$. Let $E(x)$ be an abbreviation denoting the term

$$E(x) = \exp(j\frac{2\pi}{N}x) \ .$$

Then the application of Equation (3.4) yields

$$H(u,v) = \frac{1}{4} + \frac{1}{8}\left[E(-v)+E(v)+E(-u)+E(u)\right] +$$
$$\frac{1}{16}\left[E(-(u+v))+E(-(u-v))+E(u-v)+E(u+v)\right] \quad (3.8)$$

This equation can be simplified by using first the identity

$$\cos x = \frac{1}{2}\left[\exp(jx)+\exp(-jx)\right]$$

and then simple trigonometric transformations so that it takes the form

$$H(u,v) = \frac{1}{4}(1+\cos\frac{2\pi}{N}v+\cos\frac{2\pi}{N}u+\cos\frac{2\pi}{N}v\cos\frac{2\pi}{N}u) \quad (3.9)$$

We note that H is zero whenever u or v equals $N/2$, and also that

$$H(0,0)=1 \quad H(0,\frac{N}{4})=H(\frac{N}{4},0)=\frac{1}{2} \quad H(\frac{N}{4},\frac{N}{4})=\frac{1}{4} \ .$$

Thus, high frequencies are attenuated. □

This simultaneous removal of noise and smearing of edges suggests that linear, space-invariant filters should be used cautiously in processing pictorial data. Unfortunately, the extensive and successful use of similar filters for time functions has encouraged their application in picture processing without regard to their limitations.

A similar problem exists for *high pass filters*. These produce images with sharper edges, but they also amplify high frequency noise.

Example 3.6: A simple high pass filter has the form

$$h(0,0) = b \quad\quad (3.10a)$$

$$h(1,0) = h(-1,0) = h(0,1) = h(1,0) = -a \quad\quad (3.10b)$$

Its Fourier transform is equal to

$$H(u,v) = b - 2a(\cos\frac{2\pi}{N}v+\cos\frac{2\pi}{N}u) \quad\quad (3.11)$$

The maximum value of H is $b+4a$ and is achieved when $u=v=N/2$, while its minimum is $H(0,0) = b-4a$. □

3.5 NONLINEAR IMAGE FILTERING

Filters that do not smear edges, but only remove the noise from the interior of regions, are far more complex than any of the forms given by Equation (3.3). Such filters must attempt to detect edges before they apply a smoothing function. Since edge detection is difficult on a noisy image, the problem is by no means an easy one. We outline here some of the most common approaches.

3.5.1 Directional Filters

One technique uses a linear filter that is symmetrical with respect to an axis rather than a point. Then at each pixel an effort is made to estimate the direction of an edge, if any, and the filter avoids averaging points across the edge. This idea can be implemented in a simple way by defining the following two functions of the angle ϕ that an edge forms with a coordinate axis.

ϕ	0°	45°	90°	135°
$c(\phi)$	1	1	0	−1
$s(\phi)$	0	1	1	1

Then the filter function $h(i,j,\phi)$ is defined as

$$h(0,0,\phi)=0.5, \quad h(c(\phi),s(\phi),\phi)=h(-c(\phi),-s(\phi),\phi)=0.25 ,$$

and zero for all other arguments i,j. At each pixel the values of

$$V(\phi) = [f(x,y)-f(x+c(\phi),y+s(\phi))]^2 +$$
$$[f(x,y)-f(x-c(\phi)),y-s(\phi))]^2$$

are calculated for $\phi = 0, 45°, 90°$, and 135°. Then the filter is applied for that value of ϕ for which $V(\phi)$ is minimum. Its effect is shown in Figure 3.11 (Plate 12).

3.5.2 Two-part Filters

Two-part filters are an extension of directional linear filters. First, a low pass filter is applied on the image, and then the gradient of $f(x,y)$ is calculated. This should give some idea about the location of the edges. Then a second pass is made over the filtered image using a filter whose coefficients depend on the location so that edges will not be smeared. If the original image has been lost, then a high pass filter may be used on the filtered image with large coefficients in the areas of large gradient and small coefficients elsewhere. This should restore the values of the original image in locations where the gradient has a high value. If the original image is still available, then a low pass filter could be appropriate. There exist various refinements of this approach, and readers can think of some more on their own (see Bibliographical Notes).†

3.5.3 Functional Approximation Filters

These rely on the replacement of $f(x,y)$ by a local estimate of some of its statistics. It is necessary to partition the area of an image into regions of a fixed size so that these statistics can be found. In the simplest form of the method one evaluates the mean and variance of $f(x,y)$ over each such region. If the variance is below some set threshold, then the values of $f(x,y)$ are replaced by the mean. Otherwise, the region is subdivided into smaller parts, and the process is repeated. In this way edges will be isolated. Instead of estimating the mean one can approximate $f(x,y)$ by some smooth function and then subdivide the region if the error of the approximation is too big. (See Chapter 6 for data structures and Chapter 12 for approximation techniques.) This approach is also closely connected to segmentation, which we discuss in the next chapter.

3.6 BIBLIOGRAPHICAL NOTES

The texts [2.CA], [2.HA], [2.PR], and [2.RK] cited in the previous chapter discuss the questions of filtering and edge detection.

The proof of Equation (3.4) can be found in most elementary texts on signal processing, for example [3.ST] or [3.OS]. For more information on nonlinear filters one must consult the periodical literature. See [3.NM] for the directional filters and [3.AS] for a two-part filter. Histograms are discussed in virtually all texts on image processing and pattern recognition ([3.PA], [2.PR], [2.RK], etc.). The connection between co-occurrence matrices and texture was first explored by Haralick. See his recent review paper [3.HA] for a thorough discussion of the subject of texture. Julesz [3.J1], [3.J2] has studied human discrimination of random dot patterns on the basis of their high order statistics. His studies provide further evidence for the relation between second order statistics and texture.

Theoretical work in image processing faces a serious obstacle. The lack of a mathematical measure that reflects the subjective difference in the appearance of images. For example, suppose that we

---

† The term "two-pass" could be applied to such filters, but we prefer "two-part" because a different filter is used in each pass. Thus we can distinguish these nonlinear filters from linear ones where the extra passes are simple means for implementing high order filters.

have an image $f(x,y)$ and we want to find which of two image $f_1(x,y)$ and $f_2(x,y)$ is a closer approximation to $f(x,y)$. None of the conventional measures of the difference between two functions gives results that agree with what a human observer would say. See [2.SA] for a discussion of this subject.

3.7 RELEVANT LITERATURE

[3.AS]   Abramatic, J. F. and Silverman, L. M. "Non-Stationary Linear Restoration of Noisy Images," *Proc. 18 [th] IEEE Decision and Control Conference, vol. 1,* (December 1979), pp. 92-99.

[3.HA]   Haralick, R. M. "Statistical and Structural Approaches to Texture," *Proc. Fourth Intern. Joint Conf. on Pattern Recognition,* (November 1978), pp. 45-69.

[3.J1]   Julesz, B. *Foundations of Cyclopean Perception,* Chicago: University of Chicago Press, 1971.

[3.J2]   Julesz, B., "Experiments in the visual perception of texture," *Scientific American,* **232** (1975), pp. 34-43.

[3.NM]   Nagao, M. and Matsuyama, T. "Edge Preserving Smoothing," *Proc. Fourth Intern. Joint Conf. on Pattern Recognition,* (November 1978), pp. 518-520.

[3.OS]   Oppenheim, A. V. and Schafer, R. W. *Digital Signal Processing,* Englewood Cliffs, New Jersey: Prentice-Hall, 1975.

[3.PA]   Pavlidis, T. *Structural Pattern Recognition,* Berlin, Heidelberg, New York: Springer Verlag, 1977.

[3.ST]   Steiglitz, K. *An Introduction to Discrete Systems,* New York: J. Wiley, 1974.

3.8 PROBLEMS

3.1.   Incorporate the histogram equalization algorithm, Algorithm 3.2, in the gray scale overprinting program of Problem 1.6.

3.2.   Write a program for evaluating co-occurrence matrices.

3.3.   One can define the *diagonal dominance* for a matrix with nonnegative elements as the ratio of the sum of its diagonal elements over the sum of its off diagonal elements. What type of information about the appearance of an image does the diagonal dominance, D, of a co-occurrence matrix convey? Is it possible for D to be zero? Infinity? Use the program of the previous problem to evaluate D over parts of various images.

3.4.   This problem assumes that you have been working on the image
       editor (Problems 1.5 and 2.5). You may expand it now by
       incorporating into it the procedures of Problems 3.1 and 3.2.
       The main problem that must be solved is where and how the his-
       togram or the co-occurrence matrix will be displayed.
       Hints. You have two options: you may either set aside a part of
       the screen for the display of the statistics of the area pointed to,
       or you may assign parts of the refresh memory for storing these
       statistics and then use two "color" maps (see Instruction 13 of
       Table 1.2) to switch between the two. It is advisable to scale the
       co-occurrence matrix so that it can be displayed as an image.

3.5.   Design a low-pass filter for images where it is known that most
       edges are either vertical or horizontal.

3.6.   The implementation of Equation (3.3) requires that we keep two
       copies of the image: input and output. Suppose that instead we
       traverse the image and replace the value of each pixel by the
       weighted sum of the right hand side of the equation. This
       means that the new value will be used in subsequent calcula-
       tions. Investigate the effects of such a filter.

3.7.   Consider the following nonlinear filter: at each pixel the
       difference D_v between the two neighbors above and below is cal-
       culated, and also the difference D_h between the right and left
       neighbors. If D_v exceeds D_h, then the value of the pixel is
       replaced by the weighted average of itself and its two horizontal
       neighbors, otherwise it is replaced by the weighted average of
       itself and its two vertical neighbors. (Replacement is done in the
       manner of Equation (3.3) and not as in Problem (3.6).) Investi-
       gate the effects of the filter for different combinations of weights.
       Investigate them also when the filter is applied repeatedly on an
       image.

3.8.   Devise a gadget for the amateur photographer who has more
       money than talent. This should be a black box that takes overex-
       posed or underexposed photographs and produces copies with
       correct illumination. It should also improve the appearance of
       poorly focused images. Include an option where the photogra-
       pher does not have to specify what kind of correction is desired.
       Do you think that you can offer an option for correcting shots
       when the subject has moved? When the camera has moved?

Chapter 4

SEGMENTATION

4.1 INTRODUCTION

Segmentation identifies areas of an image that appear uniform to an observer, and subdivides the image into regions of uniform appearance. It is relatively easy to define uniformity in terms of gray level or color. It is far more difficult to specify what we mean by "uniform texture."

In general, we can perform segmentation in two different ways. We may assume that we know in advance the characteristics of the regions, or we may attempt to find those characteristics during processing. As a simple example, consider segmentation by color in an image where each of the three basic colors (red, green, and blue) is assigned two bits in each pixel. In order to find the red regions of a picture, we must check whether the appropriate bits of each pixel are equal to one while the remaining bits are zero.† On the other hand, we have a tougher problem if we are asked to divide the picture into two sets of regions, of two possible colors, without being given the colors in advance. In the latter case we must either study the statistics of the image and look for modalities or examine groups of pixels and check whether they form a uniform region. Because the topic of segmentation in its full generality is beyond the scope of this text, we shall limit our

---

† The suggested solution is too simple because it detects only regions of bright red. A more realistic solution should relax these conditions.

65

coverage to some of the simplest schemes. Section 4.2 examines thresholding, Section 4.3 deals with simple edge detection, and Section 4.4 introduces some region growing techniques.

Scene analysis is a topic related to segmentation. Its goal is to provide descriptions of images in some language. It is possible to separate the two processes and do the analysis after the completion of segmentation. However, many researchers use *a priori* information about the scene to guide the segmentation. Such techniques go well beyond signal processing and algorithms and, therefore, are outside the scope of this text.

4.2 THRESHOLDING

In this technique the brightness value of each pixel is compared to a *threshold* value, and the pixel is assigned to one of two categories depending on whether the threshold is exceeded or not. The selection of the threshold value is usually made from the histogram (discussed in Section 3.2). Indeed, suppose that we deal with class 1 images that satisfy the assumptions of Example 3.1, but for which we have no information about the shape and location of regions B and C. If an image indeed consists of two regions, one predominantly light and the other dark, one can expect that its histogram will have two peaks, as shown in Figure 3.5 (Plate 7). Then a threshold T can be chosen from the values between the two peaks and the region C can be defined as the set of all pixels whose value is below T. Figure 4.1 (Plate 13) shows the result of this operation for the original of Figure 3.5 for $T = 100$. Thresholding is the simplest possible technique for segmentation (i.e., for transforming class 1 pictures into class 2 pictures). Unfortunately it is not always possible to select the value of the threshold in advance because the average brightness level may vary and one must evaluate the histogram for each image.

In general, automatic evaluation of the threshold is a nontrivial problem. The presence of two distinct peaks in the histogram is not a common occurrence. Figure 4.2a (Plate 14) shows an image that seems to be a good candidate for thresholding, but whose histogram (Figure 4.2b (Plate 14)) has only one major peak, corresponding to the background. The objects correspond to the minor peak between about 32 and 64. Figure 4.3 (Plate 15) shows the results of thresholding for $T = 100$. Sometimes it is preferable to evaluate the histogram not over all the pixels of the image but only over those that lie near the boundaries of regions. This can be implemented easily by adding a test in Algorithm 3.1 where the value of a pixel is compared to that of its neighbors. Then $H(f(P))$ is incremented only if these values differ by more than the expected amount of noise. The rationale behind this restriction is that human perception is very sensitive to changes in brightness levels and less so to absolute levels.

4.3 EDGE DETECTION

These schemes search for *edges* between regions. They use a *gradient* operator, followed by a threshold operation on the gradient, in order to decide whether an edge has been found. Then pixels that have been identified as edges must be linked to form closed curves surrounding regions. In this section we shall discuss only some of the simplest edge detectors. A common technique is to take the difference between two groups of pixels in the manner of a high-pass linear filter of the type given by Equations (3.10). In order to take into account the differences in edge orientation, we need to use more than one such filter. If we define a matrix H with $H_{ji} = h(i,j)$, then two of the simplest possible filters are given by the following forms:

$$H_{horiz} = \begin{bmatrix} -1 & -c & -1 \\ 0 & 0 & 0 \\ 1 & c & 1 \end{bmatrix} \tag{4.1a}$$

$$H_{vert} = \begin{bmatrix} 1 & 0 & -1 \\ c & 0 & -c \\ 1 & 0 & -1 \end{bmatrix} \tag{4.1b}$$

The literature contains many papers that describe filters with values of c equal to 1 or 2 (see Bibliographical Notes). Because the high-pass filters tend to enhance noise, this class of techniques is of limited value for noisy images. Figures 4.4 and 4.5 (Plates 16 and 17) show the results of tests with the edge detector of Equations (4.1) for $c = 1$ on the original of Figure 3.9 (Plate 10). Note that the selection of a threshold for deciding that we have found an edge is far simpler than the selection of a threshold for segmentation. Another example of edge detection can be seen in Figure 4.6 (Plate 18). The results here are better than those of Figure 4.5 because of the higher contrast.

There are more elaborate edge detection schemes that overcome some of the disadvantages of the simple schemes described here only at great computational cost. The examples given in Figures 4.4 to 4.6 may leave the reader with the impression that images for which edge detection gives good results are also images for which thresholding is applicable, but this is not really the case. It is probably true that simple edge detectors are appropriate only for high contrast images with little high frequency noise. However, not all such images can be segmented properly by thresholding. In particular, *low frequency* noise, which does not interfere with edge detection, can render thresholding useless.

The simplest example is an image where there is an illumination gradient, a common occurrence in practice. The human eye is contrast sensitive and smooth changes in illumination may be ignored. However, what looks like "dark" in one end of the image has the same value as what looks like "light" at the other end, so there is no way to choose a threshold for separating "dark" from "light" areas. On the other hand, a simple edge detector can do the job quite well. This conclusion may hold even in cases where the low frequency noise is not as strong, because it may be easier to choose the threshold for deciding the presence of an edge than the threshold for segmenting the whole image. Figure 4.7 provides a simple illustration of these points.

```
000000000000000000000000000000000
000000000033333300000000000000000
111111144444444444441111111111111
111111444444444444441111111111111
222225555555222555555522222222222
222225555522222255555552222222222
333666666333333333666666633333333
333666666333333336666666666333333
444777777777777777777777774444
447777777777777777777777777444
558888888555555555558888888855
588888885555555555555888888885
699999999996666666666699999999996
666666666666666666666666666666666
77777777777777777777777777777777
77777777777777777777777777777777
```

Figure 4.7 An illustration of the advantages of simple edge detection over thresholding. Readers can probably detect the shape of a letter in the figure and could also design an edge detector for finding it automatically (see Problem 4.1).

4.4 SEGMENTATION BY REGION GROWING

While edge detection and thresholding focus on the difference of pixel values, region growing looks for groups of pixels of similar brightness. In its simplest form, the method starts with one pixel, and then examines its neighbors in order to decide whether they have similar brightness. If they do, then they are grouped together to form a region. In this way regions are grown out of single pixels. More advanced forms do not start with pixels but with a partition of an image into a set of small regions. A uniformity test is then applied to each region, and if the test fails the region is subdivided into smaller elements. This process is repeated until all regions are uniform. Then regions are grown out of smaller regions, rather than pixels. The details of implementation depend strongly on the data structures used for representing an image. The topic of region growing will be discussed in Chapter 6, as an example of application of such structures. The major advantage of using small regions rather than pixels is a reduced sensitivity to noise.

4.4.1 Segmentation by Average Brightness Level

One uniformity criterion is based on the comparison of the maximum difference between the value of a pixel and the average over a region. For a region R of size N let

$$m = \frac{1}{N} \sum_{P \epsilon R} f(P) .$$

(4.2a)

Then a region is called uniform if

$$\max_{P \epsilon R} |f(P) - m| < T$$

(4.2b)

for some threshold T. We may think of this definition of uniformity as heuristic, but it is possible to provide a theoretical justification for it under certain assumptions. The following analysis illustrates many of the problems involved in region growing, and it can be used as a model for analyzing other uniformity criteria.

We shall assume that the class 1 images we deal with are actually class 2 images with zero mean Gaussian white noise added to them. This means that the probability that the value of noise is z at pixel P will be given by the following equation:

$$p_n(z) = \frac{1}{\sqrt{2\pi}\,\sigma} e^{-\frac{z^2}{2\sigma^2}}$$

(4.3a)

where σ is the standard deviation of the noise. The values of $p_n(z)$ do not depend at all on the location of the pixel P because we assumed that the noise is white. In physical terms this means that the noise affects all pixels in the same way. The probability that the brightness value at pixel P differs from its mean by more than some amount x is given by the following integral.

$$I_n(x) = \frac{2}{\sqrt{2\pi}\,\sigma} \int_x^\infty e^{-\frac{z^2}{2\sigma^2}} dz$$

(4.3b)

The factor 2 enters because we consider both negative and positive deviations from the mean. The righthand side of the above equation is known as the *error function*, *erf* (t), where t is the ratio of x over σ. Most books with mathematical tables include listings of its values. We list a few of them in Table 4.1.

Table 4.1: Error Function

t	1.0	1.5	2.0	2.5	3.0	3.5	4.0
erf (t)	0.317	0.134	0.046	0.012	0.003	0.0005	0.0001

If a region is uniform, then Equation (4.2a) is the optimal estimator of the brightness value there (see Problem 4.4). In such a case deviations of the pixel values from m will be due to the noise only and therefore the probability that Equation (4.2b) does not hold for some pixel will be given by Equation (4.3b) if we choose $z = T$. Specifically, it will equal *erf* (T/σ). For example, if we choose T in Equation (4.2b) equal to 2σ, then the probability that this condition fails for a particular pixel is 4.6 percent, while for $T = 3\sigma$ it is about 0.3 percent. We shall use $p(T)$ to denote the value of this probability. The probability of satisfying Equation (4.2b) is $1 - p(T)$ per pixel, and since N is the number of pixels per region, then we will fail to recognize a uniform region only with probability $1 - [1 - p(T)]^N$. For values of $p(T)$ much smaller than $\frac{1}{N}$, this quantity equals approximately $N \cdot p(T)$. Choosing the threshold T equal to three times the standard deviation of the noise and assuming a 16×16 square region of 256 pixels yields a probability of failure for the uniformity test equal to 54 percent (using the exact formula). If the threshold is four times the standard deviation then the same probability is found to be only 2.5 percent, a more acceptable value from a practical viewpoint. (Here both the exact and the approximate formula give similar results: 0.0253 and 0.0256 respectively).

Calling a uniform region nonuniform is not the only possible error, and we must now estimate the probability that a nonuniform region will be called uniform. In this case, differences between m and the pixel values will be due also to differences between the values of the regions of the class 2 picture. Let m_1 and m_2 be these values, and let q_i percent of the pixels of a region be pixels whose true value is m_i $(i = 1,2)$. If the region is large enough to neglect the effect of noise in estimating the mean, then the mean will be $q_1 \cdot m_1 + q_2 \cdot m_2$. If a pixel has true value m_1, then the difference between this value and the estimated mean will be

$$\delta m = m_1 - (q_1 \cdot m_1 + q_2 \cdot m_2) . \tag{4.4}$$

Consequently, the event that its observed value differs by more than T from $q_1 \cdot m_1 + q_2 \cdot m_2$ can occur by having it differ from m_1 either by $T + \delta m$, or $T - \delta m$ and the probability of either event occurring equals

$$p_1 = \frac{1}{2} \Big[P(|T - \delta m|) + P(|T + \delta m|) \Big] . \tag{4.5}$$

Therefore, p_1 is the probability that the observed value of a pixel with true value m_1 violates Equation (4.2b). The probability that none of the pixels does so is

$$p_u = (1 - p_1)^{q_1^n} \cdot (1 - p_2)^{q_2^n} \tag{4.6}$$

where p_2 is defined in a manner similar to p_1. Thus p_u is the probability of accepting a region as uniform when in fact it is not. Clearly, if δm is small compared to T, then p_1 is close to $p(T)$. If this is also true for p_2, then p_u equals approximately $[1 - p(T)]^N$, which is the same as the probability of calling uniform a region that is truly uniform. In other words, the detection of uniformity will appear to be a random event. The situation where δm is small is likely to occur when a region contains pixels of almost only one kind, therefore the error of calling it uniform is not so serious. On the other hand, if a region is an approximately equal mixture of two pixel types, i.e., if $q_1 = q_2$, so that

$$\delta m = \frac{1}{2} \Big[m_1 - m_2 \Big] , \tag{4.7}$$

then we would like it to be called uniform with a very low probability. This will happen if the difference δm is expected to be much greater in absolute value than the standard deviation of the noise, since δm will then be of comparable size to T. Under these conditions the argument of the first term in the sum of Equation (4.5) will be near zero and therefore, the corresponding probability will be near 1. The second term will have an argument equal to a high multiple of the standard deviation, so that the probability will be near zero. These assumptions yield p_1 equal to approximately 0.5 and the same value can be found for p_2. Then p_u will be approximately equal to 0.5^N. In this case the violation of Equation (4.2b) implies a nonuniform region with probability $1 - 0.5^N$. For $N = 256$ this is very close to 1.

4.4.2 Other Uniformity Criteria

The previous analysis shows that the uniformity criterion of Equation (4.2b) is likely to err on the side of calling a region nonuniform too often. This may explain, at least in part, a common experience when an image is segmented using a criterion similar to Equation (4.2b): there is a large number of small regions that do not seem to have any real counterparts in the image. A complete analysis of other criteria is beyond the scope of this text, as is a discussion of the effects of the region size N on the reliability of the estimates for the region mean (see Bibliographical Notes). A somewhat different definition of uniformity can be made by comparing the statistics over a region with the statistics evaluated over parts of it. If they are close to each other, then the region may be called uniform. Such an approach can be useful for segmentation by *texture*. One can evaluate the co-occurrence matrix over each of a group of regions and then compare the matrices. If they are similar, the union of these regions is a uniform region. In general, let $F(R)$ be a *feature* estimated over the region R. If R_{12} is the union of two adjacent but disjoint regions R_1 and R_2, then one could define a uniformity criterion by requiring that $F(R_{12})$ be close to $F(R_1)$ and $F(R_2)$. R_1 could be the already found region and R_2 a small region that is considered for addition to R_1 (see Chapter 6 for other interpretations). We must choose a threshold T' so that when the absolute value of the difference $F(R_1)$ and $F(R_2)$ is below T', we decide in favor of uniformity. An analysis similar to that of Section 4.4.1 shows that T' must be greater than the variance of $F(R)$ caused by the noise. However, in many cases this variance is much smaller than the variance of the noise itself while the variance due to nonuniformity is of the same size as before. Thus a uniformity criterion based on comparison of features is more reliable than the one given by Equation (4.2b). (Of course the mean itself is such a feature.)

4.5 BIBLIOGRAPHICAL NOTES

Advanced segmentation techniques are usually treated in the context of pattern recognition. See Chapters 4-6 of [3.PA] and Chapters 7 and 8 of [2.HA] for more elaborate edge detectors, region-growing techniques, and scene analysis. The paper by Abdou and Pratt [4.AP] provides a detailed analysis and comparison of the simpler edge detection schemes, similar to those given by Equation (4.1). Brooks [4.BR] offers a theoretical justification for various edge detectors. See [4.CP] for a treatment of segmentation as an estimation problem and a discussion of the effects of region size on the reliability of the estimates of mean, etc.

We hope that the analysis of Section 4.4 has demonstrated the need for image models. These should not be confused with the object models used in scene analysis, even though they may often be related to them. Scene analysis models tend to be deterministic while image models are primarily stochastic and have to do with the distribution of the expected values of noise and differences in region statistics. Volume 12 (1980) of the journal *CGIP* is devoted to the subject of image modeling. [4.CE], [4.DM], and [4.HA] are some of the papers there which are particularly relevant to the topic of segmentation.

[4.BA] is a recent review of scene analysis with emphasis on three-dimensional models and models of illumination. This is a topic where interaction between image processing and graphics methodologies can be very fruitful, but work in this area is only in its earliest stages.

4.6 RELEVANT LITERATURE

[4.AP]   Abdou, I. E. and Pratt, W. K. "Quantitative Design and Evaluation of Enhancement / Thresholding Edge Detectors," *IEEE Proceedings,* **67** (1979), pp. 753-763.

[4.BA]   Bajcsy, R. "Three-dimensional Scene Analysis," *Proc. Fifth Intern. Conf. on Pattern Recognition,* Miami Beach, December 1980, pp. 1064-1074. (Published by IEEE Computer Society, IEEE Catalog No. 80CH1499-3.)

[4.BR]   Brooks, M. J. "Rationalizing Edge Detectors," *CGIP,* **8** (1978), pp. 277-285.

[4.CE]   Cooper, D. B.; Elliott, H.; Cohen, F.; Reiss, L.; and Symoser, P. "Stochastic Boundary Estimation and Object Recognition," *CGIP,* **12** (1980), pp. 326-356.

[4.CP]   Chen, P. C. and Pavlidis, T. "Image Segmentation as an Estimation Problem," *CGIP,* **12** (1980), pp. 153-172.

[4.DM]   Davis, L. S. and Mitiche, A. "Edge Detection in Textures," *CGIP,* **12** (1980), pp. 25-39.

[4.HA]   Haralick, R. M. "Edge and Region Analysis for Digital Image Data," *CGIP,* **12** (1980), pp. 60-73.

4.7 PROBLEMS

4.1.   Design an edge detector for segmenting the image of Figure 4.7.

4.2.   Locating an edge on an image can be treated as a problem for finding nonuniform regions. Try to modify the analysis of Section 4.4.1 for studying the edge detectors given by Equation (4.1).

4.3.   A possible alternative to Equation (4.2b) is to compare the value
        of the root mean square error to a threshold (instead of the
        value of the maximum error). Do you think this is a reasonable
        approach?

4.4.   Prove that the value of m given by Equation (4.2a) minimizes
        the integral square error between the values of $f(P)$ and m.
        (*Note:* the proof is contained in most standard texts on statistics
        or signal processing but it may take less time to derive it than
        search for it in a book.)

4.5.   Use the editor to perform an interactive evaluation of statistics
        of images. Position a window over an area that appears uniform
        to you and then call a procedure evaluating the statistics. (Histo-
        gram is one of them.)

Chapter 5

PROJECTIONS

5.1 INTRODUCTION

In image processing, the term *projection* usually refers to mapping an image into a waveform whose values are the sums of the values of the image points along particular directions. (In graphics, as well as in some scene analysis problems, the term is commonly used to denote the mapping of a three-dimensional object to the plane with all depth information lost.) The *reconstruction* of gray scale images from their projections is one of the best known uses of computers for medical applications because it provides a strong diagnostic tool replacing some painful and dangerous techniques (see Bibliographical Notes). The technique can be extended to reconstruct a three-dimensional object from its two-dimensional projections. This is achieved by linking together a series of cross-sections. Typically, the object is a human organ (heart, brain, etc.) and the projections are radiographic or ultrasonic images, but the theory is applicable to any type of object and penetrating signal. Figure 5.1 (Plate 19) illustrates the results of such a reconstruction. We shall discuss here some of the simpler techniques, without going into any discussion of medical applications. Sections 5.2 and 5.3 describe a fundamental method for such reconstructions.

Projections have also been used for *shape analysis* and that application is discussed in Section 5.4. Finally, the Appendix is a listing of a reconstruction program implemented on a general purpose computer using gray scale overprinting for the output.

5.2 INTRODUCTION TO RECONSTRUCTION TECHNIQUES

If $d(x,y,z)$ is the density of an object at the point (x,y,z), and if the absorption of x-rays is proportional to the density by a factor k, then a (negative) radiograph parallel to the (y,z)-plane will have a brightness function:

$$p(y,z)=k\int_L f(x,y,z)dx \qquad (5.1)$$

where L is a line through the object.

If the x-rays are not along the x-axis but form an angle ϕ with it (see Figure 5.2), then the integrals will be computed along lines with equations

$$x\sin\phi-y\cos\phi=t \qquad (5.2)$$

where t is the Euclidean distance of a line from the origin. Then we have

$$p(\phi,t,z)=k\int_v d(x,y,z)\delta[x\sin\phi-y\cos\phi-t]dxdy \qquad (5.3)$$

where v is a volume surrounding the object and $\delta[]$ denotes a delta function.† The introduction of the delta function allows us to define the line of integration implicitly rather than explicitly as in Equation (5.1).

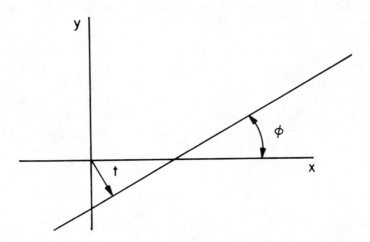

Figure 5.2   Definition of the quantities ϕ and t used in Equation (5.2)

---

† This is a function that is everywhere zero except where its argument is zero, and whose integral from $-\infty$ to $+\infty$ equals one.

In practice, projections are taken only for a fixed value of z, and a *cross-section* of the object is reconstructed and displayed. (Of course, repetition of the process for different z will yield information about the whole object.) Then we can drop the dependence on z from Equation (5.3) and, denoting by $f(x,y)$ the absorption at (x,y), we obtain

$$p(\phi,t)=\int_R\int f(x,y)\delta[x\sin\phi-y\cos\phi-t]dxdy . \qquad (5.4)$$

R is an area containing the cross-section of interest. Since we assume $f(x,y)=0$ outside the object, the exact form of R is not important.

The reconstruction of $f(x,y)$ from a set of $p(\phi,t)$ for different values of ϕ is based on a mathematical result that states that the two-dimensional Fourier transform of $f(x,y)$ can be found from the set of one-dimensional Fourier transforms of $p(\phi,t)$. Then $f(x,y)$ can be found by taking an inverse transform. This result can be proven rather easily as follows.

Let $P(\phi,w)$ be the *FT* of $p(\phi,t)$ given by the equation:

$$P(\phi,w)=\int_{-\infty}^{\infty} e^{-jwt}p(\phi,t)dt . \qquad (5.5)$$

Substituting Equation (5.4) into Equation (5.5) we find

$$P(\phi,w)=\int_{-\infty}^{\infty}\int_{-\infty}^{\infty} f(x,y)e^{-jw(x\sin\phi-y\cos\phi)}dxdy , \qquad (5.6)$$

where we have used the fact that the integrand is zero unless $t=x\sin\phi-y\cos\phi$. A comparison with Equation (2.2) shows that this is the two-dimensional Fourier transform of $f(x,y)$ calculated at frequencies $w\sin\phi$ and $-w\cos\phi$. It can be shown that the inverse Fourier transform for the two-dimensional case is given by an equation analogous to Equation (2.6), and in particular

$$f(x,y) = \frac{1}{4\pi^2}\int_{-\infty}^{\infty}\int_{-\infty}^{\infty} F(u,v)e^{j(ux+vy)}dudv . \qquad (5.7)$$

$P(\phi,w)$ is actually $F(u,v)$ in polar coordinates with $u=w\sin\phi$ and $v=-w\cos\phi$. The transformation from cartesian into polar coordinates replaces the differential $dudv$ by $|w|dwd\phi$ where $|w|$ is the determinant of the Jacobian matrix of the transformation. Thus we find

$$f(x,y) = \frac{1}{4\pi^2}\int_0^\pi d\phi\int_{-\infty}^{\infty} P(\phi,w)e^{jw(x\sin\phi-y\cos\phi)}|w|dw . \qquad (5.8)$$

Equations (5.4), (5.5), and (5.8) summarize the mathematical foundation of reconstruction by projections. Theoretically, it is possible to achieve a "perfect" reconstruction by calculating $p(\phi,t)$ for a large enough number of angles. However, many practical difficulties exist. Before we discuss these, we will examine the discrete version of these equations, since this is what is implemented in practice. Equation (5.4) is unchanged since the projection operation is always analog. Equation (5.5) becomes

$$P(\phi,w)=\sum_{k=0}^{N-1} e^{-j\frac{2\pi}{N}wk} p(\phi,k) \qquad w=0,1,\cdots N-1 \qquad (5.9)$$

where N is the number of points into which a line perpendicular to the direction of projection has been quantized. Equation (5.7) becomes

$$f(k,l) = \frac{1}{4\pi^2}\sum_{u=0}^{N-1}\sum_{v=0}^{N-1} F(u,v)e^{j\frac{2\pi}{N}(uk+vl)} . \qquad (5.10)$$

Equation (5.9) provides values of $F(u,v)$ in the form of $F(w\sin\phi,-w\cos\phi)$. Note that in this way we cannot obtain f for exactly N^2 equally spaced values of its argument. This is illustrated in Figure 5.3. We have many more values at low frequencies than at high. In the continuous case (Equation (5.8)), this lack of high frequencies is compensated for by the factor $|w|$, and therefore it is advisable to use a discrete version of Equation (5.8) rather than Equation (5.10). Much of the research in reconstruction algorithms deals in essence with the proper compensation for the nonuniform distribution of the available values of the Fourier transform.

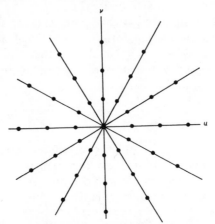

Figure 5.3 Distribution of available values of the Fourier transform. The samples (full circles) are spaced uniformly along the rays, but the distribution is not uniform in the u-v coordinate system.

5.3 A CLASS OF RECONSTRUCTION ALGORITHMS

Major practical problems in implementing reconstruction are the need for fast computation so that the results can be displayed in real time, or almost real time, and the need to keep noise and distortion low. We shall describe one popular reconstruction method, that of *convolution*.

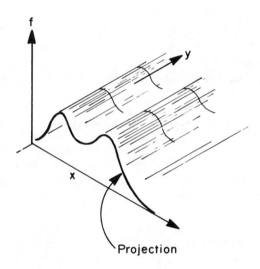

Figure 5.4 Definition of the backprojection. The curve in the f-x plane is translated along the direction of the y axis to create a cylindrical surface. That surface, viewed as a function of two variables, x and y, is the backprojection.

Let the inner integral of Equation (5.8) be defined as

$$q(\phi,t) = \frac{1}{2\pi} \int_{-\infty}^{\infty} P(\phi,w)|w|e^{jwt}dw \qquad (5.12)$$

where

$$t = x\sin\phi - y\cos\phi .$$

Then

$$f(x,y) = \frac{1}{2\pi} \int_{0}^{\pi} q(\phi, x\sin\phi - y\cos\phi)d\phi . \qquad (5.13)$$

For a fixed ϕ, $q(\phi, x\sin\phi - y\cos\phi)$ may be interpreted as a *backprojection*, i.e., a function of two variables defined from a function of a single variable, as shown in Figure 5.4. Then the reconstruction is half the average of the backprojections integrated over ϕ. (The factor 1/2 enters because the righthand side of Equation (5.13) is divided by 2π, while the integral is only from 0 to π.) The function $q(\phi,t)$ is the inverse *FT* of $P(\phi,w)|w|$, or the convolution of $p(\phi,t)$ with a function $r(t)$ whose *FT* is $|w|$, i.e.,

$$q(\phi,t) = \int_{-\infty}^{\infty} p(\phi,\tau)r(t-\tau)d\tau . \qquad (5.14)$$

From the theory of linear systems, we know that this is the output of a filter with impulse response $r(t)$ when its input is $p(\phi,t)$. (ϕ acts as a parameter.) This leads to the reconstruction Algorithm 5.1 where M is the number of angles ϕ measured, and $f_r(x,y)$ is the reconstructed function.†

Algorithm 5.1 Generic Reconstruction Algorithm

    Notation: $p(\phi,t)$ projections; $q(\phi,t)$ filtered projections; $f_r(x,y)$ reconstruction; M number of angles in calculating projections.

1.   Initialize $f_r(x,y) = 0$.
2.   **For** each measured ϕ **do:**
        Begin.
3.   Pass $p(\phi,t)$ through the filter to find $q(\phi,t)$.
4.   **For** each (x,y) **do:**
            Begin.
5. $f_r(x,y) = f_r(x,y) + q(\phi,x\sin\phi-y\cos\phi)$.
            End.
        End.
6.   **For** each (x,y) **do:**
        Begin.
7. $f_r(x,y) = \dfrac{1}{2M}f_r(x,y)$.
        End.
8.   **End of Algorithm.**

What remains, now, is the choice of the filter, and this is where the practical difficulties lie. There is no physically realizable filter with transfer function $|w|$ which does not also amplify the noise. One can say that the critical step in a reconstruction technique is the choice of $r(t)$. The following are some possible choices:

    (a) $r(t)$ is delta function and the transfer function is 1 rather than $|w|$. In this case there is no need for convolution since $q(\phi,t)=p(\phi,t)$.

---

† We use a different symbol to emphasize that is a computed function rather than the true absorption $f(x,y)$.

One simply finds backprojections from the projections $p(\phi,t)$ and calculates their average as the reconstruction. Of course, this will be distorted and the distortion can be estimated from the ratio of the transfer function of the actual filter over the transfer function of the ideal filter. In this case this ratio is $1/|w|$, i.e. a low-pass filter, so that the reconstruction will be blurred.

(b) If a is the spacing between parallel rays of the projection choose:

$$r(0) \;=\; 4/(\pi a)^2 \tag{5.15a}$$

$$r(ka) = -4/(\pi^2 a^2(4k^2-1)) \quad k=\pm 1,\pm 2,\cdots \tag{5.15b}$$

and $r(t)$ to be linear between these points. This yields

$$R(w) = \left| \frac{2}{a}\sin\frac{wa}{2} \right| \left[\frac{\sin(wa/2)}{wa/2} \right]^2 . \tag{5.16}$$

If $|w|$ is much smaller than $1/a$, then

$$R(w) \approx |w| . \tag{5.17}$$

Therefore, the reconstruction $f_r(x,y)$ will be exact if $F(u,v)$ is zero for $|u|$ and $|v|$ greater than a small fraction of $1/a$. In this case we also have a simplification of the calculation. Indeed, the algorithm is equivalent to evaluating the formula

$$f_r(x,y) = \frac{a}{2M}\sum_{j=0}^{M-1}\sum_{k=-N}^{N} p(ka,\frac{j\pi}{M})r(x\sin\frac{j\pi}{M}-y\cos\frac{j\pi}{M}-ka) . \tag{5.18}$$

This assumes uniform quantization of angle and distance. N depends on the size of the area containing the cross-section.

There are many variations of these techniques whose coverage is beyond the scope of this text. Instead, we shall give a simple example of the process of reconstruction.

Example 5.1: Let the cross-section be a circle of radius R and density one. Then its projection at any angle ϕ will be

$$p(\phi,t) = 2\sqrt{R^2-t^2} \quad \text{for } t^2\leq R^2 , \tag{5.19a}$$

$$p(\phi,t) = 0 \qquad \text{otherwise.} \tag{5.19b}$$

Note that $p(\phi,t)$ is actually independent of ϕ. Reconstruction from two backprojections at 90° without filtering yields the result expressed by the following equations, where the regions of validity of each expression are shown in Figure 5.5.

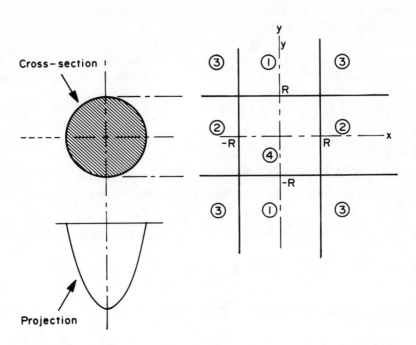

Figure 5.5 A circular cross-section (upper left) has for all angles a projection of the form shown at the lower left. The backprojection of the projection parallel to the x-axis is nonzero for Regions 2 and 4 shown at the right part of the figure. Similarly, the backprojection of the projection parallel to the y-axis is nonzero for Regions 1 and 3.

$$|x|\leq R \text{ and } |y|>R \quad \text{(Reg. 1)} \qquad f_r(x,y) = \sqrt{R^2-x^2} \qquad \text{(5.20a)}$$
$$|x|>R \text{ and } |y|\leq R \quad \text{(Reg. 2)} \qquad f_r(x,y) = \sqrt{R^2-y^2} \qquad \text{(5.20b)}$$
$$|x|>R \text{ and } |y|>R \quad \text{(Reg. 3)} \qquad f_r(x,y) = 0 \qquad \text{(5.20c)}$$
$$|x|\leq R \text{ and } |y|\leq R \quad \text{(Reg. 4)} \quad f_r(x,y) = (\sqrt{R^2-x^2}+\sqrt{R^2-y^2}) \text{ (5.20d)}$$

The factor 2 of Equation (5.19a) has been dropped because we take the average of the two backprojections. Along the perimeter of the circle $(x^2 + y^2 = R^2)$ a simple calculation shows that if

$$x = R\cos\psi \text{ and } y = R\sin\psi$$

then Equation (5.20d) yields

$$f_r(x,y) = R(|\sin\psi| + |\cos\psi|) \qquad (5.21)$$

For $0 < \psi < \dfrac{\pi}{2}$ we have

$$f_r(x,y) = R(\sin\psi + \cos\psi) = \sqrt{2}R\cos(\psi - \frac{\pi}{4}) , \qquad (5.22)$$

while the correct value is constant and equal to one. It is reasonable to normalize each projection by division by the area A found as the integral of the projection with respect to t. In the present case we have

$$A = 2\int_{-R}^{R} \sqrt{R^2 - t^2}\,dt) + \pi R^2 . \qquad (5.23)$$

so that the reconstruction becomes

$$f_r(x,y) = \frac{\sqrt{2}}{\pi R}\cos(\psi - \frac{\pi}{4}) . \qquad (5.24)$$

The plot of Equation (5.24) is shown in Figure 5.6.

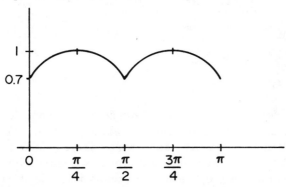

Figure 5.6 Form of the reconstructed function along the periphery of a circular region using two projections only. The vertical axis is marked in multiples of $\sqrt{2}/\pi R$.

The following are some other normalized values of $f_r(x,y)$:

$$f(0,0) = \frac{4}{\pi R} , \qquad (5.25a)$$

$$f(0,y) = \frac{2}{\pi R^2}(R + \sqrt{R^2 - y^2}) \qquad \text{if } |y| < R , \qquad (5.25b)$$

$$f(0,y) = \frac{2}{\pi R} \qquad \text{if } |y| > R . \qquad (5.25c)$$

Adding more projections will increase the values of $f_r(x,y)$ in the area of the circle but will also keep nonzero values outside it, hence the blurring. For example, adding two more projections will change the value given by Equation (5.25a) to $\frac{8}{\pi R}$ but will leave the value given by Equation (5.25c) unchanged. $\square$

5.4 PROJECTIONS FOR SHAPE ANALYSIS

In addition to their use for reconstruction, projections can be used for shape analysis because they map a two-dimensional region into a waveform. For example, alphanumeric characters are written with strokes along a few directions: vertical, horizontal, and two diagonals. Such strokes will appear as peaks in the projection along their direction and could be detected easily by any number of techniques. In this application it is practical to use only a few projections and we must also calculate Equation (5.4) explicitly rather than measure its lefthand side as the output of a physical device. We proceed with the analysis by rewriting Equation (5.4) for $\phi = 0°$, $90°$, $45°$, and $135°$.

$$p(0°,t) = \int_R f(x,t)dx \tag{5.26a}$$

$$p(90°,t) = \int_R f(t,y)dy \tag{5.26b}$$

$$p(45°,t) = \int_R f(x,x-\sqrt{2}t)dx \tag{5.26c}$$

$$p(135°,t) = \int_R f(x,\sqrt{2}t-x)dx \tag{5.26d}$$

Even though four projections are insufficient for a good reconstruction, they provide considerable information about strokes. One problem in their application is finding the appropriate discrete form for Equations (5.26c) and (5.26d). Algorithm 5.2 provides a simple implementation which assures that all projections are vectors with the same number of components and that the grid size N is even.

The operations performed in steps 6 to 13 have the effect of grouping the $2N-1$ diagonals of the $N{\times}N$ grid into N pairs, each consisting of two diagonals, except the two middle ones, which share the main diagonal. Figure 5.7 (Plate 20) and Figure 5.8 (Plate 21) show some examples.

The examples show that indeed, considerable information about the gross appearance of the character is contained in the projections. However, this does not seem to be the case with the car outline. The detection of peaks in the projections can be achieved by any technique that is appropriate in waveform analysis. Usually, the level of the noise is low and simple techniques such as thresholding or even differentiation are applicable. The method has been used for the recognition of alphabetic characters with reasonable success, even though only two projections were calculated (see Bibliographical Notes).

Algorithm 5.2 Calculating Projections for Shape Analysis

Notation: $f(i,j)$ input array of size $N \times N$; $p(k,l)$ projection array of size $4 \times N$.

1. **For** $l = 0$ to $N-1$ set $p(0,l) = \sum\limits_{i=0}^{N-1} f(i,l)$.

2. **For** $l = 0$ to $N-1$ set $p(1,l) = \sum\limits_{i=0}^{N-1} f(l,i)$.

3. Initialize $p(2,*)$ and $p(3,*)$ to zero.

4. **For** $j = 0$ to $N-1$ **do**:
   Begin.

5.   **For** $i = 0$ to $N-1$ **do**:
   Begin.

6.   Compare $i+j$ to $N-1$.

7.   **If** greater, **then** add $f(j,i)$ to $p(2,(i+j+1)/2)$.

8.   **If** less, **then** add $f(j,i)$ to $p(2,(i+j)/2)$.

9.   **If** equal, **then** add $f(j,i)/2$ to $p(2,(N/2)-1)$ and $f(j,i)/2$ to $p(2,N/2)$.

10.   Compare $j-i$ to 0.

11.   **If** greater, **then** add $f(j,i)$ to $p(3,(j-i+N)/2)$.

12.   **If** less, **then** add $f(j,i)$ to $p(3,(j-i+N-1)/2)$.

13.   **If** equal, **then** add $f(j,i)/2$ to $p(3,(N/2)-1)$ and $f(j,i)/2$ to $p(3,N/2)$.
   End.
   End.

14. **End of Algorithm.**

In order to visualize the amount of information present in these projections, we attempt to reconstruct the object outlines by filtered backprojections. The results are shown in Figure 5.9 (Plate 22) and Figure 5.10 (Plate 23). The reconstruction algorithm is similar to Algorithm 5.2 and is given as Algorithm 5.3.

The examples of reconstruction in Figures 5.7 to 5.10 suggest some of the power and limitations of the method. Details are lost when the contour is circular rather than rectilinear, as in the case of the car outline. However, because of this lack of sensitivity, the method may be appropriate for multifont character recognition. Indeed, projections may used to detect strokes along particular directions. The following example presents an analysis that may be useful in deciding how many projections to use in specific applications.

Algorithm 5.3 Reconstruction by Backprojections

Notation: $f(i,j)$ output array of size $N \times N$; $p(k,l)$ projection array of size $4 \times N$.

1.   **For** $j = 0$ to $N-1$ **do:**
   Begin.
2.   **For** $i = 0$ to $N-1$ **do:**
   Begin.
3. $g(j,i) = p(0,j) + p(1,i)$
4.   Compare $i+j$ to $N-1$
5.   **If** greater, **then** add $p(2,(i+j+1)/2)$ to $g(j,i)$
6.   **If** less, **then** add $p(2,(i+j)/2)$ to $g(j,i)$
7.   **If** equal, **then** add $1/2 \left[p(2,(N/2)-1) + p(2,N/2) \right]$ to $g(j,i)$
8.   Compare $j-i$ to 0.
9.   **If** greater, **then** add $p(3,(j-i+N)/2)$ to $g(j,i)$
10. **If** less, **then** add $p(3,(j-i+N-1)/2)$ to $g(j,i)$
11. **If** equal, **then** add $1/2 \left[p(3,(N/2)-1) + p(3,N/2) \right]$ to $g(j,i)$
   End.
   End.
12. **End of Algorithm.**

Example 5.2: Suppose that we are interested only in rectangles of particular dimensions and we want to decide how many projections we should use to detect them. We define the position of a rectangle relative to the direction of a projection by ψ, the angle formed between the largest side of the rectangle and the direction perpendicular to the projection (Figure 5.11a). For $\psi = 0$ the projection equals w over an interval equal to H, while for $\psi = 90°$ it equals H over an interval equal to w. For other values of ψ the projection has an isolated maximum, p_m. The maximum value of p_m (with respect to ψ) occurs when the direction of the projection is parallel to a diagonal of the rectangle. If w is the width and H the height, then that maximum value of p_m is $p_{max} = \sqrt{w^2 + H^2}$. This is achieved for $\psi_{max} = \tan^{-1}(H/w)$. The projection function at that angle has a triangular form, and it is nonzero over an interval equal to $w\sin\psi + H\cos\psi$, or $2Hw/p_{max}$. For $\psi < \psi_{max}$, p_m is $w/\cos\psi$, while for $\psi_{max} < \psi < 90°$, p_m is $H/\sin\psi$. The function is symmetrical with respect to $90°$, so that its plot has the form shown in Figure 5.11b. Clearly, if we use only one projection we may not detect rectangles when ψ is near $90°$. If we use four projections ($45°$ apart), then in the most unfavorable case the maximum of the detected peak will be $w/\cos(67.5°) = 2.41 \cdot w$ if $67.5° < \psi_{max}$, and $H/\sin(67.5°)$ $= 1.08 \cdot H$ otherwise. If $H/w = 5$, then $\psi_{max} = 78.7°$, and the maximum detected peak in the most unfavorable position will be about half the expected size. Figure 5.11c illustrates this position. $\square$

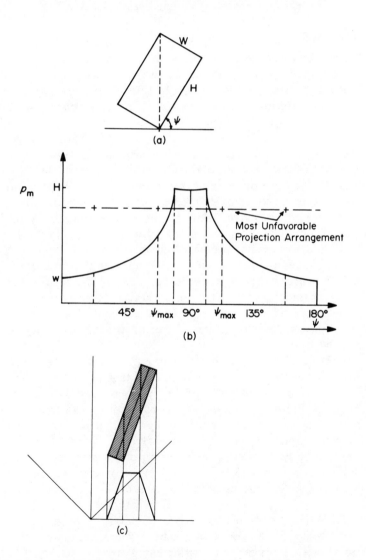

Figure 5.11 (a) Definition of the angle ψ. (b) Variation of the maximum value as a function of ψ. (c) Position where none of the projections is close to the maximum dimension of the object.

As a practical matter it is unlikely that projections by themselves can be used for recognition of the characters of the whole alphabet, but they can serve as a useful preprocessor. Many characters may be recognized strictly from their projections (e.g., L, T, I, H, etc.), while for others additional features must be used (e.g., R versus A).

5.5 BIBLIOGRAPHICAL NOTES

The abbreviation CAT refers to the use of reconstruction techniques to determine and display a cross-section of the human body from lateral x-rays. Originally, CAT stood for *Cross-Axial Tomography*, but now it is interpreted as *Computer Aided Tomography*. Machines that do reconstruction from projections are called *CAT scanners* and consist of a minicomputer, some special purpose digital hardware for computing the convolution or the transforms, graphic displays and other computer peripherals, x-ray equipment, and elaborate mechanical parts for rotating the x-ray source and receptors around the patient. These scanners have revolutionized medical diagnosis because the physician can now look at an image, while in the past the necessary information had to be obtained by exploratory surgery or by injection of fluids. Some idea of the medical implications of tomography can be seen from articles published in specialized journals such as the *Journal of Computer Assisted Tomography* (New York: Raven Press). To ensure that all x-ray beams are parallel and on the same plane it is necessary to have high mechanical precision in the equipment, which adds to the total cost. For this reason there is interest in reconstruction techniques that use nonparallel beams.

Because of the great medical importance of the subject, most of the literature appears in connection with that application. The analysis of Section 5.2 is based on a paper by Shepp and Logan [5.SL]. See [5.SS] for additional examples of reconstruction problems based on this method. There is another methodology for reconstruction based on a different principle, the fact that the evaluation of $f(x,y)$ from the projections can be expressed as the solution of a system of linear equations [5.HR]. The volume [5.HE] is collection of reviews on the subject, while the paper by Budinger [5.BU] is a concise review of reconstruction.

[5.HA], in particular [5.HH], contains a discussion of certain advanced topics in image reconstruction. The discussion of methodologies in these references is of sufficient generality to be of interest to readers whose specialty is not electron microscopy.

Projections offer a cheap way of performing some shape analysis. Their use in character recognition was first described in [5.PA]. Only vertical and horizontal projections were used but the integration was carried out separately after each gap (see Figure 5.12). Strokes were determined by a combination of thresholding and slope detection and their presence in certain locations was used to generate binary features. Then standard statistical techniques were used for the final classification. Another application of projection is described in [5.NA] where the Fourier transforms of four projections were used for the recognition of Chinese characters. [5.OT] describes a use of projections together with other features.

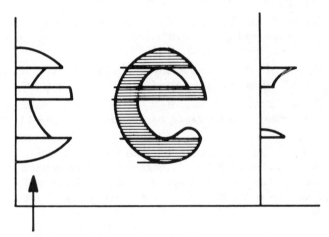

Projection is calculated over the shaded part only.

Figure 5.12 Multiply connected integral projections [5.PA]. The figure shows projections along the horizontal direction. When a gap is found during the integration, this value is given to the first projection (shown to the left above), and any subsequent values are assigned to a second projection (shown to the right above).

5.6 RELEVANT LITERATURE

[5.BU]   Budinger, T. F. "Computed Tomography: Three-Dimensional Imaging with Photons and Nuclear Magnetic Resonance," in *Biomedical Pattern Recognition and Image Processing,* K. S. Fu and T. Pavlidis, eds. Weinheim: Chemie Verlag, 1979, pp. 179-212.

[5.HA]   Hawkes, P. W., ed. *Computer Processing of Electron Microscope Images,* Berlin: Springer, 1980.

[5.HE]   Herman, G. T., ed. *Image Reconstruction from Projections,* Berlin: Springer, 1980.

[5.HH]   Hoppe, W. and Hegert, R. "Three-Dimensional Structure Determi-
         nation by Electron Microscopy (Nonperiodic Specimens)," in
         [5.HA], pp. 127-185.

[5.HR]   Herman, G. T. and Rowland, S. W. "Three Methods for Recon-
         structing Objects from X-Rays: A Comparative Study," *CGIP,* 2
         (1973) pp. 151-178.

[5.NA]   Nakimano, Y.; Nakato, K.; Uchikura, Y.; Nakajima, A., "Improve-
         ment of Chinese Character Recognition Using Projection Profiles,"
         Proc. First Intern. Joint Conf. on Pattern Recognition, Washington,
         D.C. (October 1973) pp. 172-178.

[5.OT]   Ogawa H. and Taniguchi, K., "Preprocessing for Chinese character
         recognition and global classification of handwritten Chinese charac-
         ters," *Pattern Recognition,* 11 (1979), pp. 1-7.

[5.PA]   Pavlidis, T., "Computer Recognition of Figures Through Decompo-
         sition," *Information and Control,* 14 (1968), pp. 526-537.

[5.SL]   Shepp, L. A. and Logan, B. F., "The Fourier reconstruction of a
         head section," *IEEE Trans. on Nuclear Science,* NS-21 (1974), pp.
         21-43.

[5.SS]   Shepp, L. A. and Stein, J. A., "Simulated Reconstruction Artifacts
         in Computerized X-Ray Tomography", in *Reconstruction Tomogra-
         phy in Diagnostic Radiology and Nuclear Medicine* (M. M. Ter-
         Pogossian et al., eds.), Baltimore: University Park Press, 1977, pp.
         33-48.

5.7 PROBLEMS

5.1.   Implement Algorithm 5.1 using the function given by Equation
       (5.15) for $r(t)$ (see also Appendix 5.A).

5.2.   Suppose you know that $f(x,y)$ has the form $g(x)h(y)$, where g
       and h are unknown functions. Can you use this property to sim-
       plify the reconstruction algorithm?

5.3.   We are given a function s of two variables in a tabular form:
       $N \times N$ samples. Can you think of ways to use projections to
       reduce the size of the table? You may consider two versions of
       the problem: when some error is allowed in the description of s
       and when it is not. (*Hint:* you should make certain assumptions
       about the form of s and then develop checks for verifying that
       the function described by a given table satisfies those assump-
       tions.)

5.4.   Repeat the analysis of Example 5.1 for an elliptical region.

APPENDIX 5.A: AN ELEMENTARY RECONSTRUCTION PROGRAM

The following is a FORTRAN program listing and an example of its execution implementing reconstruction. An image poster was digitized and then the projections were computed by summation, followed by the reconstruction with and without filtering. The program was written by Michael Kass, as part of a class assignment at Princeton University.†

I feel that such a project offers the student the opportunity to integrate much of the material of the first five chapters: digitization, histogram equalization, filtering, etc. In addition, it shows him or her that some of the most impressive applications of image processing are based on rather simple principles.

```
$JOB             0660142.EECS426,T=400,P=500,L=9999
C
C
C        IMAGE RECONSTRUCTION BY BACK PROJECTIONS
C
C        N PROJECTIONS ARE CALCULATED FOR
C        AN N BY N IMAGE.  THEN THE ORIGINAL
C        IMAGE IS RECONSTRUCTED BY BACK
C        PROJECTION WITH FILTERED AND
C        UNFILTERED PROJECTIONS.
C
C        ALL IMAGES ARE PRINTED WITH HISTOGRAM
C        EQUALIZATION.
C        WRITTEN BY MICHAEL KASS    3/17/80
C
C
C        VARIABLES
C        ---------
C
C        PIXEL(A,B)      ORIGINAL IMAGE
C        PIXEL2(A,B)     PORTION OF IMAGE TO BE USED
C
C        PROJ(A,B)       PROJECTION OF IMAGE ALONG ANGLE A*PI/N
C        FPROJ(A,B)      FILTERED PROJ(A,B)
C        BPROJ(A,B)      BACK PROJECTION OF THE UNFILTERED PROJECTIONS
C        FBPROJ(A,B)     BACK PROJECTION OF THE FILTERED PROJECTIONS
C
C        AX,AY           X,Y COORDINATES OF THE BEGINNING POINT OF THE
C                        INTEGRATION TO CALCULATE A PROJECTION.
C        BX,BY           COORDINATES OF THE END POINT OF THE INTEGRATION
C        P1              MIDDLE OF THE IMAGE
C        P2              MIDPOINT OF INTEGRATION PATH
C        P3              VECTOR FROM P2 TO ENDPOINT OF INTEGRATION
C
C        CNVRTD          USED TO GO FROM CHARACTER TO INTEGER REPRESENTATION
C        CNVRT
C
```

---

†It was run under the WATFIV interpreter on an IBM 3300 machine. Its execution time was 162.5 seconds and it required 17672 bytes for its object code and 155916 bytes for its arrays. The dimensions of the image were 64×64.

```
    1              LOGICAL*1 C(6,37),LINE(128),CNVRT(2),FORMS(6)
    2              INTEGER*4 PIXEL(105,128),CNVRTD
    3              INTEGER*4 PIXEL2(64,64)
    4              COMPLEX P1,P2,P3,POLAR
    5              REAL*4 INTRP2
    6              DIMENSION PROJ(64,64),BPROJ(64,64)
    7              DIMENSION FPROJ(64,64),FBPROJ(64,64)
    8              EQUIVALENCE (CNVRTD,CNVRT(1))
    9              COMMON N,SINTB2(64),COSTB2(64)
       C
       C
                   READ IN PICTURE
   10              DO 2 I=1,105
   11    1         FORMAT(128A1)
   12              READ (16,1) LINE
   13              DO 2 J=1,128
   14              CNVRTD=0
   15              CNVRT(2)=LINE(J)
   16    2         PIXEL(I,J)=CNVRTD+1
       C
       C
                   READ IN OVERPRINTING CODES
   17              DO 20 I=1,6
   18    20        READ(5,22) FORMS(I),(C(I,J),J=1,37)
   19    22        FORMAT(38A1)
       C
       C
                   INITIALIZE
   20              N=64
   21              N2=N/2
   22              DO 39 I=1,N
   23              SINTB2(I)=SIN(FLOAT(I-1)*3.141593/FLOAT(N))
   24    39        COSTB2(I)=COS(FLOAT(I-1)*3.141593/FLOAT(N))
   25              R=.5*N*2**.5
   26              P1=CMPLX(FLOAT(N2),FLOAT(N2))
       C
       C
                   SELECT A PORTION OF THE PICTURE
   27              DO 14 I=1,N
   28              DO 14 J=1,N
   29    14        PIXEL2(I,J)=PIXEL(32+I,10+J)
   30              CALL PRINT(PIXEL2,C,FORMS,N)
   31              WRITE(6,15)
   32    15        FORMAT(/15H ORIGINAL IMAGE)
       C
       C
                   CALCULATE PROJECTIONS
   33              DO 67 J=1,N
   34              DO 67 K=1,N
       C
       C
                   FIND ENDPOINTS OF INTEGRAL
   35              T=2*R*FLOAT(K-1)/FLOAT(N)
   36              P2=P1+POLAR((R-T),J)
   37              P3=(0.,-1.)*POLAR((R**2-(R-T)**2)**.5,J)
   38              AX=REAL(P2+P3)
   39              AY=AIMAG(P2+P3)
   40              BX=REAL(P2-P3)
   41              BY=AIMAG(P2-P3)
   42    68        CONTINUE
       C
       C
                   INTEGRATE
   43              SUM=0.
   44              DO 69 I=1,N
   45              X1=AX+(I-1.)*(BX-AX)/(N-1.)
   46              Y1=AY+(I-1.)*(BY-AY)/(N-1.)
   47    69        SUM=SUM+RINTRP(PIXEL2,X1,Y1,N)
   48    67        PROJ(J,K)=SUM
       C
       C
                   FILTER
   49              DO 111 I=1,N
   50              DO 111 J=1,N
   51              FPROJ(I,J)=0.
   52              DO 111 K=1,9
   53              K1=K-5
   54              IF((J+K1).GT.N) K1=N-J
   55              IF((J+K1).LT.1) K1=1-J
   56    111       FPROJ(I,J)=FPROJ(I,J)-PROJ(I,J+K1)/FLOAT(4*(K-5)**2-1)
       C
       C
                   CALCULATE BACK PROJECTIONS
```

```
57          DO 106 I=1,N
58          DO 106 J=1,N
59          R1=(((I-N2-1)**2+(J-N2-1)**2)**.5)/(2.**.5)
60          IF(J.EQ.(N2+1)) THEN DO
61          THETA1=N2+1
62          ELSE DO
63          THETA=ATAN((FLOAT(I-N2)-1.)/(FLOAT(J-N2)-1.))
64          THETA1=1.+N*THETA/3.141593
65          END IF
66   91     IF(THETA1.LT.1.) THETA1=FLOAT(N)+THETA1
67          IF(I.GT.(N2+1)) R1=-R1
68          IF((I.EQ.N2+1).AND.(J.GT.N2+1)) R1=-R1
     C
     C          SUM OVER ALL PROJECTIONS
     C
69          BPROJ(I,J)=0
70          FBPROJ(I,J)=0
71          DO 106 IPHI=1,N
72          R2=R1*COS((FLOAT(IPHI)-THETA1)*3.141593/FLOAT(N))
73          R2=R2+N2+1.
74          FBPROJ(I,J)=FBPROJ(I,J)+INTRP2(FPROJ,FLOAT(IPHI),R2,N)
75   106    BPROJ(I,J)=BPROJ(I,J)+INTRP2(PROJ,FLOAT(IPHI),R2,N)
     C
     C          PRINT BACK PROJECTED IMAGES
     C
76          DO 107 I=1,N
77          DO 107 J=1,N
78   107    PIXEL2(I,J)=BPROJ(I,J)/FLOAT(N)
79          CALL PRINT(PIXEL2,C,FORMS,N)
80          WRITE(6,108)
81   108    FORMAT(/43H RECONSTRUCTION WITH UNFILTERED PROJECTIONS   )
82          DO 109 I=1,N
83          DO 109 J=1,N
84   109    PIXEL2(I,J)=FBPROJ(I,J)/FLOAT(N)
85          CALL PRINT(PIXEL2,C,FORMS,N)
86          WRITE(6,110)
87   110    FORMAT(/41H RECONSTRUCTION WITH FILTERED PROJECTIONS   )
88          WRITE(6,120)
89   120    FORMAT(1H1)
90          STOP
91          END
```

```
92          SUBROUTINE PRINT(PIXEL2,C,FORMS,N)
     C
     C          VARIABLES
     C          ---------
     C
     C   C(A,B)        FOR INTENSITY LEVEL B, OVERPRINT C(1,B) THROUGH
     C                 C(6,B)
     C   LINE(A)       USED AS A BUFFER TO HOLD ONE LINE OF CHARACTERS
     C   FORMS(A)      CONTAINS ' ++++++' TO SIGNAL OVERPRINTING
     C   C1(A,B)       C IS DUPLICATED ACCORDING TO HISTOGRAM EQUALIZATION
     C                 SO FOR INTENSITY LEVEL B, C1(1,B) THROUGH C1(6,B)
     C                 SHOULD BE OVERPRINTED
     C   PIXEL(A,B)    CONTAINS THE INTENSITY OF THE CORRESPONDING
     C                 PIXEL
     C
     C   HIST(A)       CONTAINS THE NUMBER OF PIXELS WITH INTENSITY A
     C
     C   R             AS DESCRIBED IN PAVLIDAS'
     C   Z             HISTOGRAM EQUALIZATION ALGORITHM
     C   HINT
     C   HAVE (HAVER)
     C   LEFT(A)
     C   RIGHT(A)
     C   NEW(A)
     C   MAX           MAXIMUM PIXEL VALUE
     C   MIN           MINIMUM PIXEL VALUE
```

```
93              LOGICAL*1 C(6,37),LINE(128),FORMS(6),C1(6,128)
94              INTEGER*4 PIXEL2(64,64),HIST(128),LEFT(128),RIGHT(128)
95              INTEGER*4 R,P,Z,NEW(128),PIXEL(64,64)
96              INTEGER*4 PIX,P1,P2
        C
        C       COMPUTE MAX, MIN FOR SCALING
        C
97              MAX=0
98              MIN=1000000
99              DO 23 I=1,N
100             DO 23 J=1,N
101             PIX=PIXEL2(I,J)
102             MIN=AMIN0(MIN,PIX)
103      23     MAX=AMAX0(MAX,PIX)
        C
        C       SCALE
        C
104             DO 31 I=1,N
105             DO 31 J=1,N
106      31     PIXEL(I,J)=1+(PIXEL2(I,J)-MIN+1)*126./FLOAT
        C       (MAX-MIN+1)
        C
        C       CALCULATE HISTOGRAM
        C
107      62     DO 90 I=1,128
108      90     HIST(I)=0
109             DO 80 I=1,N
110             DO 80 J=1,N
111      80     HIST(1+PIXEL(I,J))=HIST(1+PIXEL(I,J))+1
112             HAVE=N*N/35
        C
        C       CALCULATE HISTOGRAM EQUALIZATION
        C
113             R=0
114             HINT=0
115             DO 100 Z=1,128
116             LEFT(Z)=R
117             HINT=HINT+HIST(Z)
118             K=HINT/HAVE
119             R=R+K
120             HINT=HINT-HAVE*K
121             RIGHT(Z)=R
122      100    NEW(Z)=(RIGHT(Z)+LEFT(Z))/2
        C
        C       DUPLICATE OVERPRINTING MATRIX
        C
123             DO 30 I=1,128
124             K=I*35/128+1
125             DO 30 J=1,6
126      30     C1(J,I)=C(J,NEW(I)+1)
        C
        C       PRINT OUT IMAGE
        C
127             WRITE(6,120)
128      120    FORMAT(1H1)
129             DO 60 I=1,N
130             DO 50 K=1,6
131             DO 60 J=1,N
132      60     LINE(J)=C1(K,1+PIXEL(I,J))
133      50     WRITE(6,70) FORMS(K),(LINE(I1),I1=1,N)
134      70     FORMAT(129A1)
135             RETURN
136             END
```

```
137          COMPLEX FUNCTION POLAR(B,K)
        C         CONVERTS POLAR COORDINATES TC RECTANGULAR
        C         IN THE FORM OF A COMPLEX NUMBER
138          COMMON N,SINTB2(64),COSTB2(64)
139          POLAR=CMPLX(B*SINTB2(K),B*COSTB2(K),
140          RETURN
141          END




142          FUNCTION RINTRP(MAT,X,Y,N)
143          INTEGER*4 MAT(64,64)
144          INTEGER X1,Y1,A,B,C,D
        C         INTERPOLATES INTO AN INTEGER MATRIX
        C         X,Y IS THE POINT AT WHICH THE FUNCTION
        C         REPRESENTED BY THE MATRIX IS TO BE
        C         EVALUATED.  N IS THE DIMENSION OF THE
        C         MATRIX.
145          X1=X
146          IF(X1.LE.0)  X1=1
147          IF(X1.GE.N)  X1=N-1
148          Y1=Y
149          IF(Y1.LE.0)  Y1=1
150          IF(Y1.GE.N)  Y1=N-1
151          A=MAT(X1,Y1)
152          B=MAT(X1+1,Y1)
153          C=MAT(X1,Y1+1)
154          D=MAT(X1+1,Y1+1)
155          E1=A+(B-A)*(X-X1)
156          E2=C+(D-C)*(X-X1)
157          RINTRP=E1+(E2-E1)*(Y-Y1)
158          RETURN
159          END




160          REAL FUNCTION INTRP2(MAT,X,Y,N)
161          REAL*4 MAT(64,64)
162          INTEGER X1,Y1,A,B,C,D
        C         THIS FUNCTION IS THE SAME AS RINTRP
        C         EXCEPT THAT THE MATRIX IS REAL.
163          X1=X
164          IF(X1.LE.0)  X1=1
165          IF(X1.GE.N)  X1=N-1
166          Y1=Y
167          IF(Y1.LE.0)  Y1=1
168          IF(Y1.GE.N)  Y1=N-1
169          A=MAT(X1,Y1)
170          B=MAT(X1+1,Y1)
171          C=MAT(X1,Y1+1)
172          D=MAT(X1+1,Y1+1)
173          E1=A+(B-A)*(X-X1)
174          E2=C+(D-C)*(X-X1)
175          INTRP2=E1+(E2-E1)*(Y-Y1)
176          RETURN
177          END
        $ENTRY
```

ORIGINAL IMAGE

RECONSTRUCTION WITH FILTERED PROJECTIONS

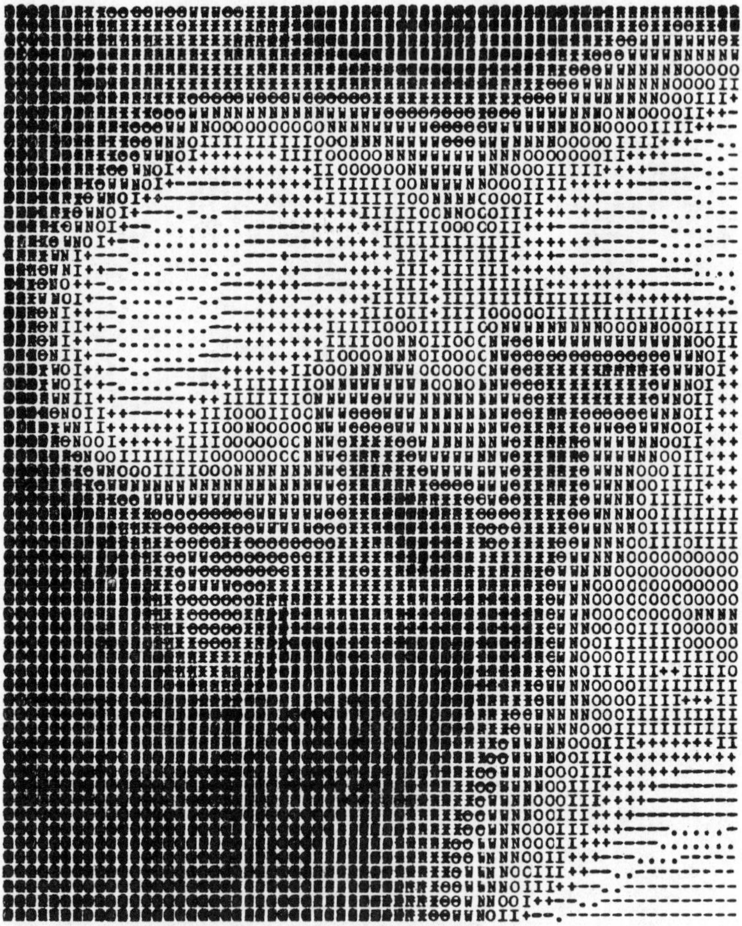

RECONSTRUCTION WITH UNFILTERED PROJECTIONS

Chapter 6

DATA STRUCTURES

6.1 INTRODUCTION

The large memory requirements associated with storing pictorial data are well known to anyone who has worked with them. For example, storing an ordinary frame of television requires at least 512x512 bytes, if we use three bits for two of the primary colors and two for the third. A black and white passport photograph requires at least a 64x64 matrix with six bits per element, well above the size of a record containing whatever other information is in a passport. (A page of single-spaced typewritten text requires about 3000 bytes.) Problems of storage, search, retrieval, transmission, etc. are particularly difficult whenever pictorial data are encountered. These difficulties are somewhat counterintuitive because humans often find it easier to deal with pictures than with text. It is far easier for us to remember the face of a new acquaintance than a page of typewritten text. The difficulty of matching such human performance on a computer can be appreciated by pointing out that, at least for some people, the recollection of the face is better when it belongs to a member of the opposite sex and that the text is remembered better if it is a piece of prose than if it is a list of names. Therefore, any data compaction techniques that depend only on signal processing are not likely to reduce the data volume to a size compatible with our intuitive expectations. The use of pattern recognition may result in higher compaction (see Example 1.1), but such processing requires a fair amount of computing so that one is still obliged to face the problem of storing and representing images on a computer.

The problem of data compaction has different forms in communications and in computing. In many applications, an image is created, transmitted, observed, and then discarded. The major consideration in communications is reducing the *bandwidth* required for transmission under the constraint that the processing must be done in time comparable to that required for generating and transmitting the image. A different situation exists in applications where a pictorial data base is needed and images must be stored for long periods. New images must be compared with old ones, or sets of images must be searched for certain features. Thus, in addition to the volume required for pictorial data, access can be a problem.

People are very good at focusing on parts of a two-dimensional display, but computers must proceed in a blind fashion. Therefore, picture traversal algorithms are very important. For discrete images, this corresponds to the traversal of a discrete grid that can be interpreted as a graph whose nodes are pixels, and whose branches connect nodes corresponding to neighboring pixels. In addition to this simple mapping, one can build other graphs corresponding to an image. In fact, because all data structures used for images are graphs, it is a good idea to start with a review of graph traversal algorithms. (Readers who are not at all familiar with graph theory should read Appendix 6.A.) There is one restriction on such algorithms when they are applied to graphs representing images. Because of their size these graphs are rarely represented in any of the usual formats (e.g., adjacency matrix, node list, etc.). For example, in the simplest case one has only the x-y coordinates of pixels and their brightness or color values. Thus, finding which nodes are adjacent to a given one is a genuine problem. If it is necessary to traverse only those parts of an image that form a uniform region, then one must decide whether the neighboring pixels belong to the same region as the current pixel. For these reasons we shall leave the term "adjacent" deliberately vague, at least in this chapter. We assume only that there is a procedure $ADJACENT(p,n,N)$ that for the node (or pixel) p returns the number n of adjacent nodes that have not been visited previously during the traversal, and the array N containing their descriptions (e.g., their x-y coordinates).

6.2 GRAPH TRAVERSAL ALGORITHMS

The traversal of a connected graph is a simple process if one starts at a point and then proceeds to those adjacent to it, while marking any place that has been already visited. If there is more than one adjacent point, then one of them is chosen as the next place to be visited and the others are put aside, so that they may be used later to resume the traversal. A convenient structure for saving these points is a *stack*. This is an array where elements are added during the search and, when the algorithm calls for it, elements are removed. The essential rule is that the last element added is removed first. Since we will encounter these operations many times in the sequel, we give them special names: *PUSH* (p,S), add pixel p to stack S; and $p = POP(S)$, remove a point from S and call it p. Algorithm 6.1 shows two simple programs implementing these functions. The value -1 is used as an indicator of an empty stack. If it is a legitimate address in some implementation, then another impossible address must be returned to indicate an empty stack.

Note that S need not be a one-dimensional array, especially in the context of image processing. There, the graph corresponds to the plane of the image, with pixels for its nodes, and adjacent nodes corresponding to adjacent pixels. To describe a point we must store both its x and y coordinates; thus, S will be an array of pairs.†

Algorithm 6.1 Stack Manipulation Procedures

Notation: i is the index of the last element of the array S.

Procedure *PUSH* (p,S)
1. Increment i by 1 and set $S(i) = p$.
2. **End.**

Procedure *POP* (S)
1. **If** i is greater than 0, **then** decrement i by 1 and **return** $S(i+1)$.
2. **else return** -1 to indicate an empty stack.
3. **End.**

During the traversal it is necessary to use two types of markings. We assume without loss of generality that initially all nodes (pixels) are marked by one. When a node (pixel) is placed on the stack it is marked by two, and when it is traversed it is marked by zero.* A basic connected graph (region) traversal algorithm using these functions is listed as Algorithm 6.2. We should also point out that we can omit

---

† This assumes that the image is stored as a two-dimensional array. The implementation of such arrays is awkward in many computer languages because the data are stored internally in a one-dimensional fashion. It is best to store the images explicitly as one-dimensional arrays, and then use pointers to address the individual pixels. In such a case the stack will be an array of pointers (see Problem 6.1).

* This notation is particularly meaningful when we deal with bilevel images. There one is interested only in the dark pixels (with value one), which are erased during the traversal.

marking pixels when they are placed in the stack. Such an omission will not affect the correctness of the traversal (see Problem 6.2), but it may cause a large growth in the size of the stack. One can construct examples where for a graph with N nodes the stack size approaches N^2. However, in many applications the form of the graph is such that the size of the stack is not a problem (see Section 8.4.4).

Algorithm 6.2 Basic Connected Graph Traversal Algorithm

Notation: Procedure $ADJACENT(p,n,N)$ receives the location of pixel p and returns the number of its neighbors n and their locations, stored in the array N.

0.   Find a node (pixel) p of the graph (region) to be traversed.
1.   Place p on the stack S.
2.   **While** S is not empty **do** steps 3-9.
     Begin.
3. $p=POP(S)$.
4.   **Repeat** steps 5-9.
             Begin.
5.   Mark p and **call procedure** $ADJACENT(p,n,N)$.
6.   **If** n equals 0, **then** exit from the loop.
7.   Set $p = N(1)$.
8.   **If** n is greater than 1, **then do** step 9.
                 Begin.
9.   For $i = 2$ to n $PUSH(N(i),S)$.
                 End.
             End.
     End.
10. **End of Algorithm.**

While the stack is a convenient data structure for region traversal, there are other problems where one wants to remove the elements from an array in the order they were put there. This data structure is called a *queue*. A function $ADD(p,Q)$, add pixel p to the queue Q, is similar to the function $PUSH$ for the stack. The function $REMOVE(Q)$ that removes a point from a queue requires more care. Algorithm 6.3 lists these functions. Note that two indices are used, indicating the start and end of the queue. This implementation is simple, but since it wastes space, one must periodically reallocate storage.

For more details on the implementation and handling of stacks and queues the reader is referred to any of the many books on algorithms and data structures (see also Bibliographical Notes).† If we

---

† For example, see pp. 44-49 of [6.AHU], or pp. 234-304 of [6.KN].

replace the stack by a queue in Algorithm 6.2 the graph is still traversed correctly, but the nodes are visited in a different order than before. Correct traversal is also possible without any of these storage constructs by using backtracking when no further advance is possible. All these graph traversal algorithms are discussed in detail in many texts.†

Algorithm 6.3 Queue Manipulation Procedures

Notation: iend is the index of the last element of the array Q.
istart is the index of the first element of Q. Initially both are equal to the first address of the array space.

Procedure $ADD(p,Q)$
1.   Increment *iend* by 1 and set $Q(iend) = p$.
2.   **End.**

Procedure $REMOVE(Q)$
1.   **if** *istart* is not greater than *iend*, **then** increment *istart* by 1 and **return** $Q(istart-1)$.
2.   **else return** -1 to indicate an empty queue.
3.   **End.**

6.3 PAGING

The simplest way of presenting pictures of class 1 is by integer matrices. If the size of the matrix exceeds that of the available fast memory, it may be necessary to subdivide it into *pages*. This seems to be a trivial process except that it may happen that the line dividing two pages is near an interesting part of the picture. To avoid repeated page swaps overlapping pages are often used. Figure 6.1 shows one possible arrangement. Such an overlap is desirable not only in order to minimize swaps but also to detect features that cannot be seen unless there is a sufficiently large area of the picture around them.

It is desirable to store such pages on a disk or tape in such a way that the geometric proximity of pages corresponds to proximity in their storage location. It can be shown that this is impossible in general (see Problem 6.5). The geometrical proximity may be preserved only with respect to a particular page. Figure 6.2 shows an example. The critical page is 5, and all pages that share a border with it are stored closer to it than pages that do not. Such strategies may be useful in allocating intermediate storage. An image is stored on tape, a page is brought in fast memory, and the pages near it are stored on a disk in way similar to that suggested by Figure 6.2. One should be aware that many

---

† For example, see pp. 176-179 of [6.AHU], or pp. 51-57 of [3.PA].

operating systems have their own strategies of space allocation and that they will not, in general, preserve geometric adjacency. In such cases it is necessary to bypass the operating system and treat disks as raw data devices.

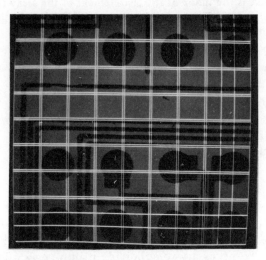

Figure 6.1   Paging arrangement: overlay of pictures on an image of a printed wiring board

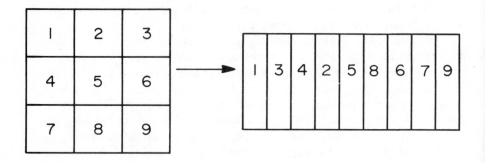

Figure 6.2   Storage arrangement for preserving geometrical adjacency with respect to page 5

6.4 PYRAMIDS OR QUAD TREES

Pyramids or quad trees are a popular data structure in both graphics and image processing. This technique is best used when the picture is a square matrix A whose dimension is a power of 2, say 2^n. Then A can be subdivided into four square matrices A_0, A_1, A_2, A_3, whose dimensions are half of A. This process can be repeated recursively n times, until the single pixel level is reached. The levels can be numbered, starting with zero for the whole picture, down to n for the single pixels. A particular square may be labeled with one of the symbols 0, 1, 2, or 3, concatenated to the label of its predecessor square. In this way single pixels will have labels that are n characters long. We can express this arrangement as a *tree,* whose nodes correspond to the squares. Nodes are connected if one of the corresponding squares immediately contains the other.

The root of the tree corresponds to the whole picture, the leaves to single pixels, and all other nodes have down degree 4. Such a tree is usually called a *quartic tree* or a *quad tree.* Figure 6.3 shows such a tree and Figure 6.4 shows the addressing notation for an 8×8 picture. Since the kth level contains 4^k squares, the tree has a total of

$$N = \sum_{k=0}^{n} 4^k = \frac{4^{n+1} - 1}{3} \approx \frac{4}{3} 4^n$$

nodes. Therefore, there are approximately 33 percent more nodes than pixels. It turns out that for many applications the tree can be stored using only 4^n locations. We discuss the creation of such a quad tree next.

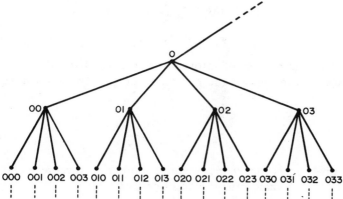

Figure 6.3   Part of a quad tree

000	001	010	011	100	101	110	111
002	003	012	013	102	103	112	113
020	021	030	031	120	121	130	131
022	023	032	033	122	123	132	133
200	201	210	211	300	301	310	311
202	203	212	213	302	303	312	313
220	221	230	231	320	321	330	331
222	223	232	233	322	323	332	333

Figure 6.4 Example showing the system for addressing the pixels of an 8×8 image according to a quad tree: the first digit identifies the first level node, the second digit the second level node, and so forth.

6.4.1 Creating a Quad Tree

We assume that we start with an image that can be accessed row by row. This is the case when it is stored on a tape or disk, or when it is digitized by a drum scan device or one based on a television camera (see Section 1.3). To form the tree, we read in two such rows, and then proceed to examine quadruples of pixels in the order shown in Figure 6.5a. For each group of four pixels with indices $2k$, $2k+1$, 2^n+2k, 2^n+2k+1 ($k = 0,1,2 \cdots, 2^{n-1}-1$), let f_0, f_1, f_2, and f_3 be the corresponding gray levels. We can create four new levels

$$g_0 = \frac{1}{4}\sum_{i=0}^{3} f_i \tag{6.1a}$$

$$g_j = f_j - g_0 \quad j = 1, 2, 3 \tag{6.1b}$$

Note that there is no loss of information in going from the f_j's to the g_j's because we can recover the f_j's from the g_j's by the formulas

$$f_j = g_j + g_0 \quad j = 1, 2, 3. \tag{6.2a}$$

$$f_0 = g_0 - \sum_{i=1}^{3} g_i . \tag{6.2b}$$

The only problem is that it may require more bits to represent the g_j's than the f_j's. We shall return to this question later.

0	1	4	5	10	11	14	15	20	21	...
2	3	6	7	12	13	16	17	22	23	...
100	101	104	105	110	111	114	115	120	121	...
102	103	106	107	112	113	116	117	122	123	...

(a)

g_0	g_4	g_{10}	g_{14}	g_{20}	g_{24}	...

$$(g_1,g_2,g_3)(g_5,g_6,g_7) \cdots (g_{75},g_{76},g_{77})$$

(b)

g_0	g_4	g_{10}	g_{14}	g_{20}	g_{24}	g_{30}	...
g_{100}	g_{104}	g_{110}	g_{114}	g_{120}	g_{124}	g_{130}	...

(c)

Figure 6.5 (a) Order in which pixels are read from an array in order to form a quad tree. Labels are in octal assuming a $64_{10} \times 64_{10}$ image. (b) Top row shows the single row produced from two rows in the original image and the bottom row shows the array of the differences. (c) Elements of the first two rows of the new image.

To form the next level of the tree, we create a new image with a row whose elements are the g_0's. At the same time we place in a separate array D the difference values g_1, g_2, g_3. Thus, we arrive at the form of Figure 6.5b. When the next two rows are read in, the index of the first element will increase by 2^{n+1}, where 2^n is the length of a row, so that the arrangement of Figure 6.5c will result. At the end we will have created a new $2^{n-1} \times 2^{n-1}$ image plus an array D of $3 \cdot 2^{2n-2}$ differences. Note that the total space is still

$$2^{2n-2} + 3 \cdot 2^{2n-2} = 2^{2n}$$

in terms of pixel numbers. The procedure can be repeated until we reach an image consisting of a single pixel. Then almost all the information will be contained in the array D. The creation process can be described by Algorithm 6.4, which uses the procedure listed as Algorithm 6.4a.

Algorithm 6.4a Creating a Level of a Quad Tree

Procedure $T.LEVEL(n,I,J,D)$

Notation: Input is image I of dimension $2^n \times 2^n$. Output is image J of dimension $2^{n-1} \times 2^{n-1}$ and array D containing the differences.

1.   **For** j from 0 to 2^n by 2 **do:**
     Begin.
2.   Place the jth row of the image I into the array p_1 and the $(j+1)^{th}$ row into the array p_2.
3.   **For** $i = 0$ to 2^n by 2 **do:**
     Begin.
4.   Set f_0 equal to $p_1(i)$,
     $\quad f_1$ to $p_1(i+1)$,
     $\quad f_2$ to $p_2(i)$,
     $\quad f_3$ to $p_2(i+1)$.
5.   Compute g_0, g_1, g_2, g_3 by Equations (6.1).
6.   Append g_0 to the image J.
7.   Append g_1, g_2, g_3 to the array D.
     End.
     End.
8.   **End of Procedure.**

Algorithm 6.4 Creating a Quad Tree

0.   **Read** image I_n of size $2^n \times 2^n$.
1.   Set *level* $= n$.
2.   **While** (*level* is greater than 0) **do:**
     Begin.
3.   Call $T.LEVEL(level, I_{level}, I_{level-1}, D_{level})$.
4.   Decrement *level* by 1.
     End.
5.   **Write** $I_0, D_1, D_2, \cdots, D_n$.
6.   **End of Algorithm.**

6.4.2 Reconstructing an Image from a Quad Tree

If an image is stored as a matrix its transmission and display proceed along rows or scan lines. Each part is displayed in full detail and if T_c denotes the time required for the complete display, in $T_c/2$ we can see only the top half of the image. This is an unsatisfactory way for browsing through pictures, especially if T_c is more than one or two seconds long. It would be better to display in $T_{c/2}$ the whole image at a coarse resolution so that the viewer can decide quickly whether there is anything interesting in it, and if there is not to abort the display.† Such a "gross-information-first" display can be implemented with quad trees.

Algorithm 6.5a Procedure *FILL* (i, x_s, y_s, x_e, y_e)

1. *win* (x_s, y_s, x_e, y_e). {define window on screen}
2. *back* (i). {set background color}
3. *erase*. {erase window area to background intensity}
4. **End of Procedure.**

Algorithm 6.5 Display of Image with Gross Information First.

Notation: Input is array D whose elements are differences from the local average except for the first element, which equals the average for the whole image.

1. Set I to the first element of array D and execute *FILL* $(I, 0, 0, 2^n, 2^n)$
2. **For** i from 0 to $n-1$ **do:**
   Begin.
3.   Set $l = 4^i$ and $u = 2^{n-i}$.
4.   **For** $j = 0$ to $l-1$ **do:**
         Begin.
5.   Read the next three elements of D: g_1, g_2, g_3.
6.   Divide j by 2^i and let q be the quotient and r the remainder. Let $y = 2qu$ and $x = 2ru$.
7.   Read g_0 from the image at location (x, y) and compute f_0, f_1, f_2, f_3 from Equations (6.2).
8.   Call *FILL* $(f_0, x, y, x+u, y+u)$.
         Call *FILL* $(f_1, x+u, y, x+2u, y+u)$.
         Call *FILL* $(f_2, x, y+u, x+u, y+2u)$.
         Call *FILL* $(f_3, x+u, y+u, x+2u, y+2u)$.
         End.
      End.
9. **End of Algorithm.**

Algorithm 6.5 describes the process. It uses a procedure *FILL* for actual display of the image, and it assumes that the image can also be read back from the device. This procedure can be implemented easily with the primitive graphic commands described in Section 1.7 (Table

---

† There is nothing special about $T_c/2$. We could have considered any other small fraction.

1.2). If a graphic display is connected to a host computer, then this is an efficient method only when the size of the window is large. For smaller sizes it is best to buffer the output by creating a matrix in main memory and then writing out with a *wpic* command (Table 1.2). When one must switch from one technique to the other, the critical window size is determined by comparing: (a) the load to the bus of the host machine when transmitting instructions to the display, (b) the relative speed for executing a *wpic* command versus a sequence of the three simple commands of *FILL* by the display controller, and (c) the over-head for creating and manipulating the buffer matrix by the host com-puter.

6.4.3 Image Compaction with a Quad Tree

The representation described in the previous two sections can be improved in a number of ways. Our first concern is to eliminate the need for increased storage (or the possibility of round-off errors) for the g_j's defined by Equations (6.1). What we need is a technique for a one-to-one mapping of four numbers onto another four.

Proposition 6.1:   Let $a_1, a_2 \cdots a_n$ be n numbers, each consisting of Q bits. The number n is assumed to be a power of two. Then their average plus the $n-1$ differences of $D_2, \cdots D_n$ from that average can be stored in $nQ + \log_2 n$ bits.

Proof: Let L be the sum of the n numbers. Let q be its quotient by n and r its remainder. Each of the n numbers q, $a_i - q$ ($i = 2, ... n$) requires at most Q bits. The remainder r requires at most $\log_2 n$ bits. $\square$

Proposition 6.1 shows that for the quad tree we must add two bits at each level, and this can certainly pile up. However, there is a trade-off between the bits for q and r and $a_i - q$. If the numbers a_i are nearly equal to each other, then r and $a_i - q$ will require very few bits, but q may require up to Q. If there are big differences between the a_i's, then q will be small and will require fewer bits. This feature can be exploited to produce representations that do not require additional space and is discussed in the next section. Here we show how the result of Proposition 6.1 can be used for increasing efficiency. Instead of transmitting the differences from the average, one can send only the differences from q (each requiring at most Q bits), plus the last q. In addition, we can transmit the remainders r, each requiring only $\log_2 n$ bits (two bits for quad trees). One can easily find that the number of remainders is

$$\frac{4^n-1}{3} \; ;$$

therefore the increase in the volume will not be 33 percent, but $(2/Q)$ times 33 percent. The reconstruction can be performed by a simple modification of the given equations.

It is possible to achieve considerable savings if the image has large uniform areas. Indeed, suppose that the three differences for a block are zero. Then, instead of placing three zeros in the array D used by Algorithm 6.4a, one can insert a single special symbol. (This could be the maximum value of brightness possible, since this value will not occur as a difference from the average). After the scanning of the whole image has been completed, repetitions of this symbol can be erased from all subsequent levels of the tree. For example, an image with one brightness value will be encoded as that value plus the special symbol (see Problem 6.6).

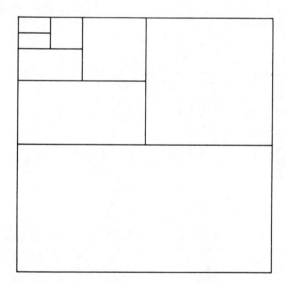

Figure 6.6 Sequence of image subdivisions for the binary tree

6.5 BINARY IMAGE TREES

Binary trees are a useful variation of quad trees and have certain advantages which are described below. Although they have been proposed only recently (see Bibliographical Notes) and have not been studied as much as quad trees have, they may be found in the long run to be a superior data structure. Figure 6.6 shows the block arrangement for the binary tree. The change in the shape of the blocks from level to level is not serious problem: it can be determined by testing whether the level index is even or odd.

A clear advantage of binary trees is the smaller change in the resolution from level to level. While for quad trees each transmission quadruples the resolution, for binary trees each transmission only doubles it. Since the total volume of data is the same in both cases, a more accurate image is formed earlier.

Another major advantage is the use of the tradeoff between average and difference so that no more bits are transmitted than in the original image. In particular g_0 and g_1 are not defined by Equations (6.1) but from a discrete approximation as shown in Figure 6.7.

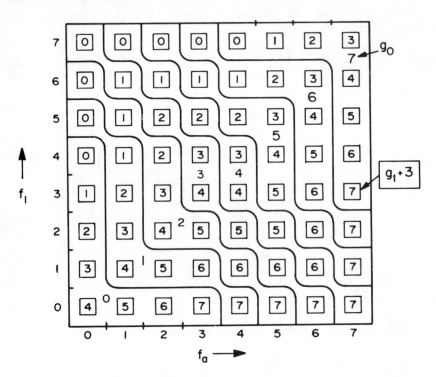

Figure 6.7   Relation determining g_0 and g_1 from f_0 and f_1. The numbers in boxes are the values of g_1, with 3 added to them so they are still in the 0-7 range. They are approximately equal to $f_0 - f_1 + 3$. The square is subdivided into regions where the unboxed numbers give the value of g_0 as an approximation to the average $(f_0 + f_1)/2$.

Figure 6.8 (Plate 24) shows a sequence of images produced by this method. The top left image has only one intensity, the average of all pixels. The first image of the third row has 4096 distinct blocks and it is transmitted in one eighth of the time of the last (fourth), which has 32,768 pixels. Most of the information is already available in the former and therefore one can decide quickly whether to continue the transmission.

6.6 SPLIT-AND-MERGE ALGORITHMS

Compaction and selective access to images are only two of the most common uses of quad (and binary) trees. Another major application of this data structure has been in image segmentation. Section 4.4 described the use of region growing and uniformity tests for image segmentation. Split-and-merge algorithms are an extension of that approach. One starts with the nodes (squares) at some intermediate level of a quad tree. If a square is found to be nonuniform, then it is replaced by its four subsquares (split). Conversely, if four squares are found that form a uniform square, they are replaced by it (merge). This process may continue recursively until no further splits or merges are possible. Algorithm 6.6 implements this idea and we shall discuss it after establishing a method for describing the nodes of the quad tree.

Note that here the tree is not used to transform an image but to guide the traversal. Thus at level q with squares that contain $2^q \times 2^q$ pixels we compute the uniformity criterion over all of the pixels without using the average value of the square. The result is again a variable resolution picture, but now we have only one copy, rather than a sequence of copies as before. Figure 6.9 (Plate 25) shows an example.

One can construct algorithms that start at single pixels and do only merge operations. One can also construct algorithms that start at the complete image and do only split operations. The former have the disadvantage that it is impossible to test many uniformity criteria on single pixels. The latter have the disadvantage of excessive computation because the split operation is more expensive than the merge operation (see Problem 6.8). Starting at an intermediate level enables us to evaluate complicated uniformity predicates without doing an excessive number of splits.

The implementation of the data structure must deal with the problem of storing squares of variable size. It is necessary to use a header for each one of them, indicating size and location in terms of x-y coordinates on the plane. If the dimension of the image is $2^n \times 2^n$, then n bits are enough for each of these quantities. Thus, $3n$ bits per square can be used to describe the coordinates of its upper left corner plus the length of its side. One can also use the indexing system described in Section 6.4. In that case the header will consist of a label at most n symbols long. Since each symbol is one of the numbers 0, 1, 2, or 3, it can be described by two bits. Providing label length information, though, requires $\log_2 n$ bits per entry. Fixed length labels can be achieved by padding with another symbol, e.g., 4, which will increase the required space to three bits per symbol. Therefore, depending on the system used, the header requires $3n$ or $(2n_i + \log_2 n)$ bits, where n_i denotes the length of a particular label. Although headers with variable length labels require less space, the increase in the complexity of implementation is probably not worth the savings in memory.

If the number of bits required to describe the characteristics of a square is m and there are N squares, then the total space required will be $N(3n+m)$. The value of m can be quite large when regions are characterized by many features. On the other hand, if the only feature used is the average brightness, m is the same as the amount required for the description of single pixels. One can compute a compaction ratio as

$$\frac{4^n \, m}{N(3n + m)} \, .$$

Eight is a typical value for both n and m, so that the variable resolution image requires less space if the number of squares is less than one quarter of the number of pixels. This is often the case, so that this implementation does not impose additional memory requirements.

The result of a split-and-merge algorithm using a quad tree needs further processing: merging of regions that are not siblings in the tree. For this we need another data structure, which will be described in Section 6.7.

Algorithm 6.6 lists the basic traversal procedure of a $2^n \times 2^n$ image starting at level q, which contains 4^q squares of size $2^{n-q} \times 2^{n-q}$ each. (Thus, the whole image corresponds to level zero, and single pixels correspond to level n.) The algorithm does not create the whole tree but only the needed parts. It maintains a linked list L, whose entries correspond to nodes of the quad tree, arranged in such a way that four successive nodes have a common parent in the tree. The index i_4 used for the traversal of the list is expressed in base 4 so that the x-y coordinates of the top left corner of the square can be found immediately (see Figure 6.4). Indeed, if $d_0, d_1, \cdots, d_k, \cdots$, are the digits of i_4, starting from the least significant, we have Equations (6.3), shown below.

Algorithm 6.6 Split-and-merge using a Quad Tree

Notation: The linked list L contains the coordinates of the top left corner and the size of squares plus pointers to the previous and next elements. The index i_4 is expressed in base 4. The input is a set of squares corresponding to a level q of the quad tree. The output is another set of squares, at different levels of the tree. The **while** conditions in steps 4 and 11 and the **if** conditions of steps 8 and 13 assume the invocation of a procedure that checks for uniformity.

1. **For** i_4 from 0 to $4^q - 1$ **do:** {Initialize}
    Begin.
2. Find the coordinates x and y from Equations (6.4).
3. Place x, y, and 2^{n-q} in the list L.
    End.
4. **While** regions are found that can be merged **do:** {Merge}
    Begin.
5. Set the index j to point to the first element of the list L.
6. **While** the end of the list L has not been reached **do:**
    Begin.
7. **If** the four regions pointed to by j, $j_1 = next(j)$, $j_2 = next(j_1)$, and $j_3 = next(j_2)$ have the same size, **then do:**
    Begin.
8. **If** their union is uniform according to the criterion used, **then** *merge* them by replacing in L the size s of the first region by $2s$ and by unlinking the other three.
9. Replace j by $next(j_3)$.
    End.
10. **Else** replace j by $next(j)$.
    End.
    End.
11. **While** nonuniform regions are found **do:** {Split}
    Begin.
12. **For** all elements of the list L **do:**
    Begin.
13. **If** the region is uniform, **then** advance along the list.
14. **Else** replace it by its four children.
    End.
    End.
15. **End of Algorithm.**

$$x = \sum_k (d_k \, modulo \, 2) \cdot 2^{n-q+k} \, , \qquad (6.3a)$$

$$y = \sum_k \lfloor \frac{d_k}{2} \rfloor \cdot 2^{n-q+k} \, . \qquad (6.3b)$$

The symbol $\lfloor x \rfloor$ denotes the greatest integer less than or equal to x. The range of the coordinates is from 0 to $n-1$. For the example of Figure 6.4, $n = q = 3$. Then index 213 corresponds to

$x = 1 \cdot 1 + 1 \cdot 2 + 0 \cdot 4 = 3$ and $y = 1 \cdot 1 + 0 \cdot 2 + 1 \cdot 4 = 5$.

The reader can verify that the box labeled 213 on that figure is indeed on the fourth column and sixth row. (We add one to the values of x and y because they are zero for the first row or the first column.) Thus the index of an entry in L points to a square region with diagonally opposite corners at (x,y) and $(x+2^{n-q}, y+2^{n-q})$. We assume that a uniformity criterion is available to decide whether a group of regions must be merged, or a single region must be split. (Such criteria have been discussed in Section 4.4.) The algorithm scans the region in such a way that when one of them is split, its first child is examined immediately for uniformity.

The above algorithm can be used for solving other problems besides image segmentation. Section 17.2 describes its use for solving a visibility problem but without any mergers (see also Problem 6.9).

6.7 LINE ENCODINGS AND THE LINE ADJACENCY GRAPH (LAG)

When a picture cannot fit in main memory it is often examined along lines parallel to a given direction (raster scan). The same form of image traversal is also common whenever television technology is used. If the picture is of class 2, it can be encoded as a sequence of lengths of particular color or brightness. It is more efficient to store such information only for the first interval of each line and store the differences in length and brightness (or color code) for the rest. Such a representation is often called *run length encoding* (RLE) although the term was originally used for bilevel images where only length information needed to be stored. Images of class 1 can also be encoded in this fashion, by approximating ranges of brightness levels by their average. If the number of intervals on a line is I, then the space required for storing lengths and brightness per line will be $I(n+m)$, where n and m have the same meaning as in the previous section. For the typical value of eight, savings will occur if I is less than half the number of pixels on the line. Therefore, run length encoding can result in significant storage savings and it is worthwhile to implement algorithms for image analysis or graphics directly on data in this form without reconstructing the image.†

The description of many algorithms for image processing using the RLE becomes easier if we use a *line adjacency graph* (LAG). The nodes of such a graph correspond to intervals, and branches connect nodes if the corresponding intervals are on adjacent lines, their projections along the scan direction overlap, and their pixels have the same

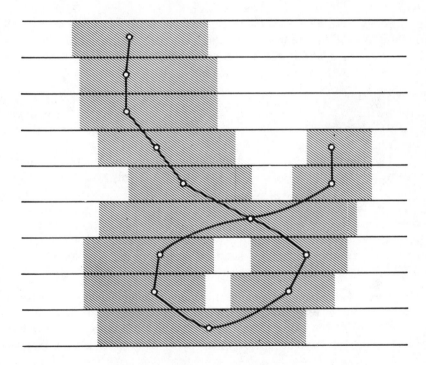

Figure 6.10 Example of a line adjacency graph

color. Figure 6.10 shows an example of a LAG. If x_i denotes the coordinates of the endpoints of the intervals, then intervals $[x_{k-1}, x_k)$ and $[x_{j-1}, x_j)$ will have overlapping projections if both following inequalities hold:*

$$x_{k-1} < x_j \text{ and } x_{j-1} < x_k . \tag{6.4}$$

---

† There are even display devices that use RLE in their refresh memory.
* Recall that $[a, b)$ is a semi-closed interval. Its points satisfy the inequality $a \leq x < b$.

The strict inequalities imply that intervals touching at only a corner are not considered overlapping. This restriction can be removed by simply making the inequalities nonstrict. Because it is easy to check the overlap conditions it is not necessary to store the line adjacency graph explicitly.

The LAG can be made directed by having branches pointing from node A to node B if the interval corresponding to node A lies above the interval corresponding to node B. Then one can speak about the *above* degree of an interval-node (number of intervals touching it on the line above) and the *below* degree of the same (number of intervals touching on the line below). We shall use the notation (a,b) to denote the degrees of a node with a standing for *above* and b for *below*. The following properties can be proven easily.

Proposition 6.2:   If a node of the LAG has degree $(0,d)$, then it corresponds to a local maximum in the vertical direction. If the degree is $(d,0)$, then it corresponds to a local minimum in the vertical direction. □

The following result, relating LAGs for different colors, is useful in some applications. It assumes that there are only two colors, X and Y, in the image and that the LAG for color X is constructed using Equation (6.4), while the LAG for color Y is constructed using the same equation after relaxing the strict inequalities to permit equality so that intervals that touch only at a corner correspond to connected nodes. (The rationale behind such an assumption is explained in Section 7.2.) Figure 6.11 illustrates the construction.

Proposition 6.3:   If a node of the LAG for color X has degree (m,n) with $n>1$ then there will be a node of the LAG for color Y with degree $(0,d)$ in the line below. Similarly, if $m>1$ there will be a node of the LAG for color Y with degree $(d,0)$ above it. The converse is also true in both cases. □

Proof: The following is a proof of the part dealing with below degree greater than one. Let $x_{1,i}$ and $x_{1,i+1}$ be the endpoints of the color X interval which corresponds to a node with below degree greater than one (see Figure 6.11a). This means that in the line below there exist interval endpoints $x_{2,j-2}$, $x_{2,j-1}$, $x_{2,j}$, and $x_{2,j+1}$ with the property of Equation (6.5), below.

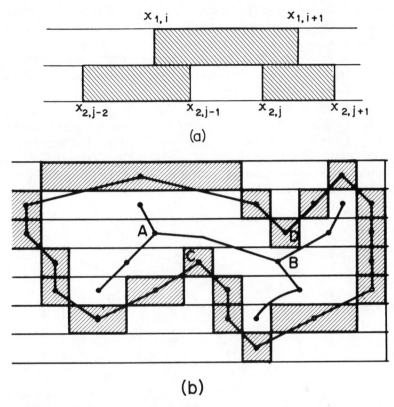

(a)

(b)

Figure 6.11 Demonstration of Proposition 6.3: (a) notations used in the proof, (b) global configuration.

$$x_{1,i} < x_{2,j-1} \text{ and } x_{2,j} < x_{1,i+1} \tag{6.5}$$

with $x_{2,j-1}$ being the right endpoint and $x_{2,j}$ the left endpoint of intervals with color X. (Figure 6.11a.) Therefore, the interval $x_{2,j-1}, x_{2,j}$ must have color Y. It would be connected to intervals of the same color on the line above if and only if one of the following inequalities holds:

$$x_{2,j-1} \leq x_{1,i} \text{ or } x_{1,i+1} \leq x_{2,j} . \tag{6.6}$$

But the set of inequalities of Equation (6.6) is the negation of the inequalities of Equation (6.5) and therefore the node corresponding to the interval $x_{2,j-1}, x_{2,j}$ (of color Y) must have above degree zero. (This is where we use the assumption about a different type of connectivity for each color: the negation of a nonstrict inequality is a strict inequality.)

Conversely, suppose that the interval $x_{2,j-1}, x_{2,j}$ has above degree zero. This means that the set of inequalities of Equation (6.6) cannot be true. Therefore, the set of inequalities in Equation (6.5) is true and there will be an interval of color X with below degree greater than one. A similar argument can be made regarding situations where the above degree is greater than one. $\square$

Proposition 6.3 implies that intervals where either the *above* or *below* degree for color X exceeds one correspond to places where the region of color Y has either a maximum in the vertical direction with color X above it (such as nodes A and C in Figure 6.11b), or a minimum in the vertical direction with the color X below it (such as nodes B and D in Figure 6.11b).

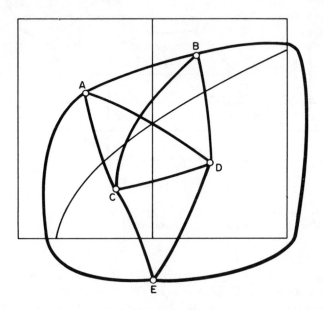

Figure 6.12   Restrictions of the definition of adjacency for regions. The image contains five regions and it is clear that the pairs (A,B), (B,D), (D,C), and (C,A) share a boundary and that the respective nodes of the RAG must be linked. Also A, B, C, and D are all linked to E. If we link the pairs (A,D) and (B,C), then the RAG becomes nonplanar. A small perturbation at the point where the four regions meet will cause only one of the pairs to be adjacent and the resulting RAG will be planar.

6.8 REGION ENCODINGS AND THE REGION ADJACENCY GRAPH (RAG)

This form is particularly suitable for class 2 pictures or approximations of pictures of class 1. A connected region of a given color can be described completely by its contour, and this usually takes much less space than a description in terms of pixels. Operations over such pictures can be facilitated if the region adjacency graph is available. The nodes of this graph correspond to regions, and two nodes are joined by a branch if the respective regions are adjacent. We should point out that the concept of adjacency must be defined carefully for discrete pictures and we shall discuss it in detail later (Chapter 7). Here we point out only that whatever definition is going to be used, it should not allow connections that will make the RAG nonplanar. In particular, when four regions meet at a corner, one should not allow both diagonal connections as shown in Figure 6.12. Figure 6.13 shows an example of the graph overlaid on a picture. It is possible to extract significant information about the picture by checking various properties of the graph.

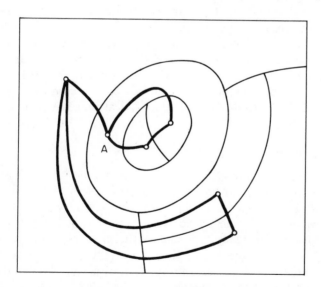

Figure 6.13 A region adjacency graph

The following is a list of some features of the RAG and the corresponding properties of the image.

(a)   The degree of a node corresponds to the number of regions adjacent to a given region. This number is usually proportional to the size of the region, and therefore nodes of high degree will correspond to large regions.

(b)   If a region surrounds other regions completely (A in Figure 6.13), then the corresponding node is a *cutnode* in the RAG. If all the regions in a picture are without holes (i.e., they are simply connected), then none of them will surround any other and the graph will have no cutnodes. Since there exist efficient algorithms (see Bibliographical Notes) for finding the cutnodes of a graph, it is possible to obtain all topological information about the picture from the RAG.

The nodes of the RAG may be labeled with information about the regions so that other properties, besides topology, may be investigated. The RAG may also be used for a sophisticated form of paging. Pages are formed by parts of a picture corresponding to small clusters of nodes (or even a single node), and this provides a more natural subdivision than an arbitrary grid system.

Finally, the RAG provides the basic data structure for segmentation by region growing, including split-and-merge algorithms. One disadvantage of Algorithm 6.6 is that at the end regions of similar features may not be merged if they do not have a common ancestor in the quad tree. The introduction of the RAG at that last stage allows the grouping of such regions.

6.9 ICONIC REPRESENTATIONS

Iconic representations are fairly complex but they are the most efficient way of storing and manipulating pictures. A picture is assumed to be subdivided into subpictures that may be arbitrary pages (as in Section 6.3), squares of a quad tree, regions resulting from a segmentation, etc. However, instead of storing all the pictures, some of them are replaced by a descriptive label. Example 1.1 illustrates one form of iconic representation. As a rule, some form of pattern recognition must be used before this form is achieved.

6.10 DATA STRUCTURES FOR DISPLAYS

The data structures described above are useful for applications where one deals with existing images. In graphics one starts with descriptions of images, and these may be in a nonpictorial form. Generally, such descriptions come in the form of piecewise polynomial functions of one variable (for curves) or two variables (for surfaces). In vector graphics, where the primitive commands display only straight lines, the functions are piecewise linear, forming polygons or polyhedra. In either case the object description is a graph with branches that are straight line segments. We may use the term *object graph* for this data structure. If the description involves curvilinear segments or high order surface patches, then we can still have an object graph, but with *labeled branches:* the labels are the coefficients of the curve or surface. Alternatively, one can use a (nonplanar) region adjacency graph whose nodes will correspond to surface patches, and if the patches are adjacent, then branches will connect the respective nodes. Such a "patch adjacency graph" is appropriate for raster graphics.

In principle, it is easy to construct displays out of such graphs. A practical challenge is to create data structures that will help solve the various problems encountered in generating the display. Presorting and introduction of additional links may be needed in order to speed up the solution of visibility problems, for example. We shall return to these questions in Chapter 17.

6.11 BIBLIOGRAPHICAL NOTES

The problems of graph traversal and the related data structures are discussed in most general books on algorithms or data structures (e.g., [6.AHU], [6.KN]). See also [3.PA] for a treatment in the context of pattern recognition. See [6.RO] and [6.DEL] for a discussion of the problem of preserving geometrical adjacency in linear storage.

The quad tree is one of the most common data structures discussed in the literature. Its first well known application was in the context of a hidden line elimination algorithm by Warnock [6.WA]. In the early seventies, it found widespread use in pattern recognition and image processing ([6.HP], [6.HS], [6.KD], [6.TP], [6.TA]). The use of the quad tree for displays with gross information first was described by Sloan and Tanimoto [6.ST]. The binary tree has been proposed recently by Knowlton [6.KK] (Figure 6.8 is from [6.KK]). Quad trees are now a popular research topic and their properties are investigated at great length. See [6.SR] for a review.

Line adjacency graphs have also been used widely, although the use is often implicit. Algorithms that perform operations on an image are described in terms of pixel and interval traversal without reference to the graph. [6.GR] is probably the earliest paper where the LAG is used (implicitly). See [3.PA] for more examples of its use in pattern recognition and image processing. [6.SH] describes an explicit use in graphics (see Chapter 8 for more on this subject).

The region adjacency graph is probably the older, more obvious data structure for image processing and most of the literature on scene analysis uses various versions of it.

6.12 RELEVANT LITERATURE

[6.AHU] Aho, A. V.; Hopcroft, J. E.; and Ullman, J. D. *The Design and Analysis of Computer Algorithms,* Reading, Mass.: Addison-Wesley, 1974.

[6.DEL] DeMillo, R. A.; Eisenstat, S. C.; and Lipton, R. J. "Preserving Average Proximity in Arrays" *CACM,* **21** (1978), pp. 228-231.

[6.GR] Grimsdale, R. L.; Summer, F. H.; Tunis, C. J.; and Kilburn, T. "A System for the Automatic Recognition of Patterns," *Proc. IEE,* **106B** (1959), pp. 210-221.

[6.HP] Horowitz, S. L. and Pavlidis, T. "Picture Segmentation by a Tree Traversal Algorithm," *Journal of the ACM,* **23** (1976), pp. 368-388.

[6.HS] Hunter, G. M. and Steiglitz, K. "Operations on Images Using Quad Trees," *IEEE Trans. Pattern Analysis and Machine Intelligence,* **PAMI-1** (1979), pp. 145-153.

[6.KD] Klinger, A. and Dyer, C. R. "Experiments on Picture Representation Using Regular Decomposition," *CGIP,* **5** (1976), pp. 68-105.

[6.KK] Knowlton, K. "Progressive Transmission of Grey Scale and B/W Pictures by Simple, Efficient and Lossless Encoding Schemes," *IEEE Proceedings,* **68** (1980), pp. 885-896.

[6.KN] Knuth, D.E., *Fundamental Algorithms,* vol. 1, Reading, Mass.: Addison-Wesley, 1973.

[6.RO] Rosenberg, A. L. "Preserving Proximity in Arrays," *SIAM J. Computing,* **4** (1975), pp. 443-460.

[6.SH] Shani, U. "Filling Regions in Binary Raster Images — a Graph-theoretic Approach," *SIGGRAPH'80,* pp. 321-327.

[6.SR] Sammet, H. and Rosenfeld, A. "Quadtree Representations of Binary Images," *Proc. Fifth Intern. Conf. on Pattern Recognition,* Miami Beach, December 1980, pp. 815-818. (Published by IEEE Computer Society, IEEE Catalog No. 80CH1499-3.)

[6.ST] Sloan, K. R., Jr. and Tanimoto, S. L. "Progressive Refinement of Raster Images," *IEEE Trans. on Computers,* **C-28** (1979), pp. 871-874.

[6.TA]   Tanimoto, S. L., "Hierarchical Approaches to Picture Processing,"
         Ph. D. Dissertation, Dept. of Electrical Engineering, Princeton
         University, August 1975, 241pp. *(Available from University
         Microfilms).*

[6.TP]   Tanimoto, S. L. and Pavlidis, T. "A Hierarchical Data Structure for
         Picture Processing," *CGIP,* **2** (1975), pp. 104-119.

[6.WA]   Warnock, J. E. "A Hidden-Surface Algorithm for Computer Gen-
         erated Half-tone Pictures," *Technical Report 4-15,* Computer Science
         Department, University of Utah, 1969.

6.13 PROBLEMS

6.1.   One disadvantage of using two-dimensional arrays is that in some
       computer languages their size must be specified during compila-
       tion. On the other hand one need fix in advance only the max-
       imum size of a one-dimensional array. Write a program using
       this concept for storing the pixels of an image and include pro-
       cedures for evaluating the x-y coordinates from the location of a
       pixel in the array. Implement Algorithm 6.2 using such an array.
       Define as adjacent pixels to p the eight pixels that can be
       reached from p by one of the directions of Figure 1.2.

6.2.   Show that one can traverse a connected component of a graph
       correctly even when a node is placed in the stack more than
       once.

6.3.   Repeat Problem 6.1 with the following change in Algorithm 6.2:
       instead of placing the pixels adjacent to p (the current pixel) on
       the stack, place p itself. How does this simplify the algorithm?
       Do you still need to use an extra marking for pixels placed in the
       stack? Do you pay any price for this simplification?

6.4.   Write a graph traversal program that prints out pairs of nodes
       connected by a path containing only nodes of degree two. (You
       may think of the graph as a communications network, where
       nodes of degree one are *terminals*, nodes of degree higher than
       two are *interchanges*, and nodes of degree two are *amplifiers*.
       Your program will produce all pairs of interchanges and termi-
       nals that have a direct connection, except for the amplifiers. For
       a similar problem in image processing, see Chapter 9.)

6.5.   This problem is related to paging. Consider a set of identical
       squares arranged on the plane so they form a matrix of $N \times N$
       squares. In this arrangement there exist $2N(N-1)$ pairs of
       squares that share a side. (Figure 6.14 shows the case for
       $N = 4$.)

1	2	3	4
5	6	7	8
9	10	11	12
13	14	15	16

Figure 6.14 Arrangement of squares for Problem 6.5.

We are now requested to arrange the squares in a linear fashion in such a way as to preserve the two-dimensional proximity as much as possible. Examine various strategies for doing this, as well as different measures of proximity. For example, if we arrange the squares in numerical order (according to the system of Figure 6.14) then direct adjacency will be preserved for $N(N-1)$ pairs. A zig-zag arrangement does the same thing for $(N-1)(N+1)$ pairs. Is there a strategy that preserves adjacency for more pairs? Other measures of proximity include maximum distance between members of pairs that used to be adjacent, average distance between such pairs, etc.

6.6.   Modify Algorithms 6.4a and 6.4 so that if the children of a node are all the same, they are not included in the quad tree.

6.7.   Given coordinates x_i and y_i of a pixel in the range 0 to $2^n - 1$, find its label according to the system illustrated in Figure 6.4.

6.8.   The major cost of a split or merge operation in Algorithm 6.6 is the need to recheck the resulting squares for uniformity. Use the analysis of Section 4.4 to show that the cost of a merge cannot exceed the cost of a split.

6.9.   Modify Algorithm 6.6 so that it finds the edges of all regions in a bilevel image.

APPENDIX 6.A: INTRODUCTION TO GRAPHS

Graph theory is an old subject with a large literature and numerous applications. It seems that knowledge of some elementary concepts of the subject can go a long way in helping a person understand most algorithms where graph theory is used in pictorial information processing. The purpose of this appendix is to introduce some of the most common concepts of graphs.

A graph is set of **points** or **nodes** connected by **lines** or **branches**. Examples of graphs are shown in Figures 6.10, 6.11b, 6.12, and 6.13. The **degree** of a node equals the number of branches incident to it. Thus all nodes of the graph of Figure 6.12 have degree four while in

Figure 6.13 the degree of the various nodes ranges from two to four. The streets of a city are an example of a graph where nodes correspond to intersections or ends of streets, and branches correspond to street segments between intersections or ends. In the "street graph" most nodes have degree four and dead end streets terminate at nodes of degree one.

A **directed graph** is one where some or all branches have a direction associated with them. In the street example the graph becomes directed if we consider one way streets. In such a graph we can talk about the **out** degree and the **in** degree of a node by counting the branches pointing away from it and the branches pointing toward it. A variation of this terminology is offered in Section 6.7.

A **path** from node A to node B is a sequence of branches that one must pass in order to go from A to B. A **circuit** is a path whose start and end coincide. A graph is said to be **connected** if there is a path between any pair of its nodes.

A **tree** is a connected graph without any circuits.

A **subgraph** of a graph G is a graph containing some or all the nodes of G and some or all its branches and no other nodes or branches. A **spanning tree** of a connected graph G is a subgraph of G which contains all the nodes of G and enough branches to make it connected without creating any circuits.

A common way of visualizing trees is to choose a node as the **root** of the tree, then draw all nodes connected to it underneath it, and so forth (see Figure 6.3). The nodes connected to A, the node above them, are called the **children** of A, and A is called their **parent**.

Chapter 7

BILEVEL PICTURES

7.1 INTRODUCTION

This chapter and the next two chapters deal with class 2 pictures where regions of fixed gray level or color are well defined. A major concern in the study of such images is the concept of *shape*, a term that is not easy to define quantitatively. One faces this problem when sampling an analog bilevel image. The size of the cells of the sampling grid must be small enough so that the shapes of regions of a given color remain unaltered in reconstructing the image. Sections 7.2, 7.4, and 7.6 deal with this and with other aspects of the digitization problem. Another set of problems in processing such images involves transforming them into a set of curves, or going back from a set of curves to plane regions. The tracing of the contour of a region is discussed in Section 7.5. Reconstructing the region from its contour, or *filling*, will be treated in Chapter 8. Instead of finding the contour, one may choose to thin a region to its skeleton, a matchstick type of figure whose curves or lines reflect the shape of the region. *Thinning* algorithms will be treated in Chapter 9.

Contour tracing, contour filling, and thinning algorithms are encountered in diverse applications, but they share many features. All of them involve traversal of a plane region and, while the process is quite simple (e.g., by using Algorithm 6.2), a number of subtle problems occur. It is easy to give precise definitions for contour tracing, contour filling, and thinning in the analog plane, provided that one deals with bounded sets that have contours satisfying certain smoothness conditions. It is rather difficult to give precise definitions in the discrete plane. We devote Section 7.3 to a discussion of discrete geometry and we return to the subject in Sections 7.6 and 7.7. Finally, because shape analysis is a major motivation for contour tracing in class 2 images, we shall devote Section 7.8 to a brief discussion of how to derive shape descriptions from contour data.

7.2 SAMPLING AND TOPOLOGY

The sampling of bilevel, or, more generally, class 2 pictures presents a special challenge because such images involve step functions. The Fourier transform of such functions is nonzero for all frequencies. Therefore, there is no finite sampling interval that permits digitization without errors. Intuitively, this seems obvious if one wants to preserve information about the exact location of the boundaries between regions. The problem can be seen in the one-dimensional case in Figure 7.1. If one is willing to tolerate an error in the location of boundaries, then it is possible to find a solution as follows.

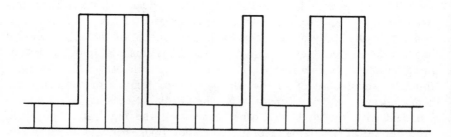

Figure 7.1 Sampling of a bilevel signal. Each peak will be preserved in the discrete version if the spacing between two samples is less than the minimum width of such peaks.

Because of the point spread function $g(r)$ (Section 2.3.2) the samples need not be equal to one of the two original levels. They will take intermediate values near the boundary between levels. In order to recover a bilevel representation the samples must be compared to a threshold between levels. This will introduce an error in the location of the boundary not more than half the length of the interval where $g(r)$ is nonzero. We assume that this interval is very small compared to the sampling interval, as it must be in any well designed digitizer.

Let h be the size of the tolerance. If the sampling interval is less than h, then we achieve the desired accuracy. No interval will be lost if the minimum width exceeds h. One can show that if the bilevel function changes values only at particular points that are located at an integer multiple of h, then its Fourier transform will be zero for high frequencies and the function can be sampled correctly. Even though this assumption is not realistic, the assumption of minimum width is, and the smaller h is in comparison to that width, the smaller is the error introduced by sampling. In particular, we can avoid *aliasing*, which for bilevel images means the loss of gaps so that the function appears to be uniform over an interval when in fact it is not.

Another approach to the sampling of bilevel signals involves their conversion into gray scale. A filter that replaces the value at a point by the average of its neighbors is a low-pass filter and reduces the Fourier transform to near zero values at high frequencies. Therefore the resulting gray scale image can be sampled without any errors, except those introduced by the averaging. This approach is not always feasible for images because there exist applications (e.g., phototypesetting) where the output is restricted to a bilevel form. If the samples are thresholded so the resulting signal is bilevel, then we introduce errors in the location of boundaries and this method is equivalent to the first one.

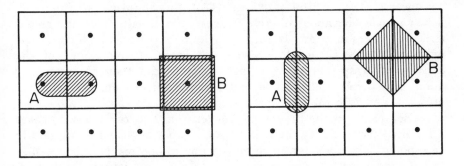

Figure 7.2 Illustration of the difficulties for establishing sampling criteria for pictures. Regions A and B are detected in the left figure but they are missing in the right figure.

The translation of the sampling problem (and its solution) to two dimensions is nontrivial. While there is only one possible form of sampling along a line (subdivision into intervals), the number of possibilities in two dimensions is infinite! One must specify not only the size of the sampling grid, but also its shape. We limit our discussion to square grids though, for the reasons discussed in Section 2.3.2. If the side of the square is h, then it is obvious that no region will be lost if all of

them are large enough so that a square of the grid can be inscribed in
the smallest region. This will be true whether the value of the sample is
determined by the center of the cell, or by an average over its whole
area.   Unfortunately this characterization is both translation- and
orientation-dependent, as can be seen from Figure 7.2. Furthermore, it
says nothing about preserving the topology of the regions. None of
these problems was present in the one-dimensional case!

From a practical viewpoint, the main concern in sampling class 2
images is to preserve shape. Preservation of shape requires that connected sets in the analog image be connected sets in the discrete image,
as well as having a number of other properties. The concern about
connectivity leads immediately to topological questions† and this is
where difficulties start. It is virtually impossible to have an intuitive
definition of topology over a set whose elements are, in a sense, isolated from each other.

However, there is a way out. Instead of considering the transformation from an analog image to a set of discrete pixels we shall consider the transformation between the analog image and its reconstruction, i.e., the analog images obtained by filling the display cells with the
color of the pixel located in the cell. Now we must deal with the relations between images that are both analog. Most of the difficulties
disappear. The practical implications of the approach are not bad.
When people talk about discrete images, they usually have the reconstructed images in mind. In particular, let I be the original image. During sampling, each pixel is given the color of the center of the
corresponding sampling cell. A new image J can then be created by
filling each display cell with the color of the corresponding pixel. Figures 7.3a and 7.3b show this process.

Before discussing the topological relations between the two images
it is necessary to clarify the terms used. Two sets A and B are said to
be topologically equivalent if there is a one-to-one mapping between A
and B, and if both the mapping from A to B, and its inverse from B
to A, are continuous ([7.KE], p. 87). In image processing, one usually
deals with the topology induced by the Euclidean metric and therefore
topological equivalence means that there is a one-to-one mapping such
that points which are close to each other are mapped to points which
are close,* and vice versa. Informally, this means that one can

---

† We shall explain shortly what we mean by *topology* for readers who are not familiar
with the term.

* Readers who feel the term "close" is not precise enough should consult a text on
analysis for the definition of continuous functions.

transform one set onto another by stretching and squeezing without tearing or cutting anything. Thus, if a region has a hole it cannot be topologically equivalent to a region without a hole, because such a transformation would require cutting.

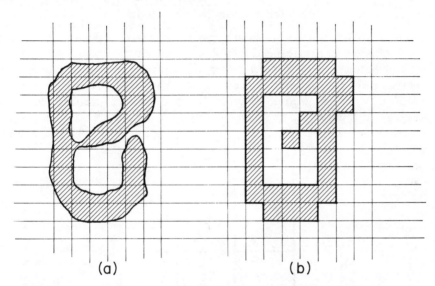

(a)　　　　　　　　　　　(b)

Figure 7.3 (a) Original and (b) reconstructed images after sampling with a square grid

There is no difficulty in defining topological concepts on either of the images shown in Figure 7.3: both are on the continuous plane where a Euclidean metric is well defined. Furthermore, one can show that they are indeed topologically equivalent. To prove this rigorously would take us beyond the scope of this text, but one can agree without resort to any formalism that, for example, both dark sets are connected, and that each has one hole. This example also shows that preserving topology might be a necessary condition, but that it is not sufficient for preserving shape. Clearly, the result of Figure 7.3b is undesirable from that viewpoint. Even though requiring that the number of connected regions of all colors be preserved is not enough, it is at least a start.

Because of the simplicity of the one-dimensional sampling criterion one may be tempted to require that the one-dimensional constraint be satisfied along all the scan lines. Unfortunately, this criterion is likely to fail along lines that are nearly tangent to the boundaries of regions. It is necessary to attack the problem directly and we shall do so in Section 7.4. We must digress first to introduce certain simple concepts from discrete geometry.

7.3 ELEMENTS OF DISCRETE GEOMETRY

As we mentioned in the Introduction, many geometrical concepts that are well defined for analog pictures have no counterparts in discrete images (sets of pixels). Therefore, it is necessary to devote some time to defining these terms for discrete images.

Definition 7.1:   Two pixels are said to be *direct neighbors* (abbreviated d-neighbors) if the respective cells share a side, and *indirect neighbors* (abbreviated i-neighbors) if those cells touch only at a corner. The name *neighbor* denotes either type. The term *N-neighbor* where $0 \leq N \leq 7$ will be used to denote that pixel whose position is marked with N in Figure 7.4. □

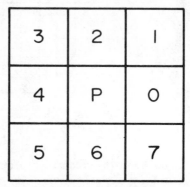

Figure 7.4   Notation used for defining the relative locations of pixels with respect to a pixel P.

Note that d-neighbors are N-neighbors with N even, while i-neighbors correspond to N odd.

Definition 7.2:   An *i-path* (or simply *path*) is a sequence of pixels $A_1, A_2, \cdots, A_n$ such that for $k > 1$, A_{k-1} is a neighbor of A_k and for $k < n$, A_{k+1} is a neighbor of A_k. The term d-path refers to a similar sequence but instead of being simply neighbors, the pixels are required to be d-neighbors. A *simple path* is one where all the pixels are distinct and no pixel has more than two d-neighbors in the path. A *closed path* is one where the first and last pixel coincide. □

Definition 7.3:   A set of pixels S is *connected* (or *i-connected*) if for every pair of pixels C and D in S, there is an i-path whose first and last elements are C and D respectively and all its other pixels belong to S. The term d-connected has the obvious meaning. □

The question of connectivity has been the subject of some

attention in the literature because of the two possible definitions. In particular people have tried to resolve the paradox illustrated in Figure 7.5.

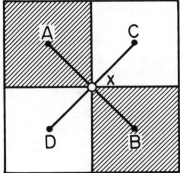

Figure 7.5 Illustration of the topological contradictions occurring in definitions of connectivity over a discrete grid

Intuitively, it is desirable to be able to transfer the concept of connectivity from the discrete plane to the analog. If a set of pixels is connected according to the above definition, then we would like to have the set of display cells connected. In the example of Figure 7.5 it is natural to assume that on the analog plane the sets of black points and white points are disjoint and that the two of them together cover the part of the plane shown, since there are no points of another color. If we define connectivity as i-connectivity, then we have a situation in which a path from A to B (see Figure 7.5) can intersect a path from C to D, even though both of them lie entirely in disjoint sets. Thus the point X must belong to both the white and the black set. If we assume d-connectivity, then neither the set of black pixels nor the set of white pixels is connected. This means that a path from A to B (or C to D) can never lie entirely within one set. Since the line segments AB and CD cross at the point X, this point must not belong to either set. But this contradicts the assumption that the black and white cells completely cover the plane region shown in Figure 7.5.

The paradox occurs because of carelessness in establishing the correspondence between pixel sets and cell sets. In the analog plane, sets may or may not contain their boundaries,† and in the present

---

† The boundary of a set S is defined formally as the set of all points in the plane with the following property. If P belongs to the boundary of S, then all circles centered at P include points of both S and its complement, no matter how small is their radius. P may, or may not belong to S.

example, the inclusion of such boundaries determines the answer to the question of connectivity. We have a number of choices: one of them is to assume that all black cells contain their boundaries (i.e., they are *closed* in a topological sense), while the white cells do not (i.e., they are *open*). Then the set of black cells is connected, and the set of white cells is not. This can be seen clearly if we define the regions of Figure 7.5 analytically after introducing a system of x-y coordinates. If Z is the size of the side of the squares, and the origin is in the lower left-hand corner, we have:

Square A	(black)	$0 \leq x \leq Z$	$Z \leq y \leq 2Z$
Square B	(black)	$0 \leq y \leq Z$	$Z \leq x \leq 2Z$
Square C	(white)	$Z < x < 2Z$	$Z < y < 2Z$
Square D	(white)	$0 < x < Z$	$0 < y < Z$

The point X has coordinates (Z,Z) and is clearly black.

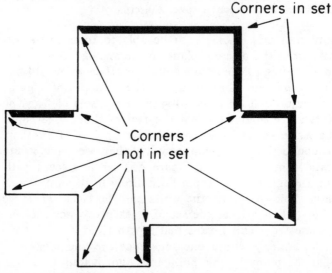

Figure 7.6 Definition of boundary inclusion depending on orientation. The heavy lines mark parts of the boundary whose points belong to the set.

When we discuss an image in terms of pixels, we obtain consistent definitions if we use d-connectivity for white pixels and i-connectivity for black pixels. This choice has been popular in the literature but it fails when we deal with pictures containing pixels of more than two colors. It is possible to assume that whether a set of cells contains certain points of its boundary depends not on its color but on the orientation of the boundary. For a union of square cells we have four directions of the outward normal to the boundary: 0, 2, 4, and 6 (in terms of the notation of Figure 7.4). We may assume that boundary points belong to the set if and only if one of the following two conditions holds: (a) the direction of the normal is 0 or 2, (b) the point is a corner with sides where the normal is 0 and 2 respectively. Figure 7.6 illustrates this. Under this condition pixels of the same color touching at a corner will be considered to be connected if and only if the direction of the bisectrix is 1. The analytical description of a rectangle under this definition will have the form

$$a < x \leq b \quad c < y \leq d \quad .$$

The choice of a definition in practice may depend on a number of factors. For example, in raster graphics lines are drawn with pixels touching only at corners. Therefore, the definition consistent with the implementation is to assume i-connectivity for the foreground intensity and d-connectivity for the background. This should be valid even in color graphics because foreground and background are well defined display parameters. The only potential problem occurs when the definition of background and foreground is changed during the formation of display, and lines of different colors cross each other. It is also possible to use more complex definitions but these are beyond the scope of this text (see [3.PA], pp. 62-64).

7.4 A SAMPLING THEOREM FOR CLASS 2 PICTURES

We proceed to study the sampling of class 2 pictures with square grids. If one requires that each region of a given color be big enough to contain a sampling cell at an arbitrary orientation, we can be sure that no region of the original image I will be missing in the reconstructed image J, but there may still be considerable shape distortions. Definition 7.4 imposes a stricter requirement and we shall prove that it leads to preservation of shape.

Definition 7.4:   A class 2 image and a square sampling grid whose cells have side size h are said to be *compatible* if the following two conditions hold: (a) There exists a number $d > \sqrt{2}h$ such that for each boundary point of each region R of a given color, it is possible to find a circle C with diameter d that is tangent to the boundary and lies entirely within R. (b) The same is also true for the complement of R. $\square$

The condition of compatibility imposes lower bounds on the width of all regions and on the curvature of their contours. In particular, no corners are allowed. This may seem a serious restriction but it is not really so. Indeed, suppose that we have a class of objects whose contours contain corners. We may choose a radius of curvature r and replace each corner by a circular arc with radius r. If r is small enough, there may be no perceived distortion in the shape of the objects, while it is now possible to find a compatible grid. Definition 7.4 has the advantage that in a number of applications it is possible to verify whether compatibility holds. For example, typesetting fonts are often defined in such a way that both the minimum width and minimum curvature can be measured.

The condition of compatibility ensures certain properties which are given next as lemmas. The term neighbor, as used below, is according to Definition 7.1, i.e., it applies to cells touching at the corners as well as at the sides.

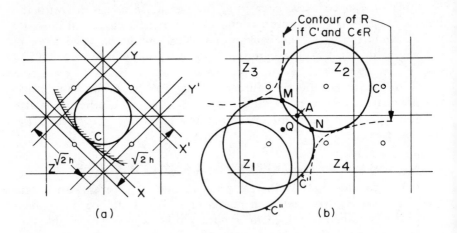

Figure 7.7   Illustrations for the proofs of (a) Lemma 7.1, and (b) Lemma 7.2

Lemma 7.1:   Under the condition of compatibility, if a sampling cell Z intersects a region R, then either the center of Z is in R, or there exists a neighbor of Z whose center is in R.

Proof: Let C be one of the circles of diameter d in R, not containing the center of Z but intersecting Z. Then C must be tangent to a line X as shown in Figure 7.7a. If C does not contain any other center, then it must also be tangent to lines X', Y, and Y'. But the distance between each parallel pair of lines is less than $\sqrt{2}h$, therefore less than d. A contradiction! □

Lemma 7.2: Under the condition of compatibility, if a region R contains the centers of two cells Z_1 and Z_2 that are neighbors, then either Z_1 and Z_2 share a side, or there is a neighbor of Z_1 and Z_2 with center in R which shares a side with each one of them.

Proof: Suppose that they do not share a side and that the centers of Z_3 and Z_4 are not in R. (Figure 7.7b.) If the corner A were in R, then it should be within a circle of diameter d which is entirely in R. C is such a circle not containing the center of Z_3 and Z_4. Consider now a similar circle containing the center of Z_1. Such a circle may intersect C (position C'), or it may not (position C''). If it does, then let M and N be the pair of the points of intersection. Both of them belong to R and any circle of diameter d containing them must also contain the center of either Z_3 or Z_4, a contradiction. If the two circles do not intersect, then there must be a point Q not belonging to R and belonging to Z_1 as shown in Figure 7.7. Then it is impossible to find a circle of diameter d containing Q and none of the centers of Z_1 and Z_2, a violation of the compatibility condition. This proves the proposition when A is assumed to be in R. A symmetrical argument can be made when A is assumed to be outside R. $\square$

Corollary: A consequence of the compatibility conditions is that all connected regions of the discrete image will be directly connected. $\square$

The banishment of corner touching is not very surprising. It was the major source of uncertainty in deciding connectivity so it had to be eliminated by a set of conditions that ensure the preservation of connectivity, among other things.

Proposition 7.1: Let A and B be two points of a set R in the analog image I, and K a curve joining them and lying entirely within R. R is mapped into a set R' in in the reconstructed image J. Then all points of K can be mapped on a curve K' which lies entirely within R' and no corresponding points of K and K' are farther apart than by a distance d.

Proof: The compatibility assumption implies that each point of K lies within a circle of diameter d contained entirely within R. Because of its size, such a circle must contain the center of a sampling cell. Therefore, we can establish a correspondence between all points of K and cell centers (Figure 7.8a). Because of Lemma 7.2 we can find a path from center to center for all these cells, and this path will cross only sides and not corners of the cells. The part of the path within each cell can be put into correspondence with the part of K which was mapped on that cell (Figure 7.8b). Clearly, we can establish a mapping between points of K and the path with the distance of respective points not exceeding d. □

Corollary: The boundaries of corresponding regions in the images I and J are no more than d units apart when the images are overlaid. □

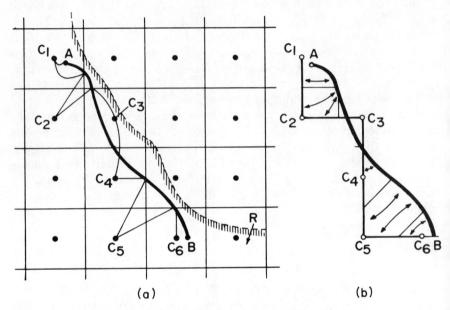

Figure 7.8   Illustrations used in the proof of Proposition 7.1

This result can be interpreted as suggesting preservation of shape between the original analog image and its reconstruction from its samples. However, one might be concerned about the possibility that some regions have been broken, or merged. We shall show next that this is not the case and that images I and J are topologically equivalent.

Theorem 7.1:   The condition of compatibility implies preservation of the topology.

Proof: We shall define a one-to-one mapping between a set and its discrete version which is continuous in both directions. If a sampling cell is contained entirely within a region, then the required mapping is the identity. If it is not, then we consider the cases of excesses and deficiencies. In the example of Figure 7.9, the triangular region KLM is a deficiency: a part of the cell that does not belong to the analog region. The region $MAPENFQBM$ is an excess because it is part of the analog region lying outside the reconstructed region. If a cell contains or is adjacent to such a part, it is subdivided into parts. The parts of the cell not belonging to any of these regions are considered as points of the analog region where all points of the discrete cell are mapped. (Thus cell *DBFH* is shrunk into *DCRGH*, the cell part *VLSMBD* into *VLTMCD*, etc.) The remaining parts are mapped into their symmetrical (with respect to the analog boundary) regions, as shown in Figure 7.9.

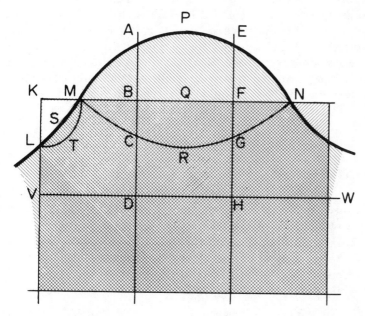

Figure 7.9 Illustration for the proof of Theorem 7.1. The original region is shaded to the left (\) and the reconstructed region to the right (/). The line segments *BD* and *FH* of the discrete image are mapped onto *CD* and *GH* of the analog. *AB* and *EF* are mapped onto *BC* and *FG*, *BQF* onto *CRG*, *APE* onto *BQF*, etc. Points *L*, *M*, and *N* are fixed. The arc *LTM* is mapped onto *LSM*, and *LSM* onto the (piecewise linear) arc *LKM*.

Because of the two lemmas we can be sure of the continuity of the transformations. In particular, Lemma 7.1 guarantees that any excess will be next to a cell with the same color. Because the lemma is valid for both a set and its complement, it also assures that filling the deficiencies will not cause the merging of any regions. Lemma 7.2 assures that no corners are touching and therefore that all the transformation can be done along sides as shown in Figure 7.9. □

This theorem, together with Proposition 7.1, implies both that the reconstructed version of a region is topologically equivalent to the analog original, and that each curve of a region can be mapped into a curve of the other region in such a way that the distance between corresponding points is of a size comparable to the size of the digitization grid. Thus, we may be justified in saying that compatible sampling preserves shape.

From a topological viewpoint, the compatibility condition implies that all analog sets are open and it ensures that the reconstructed sets are also open. This approach seems to leave open the question of how to handle thin lines that have zero thickness theoretically and topologically are not open sets. We observe that in practice lines have finite thickness and there is no way to digitize them properly unless they satisfy the compatibility condition. On the other hand we may wish to make a distinction between their reconstructions and the reconstructions of sets that have a finite thickness from a theoretical, as well as practical, viewpoint. We shall do that in Section 7.6.

7.5 CONTOUR TRACING

The concept of the boundary of a plane set in the analog plane is well defined. It is the set of all points that have the property that no matter how small a neighborhood of them is considered, it contains points both within and outside the set. The corresponding concept in the discrete plane is not at all clear. We shall give some definitions in order to clarify it. We also reserve the term contour for the discrete plane, while the term boundary will be used only when we refer to sets in the continuous plane.

Definition 7.5: The *contour* or *i-contour* of a connected set of pixels R is defined as the set of all pixels in R which have at least one d-neighbor not in R. The *d-contour* of R is the set of all pixels in R which have at least one neighbor not in R. □

7.5.1 Tracing of a Single Contour

The pixels of a contour can be traversed by a path, and it is always possible to choose a closed path for the traversal. In the sequel whenever we refer to contours, we will assume a particular form of traversal, the one given by Algorithm 7.1. This uses the concept of N-neighbor (Definition 7.1) with the notation shown in Figure 7.4. All numerical operations on N are assumed to be modulo 8. The algorithm can be described in terms of an observer who walks along pixels belonging to the set and selects the rightmost pixel available. The initial pixel A can be found in a number of ways, including a top-to-bottom, left-to-right scan of the plane. The tracing terminates when the current pixel is the same as the initial pixel. Since this is also the initial condition we use the flag *first* to distinguish the start from the return to the initial point. The loop of steps 5-9 is executed at most three times to avoid circling around a set that has only one pixel.

Algorithm 7.1 Contour Tracing Algorithm

Procedure *TRACER*

Notation: A is the starting point of the contour of the set R, C the current point whose neighborhood is examined, S the search direction in terms of the code of Figure 7.4, *first* is flag that is true only when the tracing starts, and *found* is flag that is true when a next point on the contour is found.

0. Choose a point A in the contour such that its 4-neighbor is not in the set.
1. Set the current point C to A, the search direction S to 6, and the flag *first* to *true*.
2. **While** C is different from A or the flag *first* is *true* **do** steps 3-10.
   Begin.
3.   Set the flag *found* to *false*.
4.   **While** *found* is *false* **do** steps 5-9, at most three times.
       Begin.
5.   **If** B, the $(S-1)$-neighbor of C, is in R, **then**
           Begin.
6.   Set C to B, S to $S-2$, and *found* to *true*.
           End.
7.   **Else if** B, the S-neighbor of C, is in R, **then** set C to B and *found* to *true*.
8.   **Else if** B, the $(S+1)$-neighbor of C, is in R, **then** set C to B and *found* to *true*.
9.   **Else** increment S by 2.
       End.
10.   Set *first* to *false*.
    End.
11. **End of Algorithm.**

The algorithm must be applied once for each hole of a region, in addition to one application for the external contour. Therefore, it must be combined with a search algorithm for locating holes in the interior of the region. We shall present such an algorithm shortly. This traversal produces a closed i-path and follows external contours counterclockwise and contours of holes clockwise. If a description of the contour is desired as output of the algorithm, then one can use the search directions plus the x-y coordinates of A. These coordinates are output first and then, whenever a pixel is designated as current (C), the value of S is output. Thus we can generate a chain encoding of the contour (see Section 1.2.3). Chain encodings may also be stored internally and used for the traversal of the interior of the region while looking for holes.

7.5.2 Traversal of All the Contours of a Region

Algorithm 7.2 returns all the contours of the region using the procedure *TRACER* listed above. The algorithm assumes that contours found by this procedure are placed in a queue Q. Since the contour descriptions contain both x-y coordinate pairs and chain codes, some care should be taken in the implementation of Q. In order to simplify the description of the algorithm, we assume that Q contains both the x-y coordinates P and the chain code value c. If the pixel is an initial point of a contour, then c equals 8. In practice one could have an array storing only chain codes, and use the symbol 8 to reference a separate array of starting points. Then the x-y coordinates of each new point could be obtained from the previous point plus the chain code information. The algorithm also requires that pixels identified as belonging to the contour should be marked as such on the picture. For bilevel pictures we assume that initially pixels of the region are marked by 1 and those not in the region are marked by 0. The procedure *TRACER* can be changed so that when a pixel is marked as the current point, its value is incremented by 1. Then, at the end of the tracing, pixels of the contour will have values 2 or greater. In particular, the value will be one plus the number of times the pixel has been visited during the traversal. These values are used when the interior is searched for holes. In order to avoid searching the part of the picture outside the region of interest, we adopt the following policy.

After the external contour has been found and placed in the queue Q, we start examining the contents of the latter. If we find a point located on a downward arc, we start a search to the right. Such pixels can be characterized easily by the requirement that the previous

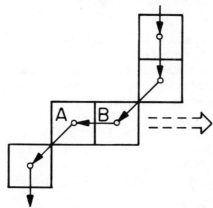

Figure 7.10 Start of an internal scan at an inflection point of the external contour. The chain code for the part of the contour shown with arrows is 665456. *B* is not selected as a starting point but *A* is.

element of the chain code must have values 4 to 7 while the next element should be in the range 5 to 7. We include the value 4 for the former element in order to take care of inflection points, as shown in Figure 7.10. Since the previous direction for the first element is not known until the last element of the chain code for that contour has been seen, its test as a starting point should be postponed until the end. (We do not include this special provision in the listing of Algorithm 7.2, in order to simplify its description.) While scanning along the horizontal direction one must search for either the start of a hole or the other side of the outside contour. The problem is complicated by the fact that there may be pixels which are common to both the external contour and the contour of a hole. If one knew that this could not happen, then one need search only for a sequence of two pixels with values 01 as a start of a hole, and for a pair with values 2 (or greater) and 0 for the external contour. The possibility of shared pixels requires the more complicated checks listed as part of Algorithm 7.2.

Algorithm 7.2 Complete Contour Tracing Algorithm.

Notation:
The queue Q contains both pixel addresses P and chain codes c. *REMOVE* as in Algorithm 6.3.

1.   Find the external contour by calling **procedure** *TRACER*. Place the points found and the chain codes in a queue Q.

2.   **While** Q is not empty **do** steps 3-8.
      Begin.

3. $(P,c) = REMOVE(C)$. **If** c equals 8 {P is the starting point}, **then** set c_0 equal to c and remove one more pixel: $(P,c) = REMOVE(C)$.

4.   **If** c_0 is between 4 and 7 and c between 5 and 7, **then do** steps 5-7.
      Begin.

5.   Starting from P search in the x-direction and examine triplets of successive pixels, A, B, C.

6.   **If** A is 0, and B is 1, **or if** A is 0, B is 2, and C is 0, **then** use B as a starting point and call **procedure** *TRACER* to append the hole contour to Q. Upon return **goto** step 8.

7.   **Else if** A is 0, B greater than 2, and Q is zero, **or if** A is 1, B is 2, and Q is zero, **then goto** step 8.
      End.

8.   Set $c_0 = c$.
      End.

9.   **End of Algorithm.**

The pattern 020 is used to indicate the start of an unscanned hole because an arc of its contour may coincide with an arc of the external contour (Figure 7.11a). The pattern 030 (or 040, etc.) indicates an already scanned hole of the same type, and since the external contour is met, the search should end. Note that regions contained entirely within holes (Figure 7.11b) are ignored. The reason is that the contour of the hole containing such a region will be seen first (scan line UU in Figure 7.11b) and its contour traced and marked. When a lower line is scanned (e.g., VV in the same figure), the scan will terminate because of the occurrence of a 120 or 030 pattern. Because hole contours, as well as external contours, stop the search, hole contours must also be used as starts. This is done automatically, since they are also placed in the queue Q.

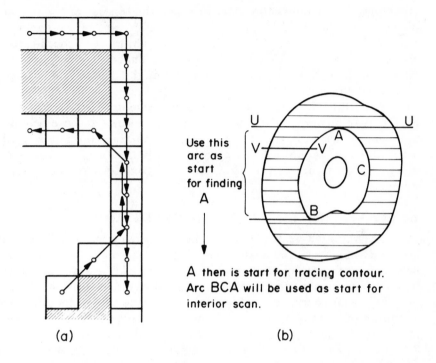

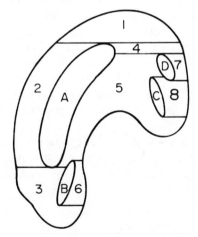

(a)   (b)

Figure 7.11 (a) An arc common to the external contour and the contour of a hole; (b) How nested regions are scanned

Figure 7.12 Order of scanning of the interior of a region

Figure 7.12 shows the order in which the interior of the region is traversed. Nested regions can be found in later scans of the picture. In order to increase the efficiency of such a search, the x-y coordinates of pixels where an internal horizontal scan has ended may be placed in a queue which should be searched after finding the contours of each connected region.

Algorithm 7.2 is efficient because elements of the picture not belonging to a contour need be scanned only once, and those belonging to a contour are scanned only twice. It does not need to mark any pixel with values greater than 3, therefore it may be modified to avoid incrementing pixel values past 3. Then one needs only two bits per pixel for storage.

7.6 CURVES AND LINES ON A DISCRETE GRID

The intuitive geometric distinction between curves or lines (having zero thickness) and plane regions (having some finite thickness) becomes fuzzy on a discrete grid. Given a set of pixels on such a grid, it is not always obvious whether the set was produced by the digitization of a thin curve or a full region. Furthermore, the Euclidean definition of a straight line as the shortest distance between two points fails if we define distance in terms of the grid. In the example of Figure 7.13 we show two i-paths between points A and B, each of them consisting of six pixels. We have lost the uniqueness of the Euclidean definition. Not only that, two such lines may intersect on more than one pixel. The reader can verify this by considering the intersection of one of the lines between A and B with a similar line between C and D. Depending on the choice of particular lines the intersection will contain anywhere from zero to four pixels ! The difficulty does not go away if we decide to find the intersection on the continuous plane and then map it on the discrete. The analog straight lines AB and CD between the centers of the respective pixels intersect at an analog point which could be mapped to any of the four pixels marked by a **bold** label in Figure 7.13.

The problem with these definitions is not just academic. In raster graphics the display of a line between two points is usually generated as an i-connected path between them and the nonuniqueness can be a source of poor displays.

C							B
		2	**2**	**2**	2	3	
	3	1	**1**	**1**	1		
A							D

Figure 7.13   Illustration of the nonuniqueness of the shortest path between two points on a discrete grid. The pixels of one path are marked by 1's and the pixels of the second by 2's. Pixels marked with a 3 belong to both paths.

Example 7.1:   A raster graphics system displays a line between points by making the lengths of segments along the dominant direction as uniform as possible. In Figure 7.14 the pixels of the line between points 0 and 7 are marked with a numerical label. Clearly, the point f belongs to that line, but the line between 0 and f, marked with lower case letters, is not a subset of the line 07, in contrast to the definitions of Euclidean geometry. (Pixel d is outside the line 07.) Suppose now that 07 is a side of polygon displayed in red color, f is the point of the intersection with some vertical line L, and that we want to color all line segments to the left of L green. What we will actually see is some green pixels (a to f) as well as one red (3) pixel to the left of L. □

			d	4e	5f	6	7
0a	1b	2c	3				

Figure 7.14   Pixels of the line between 0 and 7 are marked by a numeral while pixels of the line $0f$ (af) are marked by a lower case letter. Pixels with two labels belong to both lines.

The proper definition of thin lines is also of interest to the solution of problems such as contour filling (see Chapter 8) and region thinning (see Chapter 9). Both of these problems require the execution of geometric operations on a discrete grid. We shall introduce a criterion for distinguishing between thin curves and thick regions. Then we shall talk briefly about ways to facilitate the solution of geometrical problems.

7.6.1 When a Set of Pixels is not a Curve

Instead of going directly to the definition of thin regions we shall first define the opposite concept.

Definition 7.6:   A set of pixels R is said to be a *full region* if it has more than four pixels, its i-contour is a simple path, and the difference between the set and its i-contour is d-connected. □

Figure 7.15a shows an example of a full region. In particular, it demonstrates that a full region contains pixels besides those of its contour. (This would not have been the case if we did not include the assumption about four pixels.) In topological terms a full region corresponds to an open set.

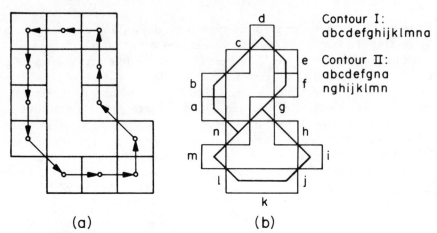

Contour I:
abcdefghijklmna

Contour Ⅱ:
abcdefgna
nghijklmn

(a)   (b)

Figure 7.15   Illustrations of Definition 7.6: (a) a full region; (b) ambiguities in the tracing of the contour that would occur without the requirement for d-connectivity.

Roughly speaking, a region is full when the sampling grid is fine enough that no boundary doubles upon itself. The requirement about d-connectivity is essential if we want to avoid ambiguous situations such as that shown in Figure 7.15b. This is a desirable property in situations where we would like the shape of the contour to reflect the shape of the object. It is also possible to fill such contours by a simple algorithm (see Section 8.3); therefore the property is important in computer graphics. The following is a sufficient condition for obtaining only full regions.

Theorem 7.2:   If the circle used in the definition of compatibility has diameter $\sqrt{10}h$ instead of just $\sqrt{2}h$, then all resulting pixel sets are full.

Proof: Figure 7.16 shows the smallest region satisfying the conditions of the theorem: it clearly encompasses at least nine pixels, which form a full region. Bigger regions can be expressed as unions of such regions and therefore can also be sampled as full sets of pixels. If the radius of the circle is R, we find that

$$R^2 = (\frac{h}{2})^2 + (\frac{3h}{2})^2 \text{ ,or, } R = \frac{h}{2}\sqrt{10} .$$

□

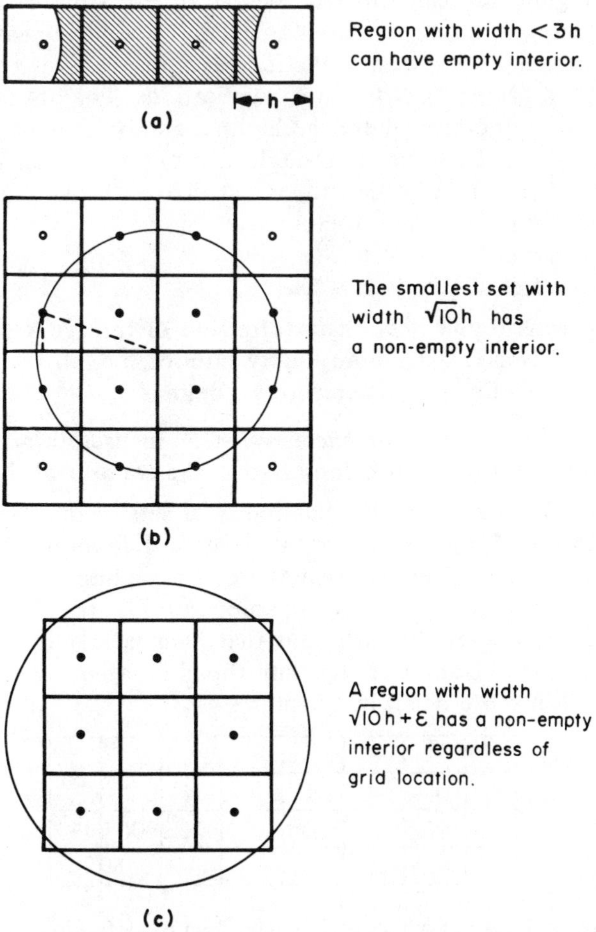

Region with width $< 3h$ can have empty interior.

(a)

The smallest set with width $\sqrt{10}h$ has a non-empty interior.

(b)

A region with width $\sqrt{10}h + \mathcal{E}$ has a non-empty interior regardless of grid location.

(c)

Figure 7.16 Illustration used in the proof of Theorem 7.2. (a) A region with width less than $3h$ which has an empty interior. (b) Calculation for determining the minimum width. (c) A region with width greater than $\sqrt{10}h$ has a nonempty interior regardless of the grid location.

The practical application of Theorem 7.2 is the specification of the grid size so that the digitization of a given set of bilevel pictures has only full regions. Let D be the diameter of the smaller inscribed circle satisfying the conditions of Definition 7.4. Then h must be chosen less than or equal to $D/\sqrt{10}$. On the other hand if we were interested only in shape preservation we could have chosen h less than or equal to $D/\sqrt{2}$. The ratio of these two grid sizes is $\sqrt{5}$. Therefore a digitization where all regions are full will require five times as many sample points as one where not all regions are full. The fivefold increase in storage requirements, as well as respective increases in processing time, is usually too high a price to pay for most applications. The only major exception is found in graphics where the high resolution may be desirable for aesthetic reasons. Even there, though, it may be necessary to deal with regions that are not full. Indeed, we shall use the lack of fullness to define lines and curves on a discrete grid.

7.6.2 When a Set of Pixels is a Curve

A rigorous topological characterization of thin curves is that they are nonempty sets that have an empty interior, i.e. all their points also belong to their boundary. Therefore we define:

Definition 7.7:   A *curve* or *lineal region* on a discrete grid is a set of pixels such that all of them belong also to the contour of the set. □

This definition allows the possibility of sets of thickness two, such as that shown in Figure 7.17. An alternative definition for simply connected thin sets is to require that there is a unique path between any pair of their points. Then the example of Figure 7.17 will not be classified as a thin set. It turns out that in most applications it makes more sense to use Definition 7.7 than the alternative. We shall discuss this question in more detail in Chapter 9.

Figure 7.17   A set which is thin according to Definition 7.7.

7.7 MULTIPLE PIXELS

Even though we have a definition for thin sets we are not yet finished with the problem. Indeed, we may have mixed regions that can be expressed as the union of full regions and lineal regions. For those, we need a definition that applies to region subsets and by extension to single pixels.

We have seen that pixels whose value after the tracing of a contour is greater than two play a special role. We shall discuss their properties after introducing certain definitions.

Definition 7.8: The *c-neighbors* of a pixel belonging to a contour C are those defined as the previous and next elements to it along the traversal defined by Algorithm 7.1. □

Note that the two c-neighbors need not be distinct. They are always distinct only when the contour is a simple path. An example of this definition is shown in Figure 7.18.

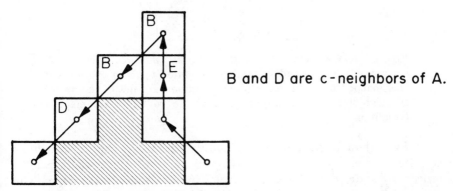

B and D are c-neighbors of A.

Figure 7.18 Definition of the c-neighbors of a contour pixel. B and D are c-neighbors of A, E is not. E and A are the c-neighbors of B.

Definition 7.9: A pixel is said to be *multiple* if one or more of the following conditions hold:

(a) It is traversed more than once during contour tracing.

(b) It has no neighbors in the interior of the region.

(c) It has at least one d-neighbor which belongs to the contour but which is not one of its c-neighbors. □

Figure 7.19 illustrates the motivation for the definition. Multiple pixels are pixels where two arcs of the contour lie, or where an arc folds. The first two conditions can be checked easily by using the markings of the procedure *TRACER* (Algorithm 7.1). Indeed, at the end of the tracing simple pixels of the contour will have value exactly 2, while multiple pixels satisfying condition (a) will have values greater than 2. A second traversal can be used to check condition (b) (no neighbor with value 1) and condition (c) (a d-neighbor with value 2 or greater and which is not a c-neighbor).

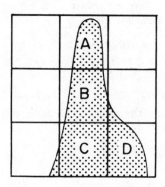

Figure 7.19 Intuitive illustration of multiple pixels. A corresponds to a boundary folding (condition b), B to two disjoint arcs mapped onto the same pixel (condition a), and C and D are adjacent pixels where disjoint arcs of the boundary are mapped (condition c).

Even though the detection of multiple pixels by contour traversals is quite simple, it may not be satisfactory in applications where parallel processing is desired. Since the verification of condition (c) depends in an essential way on such a sequential traversal we have a problem with Definition 7.9. Intuitively, we expect that sequence should not be important because we check for pixels containing two or more contour arcs, or where an arc bends, configurations that are order independent.

We proceed with a characterization of such pixels that is order independent. If a pixel is traversed more than once during the tracing of the contour of some set R, it must be only because there is no way to go from some part of R, R_1, to another part, R_2, without passing through that pixel. Therefore if the pixel is removed, the degree of connectivity of the set R will be reduced by at least one. Conversely, any pixel whose removal will reduce the connectivity of R must be traversed more than once during contour tracing. The decision on whether a pixel is essential for the connectivity of the set can be made by examining its eight neighbors. It is easy to show that P is essential for the connectivity, and only then, if its neighborhood has one of the forms shown in Figure 7.20 (or any obtained by 90° rotation). Therefore, a pixel can be classified as multiply traversed if and only if its neighborhood conforms to one of these patterns. In that diagram (and subsequent ones) the following notation is used for the pixel values:

Definition 7.10:   A number denotes the value that a pixel would be given during contour traversal: 1 for interior pixels, 2 for contour pixels traversed only once, 3 or greater for contour pixels traversed more than once. A number followed by the plus sign (+) denotes a pixel with a value at least equal to that number. 0 is for pixels not in the set. A letter, except for X, denotes that the pixel may have any nonzero value. The label X stands for any value (do not care condition). A group of pixels marked with the same symbol (e.g., A) has the property that at least one of the pixels has a value greater than zero. The star symbol (*) denotes a pixel that can have any value different from 1. $\Box$

Thus, in Figure 7.20 (left pattern), at least one of the three pixels marked with A is nonzero, and at least one of the three pixels marked with B is nonzero. Note that we can decide whether a pixel belongs to the contour without traversal. It need only have a d-neighbor that is zero.

	A	A	A			A	A	A	
	0	P	0			A	P	0	
	B	B	B			A	0	2	

Figure 7.20 Neighborhood configurations of pixels that are essential for connectivity. See the text for an explanation of the notation.

Thus we have proved:

Proposition 7.2:   Condition (a) of Definition 7.9 can be replaced by the requirement that the eight point neighborhood of a pixel exhibits at least one of the patterns of Figure 7.20 (or those obtained from them by 90° rotations). $\Box$

Condition (b) can be checked easily using a parallel algorithm. None of the eight neighbors can have label 1. This will preserve singletons (i.e. pixels without any neighbors), and endpoints (pixels with exactly one neighbor). The last observation suggests that the check for the second pattern of Figure 7.20 can be simplified by allowing all pixels marked A to be zero. Note that condition (b) also saves all lines of width two, such as the one shown in Figure 7.17.

We are left with condition (c). If a pixel satisfies this condition as

well as (a) or (b), then it will be classified as multiple anyway. Thus we
may search for a criterion that is narrower than condition (c), as long as
the pixels that it misses are caught by the other two conditions. We
shall show that for such pixels the condition can be replaced by a check
for a 3×3 pixel pattern. To this end we start with a bigger pattern (4×4)
and consider all possible configurations in it that will give rise to condition (c). The general configuration is shown in Figure 7.21.

	a_0		
a_1	a_2	a_3	a_4
c_1	c_2	c_3	c_4
b_1	b_2	b_3	b_4

Figure 7.21   Pixel labeling used in the development of an alternative form of Definition 7.9

Without loss of generality we assume that c_2 is the current pixel with
value 2 and that c_1 is its d-neighbor with value 0. (Recall that all contour pixels have such a neighbor.) Other configurations can be obtained
by rotations of 90°. Since pixel c_2 satisfies condition (c) of Definition
7.9 it must also have a d-neighbor with value greater than or equal to 2.

Proposition 7.3:   Any pixel that satisfies condition (c) of Definition
7.9 but not (a) or (b) is part of a 022+ pattern along a vertical or a horizontal line.

Proof: We shall prove the property for pixel c_2. First we consider
pixel c_3 and we show that if it does not have value 2+ (so that the proposition is not satisfied along a horizontal line), then there will be a
vertical line through c_2 with that property. If c_3 has value zero, then
pixel c_2 is either multiply traversed or an endpoint, and therefore is
classified as multiple under conditions (a) or (b). Suppose that it has
value 1. This means that pixels a_3, c_4, and b_3 cannot be zero, otherwise
c_3 would be in the contour. Because of our assumption that condition
(c) holds, either a_2 or b_2 must have value 2 or greater. We need consider only the first of these pixels because of symmetry. Let a_2 have
value 2+. If a_1 has value zero, then a_2 will be a c-neighbor of c_2 and
this means that b_2 must also be at least 2 and b_1 nonzero, the symmetric configuration. Thus we proceed assuming that a_1 is nonzero.
Now a_2 is a contour pixel that has d-neighbors c_2, a_1, and a_3 that are
not zero. Therefore pixel a_0 must be zero, and we have the pattern
022+ in pixels a_0, a_2, and c_2. □

Because of this result we can assume, without loss of generality, that c_3 in Figure 7.21 has value greater than or equal to 2. We examine next the possible configurations of the pixels marked a_1, a_2, and a_3 and those marked b_1, b_2, and b_3.

Case i: Both a_3 and b_3 are nonzero. Then c_4 must be zero, otherwise c_3 could not be a boundary pixel. If all pixels a_1, a_2, b_1, and b_2 were zero, then a_3 and b_3 would have value 2+ and c_2 would have been classified as multiple under condition (b) (no neighbors labeled 1). Therefore we must have the pattern of Figure 7.22a with at least one of these four pixels nonzero. The number of possible configurations for this pattern is quite small and one can verify that in all of them condition (c) is satisfied. (One example is shown in Figure 7.22b.)

A	A	P	X		0	0	2	X
0	2	2+	0		0	2	2	0
A	A	Q	X		2	1	1	2

(a)	(b)

Figure 7.22 Illustration of Case i: The general pattern on the left and a special case on the right

Case ii: Both a_3 and b_3 are zero. Then it is easy to verify that c_2 cannot have neighbors labeled 1, and therefore is handled under condition (b). Figure 7.23 shows the pattern for this case.

*	*	0	X
0	2	2+	X
*	*	0	X

Figure 7.23 Illustration of Case ii. Neither of the pixels marked by 2 and 2+ is essential for connectivity, but if both of them are removed the connectivity is changed.

Case iii: a_3 is not zero and b_3 is zero. (The case $a_3 = 0$ and $b_3 > 0$ is similar and we will not discuss it.) If both b_1 and b_2 are zero, then the contour passes from c_2 to c_3, and c_2 cannot be a multiple pixel unless it satisfies condition (c). The pattern is shown in Figure 7.24a with a special case in Figure 7.24b. If b_1 and b_2 are not both zero, but a_1 and a_2 are, then c_2 will have no interior neighbor, and is treated under condition (b).

X	X	P	X			2	2	1	X
0	2	2+	X			0	2	2	1
0	0	0	X			0	0	0	2

| (a) | (b) |

Figure 7.24   Illustration of Case iii: The general pattern on the left and a special case on the right

This discussion exhausts all possible configurations that occur in 3×4 pixel rectangle. If condition (c) is going to be satisfied it must be satisfied in such an area. Therefore we have proved:

Proposition 7.4:   Condition (c) is equivalent to searching for a pattern of the form given in Figure 7.25 (plus those obtained by 90° rotations).

A	A	C
0	2	2+
B	B	C

Figure 7.25   Pattern equivalent to condition (c). At least one of the pixels marked C must be nonzero. If both pixels labeled C are nonzero, then the value of the pixels labeled A and B can be anything. Otherwise, at least one of the members of each pair marked A or B must be nonzero.

Figure 7.26 shows some specific patterns of pixels. The current pixel is marked with a **bold** symbol if it is multiple.

0	2	1	1	1	1			0	2	1	1	1	1
0	0	2	1	1	1			0	0	2	1	1	1
0	0	0	P	2	1			0	0	0	P	2	1
0	0	0	2	0	2			0	0	0	0	0	2
0	0	0	0	2	1			0	0	0	0	2	1

Figure 7.26   Left: example of multiple pixel (**P**) satisfying condition (c). Note that pixel **P** satisfies neither of the other two conditions. Right: a case where this condition is not satisfied for pixel **P**.

Thus, we have found another characterization of multiple pixels.

Theorem 7.3: A pixel is multiple if it satisfies at least one of the following three conditions.

(a) Its neighborhood conforms to either of the patterns of Figure 7.20 (or those obtained by 90° rotations). The pixels labeled with A in the second pattern can have any values.

(b) It has at most one nonzero neighbor or it has no neighbors labeled 1.

(c) Its neighborhood satisfies the pattern of Figure 7.25 (or those obtained by 90° rotations). □

Clearly, it is possible to verify these conditions either in parallel or sequential fashion. We state a result linking the concept of multiple pixels to thin lines or curves.

Proposition 7.5: A lineal region consists entirely of multiple pixels. Conversely, if a region consists only of multiple pixels, it is lineal.

Proof: Since the set has no pixels other than those of its contour, none of the contour pixels will have neighbors in the interior of the region and therefore condition (b) of Definition 7.9 is valid. The proof of the converse is trivial since a multiple pixel is always a contour pixel. □

The above analysis is useful for detecting lines or operating on them on a discrete grid. We have not addressed the problem of generating such displays from equations of lines or curves. This will be treated in Chapter 10.

7.8 AN INTRODUCTION TO SHAPE ANALYSIS

Shape analysis is one of the fundamental problems in pattern recognition and is also of interest in interactive graphics. It is relevant where one must make a decision on the basis of the form of objects that he or she sees. The precise psychophysical definition of what is shape is outside the scope of this text. Certainly, terms such as "elongated" or "sharp corner" refer to shape. One could define shape by default by stating that it is the information contained in a bilevel image without considering the color of the regions. This definition limits us to the shape of silhouettes, but it is adequate for many applications and in particular for the recognition of alphanumeric characters.

One can distinguish two modes of shape recognition. In one, a person looks at the total object and makes a decision on the basis of the overall structure. This is commonly the case in the recognition of handprinted letters, especially Chinese, where one identifies strokes or other basic building blocks. In another mode one examines the contour of the silhouette, usually looking for corners, protrusions, intrusions, and other points of high curvature. An example is the recognition of silhouettes of human profiles, or the check for defects of the outlines of the circuit elements on printed wiring boards.† Of course, there are many situations where both modes must be used: an engineering drawing contains lines and letters recognizable by their structure, as well as circles or hexagons which must be distinguished from each other on the basis of their contours. Most methodologies in the past have been oriented toward one of the two modes, and since it is theoretically possible to apply them to any object, they have been used in cases where they were not well suited. Ideally, one would like to have a mixed method that could adapt itself to the mode most appropriate for the object examined.

We shall limit ourselves here to a discussion of simple contour analysis methods as used for the description of the shape of objects found in class 2 images. Structural methods will be reviewed briefly in Chapter 9. Curvature is an important feature in shape analysis, not only when it is used directly, but also when it is used indirectly. Unfortunately, a direct measurement of curvature is not always feasible because of noise. The formula given in most calculus texts requires taking a second derivative and thus cannot be used in any practical situation. On the other hand, it is possible to estimate the radius of curvature by the geometrical construction shown in Figure 7.27. Indeed, if A, B, and C are points on a curve, M and N are the midpoints of the intervals AB and BC respectively, and K the point where the normals at M and N intersect, then R, the length of BK, equals the radius of a circle passing through A, B, and C.

If the angle ABC equals ϕ, ψ denotes its complement, and the lengths of AB and BC are each equal to $2e$, then a straightforward calculation shows that

$$R = \frac{e}{\cos(\frac{\phi}{2})} = \frac{e}{\sin(\frac{\psi}{2})} \tag{7.1}$$

(see Problem 7.7). It is clear from Figure 7.27 and Equation (7.1) that R is an increasing function of ϕ. If ψ is small, as is often the case, then the curvature c which is defined as the inverse of the radius of curvature will be given approximately by

$$c = \frac{\psi}{2e} = \frac{\pi - \phi}{2e} \tag{7.2}$$

---

† This should not be confused with the so called *Gestalt* shape perception where, according to psychologists, one recognizes the shape of a figure without looking at parts.

It is possible to eliminate some of the effects of noise by calculating the curvature not on successive pixels, but on triplets, where the distance e is large compared with the spatial noise frequency. There exist many variations of this technique, but we shall not deal with them here. An indirect determination of curvature maxima can be achieved by polygonal approximations because corners will tend to be placed near such maxima.

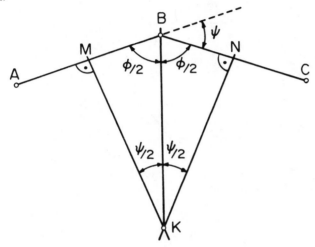

Figure 7.27 Construction used for the estimation of the radius of curvature

It is possible to proceed with a contour analysis in a number of ways. At the lowest level the methodology is based on a primitive representation such as a chain code. At a higher level the representation consists of an approximation by pieces of smooth curves (e.g., by B-splines). The latter is preferable when the data are noisy and when one looks for features involving a large part of the contour. The former is best for data with low levels of noise and localized features. Polygonal approximations have been used often not only because they detect curvature maxima, but also because they are simpler to implement than other curve fitting techniques. We shall defer discussion of such techniques until after Chapters 11 and 12, which discuss splines and approximations.

We shall discuss the detection of local features using the differential chain code of Section 1.2.3 because it provides expressions that are orientation independent. If the contour is sufficiently smooth, the only symbols present will be 0 and ± 1. The presence of ± 2 implies a 90° angle while that of ± 3 implies a 45° angle. It would be simple to associate the occurrence of such symbols with curvature maxima but this is not sufficient for locating all such maxima. For example, the sequence 01110 also represents a 45° angle.

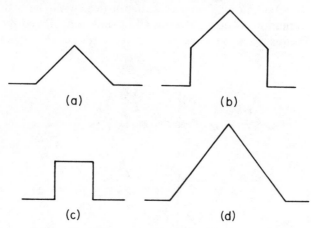

(a)   (b)

(c)   (d)

Figure 7.28   Examples of notches.   The respective differential chain codes are as follows:

(a) $\cdots 0+1-2+10 \cdots$,
(b) $\cdots 0+2-1-2-1+20 \cdots$,
(c) $\cdots 0+2-2-2+20 \cdots$,
(d) $\cdots 0+10-20+10 \cdots$.

There are four classes of arcs of interest: straight lines, corners, approximately circular arcs, and notches. A straight line along one of the chain code directions has the form 0^n. If it is not in one of these directions, then it will be of the form $(0^m+1-1)^k$ or $(0^m-1+1)^k$.[†] Because of noise the actual code may not be as regular but will always be characterized by the occurrence of $+1-1$ or $-1+1$ pairs. A circular arc, on the other hand, will be of the form $(0^m+1)^k$ or $(0^m-1)^k$, the main feature being that ± 1's will occur singly and for a given curve their sign will be fixed. A corner will contain either one of the high values of the code or a sequence of 1's with the same sign. A notch is a sharp intrusion or protrusion. It is of interest in certain applications where one wants to have very smooth contours so that the presence of a notch will indicate a defect. In terms of the chain code, a notch is a sequence of high values of the code adding up to 0 (or at most ± 1). Figure 7.28 shows some examples.

_____

[†] Actually m may vary by one from segment to segment. See [7.WU] for a precise characterization of straight line descriptions by chain codes.

One can come up with simple algorithms for detecting such features, and their applicability depends on how noise-free the data are. One useful technique is based on the definition of regular expressions or (equivalently) finite automata which match such features. For example, the following expression will recognize some of the notches shown in Figure 7.28:

0(+1 or +2)(a string of at most two negative symbols)(+1 or +2)0

Recognizing whether a long sequence represents a straight line or a circular arc is a more difficult problem. For such large-scale features it is best to use other techniques such as curve fitting (see Chapter 12).

7.9 BIBLIOGRAPHICAL NOTES

The first systematic discussions of the problems involved in defining connectivity and other topological concepts on a discrete grid can be found in [7.RO] and [7.MY]. Contour tracing is a simple enough procedure, except for the problems associated with discrete connectivity. See [7.SO] for a discussion. [7.MR] describes an algorithm that does not require labeling the image. [7.PA1] presents an algorithm that does the tracing on the basis of a run length encoding of the image.

The detailed treatment of the subject of shape analysis is beyond the scope of this text. The reader is referred to the pattern recognition literature where the subject is treated in greater length. [7.FU1], [7.FU2], [2.HA], and [3.PA] are advanced texts while [7.PA2] and [7.PA3] provide reviews of the literature. Those interested in specific applications should consult the applications literature. For example, a review of the early work on character recognition can be found in [7.UL]. Examples of contour analysis can be found in many papers. The use of concavities for the description of written symbols is emphasized in [7.AP] and [7.YM] amongst others.

7.10 RELEVANT LITERATURE

[7.AP]   Ali, F. and Pavlidis, T. "Syntactic Recognition of Handwritten Numerals," *IEEE Trans. Systems, Man, Cybernetics,* **SMC-7** (1977), pp. 537-541.

[7.FU1]   Fu, K. S. *Syntactic Methods in Pattern Recognition,* New York: Academic Press, 1974, 295pp.

[7.FU2]   Fu, K. S. (ed.) *Syntactic Pattern Recognition, Applications,* Heidelberg: Springer-Verlag, 1977, 270pp.

[7.KE]   Kelley, J. L. *General Topology,* Princeton, N.J.: Van Nostrand, 1955.

[7.MR]   Morrin, T. H. "Chain-Link Compression of Arbitrary Black-White Images," *CGIP,* **5** (1976), pp. 172-189.

[7.MY]   Mylopoulos, J. and Pavlidis, T. "On the Topological Properties of Quantized Spaces," *JACM,* **18** (April 1971), Part I pp. 239-246, Part II pp. 247-254.

[7.PA1] Pavlidis, T. "A Minimum Storage Boundary Tracing Algorithm and its Application in Automatic Inspection," *IEEE Trans. Systems, Man, Cybernetics,* **SMC-8** (1978), pp. 66-69.

[7.PA2] Pavlidis, T. "A Review of Algorithms for Shape Analysis," *CGIP,* **7** (April 1978), pp. 243-258.

[7.PA3] Pavlidis, T. "Algorithms for Shape Analysis of Contours and Waveforms," *IEEE Trans. Pattern Analysis and Machine Intelligence,* **PAMI-2** (July 1980), pp. 301-312.

[7.RO]   Rosenfeld, A. "Connectivity in Digital Pictures," *JACM,* **17** (1970) pp. 146-160.

[7.SO]   Sobel, I. "Neighborhood Coding of Binary Images for Fast Contour Following and General Binary Array Processing," *CGIP,* **8** (August 1978), pp. 127-135.

[7.UL]   Ullmann, J. R. "Picture Analysis in Character Recognition," in *Digital Picture Analysis,* (A. Rosenfeld, ed.), Heidelberg: Springer 1976, pp. 295-343.

[7.WU]   Wu, L. D. "On Freeman's Conjecture about the Chain Code of a Line," *Proc. Fifth Intern. Conf. on Pattern Recognition,* Miami Beach, December 1980, pp. 32-34. (Published by IEEE Computer Society, IEEE Catalog No. 80CH1499-3.)

[7.YM]   Yamamoto, K. and Mori, S. "Recognition of handprinted characters by outermost point method," *Proc. Fourth Intern. Joint Conf. on Pattern Recognition,* Kyoto, November 1978, pp. 794-796.

7.11 PROBLEMS

7.1.   Find the Fourier transform of a square waveform that has minimum width H, i.e., each interval where the value is constant is at least H units long. Repeat, assuming that changes in the value occur only at integer multiples of some quantity h. Compare the two transforms and study how the size of the ratio H/h affects their similarity.

7.2.   Try to estimate the proper sampling interval for digitizing the text of this page.

7.3.   Devise an algorithm for counting the number of blobs (connected sets of a given color) on a class 2 image.

7.4.   A common practical problem is the need to enlarge or reduce a bilevel image. For example, one may have a set of bilevel matrices describing alphanumeric characters and want to display it at twice or half the size. Can you devise an algorithm for doing such transformations while preserving the shape? In particular, given a set, calculate what would be the largest scaling down possible.

7.5. Implement Algorithm 7.2 and use it to count the number of blobs that are full sets, lineal sets, or mixed sets.

7.6. Let R be a connected set of pixels, and let $C(R)$ be the pixels of its contour. Show that if you remove all pixels of $C(R)$ except those that are multiple, the remaining pixels form a set that is not only connected but also topologically equivalent to R. What can you say about shape similarity?

7.7. Prove Equation (7.1).

7.8. Introduce a measure of contour smoothness using the differential chain code (for example, the proportion of nonzero values as a percent of the total). Then try to solve Problem 7.4 so that the value of this measure remains constant, or nearly constant.

Chapter 8

CONTOUR FILLING

8.1 INTRODUCTION

One of the most common problems in graphics and picture analysis is finding the interior of a region when its contour is given, i.e., transforming a class 3 picture into a class 2 picture. For example, any shading algorithm presumes the solution of this problem. In pattern recognition, many algorithms compute integrals over the area of a region and require knowledge of the interior. In phototypesetting, fonts are often described in terms of contours which are then filled to produce the final copy. The problem can be solved in many ways, which can be divided into two broad classes. In the first, one has a precise description of the contour as a polygon and decides which parts of the plane lie in the interior by considering, in effect, the line equations. Such techniques could be called polygon based but we prefer the shorter term edge filling and describe them in Section 8.2. Methods of the second class map the contour onto the discrete plane and then locate the interior by examining the values of pixels. Such pixel based techniques are discussed in Sections 8.3 to 8.5.

In addition to the above, techniques can be distinguished by the principle they use in deciding whether a point is in the interior of the polygon. Some algorithms use parity check, while others use a connectivity criterion.

Parity check algorithms are based on the fact that a straight line intersects any closed curve (such as the contour of a region) an even number of times (see Figure 8.1). If we know that the first point of the line lies outside the region, then we can traverse it and decide which segments are in the interior by counting the number of intersections. If the number is odd, then the segment belongs to the interior (*AB* and *CD* in Figure 8.1), otherwise it does not (*BC* in Figure 8.1). All edge filling algorithms use parity check. The principle can also be used by pixel based algorithms, but one is faced with a serious problem. It is possible to have points from two or more sides mapped on the same pixel (see Section 7.6), and this produces an incorrect count of the number of intersections. One also has to be careful about lines that are tangent to the contour: the point of contact must be counted twice as an intersection. We suggest ways for overcoming these problems, at least partially, in Section 8.3.

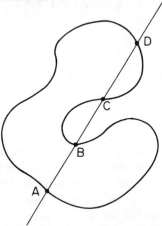

Figure 8.1   Illustration of the parity principle for deciding which points belong to the interior of a closed curve

Connectivity filling assumes that an interior point (seed) is given, in addition to the contour. One then performs a traversal of the plane to find all pixels that can be reached from the seed without crossing the contour. The process can be modeled as a graph traversal by using some of the data structures discussed in Chapter 6. Connectivity filling is appropriate only for pixel based algorithms because it requires random access to the pixels of the interior. The filling is best done on the refresh memory of a raster graphics device or its exact copy in main memory. The major advantage of connectivity filling is that it is robust with respect to contour irregularities as long as the contour is a closed curve. Its major disadvantage is the need to know an interior point in advance. Therefore, it is well suited for interactive graphics where a user draws a contour (possibly quite irregular) and then points to its interior (thus providing the seed) and requests that it be filled. We discuss algorithms based on connectivity in Section 8.4.

It is possible to combine connectivity and parity filling in various ways and come up with new algorithms. Such combinations are implemented easily if we use a common data structure. It turns out that the line adjacency graph for the contour (C-LAG) is suitable for both. Clearly, it is justified for a pixel based parity check algorithm where the emphasis is on the contour. While a line adjacency graph for the interior (I-LAG) is the commonly used data structure for connectivity algorithms, Proposition 6.3 suggests a way for using the C-LAG for them. Let us assume d-connectivity for the interior, i-connectivity for the contour, color X for the interior, and color Y for the contour pixels. Then Proposition 6.3 becomes:

Proposition 8.1: If a node of the I-LAG has degree (m,n) with $n>1$ then there will be a node of the C-LAG with degree $(0,d)$ in the line below. Similarly, if $m>1$ there will be a node of the C-LAG with degree $(d,0)$ above it. The converse is also true. $\square$

Therefore, instead of checking the degree of the nodes of the I-LAG (as needed for a graph traversal), we may check the degree of the nodes of the C-LAG. Such a choice has two practical advantages. One is that it allows the combination of the parity check and connectivity algorithms. The other is a possible increase in speed. Evaluating the degree of a LAG requires examination of three lines at a time. For the I-LAG these lines can be quite long while the contour intervals tend to be much shorter. Because of the possibility for combinations we shall use the C-LAG for both types of algorithms.

8.2 EDGE FILLING

Edge or polygon based filling is also called *scan conversion filling* although all these terms are sometimes used for other purposes. The sides of the polygon, or edges, are sorted and marked in such a way as to preserve all topological information. Then the parity check is performed by a simple, one-pass algorithm and the actual filling does not require random access to the pixels. It can be done equally well in a raster graphics or a vector graphics device. It is particularly well suited for applications where the same contour is displayed repeatedly, such as in phototypesetting, because the computationally expensive presorting and marking has to be performed only once.

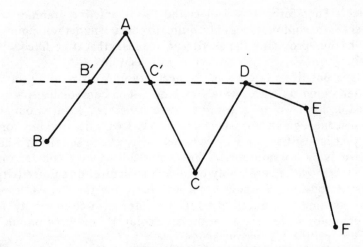

Figure 8.2 Edge fill: within each horizontal slice there is an even number of edges and the interior of the region is between the first and second, third and fourth, etc.

We start with the sequence of the sides (edges) of a polygon approximating the contour. For each side we are given the coordinates x_i, y_i of the corner with maximum y, or minimum x if the line is horizontal, and the differences $\Delta x, \Delta y$, which yield the coordinates of the other corner if added to the first. An edge filling algorithm proceeds by first sorting the sides according to the y_i value and the x_i value for edges with the same y_i. If there is still a tie, Δx is used, and finally Δy. When sorting is done according to these differences, the smallest† goes first. Thus, in the example of Figure 8.2, AB will precede AC because Δx is negative for AB and positive for AC. Next, the algorithm finds the maxima in the y direction and detects the intersections of edges with lines parallel to the x-axis. In the example of Figure 8.2 the line through D produces two such intersections, B' and C'. These lines divide the picture into slices with the property that each slice contains an even number of edges and the interior of the region is between odd-numbered and even-numbered edges.

The sorted edges are placed in a waiting list and the filling is done by maintaining an active list containing the edges present in each slice. The process starts from the highest value of y and proceeds toward the lowest. Various flags are inserted in the waiting list of edges to indicate the following circumstances.

---

† in an algebraic sense, i.e. all negative values are considered smaller than all positive.

(a) How many edges to transfer next: one if we are along a side, two if we are at a maximum, possibly more if we have more than one maximum for the same value of y. (This is not as unlikely as it sounds. For example, a contour of the letter **W** for certain fonts has three maxima for the same y.)

(b) Whether a new pair of edges must be read before the end of the current pair is reached. This will be the case when the line through the maximum intersects one of the current edges.

(c) Whether at the end of this edge we should not read any more because it corresponds to a minimum in the y direction.

For the example of Figure 8.2, the first pair of edges is read (AB and AC), together with the y value, y_{max}, of any maxima in the same slice (D). The region between the edges with y greater than y_{max} ($B'AC'$) is filled and then the next pair of edges is read (CD and DE). Now we have an active list of four edges and the regions between the first and second and third and fourth of them are filled. Maxima are clearly identified as such and there is no problem with the parity count there, in contrast to pixel based parity fill (see Section 8.3). When an edge ends the next one is read from the sorted list (EF) and is added to the active list. However, we should distinguish the case where two edges end simultaneously (AC and DC) and there is no need to add any new elements to the active list. This should be indicated by an appropriate flag.

Table 8.1: Edge description for the contour of Figure 8.2

Side	x	y	Δx	Δy	Flag (a)	Flag (b)	Flag (c)
AB	x_A	y_A	$x_B - x_A$	$y_B - y_A$	2	y_D	1
AC	x_A	y_A	$x_C - x_A$	$y_C - y_A$	1	-	0
DC	x_D	y_D	$x_C - x_D$	$y_C - y_D$	2	-	0
DE	x_D	y_D	$x_E - x_D$	$y_E - y_D$	1	-	1
EF	x_E	y_E	$x_F - x_E$	$y_F - y_E$	1	-	1
...	...	...	...	...	...	...	...

The form of the waiting list in the case of Figure 8.2 is given in Table 8.1. Subscripts correspond to the labels of points in the figure. The value given under flag (a) is the number of edges to be transferred simultaneously from the waiting list into the active list: 2 means the current edge plus the next one and 1 means only the current edge. Flag (b) gives the y value where a new pair of edges must be moved into the active list. Flag (c) gives the number of new edges to be read at the end of the current edge.

Algorithm 8.1 Edge Filling

    Notation: Each side is specified by the y and x values of its highest end-
point, unless it is horizontal. Then the (x,y) values of its leftmost point
are selected. Δx and Δy are the difference between the coordinates of
the second point and the one chosen to represent the line. The subscript
i refers to the original indexing of the sides. The labels of the sides are
the same as the flags of Table 8.1.

1.   Sort all sides according to the value y_i (greater first). Break ties
    by sorting first according to the value of x_i and then according to
    Δx and Δy, negative values preceding positive. {Preparation of
    waiting list.}

2.   **For** all pairs of successive sides that have the same y **do:**
      Begin.

3.   Draw a line through the point where such edges meet and
      find its intersection with all other sides. {Clearly, one need
      consider only sides coming ahead in the list.}

4.   **For** the first intersected edge, label its entry in the waiting
      list with the value of y where the intersection occurs.
      End. {Waiting list is now ready.}

5.   **While** the waiting list is not empty **do:**
      Begin.

6.   **If** the active list is empty **or** the value of y is below the
      lower endpoint of one of its members, **then** remove those
      members and transfer from the waiting list to the active list
      as many elements as indicated by the labels.

7.   Fill the space between alternate members of the active list.

8.   Decrement y.
      End.

9.   **End of Algorithm.**

    Clearly, the format of Table 8.1 contains redundant information.
For example, one could dispense with almost all values of x_i and y_i
(see Problem 8.2). We do not discuss the encoding problem here in
order not to obscure the basically simple form of the algorithm. The
process is described in detail as Algorithm 8.1. The sorting of step 1
can be performed by any of the numerous algorithms available in the
literature. The way the tie breaking is performed guarantees that edges
meeting at a maximum will be stored in successive locations, with the
one having positive slope first. Step 2 looks at maxima. Since the y
value associated with each edge is that of the endpoint corresponding to
the larger of the two values, equality of y in two successive edges
means a maximum. Because of the tie breaking rule in sorting, a simple geometric argument can be used to show that one does not have to

check the x value. Steps 1 to 4 prepare the waiting list and have to be performed only once for each contour. Steps 5 to 9 do the actual filling.

The algorithm does not distinguish between contours of holes and external contours and is not restricted to simply connected regions. It will correctly fill groups of regions if their contours have been sorted together. (For example, it will fill the contour of the letter "i".)

The description given here does not provide for the case that parts of the contour are horizontal lines. However, the algorithm is easily modified to handle such contours correctly (see Problem 8.1).

8.3 CONTOUR FILLING BY PARITY CHECK

Although the implementation of a parity check is trivial in an edge filling algorithm it is nontrivial in the discrete plane. In addition to the difficulty of identifying tangents, which must be counted as double points, one must worry about multiple pixels that can throw off the count of intersections. The difficulties of defining lines and intersections of lines and curves detailed in Chapter 7 should be a warning about the risks of the approach. We shall present here an algorithm using the C-LAG and then show that for full regions it gives correct results. Algorithm 8.2 shows the basic operation of a parity check.

Algorithm 8.2 Trivial Parity Check on the Plane

0. Establish an x-y coordinate system.
1. **For each** y **do** steps 2-6.
        Begin.
2.   Set *count* equal to zero.
3.   **For each** x from left to right **do** steps 4 and 5.
            Begin.
4.   **If** (x,y) belongs to the contour **then** increment *count*.
5.   **Else if** *count* is odd, **then** pixel (x,y) is in the interior of the region.
            End.
        End.
6. **End of Algorithm.**

Clearly, Algorithm 8.2 is incorrect. First, it counts pixels rather than intervals of adjacent pixels which have the contour color. (Recall that on the discrete plane the intersection of two curves is not always a single pixel.) Second, it does not look for extrema. We can develop a correct algorithm, at least for full regions, if we count intervals rather than pixels, and if we examine the lines above and below the one used for the parity test. If one of them does not intersect the contour in the neighborhood of the current intersection, then we know that the current line is a tangent.

Algorithm 8.3 Pixel Based, Parity Check Filling Algorithm.

> *Notation: count* is the number of intersections of the contour with the current horizontal line. The variables *above* and *below* are the degrees of the C-LAG returned by *LINK*.

1. **For** each y **do** steps 2-11.
    Begin.
2. Set *count* to zero
3. Set x to the leftmost value of the grid.
4. **While** x is less than or equal to the rightmost value of the grid **do** steps 5-11.
    Begin.
5. **If** (x,y) does not belong to the contour, **then do** steps 6 and 7.
    Begin.
6. **If** *count* is odd, **then** mark (x,y) as belonging to the interior.
7. Increment x.
    End.
8. **Else do** steps 9-11.
    Begin.
9. Call **procedure** *LINK*.
10. **If** both *above* and *below* equal 1, **then** increment *count*.
11. **If** the sum *above* + *below* is not 0 or 2, **then** set the error flag.
    End.
    End.
    End.
12. **End of Algorithm.**

The contour line adjacency graph (C-LAG) offers a convenient data structure: its nodes correspond to intersections of the contour with a horizontal line. For a maximum the *above* degree is zero, and for a minimum the *below* degree is zero. If the contour has no multiple points, then an intersection of an arc with a horizontal line will have degree (1,1) in the C-LAG. Furthermore, extrema will have degrees (0,2) or (2,0). All other degree pairs are illegal configurations if the region is full. Algorithm 8.3 implements these ideas. It uses the procedure *LINK* (listed as Algorithm 8.3a) for finding the degrees of the nodes of the C-LAG by counting the number of intervals overlapping with the current one. It also assumes that x and y are measured in units of the grid cell size. The error flag in the listing of the algorithm signifies the occurrence of degrees other than the legal pairs (1,1), (0,2), and (2,0). Figure 8.3 shows some examples of the values of the degrees of the LAG for various pixel configurations.

Algorithm 8.3a Finding the Degree of a Node in the LAG

Procedure *LINK*

Notation: dy is the increment in the value of y from line to line. If the the origin of coordinates is at the lower left corner of the display, then dy is positive. Otherwise it is negative. dx is the increment in the values of x. Usually, both dx and dy equal one.

0.   Input is pixel on contour (x,y). Output is values of *above* and *below*.

1.   Set the counters *above* and *below* to zero.

2.   **If** $(x-dx,y+dy)$ belongs to the contour, **then** increment *above*.

3.   **if** $(x-dx,y-dy)$ belongs to the contour, **then** increment *below*.

4.   **While** (x,y) belongs to the contour **do** steps 5-7.
        Begin.

5.   **If** $(x,y+dy)$ belongs to the contour and $(x-dx,y+dy)$ does not, **then** increment *above*.

6.   **if** $(x,y-dy)$ belongs to the contour and $(x-dx,y-dy)$ does not, **then** increment *below*.

7.   Increment x.
        End.

8.   **If** $(x-dx,y+dy)$ does not belong to the contour and $(x,y+dy)$ does, **then** increment *above*.

9.   **if** $(x-dx,y-dy)$ does not belong to the contour and $(x,y-dy)$ does, **then** increment *below*.

10.   **Return** location of pixel (x,y) and values of counters *above* and *below*.

11.   **End of Algorithm.**

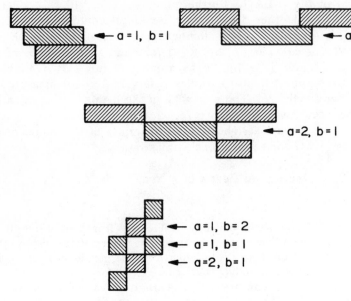

Figure 8.3   Examples of configurations of interval overlaps with the values of the counters used in Algorithm 8.3/3a. *a* stands for *above* and *b* for *below*.

8.3.1 Proof of Correctness of Algorithm 8.3

We must study the conditions under which the error flag is set. It turns out that this can happen only around multiple pixels. Since a boundary is a closed curve, it is true that it will intersect a convex plane set (e.g., the cell corresponding to a pixel) an even number of times. A simple pixel contains only one such arc and therefore should have exactly two neighbors on the contour. The same will also be true for a set of simple pixels, and in particular for a set of adjacent pixels along the horizontal line. On the other hand, a multiple pixel may have more than two neighbors on the contour, or only one. Then the tracking of the contour may not correspond to the tracking of the boundary. The situation is complicated further because we deal with intervals rather than single pixels. Figure 8.4 shows a contour with a number of multiple pixels where the parity count is not correct, which causes the error flag to be set. Table 8.2 lists the degree values of the corresponding LAG nodes and the proper changes in *count* if one wanted to do the filling correctly.

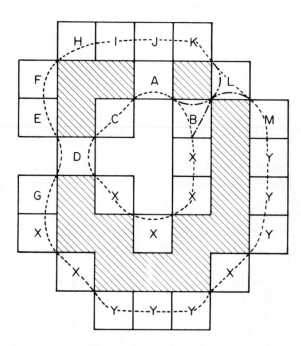

Figure 8.4 Interpretations of boundary tracing corresponding to a pixel with three neighbors. Pixels of the interior are shown shaded.

At first glance, it might seem that pixels B and L are not multiple, according to the definitions of Chapter 7. However, it is possible to have a contour arc through pixels B, L, K, and A, and another arc through X, B, L, M, Y, $\cdots$, etc. A similar ambiguous situation was shown in Figure 7.15b and motivated the requirement that full regions have an interior that is d-connected. It should be mentioned that a multiple pixel does not always cause the error condition.

Table 8.2: Problem Intervals in Figure 8.4

Interval	Degree	Proper Count
(H-K)	(0,3)	0
(A)	(1,2)	0
(D)	(2,2)	2
(B)	(2,1)	1
(L)	(1,2)	1

These examples illustrate a rather extreme case and in many applications the sampling grid is sufficiently fine that multiple pixels do not occur. We shall show that under such conditions Algorithm 8.3 is correct.

Theorem 8.1:   If a region is full, then the only degree pairs possible for its contour are (0,2), (2,0), and (1,1).

Proof: We prove the theorem by showing the impossibility of the occurrence of other pairs. First, we examine the case of a degree pair (0,1). If the current interval and the one below it each contain only one pixel, then we have a pixel whose c-neighbors coincide (Figure 8.5a). If the interval below has two pixels, then they are d-neighbors of each other (Figure 8.5b). If it has more than two pixels, then some of them are d-neighbors of the contour pixels in the line above (Figure 8.5c). The last two situations occur regardless of the number of pixels in the current interval. All three configurations violate the conditions of

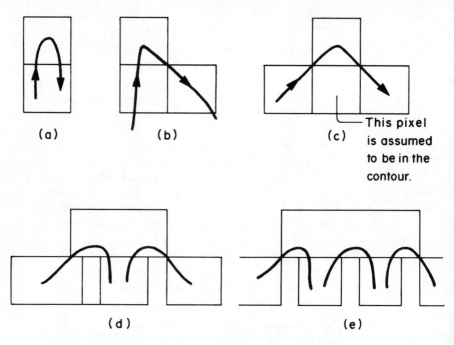

Figure 8.5   Illustration used in the proof of Theorem 8.1: (a) (0,1) degree with one pixel in the line below; (b) (0,1) degree with two pixels in the line below; (c) (0,1) degree with three pixels in the line below; (d) (0,3) degree; and (e) (0,4) degree.

Definition 7.6 and therefore cannot occur when the region is full. The case of (1,0) is treated in a similar manner. We must now show that if the region is full, neither degree can exceed 2. First, if the degree is odd, it means that one of the branches is multiply traversed (Figure 8.5d). If the degree is even then some pixels must have more than two d-neighbors in the path (Figure 8.5e). □

Corollary: If Algorithm 8.3 examines the contour of a full region, then the error flag (step 11) is never set. □

  Therefore, contours of full regions can be filled by a relatively simple algorithm, examining only a few lines at a time. If the region is not full, then such an algorithm may fail, as shown in Figure 8.4 and Table 8.2. Unfortunately, for regions that are not full, the algorithm not only fails, but does so without setting the error flag. Figure 8.6 shows such an example. There, the top node has degree (0,2) but the corresponding interval contains four boundary arcs. Note that there is no way that a pixel based parity check algorithm can fill such a contour correctly, unless it traverses the contour more than once. It is possible to fill correctly an arbitrary region R if we consider the contour of R as a region and traverse it to find a new contour while marking pixels with their multiplicity (see Bibliographical Notes).

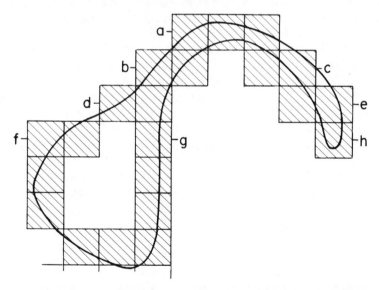

Figure 8.6 A contour that cannot be filled properly by Algorithm 8.3. Furthermore, the error flag is not set until after some erroneous filling: the pixel between intervals b and c.

8.3.2 Implementation of a Parity Check Algorithm

A pixel based parity check has certain advantages over an edge filling because both the sorting according to y, and the interpolation between the given points (if there are gaps in the values of y) are not done in the host computer, but on the display device. One can first display the contour by using a $vec(x,y)$ command (see Section 1.7, Table 1.2). In this way the interpolation is performed by the device hardware without any cost to the host computer. This also achieves the correct sorting of the points, since the process of display can be thought of as a "bucketsort." Two options are then open. In one, the algorithm can be implemented in the microprocessor controlling the display device. In this case the grid is the refresh memory. In the other, a group of three lines are read in the host memory by using a *rpic* instruction (see Section 1.7, Table 1.2). The parity check is performed there and then the middle line is written back. The price that one pays for this convenience is that only full regions are filled correctly.

8.4 CONTOUR FILLING BY CONNECTIVITY

If we know a point of the interior, then we can use it as a *seed* and propagate its color to adjacent pixels until the contour is reached. The algorithm can be described recursively in simple terms: Let c be the color of the seed S, and F be the filled region at some step. We set $F = \{S\}$ initially, and then at each step we add to F all pixels whose color is c and who have a direct neighbor in F. Thus, the contour filling is performed on the basis of connectivity. The name "seeding algorithm" is also used to describe such a process. The assumption about knowing a seed is realistic in interactive graphic systems, where a user may point a lightpen or a cursor to the interior of a contour. It is also valid in systems where a solid is defined by the vertices of an approximating polyhedron and different views are displayed on the graphics screen. Interior points of the various resulting polygons may be computed easily. In picture processing systems a point of the interior may be found as one directly adjacent to a contour pixel, and may be marked when the contour is extracted. A partial parity check may also be used as a preprocessor.

Connectivity filling is less likely to produce spillovers than filling based on the parity check. Indeed, the current color of the interior is known and a pixel is not filled unless it is of that color. Spillover can occur only when the given contour is not closed. The price that we pay for the assurance against spillover is that regions that have more than one component require a seed for each component.

8.4.1 Recursive Connectivity Filling

The interior can be traversed in a number of ways by using the data structures of Chapter 6. The simplest algorithm in terms of program length uses the pixel grid and is based on recursion. It is listed as Algorithm 8.4. The four d-neighbors of the seed are examined, and for each one of them that does not belong to the contour we call *FILL* again with that neighbor as seed. A slight modification could make it fill any pixel with the color of the seed.

Algorithm 8.4 Recursive Fill

Notation: seed is the given pixel and C is the color of filling. The contour pixels already have that value. The variable p_N denotes the N-neighbor of p, $0 \le N \le 7$ (see Definition 7.1).

1.   **Call** *FILL* (*seed*).
2.   **End of Algorithm.**

Procedure FILL (*p*)

F1.   Set the color of p to C.
F2.   **For** $N = 0, 2, 4, 6$ **do:**
            Begin.
F3.   **If** the color of p_N is not C, **then call** *FILL* (p_N).
            End.
F4.   **Return**

The apparent simplicity of this algorithm is misleading because each time a subroutine is called there is a certain computational cost that is not obvious in the listing. We shall return to this point in Section 8.5.

8.4.2 Nonrecursive Connectivity Filling

Instead of passing all the bookkeeping of the traversal to the system handling the subroutine calls, we might want to do that ourselves, more efficiently. For raster graphics, the LAG is a particularly convenient data structure. In its simplest form, the algorithm starts from the seed and proceeds to the left until a contour pixel is found. Then a scan to the right is repeated until the contour is seen again. Then the next line is filled and so forth until the lowermost part of the contour is reached. The process is repeated for the part of the region above the starting pixel. This is a simple enough process but one can easily see that it fills a contour successfully only if the region is convex. It can be modified to fill nonconvex regions by the use of a stack where pixels near maxima or minima of the contour are placed. Subsequently, these pixels are popped from the stack and used as seeds. In the example of Figure 8.7, pixels A, B, and C would all be placed in the stack while the shaded part is filled. Pixels D and E will be placed there later, during the traversal of the unshaded part. Although the basic idea is quite simple, its proper implementation requires care.

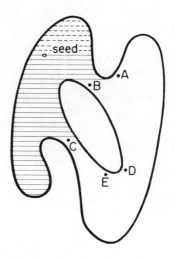

Figure 8.7 Connectivity filling for a nonconvex region. For the given seed, one proceeds downward filling the part shaded by complete horizontal lines. Then one returns to the seed and goes upwards filling the part shaded with broken lines.

Before describing the main algorithm we outline certain procedures used by it.

8.4.3 Procedures used for Connectivity Filling

We shall use the term pixel address to denote the description of the location of the pixel. This can be a pair of x-y coordinates, a pointer to an array, etc. If p is the address of pixel A, the expression $p-1$ denotes the address of the pixel to its left (on the same horizontal line), and $p+1$ the address of the pixel to its right. One of these addresses is not defined for the rightmost and another for the leftmost pixels of each line. Any implementation of the algorithms must make special provisions for such pixels but we do not want to complicate our description with such special cases.

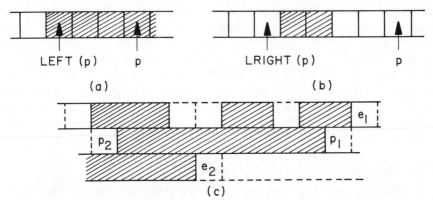

Figure 8.8 (a) Definition of *LEFT*(*p*). (b) Definition of *LRIGHT*(*p*). (c) Definition of pixels p_1, p_2, e_1, and e_2. The argument *p* of the procedure *LINK* is any pixel in the shaded zone between p_2 and p_1.

The procedure *LEFT*(*p*) returns the address of the leftmost pixel of the fixed color interval containing *p* (Figure 8.8a). The procedure *LRIGHT*(*p*) is defined as

$$LRIGHT(p) = LEFT(LEFT(p)-1)-1,$$

i.e., it returns the address of the rightmost pixel to the left of *p* which has the same color as *p*, and has the property that there is at least one pixel of different color between the two (Figure 8.8b). The implementation of such procedures is straightforward.

The degrees of a node (interval) of the LAG containing the pixel *p* are found by the procedure *LINK*(*p*) given as Algorithm 8.3a. A slight modification is necessary in order to specify the addresses of pixels e_1 and e_2 shown in Figure 8.8c. If any of these pixels is not defined, the returned address is zero. (If zero is a legitimate address, then the implementer can choose some other value to initialize e_1 and e_2 inside *LINK*.)

Because the seed may be given in the middle of a region, it is necessary to do the filling in both directions from it, as shown in Figure 8.7. Such a bidirectional traversal is not necessary for any other pixel from the stack. Instead of having a special procedure for the traversal of the first region, it is best to pay some attention to the initialization. If the pixel *seed*$_{above}$, directly above the seed, is not in the contour then *LEFT*(*seed*$_{above}$) should be placed in the stack with an indication that it should be used to start an upward scan. This is expected to be the

usual case in interactive graphics because a user is likely to provide a
pixel far from the contour as a seed. If the pixel above the seed is on
the contour, then we proceed as follows. First we examine the degree
of that contour interval through a call to *LINK*. If it has degree (0,2),
then the seed was chosen just below a maximum, so there is no need
for an upward scan. Otherwise, the seed was chosen just beneath a
nearly horizontal arc of the contour. Then we replace the seed by
LEFT(*seed*) and call *LINK* for the contour interval to the left of the
seed. The pixel e_1 is then chosen as a seed for an upward scan.

8.4.4 Description of the Main Algorithm

The algorithm can be described informally as follows. It fills horizontal lines by proceeding from left to right starting from a pixel
immediately to the right of the contour. (This can be found in the first
line by a call of *LEFT*(*seed*).) Let p be that pixel. Before filling, a call
to $LINK(p-1)$ is performed to investigate the C-LAG of the left contour interval. If *above* and *below* are both one, then we have a simple
arc and we specify the locations for the next scan line. If the direction
of vertical scan has the value "down", then we set $p_{next} = e_2$, otherwise
$p_{next} = e_1$. Then we proceed, filling horizontally starting from p until a
contour pixel is found. Let p_{right} be the address of the last interior
pixel. We next call $LINK(p_{right}+1)$. If it returns *above* and *below* both
equal to 1, then we replace p by p_{next} and repeat the process.

The interesting cases are where *above* and *below* are not both one
at both ends. In particular if one of them is zero, then we know that
we have an extremum and we must either place a pixel on the stack or
terminate the filling in a particular direction. This is the essential part
of the algorithm that is next described.

Algorithm 8.5 is based on these ideas. Besides the stack S, it also
uses a stack S_d to store the proper direction at the same time that it
places an address in S. (Of course, it is possible to use a single stack
whose elements are a pair of values, the pixel address and the direction.) *POP*(*stack*) is as listed in Algorithm 6.1. Step 3 examines the
direction of the scan and sets up certain variables accordingly. In particular, $u = 1$ means that e_1 will be selected as the next pixel, while
$u = 2$ will cause e_2 to be selected. The use of these variables eliminates the need to have separate codes for upward and downward
traversal. The loop consisting of steps 5-17 is the main part of the
algorithm. In order to scan the top part of the picture we must place
the seed on the stack twice.

Step 5 examines whether the next pixel is a legal address, or
whether it has already been filled. In either case, the algorithm exits

from the inner loop and executes step 1. If the stack is not empty, a new pixel is popped and the whole process is repeated. If the next pixel is a legal address and is not yet filled, then it becomes the current pixel (step 6). Step 7 evaluates the degrees of the C-LAG at the left end.

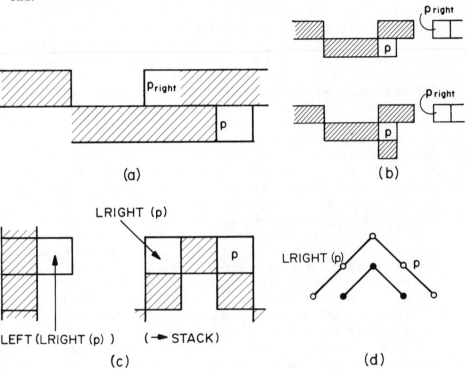

Figure 8.9 (a) and (b) Configurations that cause the condition in brackets ([...]) of Step 8 of Algorithm 8.5 to be true, when scanning in a downward direction. However, only (a) indicates that a bottom has been reached and filling in that direction stops. (c) When the left contour is examined, and the configuration shown is found, pixel *p* is placed in the stack. (d) The two LAGs for configuration (c).

Step 8 performs the first nontrivial operation: it checks whether we have reached the end of the interior in the direction of the scan. If the scan direction is downward and *above* exceeds one, we must have reached either a bottom, as shown in Figure 8.9a, or one of the configurations shown in Figures 8.9b. The former case is detected by verifying that the current pixel *p* is to the right of p_{right}, and therefore outside the contour. Then filling in that direction is terminated and the algorithm exits from the loop. Otherwise we know that the current pixel is indeed in the interior. (If the scan direction is upward, we have a similar test for checking whether we reached a top.)

Step 9 checks whether both the above and below degrees are nonzero and sets aside the starting point in the next line. We do not insist that both degrees be one, even though nodes with degree (1,2) or (2,1) are impossible for full regions. For most pixels of the contour the conditions of this step will be true and the algorithm will proceed directly to step 14. If at least one of the degrees is zero, then we know that we must place a pixel in the stack (according to Proposition 8.1), and some caution is required in defining p_{next}.

Placement in the stack is performed in step 10. Figure 8.9c shows the pixel arrangement when *above* $= 0$. Note that the existence of the contour arc shown to the left is guaranteed if the contour is indeed closed. Otherwise, the pixels on the line above p will have the same color as p and will not be bounded to the left. Figure 8.9d shows the relation between the C-LAG (full circles for nodes) and the I-LAG (open circles for nodes) in that case.

Having either of the degrees zero means that we must be careful in defining the starting point for the next scan line. If we are proceeding downward and the above degree is zero but the below degree is not, then there is no problem. This check is performed in step 11 together with a similar check for the case of upward traversal. The configuration of the contours when the conditions in step 11 are true during a downward traversal is shown in Figure 8.10a.

Step 12 handles the case when there are no contour pixels in the next line (according to the scan direction) connected to the contour. This configuration is shown in Figure 8.10b for a downward direction. It examines the pixel directly ontop (p_{ontop}) or directly under (p_{under}) the current one. If that pixel is not filled, then it selects as the next pixel one on the same line that is immediately to the right of the contour. (See the comments in step 10 regarding the existence of such a contour arc.)

Step 14 does the actual filling of the line. It is the step that sees most of the pixels. For each pixel it checks whether the pixel has the color of the contour, and if not it fills the pixel with the appropriate color.

Algorithm 8.5 Filling by Connectivity

Notation: p_{next} is the pixel which will be used to start the filling on the new line. p_{other} can have the value p_{ontop} or p_{under} and is the pixel lying directly on top or directly under the current one. S is a stack of seed addresses and S_d a stack of directions for the traversal of the LAG.

0.   Input is the image array, the address of an interior pixel *seed*, and possibly a second pixel *seed*$_{ontop}$. *LEFT*(*seed*) is placed in S and the direction *down* in S_d. If the second pixel is given, *LEFT*(*seed*$_{ontop}$) is also placed in S and the direction *up* in S_d.

1.   **While** the stack S is not empty **repeat** steps 2-19

       Begin.

2. p_{next} = POP(S), *dir* = POP(S_d), p_{right} = X_{max}

3.   **If** *dir* equals *down*, **then** set $u = 2$, *other* = *under*. **Else** $u = 1$, *other* = *ontop*.

4.   **Repeat** steps 5-16

              Begin.

5.   **If** p_{next} equals zero **or** if p_{next} is filled, **then exit** from the loop.

6. $p = p_{next}$

7.   *LINK* $(p-1)$ {check left contour}

8.   **If** [(*dir* equals *down* and *above* exceeds 1) or (*dir* equals *up* and *below* exceeds 1)] and p is to the right of p_{right} **then exit** from the loop.

9.   **If** both *above* and *below* exceed zero, **then** set $p_{next} = e_u$.

           Else do:

                Begin.

10.   **If** p is not already filled, **then** place in S the address *LEFT*(*LRIGHT*(p)) and in S_d the value *dir*.

11.   **If** (*above* equals zero and *below* does not and *dir* equals *down*) **or** (*below* equals zero and *above* does not and *dir* equals *up*), **then** set $p_{next} = e_u$.

12.   **Else if** p_{other} is not filled, **then** set p_{next} = *LEFT*(p_{other}).

13.   **Else** set $p_{next} = 0$.

                End.

14.   Fill the line starting from p and let p_{right} be the last pixel before the contour.

15.   *LINK* $(p_{right}+1)$ {check right contour}

16.   If either *above* or *below* equals 0 and if p_1 is not filled,
                       then do:
                           Begin.
17.   Place p_1 in stack S
18.   **If** *above*>0, **then** place *up* in S_d.
19.   **Else** place *down* in S_d.
                           End.
                       End.
               End.
20.   **End of Algorithm.**

Step 15 checks the degree of the C-LAG at the node corresponding to the right contour arc. If either of the degrees is zero, then the
pixel on the other side of the contour arc (p_1 in Figure 8.10c) is placed
in the stack, together with the appropriate direction. (Steps 15 to 17.)
Figure 8.10d shows the configuration in terms of the two LAGs.

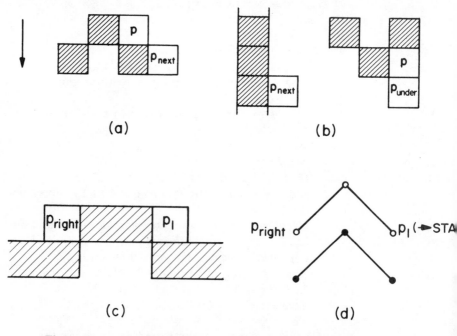

(a)   (b)

(c)   (d)

Figure 8.10 (a) Configuration when the conditions of step 11 are
true. (b) Configuration when the conditions of step 12 are true.
(c) When the right contour is examined, and the configuration
shown is found, pixel p is placed in the stack. (d) The two LAGs
for configuration (c).

We observe that at most two nodes at a time are placed on the stack. However, all nodes connected to a given one are eventually either placed in the stack or filled. In the example of Figure 8.11, let C be the first node visited during an up traversal. Then B and D are placed on the stack. Whenever D is visited again (either by being pulled from the stack or by being reached from another node), E will be placed in the stack.

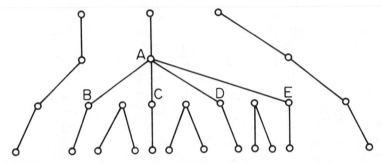

Figure 8.11 If C is the first visited node, nodes B and D are placed in the stack. Node E will be placed only when D is visited again.

One can also show that for a full region Algorithm 8.5 does the filling correctly. Indeed, in this case the only pixels placed on the stack are those that are adjacent to maxima or minima in the vertical direction.

8.5 COMPARISONS AND COMBINATIONS

If we compare the pixel based algorithms in terms of program length, Algorithm 8.4 is clearly the simplest one, followed by the parity check, Algorithm 8.3, with Algorithm 8.5 last. In some ways the computations performed by the last two algorithms are the same. Both use the same data structure and the same basic procedure. They make a subroutine call only at contour points, so that the number of such calls equals approximately the number of horizontal contour intervals (in other words, the number of nodes in the C-LAG). Pixels in the interior of the region are addressed in a sequential fashion and for each one of them only a simple test is done: whether they are on the contour or not. The sequential addressing can be implemented very efficiently with *index registers* on most machines. On the other hand the recursive algorithm makes about four subroutine calls for each pixel of the interior. Such calls are expensive because of the need to save registers, as well as the necessary information for returning to the original point. Machines that have a hardware implementation of a stack can perform the last operation efficiently. Therefore the major cost of the recursive algorithm is the cost of saving memory locations during subroutine calls (in case both the calling and the called program use those registers). While such a cost is quite high when one uses a high level language, it might be possible to devise implementations in assembly language where the cost is modest (see Problem 8.5).

We next compare the two nonrecursive algorithms to each other. Connectivity filling has two major advantages: (a) it will not leak as long as the contour is connected, (b) the computation time is proportional to the area to be filled instead of to the area of a rectangle circumscribing the contour as is the case with parity check algorithms. Its major disadvantages are: (a) the need to know a point of the interior, which in some applications may be difficult to find, (b) if a figure has a connected contour but a nonconnected interior, then only the part containing the seed will be filled (a parity check algorithm will fill all parts), (c) the interior is not traversed in raster order, which may cause excessive communication between the host computer and the controller of the graphic display. This disadvantage is relevant in the context of the discussion of Section 8.3.2. If we cannot program the microprocessor, then we may read all the horizontal lines in sequence, keeping three of them in main memory at a time, and evaluate the degrees of the LAG there. In a parity check, once a line has been examined, it does not have to be examined again. This is not the case with a connectivity algorithm. (Because of this factor it is also necessary to do the filling with a different intensity than that used for the contour.) Thus the actual computational cost may be higher because of the larger number of input and output operations.

Because both types of algorithms use the same basic procedure, *LINK*, it is possible to create a combined algorithm that fills some parts of an image by a parity check and others by seeding. This can be important in applications where it is difficult to determine a seed in advance. It can be achieved by running Algorithm 8.3 without filling intervals, and not exiting if the error flag is set. When a line that does cause an error condition is found, then a seed is chosen. It is possible to relax the condition on the degrees and require that they be greater than or equal to one, rather than equal to one. (This relaxed form was used in the implementation that produced the examples shown in Figure 8.12 (Plate 26) and Figure 8.13.) Filling can then proceed by connectivity in order to avoid scanning outside the contour area.

Conversely, we may choose parity check as the basic algorithm and then revert to connectivity when we come across lines where the interior is not well defined on the basis of parity. Such an algorithm will not miss parts of the interior that are not connected to the region containing the seed.

It is also worth pointing out that Algorithm 8.5 does most of the computation around extrema of the contour in the vertical direction, points which are relatively rare. Figure 8.12 (Plate 26) shows an example of a region filled by Algorithm 8.5 with a different gray level used each time a pixel is taken from the stack. The algorithm can be easily adapted to fill with patterns, rather than uniformly, by selecting a fill color according to the address of the pixels. One such example is shown in Figure 8.13.

```
      1 1 1 1 1 1 1 1 1                The _ prob l
      1a1a1a1a1a1a1a1a1                em_of_filling_the
      1aaaaaaaaaaaaaaaa1               _contour_of_a_regi
      1aaaaaaaaaaaaaaaa1               on_with_a_given_co
      1aaaaaaa111aaaaaa1               lor_has_been_attac
      1aaaaaaa1   1aaaa1               ked_by_tw    o_meth
      1aaaaaaa1   1aa1                 odologies       _In
      1aaaaaaa1   11                   _one_the_       co
      1aaaaaaa1                        ntour_is_
      1aaaaaaa1                        intersect
      11aaaaaaaaa1111111               ed_by_a_set_of_hor
      1aaaaaaaaaaaaaaaaa1              izontal_line_and_pix
      11111aaaaaaa11aaaaa1             els_are_filled_if_th
           1aaaaa1  11111              ey_lie_   to_th
           1aaaaa1                     e_right
            1aaaaa1                    _of_an_
             1aaaaa1                   odd_num
              1aaaa11                  ber_of_
      11       1aaaaa11             in     tersecti
      1aa1     1aaaaaa11            ons_     (assuming
      1aa1   1aaaaa11               _tha   t_the_le
      1aa11aaaaa1                   ftmost_part
      1aaaaaaa1                     _of_the_l
       1111111                      ine_is_
```

Figure 8.13 *Left*: a contour (marked by 1's) filled uniformly. *Right*: both the contour and the interior have been replaced by text. Spaces were replaced by underlines (_).

8.6 BIBLIOGRAPHICAL NOTES

Edge fill is the oldest and probably the most widely used filling algorithm in graphics. Its use is clearly justified in applications where the same contour is displayed repeatedly, as in phototypesetting. Two-dimensional animation where contours may be subject to translation but not rotation is another application where edge fill is appropriate. Algorithm 8.1 is a variation of the "YX" algorithm described in [1.NS], modified on the basis of certain observations on the algorithms implemented in phototypesetters. The major effort in such algorithms goes into the proper encoding of contours. Such algorithms can be rather wasteful in applications where a given contour will be filled very few times. It is best to use pixel based algorithms there, especially in a raster graphics environment. One must pay a price for discarding the analog topological information about the contour, although in certain applications that information was never available. A number of papers suggest methods for solving the problem when the contour is given as a collection of pixels without any order. [8.DU], [8.ME], and [8.PA] use modifications of the parity check. The last reference presents extensions of Algorithm 8.3 which correctly fill regions that are not full, provided that there exist no pixels containing more than two contour arcs, or two contour arcs, one of which forms an extremum in the y direction. Connectivity algorithms have been presented in [8.LI], [6.SH], and [8.SM]. The algorithm of [8.LI] is not correct and this was pointed out in [6.SH] where a correct algorithm was presented, traversing, in effect, the I-LAG.

8.7 RELEVANT LITERATURE

[8.DU]   Dudani, S. A. "Region Extraction Using Boundary Following," C. H. Chen, ed. *Pattern Recognition and Artificial Intelligence* New York: Academic Press, 1976, pp. 216-232.

[8.LI]   Lieberman, H. "How to Color in a Coloring Book," *SIGGRAPH'78*, Atlanta, Georgia , (August, 1978), pp. 111-116. Published by ACM.

[8.ME]   Merrill, R. D. "Representation of Contours and Regions for Efficient Computer Search," *CACM*, **16** (1973), pp. 69-82.

[8.PA]   Pavlidis, T. "Filling Algorithms for Raster Graphics," *CGIP*, **10** (1979), pp. 126-141.

[8.SM]   Smith, A. R. "Tint Fill," *SIGGRAPH'79*, Chicago, Illinois, (August, 1979), pp. 276-283. Published by ACM.

8.8 PROBLEMS

8.1.   The edge fill algorithm of Section 8.2 has no provision for horizontal edges. Modify it so that figures with such edges are handled correctly.

8.2.   Derive a format for the waiting list that stores only Δx and Δy plus the y values at extrema and as little other information as possible.

8.3.   Modify Algorithm 8.3a so that it calculates the values of e_1 and e_2 needed in Algorithm 8.5.

8.4. Estimate the cost of filling a circle by an edge fill, a parity check fill, and a connectivity fill. Repeat for the case of a circular ring.

8.5. (This problem assumes that you are familiar with assembly language.) Devise an implementation of Algorithm 8.4 that does not use any registers for saving the results of the computation so that their contents can be discarded when calling or returning from a subroutine. Then subroutine calls can be almost as inexpensive as *jump* instructions. Compare this with the cost of implementing the nonrecursive algorithms.

Chapter 9

THINNING ALGORITHMS

9.1 INTRODUCTION

Thinning algorithms have been studied widely in picture processing and pattern recognition because they offer a way of simplifying pictorial forms. Figure 9.1 illustrates a motivation for a thinning algorithm. The shaded pixels represent a quantization of a line drawing to be mapped back into a set of lines. In Sections 7.6 and 7.7, we have already discussed how the concept of thinness can be defined over a discrete grid. We shall use that analysis here as the basis for thinning algorithms.

It is possible to define thinning in a mathematically rigorous way on the continuous plane as follows.

Definition 9.1: Let R be a plane set, B its boundary, and P a point in R. A nearest neighbor of P on B is a point M in B such that there is no other point in B whose distance from P is less than the distance PM. If P has more than one nearest neighbor, then P is said to be a *skeletal* point of R. The union of all skeletal points is called the *skeleton* or *medial axis* of R. $\Box$

This definition implies that skeletal points are centers of circles contained entirely within R, with the property that there is no other circle with the same center and greater radius contained in R. Figure 9.2 shows some examples of skeletons with some of their major features. One can see that they are very sensitive to noise, since a small disturbance of the boundary not only causes a disturbance in one branch but also causes the creation of new branches. As a matter of fact, we have the following result.

```
        XXX    X                              XXXX        XXXXXXXXX
     XXXXXXXXXXX                            XXXXXXX    XXXXXXXXXXXX
    XXXXXXXXXXXXXXX              XXXXXXXXXXXXXXXXXXXXXXXXXXXXXXXXX
   XXXXXXXXXXXXXXXXXX            XXXXXXXXXXXXXXXXXXXXXXXXXXXXXXXXX
    XXXXX      XXXXXXX           XXXXXXXXXXXXXXXXXXXXXXXXXXXXXXXXXXX
   XXXXX          XXXXXXXX       XXXXXXXXXXXX          XXXXXXXX
  XXXXX              XXXXXXX     XXXXXXXXXXX            XXXXXXX
  XXXXX              XXXXXXX     XXXXXXX               XXXXXXX
  XXXXX              XXXXXXX     XXXXXX                XXXXXXX
  XXXXX             XXXXXXXX     XXXXX                 XXXXXXX
 XXXXXXX            XXXXXXXX     XXXXX                 XXXXXXX
XXXXXXXXXXXXXXXXXXXXXXXXXXXXXXX  XXXXX                 XXXXXXX
XXXXXXXXXXXXXXXXXXXXXXXXXXXXXX   XXXXX                 XXXXXXX
XXXXXXXXXXXXXXXXXXXXXXXXXXXXX    XXXXX                 XXXXXXX
 XXXXXXX                         XXXXX                 XXXXXXX
 XXXXXX                          XXXXX                 XXXXXXX
 XXXXX                           XXXXX                 XXXXXXX
 XXXXX                           XXXXX                 XXXXXXX
 XXXXXXX                         XXXXX                XXXXXXXX
 XXXXXXX                         XXXXX                 XXXXXXX
 XXXXXXX                         XXXXX                 XXXXXXX
 XXXXXXX                         XXXXX                 XXXXXXX
 XXXXXXXX           X            XXXXX                 XXXXXXX
 XXXXXXXXX         XXX           XXXXX                 XXXXXXX
 XXXXXXXXX         XXX           XXXXX                 XXXXXXX
 XXXXXXXXXX       XXXX           XXXXX                 XXXXXXX
 XXXXXXXXXX       XXX            XXXXX                 XXXXXXX
 XXXXXXXXXXX     XXXXX           XXXXX                 XXXXXXX
XXXXXXXXXXXXXXXXXXXXXXXXX        XXXXX                 XXXXXXX
 XXXXXXXXXXXXXXXXXXXXXXX         XXXXXXXXX             XXXXXXX
 XXXXXXXXXXXXXXXXXXXXX           XXXXXXXXX            XXXXXXXX
  XXXXXXXXXXXXXXXXXX             XXXXXXXXXXXX         XXXXXXXXXXX
   XXXXXXXXXXXXXX                XXXXXXXXXXXXXXX   XXXXXXXXXXXXXXXXXX
    XXXXXXXXX                    XXXXXXXXXXXXXX    XXXXXXXXXXXXXXXXX
```

Figure 9.1 Illustration of the need for thinning algorithms: A line drawing or text must be digitized at a high enough resolution to assure that no lines will be broken and that the ends of the serifs will be preserved (see Chapter 7). Such a resolution will cause a width of more than two pixels in other locations. Thinning is required in order to recapture the lineal structure of the input without destroying its connectivity.

Proposition 9.1:   If P is the curvature center of a point of the boundary B of a plane set R where the curvature of B has an isolated maximum, then there exists a branch of the skeleton terminating at P.

Proof: An isolated curvature maximum means that a circle tangent to the boundary at that point (M) has a smaller radius than circles tangent at neighboring points. Furthermore, by the definition of tangent curves, the circle has more than one point in common with the curve, and hence its center (P) is part of the skeleton. Any larger circle will be tangent at two points in the neighborhood of M, and therefore its center will be part of the skeleton, but farther away from P. □

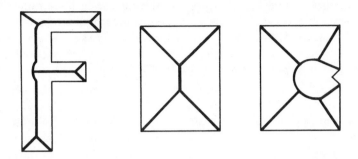

Figure 9.2   Examples of skeletons: (a) the lineal structure of the silhouette corresponds closely to that of the medial axis; (b) no simple correspondence exists between skeleton branches and object structure; (c) small amounts of noise alter the form of the skeleton drastically.

Another observation that one can make from Figure 9.2 is that for objects that are thin to start with, the skeletons provide substantial information about their shape. This is not the case with thick objects, as shown in Figure 9.2b.

The translation of the concept of the medial axis in the discrete plane is by no means obvious or even feasible because of the difficulty of defining equality of distance between pixels over a discrete grid. Therefore, much is left to the intuition of the individual implementer. One possible choice is to extend Definition 9.1 to the discrete plane. One could define a discrete version of the circle and then search for "circles," contained entirely within the set and having the property that there is no greater "circle" with the same center contained in the set. As such an approach requires extensive calculations, it has not been very popular. Most of the literature on thinning deals with algorithms defined directly on a discrete grid. We shall present two such algorithms in this chapter. Both are based on the concept of multiple pixels (Definition 7.9 and Theorem 7.3), although the first one makes use of only part of the definition. Both algorithms modify the concept somewhat in order to find skeletons that have the width of a single pixel only, whenever possible. (Recall that one can have lineal sets with width two, such as shown in Figure 7.17.) For this reason we shall use the term *skeletal* rather than multiple to describe the basic approach that both algorithms take.

Definition 9.2:   The *skeleton* of a set of pixels R is a set found as follows.   First, the skeletal pixels and the contour pixels of R are determined.   Then, all the contour pixels that are not skeletal are removed and the set thus found replaces R.   The process is repeated until a set consisting of only skeletal pixels is left.   □

The reader who is annoyed by the circularity of this definition may substitute "multiple" for "skeletal." Verifying whether a pixel is multiple requires the examination of only its immediate neighborhood and thus the transformations implied by Definition 9.2 can be implemented by local operations (see Section 7.6.2). The important part is the assumption that one can decide for each set that certain pixels are skeletal, and keep them, and that other pixels are definitely not skeletal, so one can discard them. We also recall that it can be decided without any previous knowledge whether a pixel belongs to the contour or not, since all such pixels must have a d-neighbor with value zero.

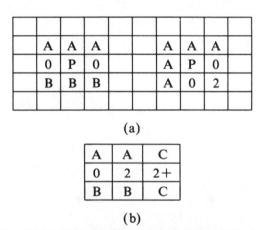

(a)

(b)

Figure 9.3   Neighborhood patterns of multiple pixels (a) At least one of each group of pixels marked with A or B must be nonzero. (b) At least one of the pixels marked C must be nonzero. If both pixels labeled C are nonzero, then the value of the pixels labeled A and B can be anything. Otherwise, at least one of the members of each pair marked A or B must be nonzero.

9.2 CLASSICAL THINNING ALGORITHMS

Most of the algorithms in the literature define skeletal pixels as only those that fit either of the patterns of Figure 7.20 or Figure 9.3a†, i.e. they satisfy condition (a) of Theorem 7.3. In order to preserve pixels that satisfy the other conditions they impose a very specific order by which condition (a) is checked. Note that condition (a) is in effect a connectivity criterion and if it is applied sequentially to an image, a simply connected (i.e., without holes) region will be shrunk to a single pixel, which, of course, is not what we want.

This difficulty may be overcome by examining pixels in parallel and by extending Definition 9.2 to require that if a pixel was labeled as skeletal during one iteration it cannot be erased later on. Thus, if Q is a horizontal array of pixels, removal of any one of the pixels in the middle will violate the connectivity condition. Therefore, only the two end pixels of the array will be removed and the rest will be considered final. However, one more difficulty remains, because if an array consists of pairs of pixels such as those shown in Figure 7.17, then none of them is critical for the connectivity and all of them will be deleted. This last obstacle can be circumvented by a mixture of parallel and sequential processing. We do not check all contour pixels at the same time but only those whose N-neighbor is zero, where N takes the values 0, 2, 4, and 6 in sequence. Then an array of thickness two will first be thinned to thickness one, and some of its pixels will thereby be preserved. In such algorithms it is necessary to mark skeletal pixels in a specific way, otherwise they would be deleted in a subsequent iteration when they are not required for connectivity. Algorithm 9.1 implements this method. It assumes a bilevel input with pixels labeled 0 or 1. During the process, pixels of the set to be thinned are also marked by 2 or 3, so that while checking the neighborhood patterns, we must accept those values as denoting the presence of a pixel.

The pattern matching operation of step 9 is done easily by forming a string whose values are those of the eight neighbors of p. Then one need compare only two strings. An example of the application of the algorithm is shown in Figure 9.4.

---

† We repeat Figures 7.20 and 7.25 as part of Figure 9.3 because of frequent references to them in this chapter.

Algorithm 9.1 Classical Thinning Algorithm.

Notation: I is the input image. *P* is the set of patterns of neighborhoods of skeletal pixels shown in Figure 9.3a, including also a 90° rotation of the first pattern and three 90° rotations of the second pattern. Flag *remain*, when set to true, is used to denote that nonskeletal pixels may remain. Flag *skel* is set to true when the neighborhood of a pixel matches one of the patterns in *P*. A "one" in the pattern matches any nonzero element of the neighborhood.

1.   Set the flag *remain* to true.
2.   **While** *remain* is true **do** steps 3-12.
         Begin.
3.   Set *remain* to false. {No change has been made.}
4.   **For** *j* = 0,2,4, and 6 **do** steps 5-12.
                Begin.
5.   **For** all pixels *p* of the image *I* **do** steps 6-10.
                    Begin.
6.   **If** *p* is 1 **and if** its *j*-neighbor is 0 **then do** steps 7-10.
                        Begin.
7.   Set flag *skel* to false.
8.   **For** all patterns *P* **do** step 9.
                            Begin.
9.   **If** the neighborhood of *p* matches the pattern *P*, **then** set *skel* to true and exit from the loop.
                            End.
10.   **If** the flag *skel* is true, **then** set *p* to 2 {skeletal pixel}, **else** set *p* to 3 {deletable pixel} and also set *remain* to true.
                        End.
                    End.
11.   **For** all pixels *p* of *I* **do** step 12.
                    Begin.
12.   **If** *p* is 3, **then** set *p* equal to 0.
                    End.
                End.
         End.
13. **End of Algorithm.**

```
         ---   -
        ------------
      ---00000000----                ----        ---------
     ---00--------0----           -------     -----------
     --0--       --0----        ----------------0000-----
     ---0-        ---0----       --0--------000000----00----
     --0-         ---0----       ---0000-0000-----------0----
    ---0-          --0----       -----0-----          ----0----
    --0--          --0----       ----0-----           --0----
    --0--          ---0----      ---0-----            ---0----
    ---0---        ---0----      --0---               ---0---
    ---0-------------0-----      --0---               ---0---
    ----00000000000000000000-----  --0---             ---0---
    ---0----------------------      --0---            ---0---
    --0----                         --0---            ---0---
    --0---                          --0---            ---0---
    --0---                          --0---            ---0---
    --0---                          --0---            ---0----
    --0----                         --0---            ---0---
    --0----                         --0---            ---0---
    --0----                         --0---            ---0---
    ---0---                         --0---            ---0---
    ---0----                        --0---            ---0---
    ---0----           -            --0---            ---0---
    ---0-----        ---            --0---            ---0---
    ---0-----        -0-            --0---            ---0---
    ---0-----       --0-            --0---            ---0---
    ----0-----      -0-             --0---            ---0---
    ----0----------00-              --0---            ---0---
    ----00---------00--             ----0----         ---0---
    ------00----00000---            ----0----         ---0----
    ------0000------                ----00-----       ----0-0----
        ------------                ----00----------  ---000---000---
         ---------                  ------------      --0--------0-..
```

Figure 9.4 Operation of classical thinning algorithm. Deleted pixels are denoted by "-" and pixels of the skeleton by "O".

9.3 ASYNCHRONOUS THINNING ALGORITHMS

Although the classical algorithm specifies a strict sequence of operations, it is not hard to remove that constraint. Purely parallel processing is not very efficient for images because most processing algorithms operate, in effect, near edges, so that processors assigned to pixels inside large uniform areas would be idle most of the time. On the other hand, assigning a processor to a matrix of, say, 32×32 pixels and having it process them sequentially ensures a more uniform distribution of workload. Such a decision imposes the following constraints on the nature of the algorithms that can be used:

(1) Since we use parallelism, algorithms that are essentially sequential are not acceptable.

(2) In order to avoid problems at the junction of the domain of two processors we must allow each processor to look at parts of the domain of its neighbors but processors must not be allowed to write on each other's domain. Therefore, the algorithm must be allowed to modify the value of the current pixel but not the values of its neighbors. (This is an essential requirement of all parallel algorithms; one must avoid having two or more processors trying to write on the same memory location. The definition of current may vary with the

algorithm, though.) To keep the amount of communication between processors down, we may also insist that a processor looks only at the pixels surrounding the current one.

(3) Because part of the processing is sequential, the data and the algorithm must be organized in such a way that when pixels are marked, it does not affect the decision for subsequent steps, at least up to some limit when the processors may be resynchronized. Keeping two copies of the image matrix (one for reading, the other for writing) is not an efficient solution.

Any algorithm that satisfies the above three constraints also has the advantage that it could be implemented either in pure sequential or in pure parallel fashion. It turns out that the characterization of multiple pixels contained in Theorem 7.3 can be used to design such an algorithm.

The only problem with this approach is that the resulting skeleton requires editing because we have kept both pixels of paths with width two. We can achieve single pixel thickness by establishing an orientation preference and deleting one of each pair of adjacent multiple pixels if such a deletion will not affect connectivity.

Definition 9.3:   If the 4- or 2- neighbor of a multiple pixel is zero, then the pixel is labeled as removable, provided that it does not already have a neighbor labeled as removable. □

The last precaution is necessary to prevent getting a disconnected object in cases similar to that shown in Figure 9.5.

1	1	2	0	0	0
2	2	d	0	0	0
0	0	4	4	3	3
2	2	1	d	0	0
1	1	1	2	0	0

Figure 9.5 Pattern demonstrating the need for the use of an additional label before removing *multiple* pixels. Interior pixels are marked by 1, contour pixels that do not match any of the critical patterns are marked by 2, contour pixels that match one of the patterns of Figure 9.3a are marked by 3, and contour pixels that match the pattern of Figure 9.3b are marked by 4 or d. Both pixels labeled 4 have a 4- or 2-neighbor which is zero, but one of them must be kept.

Algorithm 9.2 Basic Thinning Algorithm

Notation: R is the set of 1's in the input image. $B(R)$ is the boundary of R and $M(R)$ the set of multiple pixels of R

1.   **Repeat** steps 1-4.
         Begin.
2.   Find the set $B(R)$ consisting of all pixels of R which have a d-neighbor outside R.
3.   Identify the set $M(R)$ of all multiple pixels in $B(R)$.
4.   **If** $B(R)$ equals $M(R)$ **then exit.**
5.   Replace R by $R - (B(R) - M(R))$.
         End.
6.   **End of Algorithm.**

Algorithm 9.2 implements Definition 9.2. It is independent of the way that multiple pixels are defined.

9.4 IMPLEMENTATION OF AN ASYNCHRONOUS THINNING ALGORITHM

The three conditions of Theorem 7.3 can be checked as follows. We define five 8-bit registers, bdr_1, bdr_2, bdr_3, bdr_4, and bdr_5, whose bits are set depending on the value of the neighbors of a pixel. Using the notation of Figure 7.4, we assign the 0-neighbor to the most significant bit, the 1-neighbor to the second most significant bit, and so forth. If the value of a pixel is j, then the corresponding bits are set in all the bytes bdr_k, $k \le j$. Initially, all pixels have value zero or one, so that only bits in bdr_1 can be set. When a pixel is found to belong to the contour, then its value is set to 2, so that after this operation, bits in bdr_2 may be set. We can express the occurrence of the patterns of Figure 9.3 in a simple way, as bit operations between these registers and masks. The masks are expressed as octal numbers. For example, the pixels marked with A in the first pattern of Figure 9.3a correspond to 160_8. We shall use the notation $a \& b$ to signify a bitwise *AND* between the strings a and b so that $bdr_1 \& 160_8$ will have the bits that correspond to the nonzero 1-, 2-, and 3-neighbors of the current pixel set to one. Patterns obtained by 90° rotation can be checked easily by shifting the bits in each register by two positions. Therefore we will not worry about them in the sequel. (For each stated criterion there are one or three more found by this shift operation.) We have the following simple result.

Proposition 9.2:   The following statements and their converses are true.

(a)   A pixel belongs to the contour if $bdr_1 \& 252_8$ does not equal 252_8.

(b)   The neighborhood of a pixel has the configuration of Figure 9.3a (left) if $bdr_1 \& 160_8 \neq 0$ and $bdr_1 \& 7 \neq 0$ and $bdr_1 \& 210_8$ equals 0.

(c)   The neighborhood of a pixel has the configuration of Figure 9.3a (right) if $bdr_1 \& 202_8$ equals 0 and $bdr_1 \& 1 \neq 0$.

(d)   A pixel has no neighbors in the interior of the set if bdr_1 equals bdr_2.

(e)   A pixel satisfies the pattern of Figure 9.3b if $bdr_2 \& 200_8 \neq 0$ and $bdr_1 \& 10_8$ equals 0, and if one of the following conditions hold:

(e1) $bdr_1 \& 100_8$ and $bdr_1 \& 1$ are both greater than 0;

(e2)   only one of the quantities in (e1) is greater than 0, and both $bdr_1 \& 60_8$ and $bdr_1 \& 6$ are greater than 0. $\square$

Proof: All statements can be proven by direct application of the definitions. For example, in part (e) the string 200_8 selects the 0-neighbor (the most significant bit of the pattern is one). The *AND* operation ($\&$) with bdr_2 returns one if the 0-neighbor is in the boundary and zero otherwise. The string 10_8 selects the 4-neighbor and the *AND* operation with bdr_1 returns one if that pixel is nonzero, and zero otherwise. Therefore those two conditions check for the pattern exhibited by the three pixels in the middle row of Figure 9.3b. $\square$

Algorithm 9.3 uses these results. Step 4 locates pixels that belong to the boundary, step 5 checks part of condition (b) of Theorem 7.3, and step 6 performs the test listed in Proposition 9.2(b). Step 8 labels pixels that have no interior neighbors, and step 9 checks for the pattern of Figure 9.3b. Steps 11 and 12 check for the conditions of Definition 9.3. At step 15 all pixels labeled by 2 or 5 are erased. Steps 6, 9, 11, and 12 must be performed for additional orientations that are obtained by shifting the bit pattern by two positions.

The algorithm can be implemented by a mixture of parallel and sequential processing without any difficulty because the labeling operation does not affect the values of the low order registers, i.e., the value of bdr_j is independent of the value of bdr_k $(k > j)$. Finding the contour and checking some of the conditions requires knowledge of only bdr_1. Therefore each processor can perform a set of pattern matching operations in an asynchronous way and wait until all of them have reached the same point before proceeding further.

Algorithm 9.3 Asynchronous Thinning Algorithm

Notation: C is the iteration counter plus five. The flag *erase* indicates whether any pixels have been erased.

1. Set counter C to five and flag *erase* to true.
2. **While** *erase* is true **do:**
        Begin.
3.   Increment C.
4.   Locate the contour pixels according to Proposition 9.2(a) and for each one of them **do:**
            Begin.
5.   **If** bdr_1 has at most one nonzero bit, **then** label the pixel with 3.
6.   **If** the conditions (b) or (c) of Proposition 9.2 hold, **then** the pixel is given the label 3.
            End.
7.   **Wait. For** all pixels **do:**
            Begin.
8.   **If** bdr_1 equals bdr_2 **then** the pixel is labeled with 4.
9.   **If** a pixel is on the contour and **if** the condition (e) of Proposition 9.2 holds **then** label the pixel with 4.
            End.
10.   **Wait. For** all pixels **do:**
            Begin.
11.   **If** $bdr_4 \& 10_8$ equals 0, **then** label the pixel with 5.
12.   **If** $bdr_4 \& 40_8$ equals 0 and bdr_5 is zero, **then** label the current pixel with 5.
13.   **If** a pixel has label 3 or 4, **then** it is classified as skeletal and it is labeled with C.
            End.
14.   **Wait. For** all pixels **do:**
            Begin.
15.   Erase all pixels with labels 2 and 5. If no pixels are erased flag *erase* is set to false.
            End.
        End.
16. **End of Algorithm.**

The listing of the algorithm assumes that we provide each processor with a segment of the picture and that each processor can read the pixels adjacent to the borders of its region but cannot write on them. Therefore, there is no need to take special care of the frame, except when going outside the active region. The keyword **wait** means that at these steps each processor waits for the others to finish. In certain applications it may be desirable to preserve thickness information. The algorithm can accomplish that easily by using the iteration number to mark each pixel when it is classified as skeletal for the first time. This will require the use of additional memory but otherwise its implementation is very simple. C denotes the number of iterations plus five, so that skeletal pixels can be labeled with numbers that do not interfere with the labeling necessary for the main operation of the algorithm. Such labeling can be used to reconstruct an approximation of the original region from the skeleton (see Problem 9.5). Figure 9.6 shows an example of implementation over digitized alphanumeric characters.

Figure 9.6   Operation of an asynchronous thinning algorithm. Deleted pixels are marked by "-" and pixels of the skeleton by "o".

9.5 A QUICK THINNING ALGORITHM

The algorithms of the previous sections perform the thinning operation in a systematic manner over an area of the image. However, there exist applications where it is not practical to store the complete image in memory and where one would like to perform thinning in a simpler fashion. Algorithm 9.4 does a very simple form of thinning but for many objects it will fail to detect parts of the skeleton. On the other hand, it is much faster than any of the algorithms of the previous sections, and it may not be a bad idea to use it as a preprocessor, even when the objects do not consist primarily of thin lines. In that case one could apply one of the general thinning algorithms to the parts of the silhouette that have not been thinned.

The algorithm proceeds line by line and needs to keep in memory only a small number of lines, or parts thereof. For simplicity, we describe it in terms of traversal of the line adjacency graph (LAG), but that graph does not have to be stored explicitly. (See Chapter 8 for a parallel treatment.) The concepts of vertical, horizontal, and diagonal paths are essential for the operation of the algorithm and are defined as follows.

Definition 9.4a: A vertical path of the LAG is one where the width of all nodes is below a given threshold w_0 and the number of nodes exceeds a given value N_0. □

Definition 9.4b: A horizontal path of the LAG is one where the width of all nodes exceeds a threshold $N_0 \cdot v_s$, the number of nodes is below w_0/v_s, and nodes on either side of the path have width greater than or equal to w_0. (v_s denotes the spacing between scan lines.) □

Definition 9.4c: A diagonal path of the LAG with slope ϕ is one where all the centers are approximately collinear (this can be verified by one of the algorithms of Chapter 12), the slope of the line passing through them is ϕ, the width of all the nodes is below $w_0 \sin\phi$, and their number exceeds $N_0 \cos\phi$. □

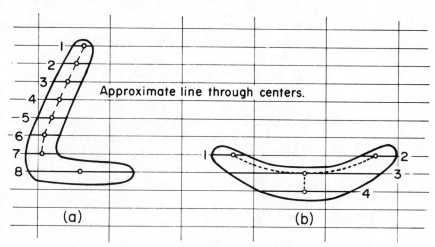

Figure 9.7 Examples of silhouettes where Algorithm 9.4 operates successfully (a) and unsuccessfully (b).

Example 9.1: Figure 9.7a shows a silhouette and the respective LAG. It is seen that two branches are clearly identified and found by Algorithm 9.4. Because all the widths are small, the subpath 1-7 is interpreted as a vertical stroke. Node 8 is a subpath by itself and is interpreted as a horizontal stroke. If node 7 were not included in the first subpath it could have been used as a connecting node between the two strokes found. In Figure 9.7b, the same algorithm fails to find the curved stroke. If node 3 were by itself it would have been classified as a horizontal stroke, but the presence of node 4 disqualifies it. □

Algorithm 9.4 Fast Thinning Algorithm

1.   Form the LAG and label each node with the location of the center and the width of the respective interval.
2.   Use a graph traversal algorithm (e.g. Algorithm 6.2) to find all paths consisting of nodes with degree (1,1), possibly starting and/or ending with nodes of degree (1,0) or (0,1).
3.   **While** any of the conditions of steps 5, 6, and 8 have been found to be true **do**:
      Begin.
4.   **For** each path found in step 2 **do**:
          Begin.
5.   **If** a path contains a subpath that is vertical, **then** all nodes of the subpath should be labeled as belonging to such a branch.
6.   **If** a path contains a subpath that is horizontal, **then** all nodes of the subpath should be labeled as belonging to such a branch.
7.   **If** neither of the conditions stated in steps 5 and 6 is true, **then do**:
              Begin.
8.   Search for a diagonal subpath. **If** one is found and its slope equals ϕ, **then** all nodes of the subpath should be labeled accordingly.
              End.
          End.
      End.
9.   **End of Algorithm.**

9.6 STRUCTURAL SHAPE ANALYSIS

In our brief introduction to shape analysis in Section 7.8 we mentioned that in many cases shape is perceived on the basis of the overall structure. The results of thinning algorithms can be used as the basis for such a structural analysis and we shall review this application here. In general, a structural analysis must identify the elementary building blocks of an object whose silhouette is available as part of a class 2 image. This can be done directly by decomposition into some primitive, simple shapes. For example, one could express the silhouette as a union of some of its convex subsets. Such methods, although theoretically possible, have substantial computational requirements. It is possible to achieve similar results at a lower cost by analysis of skeletons. One should keep in mind that although this method is theoretically applicable to any object, it yields reasonable results only for objects that are thin to start with.

In practice, shape analysis based on thinning methods can be used for the recognition of line drawings or alphanumeric characters, objects which are likely to appear in an interactive graphics environment. Additional methods for decomposition can be found in the literature cited in the Bibliographical Notes. A major obstacle in the application of structural techniques has been the lack of convenient classification algorithms. The complete treatment of the subject is beyond the scope of this text, but the following is a summary of major problems.

(1) The results of structural analysis are best expressed as a graph. It is possible to describe these graphs in terms of graph grammars, but this does not seem to be a fruitful method in spite of its theoretical attraction. There are at least two reasons: first, it is very difficult to infer grammars from samples of data, and second, it is very difficult to parse graph grammars.

(2) An alternative to graph grammars is to define certain logical functions on the (labeled) graph, for example, "there exist two vertical strokes." Then one can establish a decision tree or define binary vectors whose components correspond to these logical functions. Such vectors can then be classified according to appropriate statistical rules. The challenge here is the selection of the logical functions. There are no automatic procedures for doing so.

9.7 TRANSFORMATION OF BILEVEL IMAGES INTO LINE DRAWINGS

Thinning by itself does not quite accomplish the goal of transforming a class 2 image into a class 3 image. The skeletons obtained by Algorithms 9.1 and 9.3 are still bilevel images, although with very few black pixels. This image is equivalent to a graph whose nodes are the black pixels and whose branches connect pixels with their neighbors. We can transform this graph into another where there are no nodes of degree two as follows.

We start a traversal of the bilevel image containing the skeleton using Algorithm 6.2, or a similar algorithm. In addition to the stack S we create a buffer T where we place the coordinates of all points that correspond to nodes of degree two. If a node has degree other than two we output its coordinates and we check whether the buffer has any points in it. If it does, then we output a description of them together with the coordinates of the last node with degree other than two that we have seen. We shall explain this process in terms of an example.

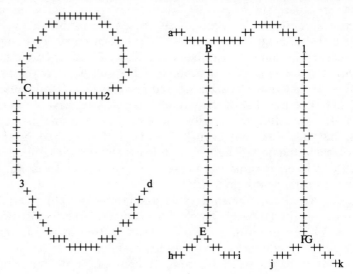

Figure 9.8 A skeleton as a graph: nodes of degree two are marked with a "+" or a number, nodes of degree one with a lower case letter, and nodes of degree three with a capital letter.

Figure 9.8 shows the skeleton of the example of Figure 9.6. In order to traverse the graph we need a starting node for each connected component. Such nodes can be found from a top to bottom, left to right scan of the bilevel image containing the skeletal pixels. In general, this will be a node of degree two, as is the case with both components of Figure 9.8. We may start traversing the graph without producing any output until we find a node of degree other than two. If no such node can be found, then the graph is a single loop and we may output that description only. For this example, let us assume that we start with node "d" for the first connected component, and node "a" for the second. Starting from "d" we find that "C" is the next node of degree other than two. We then output the pair "d" and "C" plus a description of the pixels in between that were stored in the buffer T. There are a number of choices for such a description. One is to output the chain code of the path they form. Here, it will be

$$5^3 6 5 4 5^2 4^2 5 4^5 3 4^2 3^4 2 3^3 2^9 1^2$$

where exponents denote repeated symbols. Another choice is to output descriptions of lines and circular arcs. Here, such a description will be the radius and center of a circular arc from point "d" to the point "3", plus a straight line from that point to "C". In order to obtain such a description one must use the techniques of curve fitting, and in particular those of piecewise approximations described in Chapter 12. Then pixel "2" will be selected by an algorithm such as Algorithm 12.1.

From node "C" the top loop will be traversed, ending back on "C". In this case a description by curves will contain the radius and center of an arc from "C" to "2" and the straight line from "2" to "C".

For the second component, the first output will be the pair of pixels "a" and "B", with the branch between them described as a line. From "B" we may next find "E", and from "E", "h". In order to continue that traversal we must take a node from the stack S, in this case the neighbor of "E" to its lower right. Then the next branch will be from "E" to "i", and so forth. The results of such a traversal are summarized in Table 9.1. The exact sequence of the branches depends on the order in which we scan the neighborhood of each pixel. Here we have chosen to look in an increasing order of the direction marked in Figure 7.4. We have added certain orientation information in the description of the branches. This can be obtained by the techniques of curve fitting described in the next three chapters.

Table 9.1: Description of Figure 9.8

End points	Branch description
d,3	upward arc
3,C	vertical line
C,2	downward arc
2,C	horizontal line
a,B	right diagonal line
B,E	vertical line
E,h	left diagonal line
E,i	right diagonal line
B,1	downward arc
1,F	vertical line
F,G	too small a branch†
F,j	left diagonal line
F,k	right diagonal line

†Point G is considered identical to F.

We do not present an explicit algorithm for obtaining such descriptions because the exact implementation of the traversal can be done in a number of different ways, depending on the application.

9.8 BIBLIOGRAPHICAL NOTES

The medial axis transformation was first proposed in [9.BL]. [9.MO] describes a solution on the analog plane by approximating boundaries with polygons, and then solving systems of linear equations for the loci of equidistant points. The classical thinning algorithm is essentially one proposed originally in [9.SR], and further developed in [9.TA]. Other early work includes [9.HI], [9.PF], [9.RO], and [9.RP]. The connection between specific patterns of neighborhoods and multiplicity of traversal is shown in [9.YTF]. Sequential algorithms that thin sets by peeling off boundary pixels are described in [9.ACL] and [9.PA]. (Such algorithms have the advantage that they are faster to implement on the usual general purpose sequential computers than parallel algorithms.)

Examples of simple structural descriptions can be found in [9.BE], [6.GR], [9.HTW], and [9.NAM]. [6.GR] uses the LAG for a decomposition procedure. The method described in [9.NAM] performs, in effect, an analysis of the LAG in order to find the skeleton. [9.BE] describes a direct thinning algorithm and uses it for numeral recognition. It is interesting to note that although structural descriptions were proposed quite early (as far back as 1959), they have found limited use in practice. The most likely reason is that they tend to have more extensive computational requirements than purely heuristic techniques. As the price of computing decreases, though, one expects their implementation to become inexpensive. Therefore, they should be kept in mind as potential candidates in any system design. See [3.PA], [7.FU1], [7.FU2] for more on structural techniques.

9.9 RELEVANT LITERATURE

[9.ACL] Arcelli, C.; Cordella, L. P.; and Levialdi, S. "From Local Maxima to Connected Skeletons," *IEEE Trans. Pattern Analysis Machine Intelligence,* **PAMI-3** (1981), pp. 134-143.

[9.BE] Beun, M. "A flexible method for automatic reading of handwritten numerals," *Philips Technical Review,* **33** (1973), Part I: pp. 89-101. Part II: pp. 130-137.

[9.BL] Blum, H. "A Transformation for Extracting New Descriptions of Shape," *Symposium on Models for the Perception of Speech and Visual Form,* M.I.T. Press, 1964.

[9.HI] Hilditch, C. J. "Linear Skeletons from Square Cupboards," *Machine Intelligence,* **4** (1969), pp. 403-420.

[9.HTW] Hattich, W.; Tropf, M.; and Winkler, G. "Combination of statistical and syntactical pattern recognition - applied to classification of unconstrained handwritten numerals," *Proc. Fourth Intern. Joint Conf. on Pattern Recognition,* Kyoto, November 1978, pp. 786-788.

[9.MO] Montanari, U. "Continuous Skeletons from Digitized Images," *JACM,* **16** (1969), pp. 534-549.

[9.NAM] Naito, S.; Arakawa, H.; and Masuda, I. "Recognition of hand-printed alphanumerics and symbols based on centroid lines," *Proc. Fourth Intern. Joint Conf. on Pattern Recognition,* Kyoto, November 1978, pp. 797-801.

[9.PA] Pavlidis, T. "A Thinning Algorithm for Discrete Binary Images," *CGIP,* **13** (1980), pp. 142-157.

[9.PF] Pfaltz, J. L. and Rosenfeld, A. "Computer Representation of Planar Regions by Their Skeletons," *CACM,* **10** (1972) pp. 119-125.

[9.RO] Rosenfeld, A. "A Characterization of Parallel Thinning Algorithms," *Information and Control,* **29** (1975), pp. 286-291.

[9.RP] Rosenfeld, A. and Pfaltz, J. L. "Sequential Operations in Digital Picture Processing," *JACM,* **13** (1966), pp. 471-494.

[9.SR] Stefanelli, R. and Rosenfeld, A. "Some Parallel Thinning Algorithms for Digital Pictures," *JACM,* **18** (1971), pp. 255-264.

[9.TA]   Tamura, H. "A Comparison of Line Thinning Algorithms from Digital Geometry Viewpoint," *Proc. Fourth Intern. Joint Conf. on Pattern Recognition,* Kyoto, November 1978, pp. 715-719.

[9.YTF]   Yokoi, S.; Toriwaki, J. I.; and Fukumura, T. "An Analysis of Topological Properties of Digitized Binary Pictures Using Local Features," *CGIP,* **4** (1975), pp. 63-73.

9.10 PROBLEMS

9.1.   Write a program implementing Algorithm 9.1.

9.2.   Complete the proof of Proposition 9.2.

9.3.   Is it possible to reduce the number of labels used in Algorithm 9.3? In particular, can we dispense with the use of the label "3" for skeletal pixels?

9.4.   Write a program implementing Algorithm 9.3.

9.5.   Design an algorithm for reconstructing thick regions from skeletons produced by Algorithm 9.3. Use the following rule: starting with the higher labels, for all pixels having a given label convert all of their zero neighbors to pixels with label one less and then replace the original label by 1. Repeat until all nonzero pixels have label one. Compare the results when you label only the direct neighbors with the results when all eight neighbors are labeled. The following example shows the sequence of transformations for a simple figure under the direct neighborhood rule.

```
       thin           ->            expand
---1----------3--------6------------6
----11---------22------6------------66
----111-------212------7-----------666
----1111------2212------7-----------666
------11--------22------------------6
```

(Recall that Algorithm 9.3 adds 5 to the iteration label.)

9.6.   If you are familiar with an assembly language use it to write a program for finding the strings bdr_k and for checking the bit patterns listed in Proposition 9.2 and Algorithm 9.3. Include the shift operation to check the form of patterns rotated by 90°.

Chapter 10

CURVE FITTING AND CURVE DISPLAYING

10.1 INTRODUCTION

In Section 7.6 we discussed how one can define a curve on a discrete grid, and in Section 9.7 we discussed how to derive curves from skeletons. The representation of a curve as a sequence of pixels may be adequate for some applications, but for others we would like to have a mathematical expression for it. Such an expression may be far more compact than the discrete forms, as a comparison between Figure 9.8 and Table 9.1 shows. Finding a curve that passes through a set of given points is the problem of *interpolation,* while finding a curve that passes near a set of given points is the problem of *approximation.* We shall use the term *curve fitting* to refer collectively to both of them. The problem of *curve displaying* is also of interest: given a mathematical expression, identify the pixels that must be marked so that an image of the curve described by the expression is displayed. The problem is by no means trivial, even in the case of straight line displays (Section 7.6).

Often, the two problems occur in a combined form. The set of points that must be fitted by a curve is not dense, as in the example of Figure 9.9, but sparse. Then we must connect these points with curves and display them on a grid where there are many more pixels on the curve than in the original set of points.

Curve fitting problems occur in design and manufacturing, as well

215

as in graphics, image processing, and pattern recognition. For example, the surface of the body of a car may be specified by a set of discrete points determined by engineering and styling considerations. In order to use computer controlled tools, we need a mathematical description of a smooth surface passing through all these points. This is one of the earliest major uses of graphics in industry. Another application involves the representation of experimental data, for display purposes or for automatic pattern recognition. In the pattern recognition case, the mathematical description of the contour of an object may provide information about the class to which the object belongs. The exact requirements for the curves or surfaces depend on the application, but the solution of all such problems depends on a common methodology that will be the subject of this and the next three chapters.

From a mathematical viewpoint, interpolation problems are probably easier to solve, but approximation may be more realistic in many applications, where the exact values of the data are subject to corruption by noise. A compromise between the two is to select a set of guiding points, which can be defined interactively by the user, and then to pass a curve (or surface) near these points. We shall emphasize such techniques in this text. The satisfactory display of curves requires the solution of some difficult problems in discrete geometry, but *ad hoc* solutions are common, with mixed qualitative results.

Choosing the form of the mathematical functions for curve fitting is often a critical question. Although polynomials come to mind first, they are usually poor choices. The most popular techniques use piecewise polynomial functions of various types. For approximations, one must also be concerned with choosing a criterion for the quality of approximation. Specification of a maximum distance of the points from the curve or surface seems a reasonable choice, but it often requires solving difficult computational problems. In general, one must compromise between what is intuitively desirable and what is computationally feasible.

We start with polynomial curve fitting. Piecewise polynomial curve fitting will be discussed in the next two chapters. The emphasis there will be on B-splines and polygonal approximations, while in this chapter we shall focus on Bezier polynomials. We will cover some techniques for surface fitting in Chapter 13.

The efficient display of curves requires that the displayed points be generated at a low level, usually by the hardware of the display device. This limits the number of curve classes that can be displayed efficiently. The two most common types are straight lines and circular arcs. (When there is no fear of confusion we shall refer to them as lines and arcs respectively.) These seem to be sufficient for many applications because is possible to display more complex curves through them. We shall discuss their display problems in Section 10.7.

10.2 POLYNOMIAL INTERPOLATION

Let $(x_1,y_1),(x_2,y_2), \cdots (x_n,y_n)$ be a sequence of points on the plane with $x_i \neq x_j$ for $i \neq j$. One can immediately obtain the formula for an interpolating polynomial of $(n-1)^{th}$ degree

$$p_n(x) = y_1 \frac{(x-x_2) \cdots (x-x_n)}{(x_1-x_2) \cdots (x_1-x_n)} + y_2 \frac{(x-x_1)(x-x_3) \cdots (x-x_n)}{(x_2-x_1)(x_2-x_3) \cdots (x_2-x_n)}$$

$$+ \cdots + y_n \frac{(x-x_1) \cdots (x-x_{n-1})}{(x_n-x_1) \cdots (x_n-x_{n-1})} \tag{10.1}$$

or, in more concise fashion,

$$p_n(x) = \sum_{i=1}^{n} y_i \prod_{j \neq i} \frac{(x-x_j)}{(x_i-x_j)} \tag{10.1'}$$

We can see that y_i is multiplied by a fraction that equals one when $x = x_i$ but is zero when x takes another value from among the given coordinates. For the special case $n = 2$ we find the equation of a line joining two points:

$$p_2(x) = y_1 \frac{x-x_2}{x_1-x_2} + y_2 \frac{x-x_1}{x_2-x_1} \tag{10.2}$$

A major disadvantage of polynomial interpolation is that the curve may oscillate significantly between the given points. An example illustrates the problem.

Example 10.1:   The following five points are given: (0,0), (1,3), (2,0), (3,0), and (4,0). The interpolating polynomial is

$$p(x) = -\frac{1}{2}x(x-2)(x-3)(x-4) \tag{10.3}$$

and is shown in Figure 10.1a. It has three extrema, approximately at (0.67,3.46), (2.46,−0.47), and (3.5,0.66). One might have liked the polynomial to be near zero on the interval [2,4] and have a maximum at, or be symmetrical around, $x = 1$, but it has neither property. □

The reason for this behavior of interpolating polynomials is that a polynomial is a sum of powers of x. Such functions have the property that their value over the whole interval is determined by their value over an arbitrarily small subinterval. While we try to manipulate the coefficients so that the sum takes the desired values at a few points, the value of the terms at other points is beyond our control. Since each term may be quite large, it is not surprising to have large deviations. Thus, there is no way to force a zero value throughout the subinterval [2,4] in Example 10.1. It may be instructive at this point to look at a piecewise polynomial interpolation.

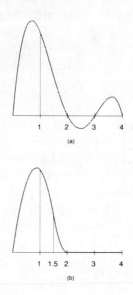

Figure 10.1 Comparison of: (a) polynomial, and (b) piecewise polynomial interpolations

Example 10.2: The same five points are interpolated by a piecewise quadratic polynomial. An intermediate point at $(1.5, 1.35)$ is introduced and the following solution is found:

$$
\begin{array}{llll}
p_a(x) & = & 6x(0.6-0.7x) & 0 \leq x \leq 1.5 & (10.4a) \\
p_b(x) & = & 5.4(x-2)^2 & 1.5 \leq x \leq 2 & (10.4b) \\
p_c(x) & = & 0 & 2 \leq x \leq 4 & (10.4c)
\end{array}
$$

Methods for the selection of the intermediate point are discussed in Section 12.4. Here we observe that the approximation is continuous and has a continuous first derivative, so that the smooth plot of Figure

10.1b is obtained. Although there is no symmetry around $x = 1$ there is symmetry around $x = 0.857$, and the value of the function there is 3.09. (Exact symmetry could have been achieved by using four intervals: [0, 0.5], [0.5, 1.5], etc.) □

These examples illustrate that polynomial interpolation is useful only over relatively small intervals. It deserves attention only because it is used as a basis for more appropriate forms of curve fitting. However, one should not conclude that piecewise polynomial interpolation is always better than polynomial interpolation. If the domain of the data is not subdivided properly, then any advantages of the piecewise approximation can be completely lost.

Sometimes, in addition to a set of points, one is also given the tangent that the curve passing through them must have at each one. The expression for the interpolating polynomial in this case is rather cumbersome, and it is omitted from this text. The reader can find it in texts on advanced calculus or numerical analysis. Here we list only the formula when two points and their tangents are given: (x_1, y_1, y'_1) and (x_2, y_2, y'_2).

$$p(x) = \left[y'_1 - \frac{y_1 - y_2}{x_1 - x_2} \right] \frac{(x-x_2)^2(x-x_1)}{(x_1-x_2)^2} +$$

$$\left[y'_2 - \frac{y_1 - y_2}{x_1 - x_2} \right] \frac{(x-x_1)^2(x-x_2)}{(x_1-x_2)^2} +$$

$$y_1 \frac{x-x_2}{x_1-x_2} + y_2 \frac{x-x_1}{x_2-x_1} \tag{10.5}$$

In general, this will be a cubic polynomial. It will be linear if, and only if, y'_1 and y'_2 equal the slope of the line between (x_1, y_1) and (x_2, y_2), and quadratic if and only if the average of y'_1 and y'_2 equals the same slope.

Example 10.3: The two points are $(0,0)$ and $(1,1)$ with slopes 0 and s respectively. Then

$$p(x) = (s-2)x^3 + (3-s)x^2 \tag{10.6}$$

Figure 10.2 illustrates two cases, for $s = 1$ and $s = 16$. The second interpolation is certainly unappealing. On the other hand, the following piecewise approximation produces a reasonable result for $s = 16$.

$$p_a(x) \quad = \quad 0 \qquad\qquad\qquad 0 \le x \le \frac{7}{8} \qquad (10.7a)$$

$$p_b(x) \quad = \quad 64(x - \frac{7}{8})^2 \qquad \frac{7}{8} \le x \le 1 \qquad (10.7b)$$

This is shown on Figure 10.2 with a broken line. $\square$

The example illustrates that the specification of tangents may result in very substantial oscillations because a polynomial has a constant derivative of some order (here, third because we have a cubic polynomial) and therefore it cannot make very sharp turns.

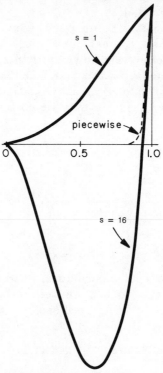

Figure 10.2 Polynomial and piecewise polynomial interpolations when the tangents at the endpoints are given. The broken line shows a piecewise approximation for $s = 16$.

10.3 BEZIER POLYNOMIALS

This class of polynomials has been used in interactive graphics to obtain approximate solutions to curve fitting problems. Instead of using the data points directly to specify a polynomial, a set of guiding points is specified interactively to achieve the desired form. The polynomials have the parametric form of Equation (10.8) rather than the explicit form $y = p(x)$.

$$x = p_x(t) \tag{10.8a}$$

$$y = p_y(t) \tag{10.8b}$$

If (x_0,y_0), (x_1,y_1), $\cdots (x_m,y_m)$ denote the guiding points, the corresponding Bezier polynomial is defined by

$$p_x(t) = \sum_{i=0}^{m} C_i^m t^i (1-t)^{m-i} x_i \tag{10.9a}$$

$$p_y(t) = \sum_{i=0}^{m} C_i^m t^i (1-t)^{m-i} y_i \tag{10.9b}$$

where C_i^m denotes the number of combinations of m objects taken i at a time, and is given by:

$$C_i^m = \frac{m!}{i!(m-i)!} . \tag{10.10}$$

This expression is not convenient for computation, and C_i^m is best calculated from the following recursive formula:

$$C_i^m = C_i^{m-1} + C_{i-1}^{m-1} . \tag{10.10'}$$

It is often convenient to write Equations (10.9) in a vector form by defining:

$$\boldsymbol{P}(t) = \begin{bmatrix} p_x(t) \\ p_y(t) \end{bmatrix} \text{ and } \boldsymbol{P}_i = \begin{bmatrix} x_i \\ y_i \end{bmatrix} \tag{10.11}$$

so that

$$\boldsymbol{P}(t) = \sum_{i=0}^{m} C_i^m t^i (1-t)^{m-i} \boldsymbol{P}_i . \tag{10.12}$$

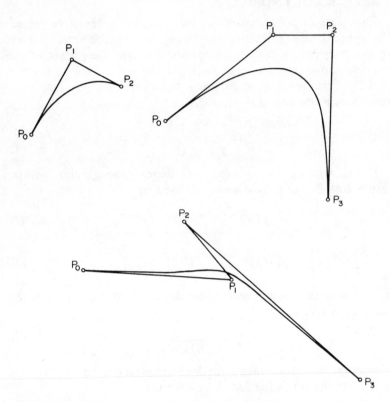

Figure 10.3   Examples of Bezier polynomials with three and four guiding points

Figure 10.3 shows one Bezier polynomial for $m = 2$ and two for $m = 3$. The last example demonstrates that the placement of the guiding points to achieve a given form is not at all obvious to the inexperienced person. This is a serious defect of the method. It seems that the main reason for its popularity is that computer programs implementing Bezier polynomials are far easier to write than programs for better techniques.

It is possible to use Equation (10.12) not only for two-dimensional vectors P (as defined by Equation (10.11)), but for vectors of any dimension. This can be convenient for the description of space curves. It is obvious from Equation (10.12) that

$$P(0) = P_0 \quad \text{and} \quad P(1) = P_m , \tag{10.13}$$

so the useful range of the parameter t is 0 to 1.

The derivative of $P(t)$ is

$$P'(t) = -m(1-t)^{m-1} P_0 +$$

$$\sum_{i=1}^{m-1} C_i^m [\, it^{i-1} (1-t)^{m-i} - (m-i)t^i (1-t)^{m-i-1} \,] P_i + mt^{m-1} P_m \; . \quad (10.14)$$

We observe that

$$P'(0) = m(P_1 - P_0) \quad \text{and} \quad P'(1) = m(P_m - P_{m-1}) \; , \quad (10.14')$$

so that a Taylor expansion near zero yields

$$P(t) = P(0) + tP'(0) + O(t^2) \approx P_0(1-mt) + mtP_1 \quad (10.15a)$$

and an expansion near one yields

$$P(t) = P(1) - (1-t)P'(1) + O((1-t)^{2)}$$

$$\approx P_m[1-m(1-t)] + m(1-t)P_{m-1} \quad (10.15b)$$

Thus for $t \to 0$ and $t \to 1$ the Bezier polynomial lies on the lines joining P_0 and P_1 and P_{m-1} and P_m, respectively, which means that these lines are tangents of the curve at P_0 and P_m. Furthermore, since

$$\sum_{i=0}^{m} C_i^m t^i (1-t)^{m-i} = (t+1-t)^m = 1$$

the Bezier polynomial lies inside the convex hull of the guiding points.

10.4 COMPUTATION OF BEZIER POLYNOMIALS

Next we derive a recursive relation for Bezier polynomials that also has a convenient graphical interpretation. We rewrite Equation (10.12) as

$$P(t) = (1-t)^m P_0 + \sum_{i=1}^{m-1} C_i^m t^i (1-t)^{m-i} P_i + t^m P_m \quad (10.16)$$

and then use Equation (10.10a) to split the sum into two terms, and find that

$$P(t) = (1-t)^m P_0 + \sum_{i=1}^{m-1} C_i^{m-1} t^i (1-t)^{m-i} P_i +$$

$$\sum_{i=1}^{m-1} C_{i-1}^{m-1} t^i (1-t)^{m-i} P_i + t^m P_m$$

or

$$P(t) = (1-t)[(1-t)^{m-1}P_0 + \sum_{i=1}^{m-1} C_i^{m-1} t^i (1-t)^{m-1-i}P_i] +$$

$$t[\sum_{i=1}^{m-1} C_{i-1}^{m-1} t^{i-1}(1-t)^{m-i}P_i + t^{m-1}P_m] . \qquad (10.17)$$

We observe that the terms inside the first pair of brackets form the Bezier polynomial for the points P_0, P_1, $\cdots P_{m-1}$, while those inside the second pair form the polynomial for P_1, P_2, $\cdots P_m$. If we introduce the notation $P_{kl}(t)$ to denote the Bezier polynomial for P_k, P_{k+1}, $\cdots P_l$, then Equation (10.17) can be rewritten as

$$P_{0m}(t) = (1-t)P_{0,m-1}(t) + tP_{1m}(t) \qquad (10.18a)$$

or

$$P_{0m}(t) = P_{0,m-1}(t) + t[P_{1m}(t) - P_{0,m-1}(t)] . \qquad (10.18b)$$

In other words, a Bezier polynomial can be found from two other such polynomials by joining corresponding points (i.e., for the same t) with a line and dividing that line in proportion to t. Since this procedure can be used to derive the first two polynomials, we arrive at Algorithm 10.1.

Algorithm 10.1 Geometric Algorithm for Bezier Polynomials

Notation: At each iteration R_i are the old guiding points and Q_i the new guiding points.

1.   **For** each value of t from 0 to 1 by Δt **do:**
        Begin.
2.   **For** i from 0 to m set $R_i = P_i$.
3.   Set $n = m$.
4.   **While** $n > 0$ **do:**
            Begin.
5.   **For** i from 0 to $n-1$ set $Q_i = R_i + t(R_{i+1} - R_i)$.
6.   Decrement n by one.
7.   **For** $i = 0$ to n set $R_i = Q_i$.
            End.
8. $P(t) = R_0$.
        End.
9.   **End of Algorithm.**

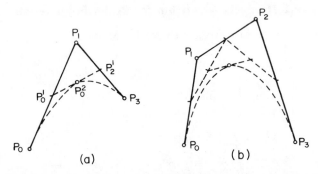

Figure 10.4 Geometric construction of Bezier polynomials for $t = 0.5$. Each new set of guiding points is defined as the midpoints of the sides of the polygon formed by the previous set. When we are down to only one guiding point, then we have a curve point.

This algorithm can also be implemented graphically because the operation of step 5 is equivalent to selecting a point on the line segment joining R_i and R_{i+1} at a distance from R_i equal to a fraction t of the length of that line segment. Thus, if t equals m/n, the segment is divided into n parts and the new guiding point is at the end of the mth such part after the old guiding point. Figure 10.4 illustrates the geometric construction for $m = 3$ and $m = 4$ for $t = 1/2$. Because all the vectors are two-dimensional, step 5 requires $6n$ scalar operations: one addition, one subtraction, and one multiplication per component. Then the whole algorithm requires

$$\sum_{n=1}^{m} (6n) = 3m(m+1) \qquad (10.19)$$

operations for each value of t, without any preprocessing, or use of intermediate storage. Using Equation (10.12) while keeping tables for t^i and $(1-t)^{m-i}$, plus having the values of the binomial coefficients available, requires $m(m+5)$ scalar operations.

An even faster algorithm can be found by rewriting Equation (10.12) as

$$P(t) = (1-t)^m \sum_{i=0}^{m} C_i^m \left[\frac{t}{1-t}\right]^i P_i \qquad (10.20a)$$

or

$$P(t) = (1-t)^m \left\{ \frac{t}{1-t} \left[\sum_{i=1}^{m} C_i^m \left(\frac{t}{1-t}\right)^{i-1} P_i \right] + P_0 \right\} \qquad (10.20b)$$

Algorithm 10.2 Horner's Algorithm for Bezier Polynomials.

1.   **For** each value of t from 0 to 0.5 by Δt **do:**
      Begin.
2.   Evaluate $(1-t)^m$.
3. $Q_0 = P_m$.
4.   **For** $i = 1$ to m **do:**
          Begin.
5.
$$Q_i = \frac{t}{1-t}\, Q_{i-1} + C^m_{m-i}\, P_{m-i}$$
          End.
6. $P(t) = (1-t)^m\, Q_m$.
      End.
7.   **For** each value of t from 0.5 to 1 by Δt **do:**
      Begin.
8.   Evaluate t^m.
9. $Q_0 = P_0$.
10.   **For** $i = 1$ to m **do:**
          Begin.
11.
$$Q_i = \frac{1-t}{t}\, Q_{i-1} + C^m_i\, P_i$$
          End.
12. $P(t) = t^m\, Q_m$
      End.
13.   **End of Algorithm.**

Finding the value of $P(t)$ from the term in brackets of Equation (10.20b), assuming that the values of $(1-t)^m$, $t/(1-t)$, and the binomial coefficients are available, requires eight scalar operations. A similar computation is required for the evaluation of each polynomial in the brackets so that the total effort is $8m+m = 9m$, where the second term in the sum is for the calculation of $(1-t)^m$. This is actually Horner's algorithm for Bezier polynomials. For small values of m ($m<5$) the geometric algorithm is more convenient because of its small overhead, but for larger values, Horner's is preferable. In the interest of accuracy, it is best to use a dual of Equation (10.20) to calculate values for t greater than 0.5. Then the multiplier $t/(1-t)$ will always be less than 1. This process is listed as Algorithm 10.2.

It is possible to follow the guiding points more closely by using more than one at each location. Figure 10.5 shows the effect for the example of Figure 10.4a. It can be seen that the extra multiplicity of the middle point affects the results mostly locally. An analytical demonstration of this trend can be made on the basis of Equation (10.14). The term in brackets is the derivative with respect to t of the coefficient of P_i in Equation (10.12). A simple calculation shows that the derivative is zero for $t = t_i \equiv i/m$, so that the coefficient of P_i is maximum for $t = t_i$. One can also verify that the value of the coefficient drops fast toward zero for t different than t_i. Therefore, for any given t there only a few guiding points that affect the shape of the curve: those for which t_i is near the given t. Increasing the multiplicity of a point increases the interval of values of t where that point is dominant in determining the shape of the curve.

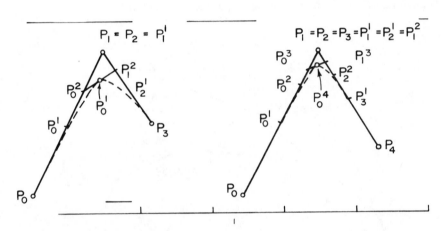

Figure 10.5 Geometric construction of Bezier polynomials with multiple guiding points

Intuitively, one can think of a Bezier polynomial as a magnetized elastic band attached to the first and last point, with magnets placed at all other points. The band is then attracted toward each point, and the stronger the intensity of the magnet there (i.e., the higher its multiplicity), the closer it will move toward that particular point. If the multiplicity tends to infinity, then the Bezier polynomial tends to the polygonal arc formed by the guiding points.

10.5 SOME PROPERTIES OF BEZIER POLYNOMIALS

A curve generated by a Bezier polynomial has the interesting property that any segment of it can also be generated by some Bezier polynomial [10.BE]. This feature turns out to be useful in the definition of surfaces (see Chapter 13) and we shall state and prove formally one special case. There a new set of guiding points is derived recursively from the original ones by replacing a pair of points by their midpoint. If k is the number of the iteration, then we define

$$P_i^0 = P_i \tag{10.21a}$$

and we have the following relation for generating additional guiding points.

$$P_0^k = P_0 \quad k \geq 1 \tag{10.21b}$$

$$P_i^k = \frac{1}{2}\left[P_{i-1}^{k-1} + P_i^{k-1}\right] \quad k \geq 1, i \geq 1 \tag{10.21c}$$

Figure (10.6) illustrates how such points are distributed.

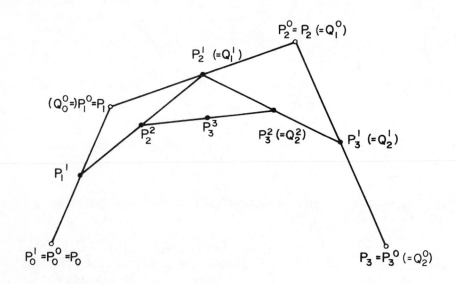

Figure 10.6   Arrangement of the additional guiding points for a Bezier polynomial

Next, we state and prove a theorem that defines how the additional guiding points are used. In this way we can find a closer delineation of the form of the curve, as shown in the example of Figure 10.6. There the initial definition contains only two guiding points in addition to the two endpoints. As a result of Theorem 10.1, the curve can be drawn with five guiding points in addition to the endpoints.

Theorem 10.1: For $0 \leq t \leq 0.5$, the values of $P(t)$ are given by the values of a Bezier polynomial $P_a(s)$ $(0 \leq s \leq 1)$ with guiding points P_0^0, $\cdots$,P_i^i, $\cdots$,P_m^m. For the range $0.5 \leq t \leq 1$, the values of $P(t)$ are the values of a Bezier polynomial $P_b(s)$ $(0 \leq s \leq 1)$ with guiding points P_0^m, $\cdots$,P_i^{m-i}, $\cdots$,P_m^0.

Proof: The proof is by induction and it is based on Equation (10.18a) repeated here.

$$P_{0m}(t) = (1-t)P_{0,m-1}(t) + tP_{1m}(t) .$$

This equation can be rewritten in the following two ways:

$$P_{0m}(t) = (1-2t)P_{0,m-1}(t) + 2t\left[\frac{P_{0,m-1}(t) + P_{1m}(t)}{2}\right], \qquad (10.22a)$$

and

$$P_{0m}(t) = 2(1-t)\left[\frac{P_{0,m-1}(t) + P_{1m}(t)}{2}\right] + (2t-1)P_{1m}(t) . \qquad (10.22b)$$

If we set $m = 1$, then we observe that $P_{00}(t) = P_0$ and $P_{11}(t) = P_1$. Substituting from Equation (10.21), we find that for $m = 1$

$$P(t) = (1-2t)P_0^0 + 2tP_1^1 , \qquad (10.23a)$$

and

$$P(t) = [1-(2t-1)]P_1^1 + (2t-1)P_1^0 . \qquad (10.23b)$$

Substituting $s = 2t$ in Equation (10.23a), we see that the values of $P(t)$ for $0 \leq t \leq 0.5$ are given by the right hand side for $0 \leq s \leq 1$ which is then a Bezier polynomial with guiding points P_0^0 and P_1^1. Similarly, the substitution $s = 2t-1$ in Equation (10.23b) shows that the right hand side is a Bezier polynomial with guiding points P_1^1 and P_1^0, and that while s varies from 0 to 1 it gives the values of $P(t)$ for t varying from 0.5 to 1. Therefore, the theorem is proven for $m = 1$.

For the general induction step assume that the theorem is valid for $m-1$. Then we can write

$$P_{0,m-1}(t) = \sum_{i=0}^{m-1} P_i^i C_i^{m-1} s^i (1-s)^{m-1-i} \qquad s \equiv 2t \qquad (10.24a)$$

and

$$P_{1,m}(t) = \sum_{i=0}^{m-1} Q_i^i C_i^{m-1} s^i (1-s)^{m-1-i} \qquad (10.24b)$$

for the proper points Q_i^i. It can be easily verified that

$$Q_i^i = P_{i+1}^i \qquad (10.25)$$

and therefore

$$\frac{1}{2}\left\{P_i^i + Q_i^i\right\} = P_{i+1}^{i+1} \qquad (10.26)$$

Substituting Equations (10.24) into Equation (10.22a) yields

$$P_{0m}(t) = \sum_{i=0}^{m-1} P_i^i C_i^{m-1} s^i (1-s)^{m-i} +$$

$$\sum_{i=0}^{m-1} \frac{P_i^i + Q_i^i}{2} C_i^{m-1} s^{i+1} (1-s)^{m-1-i} \qquad (10.27)$$

Because of Equation (10.26), the second term equals

$$\sum_{i=0}^{m-1} P_{i+1}^{i+1} C_i^{m-1} s^{i+1} (1-s)^{m-(i+1)} .$$

This can also be written as

$$\sum_{i=1}^{m} P_i^i C_{i-1}^{m-1} s^i (1-s)^{m-i} ,$$

so that the terms in Equation (10.27) can be rearranged to yield

$$P_{0m}(t) = P_0^0 C_0^{m-1} (1-s)^m +$$

$$\sum_{i=1}^{m-1} P_i^i \left[C_i^{m-1} + C_{i-1}^{m-1}\right] s^i (1-s)^{m-i} + P_m^m C_{m-1}^{m-1} s^m \qquad (10.28)$$

The binomial coefficients in the first and last term equal one, while their sum in the second term equals C_i^m because of Equation (10.10a). Therefore we obtain an expression identical to Equation (10.24a), except that $m-1$ has been replaced by m. This completes the proof for $0 \le t \le 0.5$. The proof for $0.5 \le t \le 1$ is left as an exercise. $\Box$

10.6 CIRCULAR ARCS

We now turn our attention to certain display problems. We shall discuss questions that arise because of the discrete nature of the data in the next section. Here we present a special problem that occurs often in graphics applications: finding a circular arc of a given radius r that joins two given points, P_1 with coordinates (x_1, y_1), and P_2 with coordinates (x_2, y_2). To this end we must find the coordinates of the center and then select the proper arc from among four possible solutions. We start this computation by first determining the coordinates of the midpoint P_m of the line L joining the two endpoints.

$$x_m = \frac{x_1 + x_2}{2} \tag{10.29a}$$

$$y_m = \frac{y_1 + y_2}{2} \tag{10.29b}$$

Let the half differences in coordinates be denoted by

$$x_{12} = \frac{x_1 - x_2}{2} \qquad y_{12} = \frac{y_1 - y_2}{2} \tag{10.30}$$

The center lies on the normal to L passing through its midpoint. If x_{12} is zero (the line L is vertical), then the center of the circle has y coordinate

$$y_c = y_m \tag{10.31a}$$

and the following two possible values for x_c.

$$x_c = x_m \pm \sqrt{r^2 - y_{12}^2} \tag{10.31b}$$

If L is not vertical then we must do some more work. First, we compute the slope of the line L,

$$u = \tan\phi = \frac{y_{12}}{x_{12}} \tag{10.32}$$

(see Figure 10.7), and second, we compute the square of distance d between the center and the midpoint

$$d^2 = r^2 - (x_{12}^2 + y_{12}^2) \tag{10.33}$$

If d^2 negative, then the radius given is too short, and the diameter of the circle is less than the distance between the points. If it is zero, the center coincides with the midpoint. Otherwise we have two possible sets of values for the center

$$x_c = x_m \pm \frac{du}{\sqrt{1 + u^2}} \tag{10.34a}$$

$$y_c = y_m \mp \frac{d}{\sqrt{1 + u^2}} \tag{10.34b}$$

The expressions involving u are the sine and cosine of the angle ψ shown in Figure 10.7. (Recall the trigonometric identities giving the sine and cosine of an angle in terms of the tangent.) Equations (10.34) require computing more square roots than necessary. If we substitute d from Equation (10.33), and u from Equation (10.32) we obtain

$$x_c = x_m \pm y_{12} \sqrt{\frac{r^2}{x_{12}^2 + y_{12}^2} - 1} \qquad (10.35a)$$

$$y_c = y_m \mp x_{12} \sqrt{\frac{r^2}{x_{12}^2 + y_{12}^2} - 1} \qquad (10.35b)$$

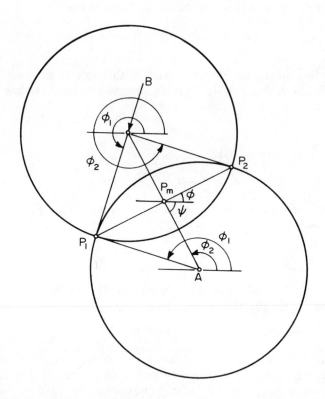

Figure 10.7   Illustration of the construction for finding a circular arc joining two points with a given radius. *AB* is the line segment *L* referred to in the text.

Figure 10.7 illustrates the two center locations. For each center we also have two possible arcs, so that, in general, the problem of joining two points with an arc of a given radius has four solutions. Even if we specify a direction, clockwise or counterclockwise, we are still left with two solutions. Usually one wishes to choose the shorter arc of the two. (Of course, if *d* is zero both arcs have the same length.) If we define

$$x_{1c} = x_1 - x_c \qquad y_{1c} = y_1 - y_c \qquad (10.36a)$$

$$x_{2c} = x_2 - x_c \qquad y_{2c} = y_2 - y_c \qquad (10.36b)$$

we can compute the angle with the x-axis formed by the line joining each point and the center. (See Figure 10.7 for notation.)

$$\phi_1 = \arctan(y_{1c}, x_{1c}) \qquad (10.37a)$$

$$\phi_2 = \arctan(y_{2c}, x_{2c}) \qquad (10.37b)$$

where the function arctan returns an angle between 0 and 2π. If the difference $\Delta\phi = \phi_1 - \phi_2$ is positive (as it is in Figure 10.7 for the lower location of the center, "A"), then a clockwise arc from the first point to the second point has length $r\Delta\phi$. If the difference is negative (as when we choose the top location for the center in Figure 10.7, "B"), then a counterclockwise arc has length $-r\Delta\phi$. These formulas allow the selection of the shortest arc with a given orientation.

Sometimes we have available a third point P_3, and wish to select the arc that passes closest to that point. If (x_3, y_3) are its coordinates, then we can calculate its distance from both centers, and select the center whose distance is the most nearly equal to the radius. If P_3 lies to the same side of the line $P_1 P_2$ as the center of the chosen circle, then we must select the larger of the two arcs, otherwise we select the smaller. This decision can be made by computing the projection of the line segment $P_3 P_c$ on the line L. (P_c denotes the center of the circle: either "A" or "B" in Figure 10.7.) The following lemma is easily proven by a simple geometrical calculation:

Lemma 10.1: Let K, L, and M be three points on the plane. Let $(KL)_x$ denote the signed difference of the x coordinate of K minus the x coordinate of L. $(KL)_y$, $(ML)_x$, etc. are defined similarly. Then the length of the projection of the segment KL on the segment ML equals $(KL)_x(ML)_x + (KL)_y(ML)_y$ divided by the length of ML. $\square$

The lemma can be applied directly in our case by taking P_3 for K, the center of the selected circle for L, and the other center for M. Because we are comparing the projection with half the length of the distance between the centers, the division by the length may be omitted (see Problem 10.10).

Example 10.4: We want to draw an arc of radius 10 from the origin $(0,0)$ to the point $(5,5)$, passing near the point $(3,4)$. We find $x_m = y_m = 2.5$, $u = 1$, and

$$d^2 = 100 - \frac{50}{4} = 87.5$$

or $d = 9.354$. Equations (10.34) then yield the following values

$$x_c = 2.5 \pm \frac{9.354}{\sqrt{2}}$$

$$y_c = 2.5 \mp \frac{9.354}{\sqrt{2}}$$

or two candidates for the center of the arc: (8.115,−4.115) and (−4.115,8.115). The distance of the third point from the first candidate is 9.59 while the distance from the second candidate is 8.76. The first value is closer to the radius 10, and therefore we select (8.115,−4.115) as the center. Using Equation (10.36) we find

$$x_{1c} = -8.115 \qquad\qquad y_{1c} = 4.115$$

$$x_{2c} = -3.115 \qquad\qquad y_{2c} = 9.115$$

and from a table of trigonometric functions (or any scientific calculator) we find that $\phi_1 = 2.67rad$ and $\phi_2 = 1.90rad$ so that the length of the clockwise arc is $(2.67 - 1.90) \times 10 = 7.7$. Clearly, the clockwise arc is shorter than the counterclockwise since the circle has a circumference of 31.4. The numerator of the expression given in Lemma 1 is found to be $(3 - 8.115) \cdot (-4.115 - 8.115) + (4 + 4.115) \cdot (8.115 + 4.115)$ which equals $12.23 \cdot (8.115 - 5.115)$ or 36.69. This is less than twice d^2, therefore we must select the larger of the two arcs. Thus the arc must be drawn clockwise. ☐

10.7 DISPLAY OF LINES AND CURVES

In general, a mathematical curve on the plane can be given in one of two forms: parametric representation

$$x = X(t) \qquad y = Y(t) \tag{10.38}$$

or expression

$$f(x,y) = 0 \tag{10.39}$$

The former is usually more convenient for producing a display: t is evaluated for a series of values $t_1, \cdots, t_i, \cdots, t_n$ and the pixels with the rounded values of $X(t_i)$ and $Y(t_i)$ as coordinates are displayed. The actual display may consist of single pixels, or lines joining them. A critical choice is the number of points to be displayed. If they are chosen too far apart, then the curve will have the appearance of a dotted line (if only points are displayed), or a polygon (if the points are joined with lines). Choosing them too close together may result not only in excessive computation but also in a curve that appears too thick in parts. If $X'(t)$ and $Y'(t)$ are the derivatives with respect to t of

$X(t)$ and $Y(t)$, then the distance d between points for values of t Δt units apart is given approximately by

$$d = \Delta t \sqrt{X'(t)^2 + Y'(t)^2} \tag{10.40}$$

Thus the value Δt should be chosen differently in different parts of the curve. Unfortunately, it is not always easy to evaluate Equation (10.40). For example, in the case of Bezier polynomials one must substitute in it the terms from Equation (10.14). When the points are joined by lines we want to avoid sharp angles and this depends on the curvature. The curvature is inversely proportional to d so that an altogether different spacing strategy may be required. Clearly, displaying a smooth curve through a set of points requires more than just finding the mathematical equation of such a curve.

Example 10.5: We want to display the parabola

$$x = t \qquad y = t^2$$

We calculate first the distance between a pair of points as a function of t. We have:

$$\Delta x = x_{i+1} - x_i = t_{i+1} - t_i = \Delta t$$
$$\Delta y = y_{i+1} - y_i = t_{i+1}^2 - t_i^2$$

Then the distance d_i will be

$$d_i = \sqrt{(\Delta x)^2 + (\Delta y)^2} = \Delta t \sqrt{1 + (t_{i+1} + t_i)^2}$$

i.e., it is an increasing function of t. Note that $t_i + t_{i+1}$ equals $y'(t)$ at some intermediate point. If we are going to plot points only, then Δt should be chosen inversely proportional to t. □

10.7.1 Display of Curves through Differential Equations

The form $f(x,y) = 0$ can be handled similarly to the parametric if we can solve with respect to one of the variables. Another approach is based on the differentiation of Equation (10.39). Since $f(x,y)$ is constant, its total differential will be zero, so that we have

$$\frac{\partial f}{\partial x}dx + \frac{\partial f}{\partial y}dy = 0 \tag{10.41}$$

We introduce the notation

$$F_x(x,y) = \frac{\partial f}{\partial x} \qquad F_y(x,y) = \frac{\partial f}{\partial y}$$

to obtain

$$\frac{dy}{dx} = -\frac{F_x(x,y)}{F_y(x,y)} \qquad (10.42)$$

This is a differential equation which has the desired curve as a solution. It was a common method of producing curve displays in analog devices because many such equations can be simulated by relatively simple electronic circuits. A discrete approximation of the equation can be written as

$$x_{k+1} - x_k = \qquad -cF_y(x_k,y_k) \qquad (10.43a)$$
$$y_{k+1} - y_k = \qquad cF_x(x_k,y_k) \qquad (10.43b)$$

where c is an arbitrary constant. If we start at (x_0,y_0), then we can find the remaining points from Equation (10.43). Clearly, the size of c determines the density of the points found. We have the same problems as in the case of plotting a curve given in the form of Equation (10.38). There is, though, a significant new difficulty here. Because Equation (10.43) is only an approximation to Equation (10.42) there is a possibility that the resulting curve may diverge significantly from what is desired. A complete discussion of this point involves questions of numerical stability and is beyond the scope of this text (see Bibliographical Notes). The following example illustrated the problem and a remedy in a simple case.

Example 10.6: The equation of a circle of radius r with center at the origin is

$$x^2 + y^2 = r^2$$

so that here Equations (10.43) become

$$x_{k+1} = x_k - 2cy_k \qquad (10.44a)$$

$$y_{k+1} = y_k + 2cx_k \qquad (10.44b)$$

If we wish to have $y_0 = r$ and $x_0 = 0$ then we can show that the above difference equations have as a solution

$$x_k = r(\sqrt{1 + 4c^2})^k \sin(k\phi) \qquad (10.45a)$$

$$y_k = r(\sqrt{1 + 4c^2})^k \cos(k\phi) \qquad (10.45b)$$

where ϕ is an angle whose tangent equals $2c$.† We observe that both x

---

† Readers unfamiliar with the theory of difference equations can substitute Equations (10.45) into Equations (10.44) and verify that both sides have the same value. In the process they should use the fact that the expression $\sqrt{1 + 4c^2}$ equals $1/\cos\phi$.

and y are proportional to a power of a number greater than one, namely the square root of $1 + 4c^2$. Therefore, their values will increase without bound as k increases and the resulting curve will be an outward spiral rather than a circle, certainly not a desirable result. Let us now select a number b with the property that

$$b^2 + 4c^2 = 1$$

and replace Equations (10.44) by

$$x_{k+1} = bx_k - 2cy_k \tag{10.46a}$$

$$y_{k+1} = by_k + 2cx_k \tag{10.46b}$$

The selection of such a parameter will be possible if c is less than $1/2$. Then the solution becomes

$$x_k = r\sin(k\phi) \tag{10.47a}$$

$$y_k = r\cos(k\phi) \tag{10.47a}$$

while ϕ is now an angle with tangent $2c/b$. Clearly, the points given by Equations (10.47) lie on a circle, and the arc between successive points equals $r\phi$. $\square$

The selection of the value of c must be made so that the points are sufficiently close. In the previous example the critical factor is the ratio $2c/\sqrt{1 - 4c^2}$.

10.7.2 Effect of Round-off Errors in Displays

The selection of the proper sampling step of the curve is not the only problem in producing a good display. The detailed structure of the display of the curve is also affected by the round-off error in the values of $X(t)$ and $Y(t)$. Indeed, all displays have a finite resolution and must select the pixel with coordinates closest to the computed values and display that point rather than one whose coordinates are exactly $X(t), Y(t)$ (or x_k, y_k if the method of the previous subsection is used.) Some of the problems were discussed in Section 7.6 on the definition of straight lines on a grid. Suppose that we want to display the straight line from a point (x_1, y_1) to another, (x_2, y_2). The points of the line are defined by Equation (10.2), and we may use that equation to find the values of y for different values of x.

Example 10.7: Let $x_1 = y_1 = 0$ and $x_2 = 40$, $y_2 = 17$. Then Equation (10.2) becomes

$$y = \frac{17}{40}x$$

If we roundoff to the nearest integer we obtain the following table

Table 10.1: Comparison of Exact and Rounded-off Coordinates

x	1	2	3	4	5	6	7 $\cdots$
exact y	0.425	0.85	1.275	1.7	2.125	2.55	2.975 $\cdots$
rounded y	0	1	1	2	2	3	3 $\cdots$

that yields an i-connected path. If the slope is greater than one then we should use y as the independent variable. $\square$

This example shows that the line resulting from the truncated y has a staircase appearance that can be aesthetically unappealing. We mentioned in Section 7.6 that if C is a point on the line between A and B, the displayed line between A and C may not be part of the line AB, as demonstrated in Example 7.1. If we have a display device with gray scale, then we may choose not to display all the points at the same brightness. At points where the exact and truncated values are close, for example for $x = 2$, 5, 7, etc., a single pixel is displayed at full brightness. For other points two pixels are displayed at a reduced brightness. Then the resulting line appears smoother. The same technique can be used for the display of arbitrary curves. A complete discussion of such methods is beyond the scope of this text (see Bibliographical Notes). The reader should also keep in mind that there are many applications, such as phototypesetting, where the display must be bilevel.

Further difficulties may arise when display calculations are done in display processors. Because these processors usually have only low-precision integer arithmetic, the mathematical coefficients of a curve may have to be rounded so severely that curves may not even pass through points known to be on them.

Example 10.8: We want to join the point (0,0) to the point (17,11) with an arc of a circle whose center is on the x-axis. The equation of the circle has the form

$$x^2 - 2x_c x + y^2 = 0$$

and we find easily that $2x_c = 410/17 = 24.1176 \cdots$. This is rounded to 24 so that we must use the following equation for plotting

$$F(x,y) = x^2 - 24x + y^2 = 0$$

We find that $F(17,11) = 2$ so that the endpoint does not belong to the curve. $\square$

Having the endpoint outside the curve may not be too bad if the point is included in the displayed pixels but this depends entirely on the precise rule used for plotting (see Problem 10.9). Therefore, one should not use an equality check for deciding when to stop drawing a curve, unless a careful analysis shows that this will not cause problems. Alternative termination criteria check for equality of one of the coordinates only, and then test if the other differs by less than one. (Unfortunately, certain commercial implementations of conic drawing routines use equality checks and keep producing pixels of a curve as long it does not pass through the given endpoint.)

10.8 A POINT EDITOR

Curve fitting in computer graphics requires the specification of a set of parameters so that the curve computed from them has the desired shape. It is often quite difficult to select the proper values of these parameters in advance and the need for interactive design arises. In the case of Bezier polynomials we must have means to enter a set of guiding points, and compute and display the polynomial. If the form of the result is not acceptable, we should be able to modify the location of the guiding points, to insert new ones, or to delete some. A basic tool for such operations is an interactive graphics editor. We shall use the term point editor (as distinct from a text or a picture editor) to describe such a facility. A point editor can be used for a number of other things besides curve fitting. Its appearance in this chapter does not imply that specification of Bezier polynomials is its major application.

There are two important considerations in the design of a point editor: the data structure used for the storage of the points and the means of entering and addressing (pointing to) points.

10.8.1 A Data Structure for a Point Editor

The simplest possible structure is a two-dimensional array of the (x,y) coordinates of the points. However, this makes insertion and deletion of points very cumbersome. It is best to use a linked list. The list elements consist of four entries: x coordinate, y coordinate, address of previous element on the list, (p), and address of next element on the list, (n). This could be implemented as four one-dimensional arrays with the array index used as an address.

Example 10.9: Suppose we start with the points (5,8), (11,22), and (14,18). Then the list entries will be:

$$(5,8,0,2), (11,22,1,3), (14,18,2,0).$$

0 denotes a pointer to a nonexisting element, and thus marks the first and last points of the list (see Figure 10.8a). If we insert the point (9,10) between the first and the second, then the list will be:

$$(5,8,0,4), (11,22,4,3), (14,18,2,0), (9,10,1,2).$$

(Figure 10.8b.) Deleting the last point of the sequence (third on the list) will result in

$$(5,8,0,4), (11,22,4,0), (14,18,3,3), (9,10,1,2).$$

(Figure 10.8c) where we have used self-pointing for the deleted point. Interchanging the second and last points produces the following:

$$(5,8,0,2), (11,22,1,4), (14,18,3,3), (9,10,2,0).$$

(Figure 10.8d.)

□

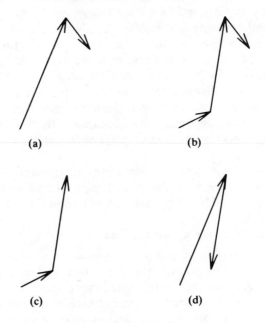

Figure 10.8   Point arrangement used in Example 10.9

An even better way of implementing the linked list is offered by array structures and pointers. Conceptually the manipulation of the data is the same as shown above, but it introduces a simpler notation when describing the algorithm. We define the structure *point* as follows:

$$struct\ point\ =\ \{x,y,p,n\}$$

PLATES

PLATES

TABLE OF CONTENTS

Plate 1

Figure 2.3 Digital image with 256×256 samples and 256 gray levels

Plate 2   Graphics and Image Processing

Figure 2.4   Digital image with 64x64 samples, reconstructed on a large display

Figure 2.5   Digital image with 32x32 samples, reconstructed on a large display

Figure 2.9   A copy of Figure 2.3 quantized in 8 levels (three bits)

Figure 2.10   A copy of Figure 2.3 quantized at four levels (two bits)

Plate 4   **Graphics and Image Processing**

Figure 2.11   Dithered version of Figure 2.9

Figure 2.12   Dithered version of Figure 2.10

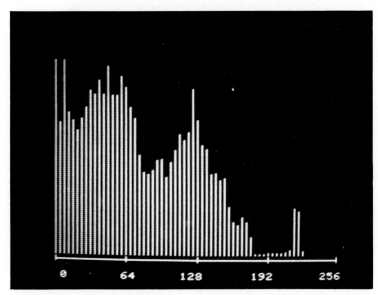

Figure 3.3 An image and the corresponding histogram that shows that not all brightness levels are used effectively

Plate 6   Graphics and Image Processing

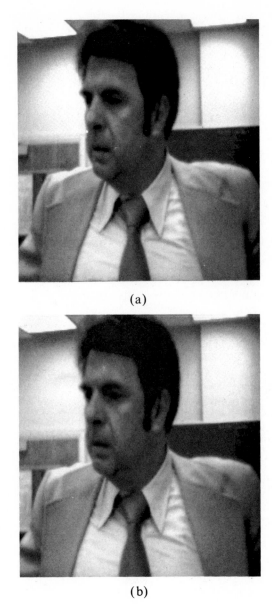

(a)

(b)

Figure 3.4   Results of histogram equalization for the original of Figure 3.3. The image at the top was produced by Rule 1 and that at the bottom by Rule 2.

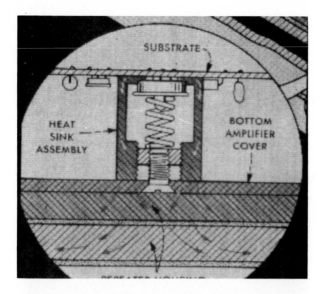

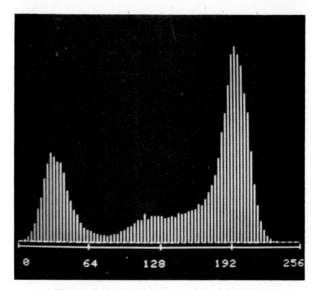

Figure 3.5 An image and its histogram

Plate 8　　　　　　　　　　　**Graphics and Image Processing**

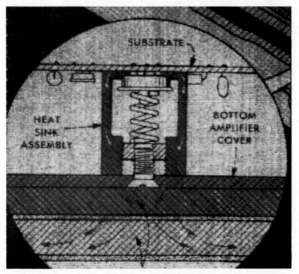

Figure 3.6　Deterioration in the appearance of a picture because of histogram equalization

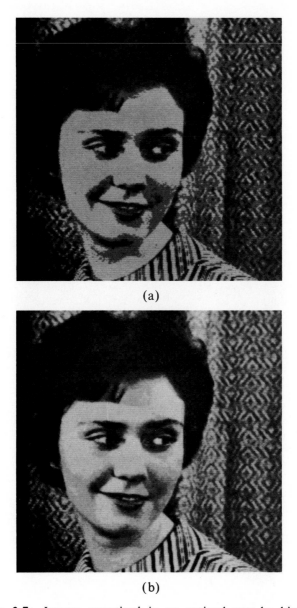

(a)

(b)

Figure 3.7   Images quantized in an optimal way by histogram equalization: (a) with four levels, and (b) with eight levels. The appearance is clearly superior to that obtained with the uniform quantization shown in Figures 2.9 and 2.10.

Plate 10   Graphics and Image Processing

Figure 3.9   Original of the image used for illustrating the effects of filtering in Figure 3.10

(a)

(b)

Figure 3.10   (a) A noisy image and (b) the effect of linear filtering on it

Plate 12   **Graphics and Image Processing**

(a)

(b)

Figure 3.11   Effects of a directional low-pass filter on the original of Figure 3.10a: (a) one pass, (b) three passes.

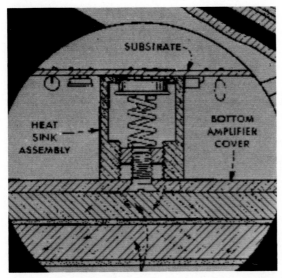

Figure 4.1 Thresholded image for $T = 100$ of the original of Figure 3.5

Plate 14   Graphics and Image Processing

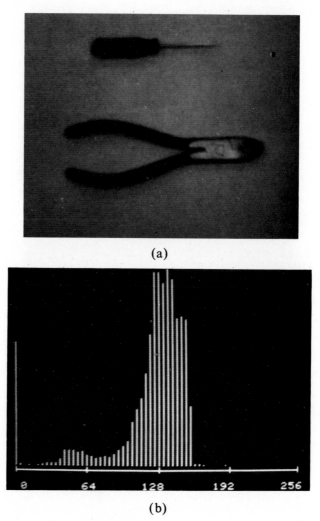

(a)

(b)

Figure 4.2 (a) Original image (256×256 pixels); (b) gray level histogram.

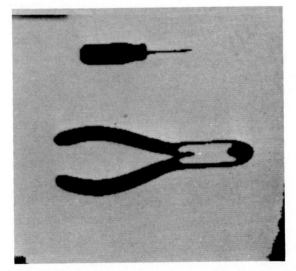

Figure 4.3   Results of thresholding for $T = 100$ for the original of
Figure 4.2a

Plate 16   **Graphics and Image Processing**

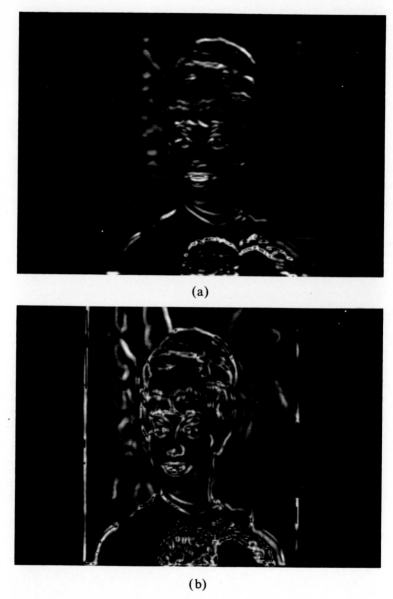

(a)

(b)

Figure 4.4   (a) Horizontal gradient image, (b) edges found from both the vertical and the horizontal gradient.

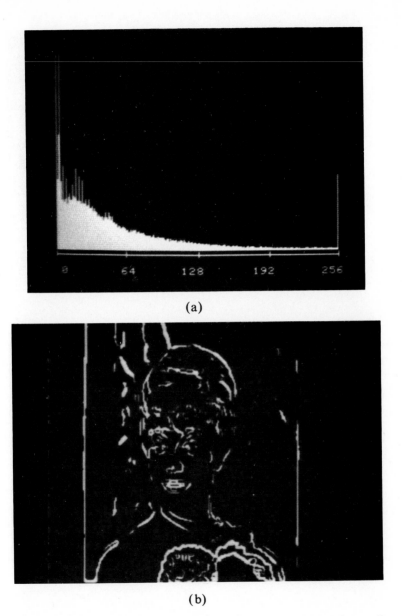

(a)

(b)

Figure 4.5 (a) Histogram of Figure 4.4b, (b) thresholded form of
Figure 4.4b for $T = 128$.

Plate 18   Graphics and Image Processing

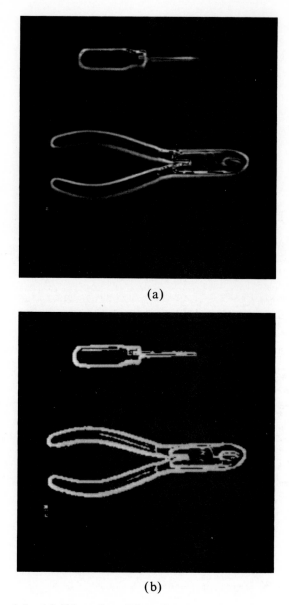

(a)

(b)

Figure 4.6   (a) Edges found from both the vertical and horizontal gradients for the original of Figure 4.2a, (b) thresholded form of (a) for $T = 64$.

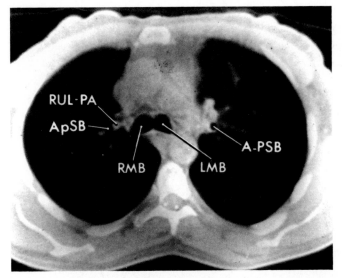

Figure 5.1 Reconstruction of a cross-section of a human body at upper chest level showing details of the bronchi. The label RUL-PA points to a pulmonary artery. The other labels identify bronchi. (From Naidich, D. P.; Terry, P. B.; Stitik, F.P.; and Siegelman, S. S. "Computed Tomography of the Bronchi: 1. Normal Anatomy" *Journal of Computer Assisted Tomography,* **4** (1980), pp. 746-753.) *(Courtesy S. S. Siegelman. Copyright © 1980 Raven Press)*

Plate 20   **Graphics and Image Processing**

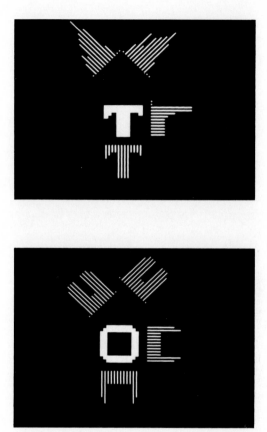

Figure 5.7 Binary matrices representing printed characters surrounded by the respective projections found by Algorithm 5.2

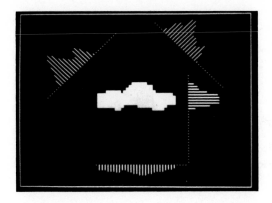

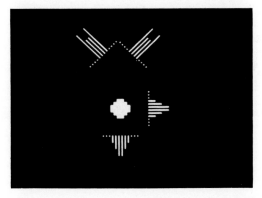

Figure 5.8 Binary matrices representing the outline of a car and a circular disk surrounded by the respective projections found by Algorithm 5.2

Plate 22   Graphics and Image Processing

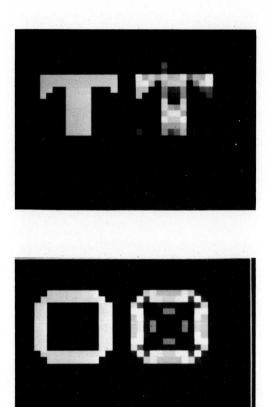

Figure 5.9   Reconstruction of the examples of Figure 5.7 using filtered backprojections

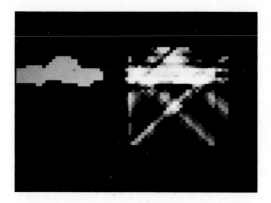

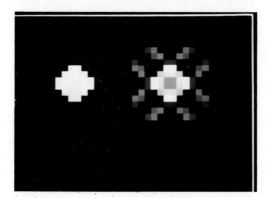

Figure 5.10   Reconstruction of the examples of Figure 5.8 using filtered backprojections

Plate 24   Graphics and Image Processing

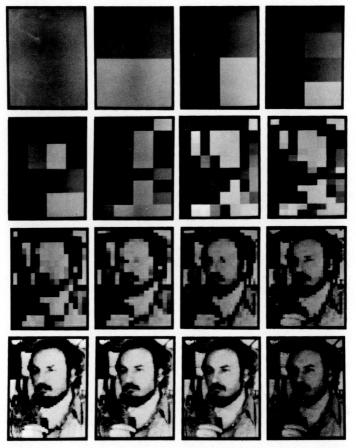

Figure 6.8 Sequence of images produced by successive transmission of elements of the binary tree. (From Knowlton, K. "Progressive Transmission of Grey Scale and B/W Pictures by Simple, Efficient and Lossless Encoding Schemes," *IEEE Proceedings,* **68** (1980), pp. 885-896.)
(Courtesy of K. Knowlton. Copyright © 1980 IEEE)

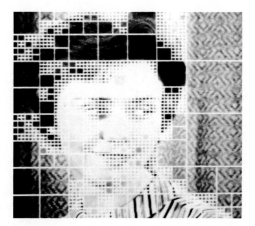

Figure 6.9   Use of a quad tree in a split-and-merge algorithm.
The uniformity criterion was based on an evaluation of the co-
occurrence matrix. The boundaries of the squares are overlaid on
the original image. Initially, the image was divided into 64 squares.
Some of them have been merged while others have been split.

Plate 26   **Graphics and Image Processing**

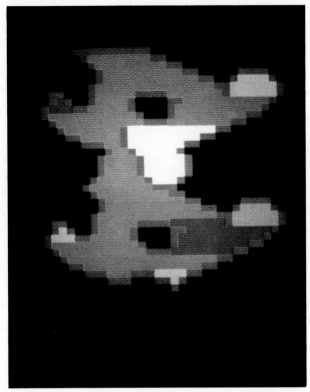

Figure 8.12 Sequence in which different parts of the interior are filled. The parity check preprocessor finds a seed near the left top of the interior. Filling proceeds on the basis of connectivity. Each gray level corresponds to one popping from the stack.

Figure 13.4 Shading of a sphere using the technique of Example
13.7. Left, a matte sphere ($g/d = 1/10$) and right, a glossy sphere
($g/d = 10/1$).

Plate 28   **Graphics and Image Processing**

Figure 17.1 The use of shading and reflection produce a realistic scene from a description consisting of 36 bicubic patches in addition to a number of polygons. (From "A 3-Dimensional Representation for fast Rendering of Complex Scenes" by S. M. Rubin and T. Whitted, in *SIGGRAPH'80*, pp. 110-116.)
(Courtesy of Turner Whitted. Copyright © 1980 ACM)

Figure 17.2 The use of shading, hidden surface elimination, and perspective projection create a scene that is difficult to distinguish from a painting. The objects of the scene were described by 32,000 polygons. (From "A Software Test-Bed for the Development of 3-D raster Graphics Systems" by T. Whitted and D. M. Weimer, in *SIGGRAPH'81*, pp. 271-277.)
(Courtesy of David M. Weimer. Copyright © 1981 ACM)

(We assume that the reader is familiar with structures and pointers that are used in many programming languages.) The points of the curve would be stored in an array consisting of such structures. We shall use the value 0 as before (pointing to nowhere) and the value L to denote the first available free location in memory. The symbol q will denote the pointer to the current location.† Thus, to draw a line between the current point and the one before it we can use the following commands (see Section 1.7, Table 1.2):

$$setp((q{-}{>}p){-}{>}x,(q{-}{>}p){-}{>}y)$$
$$vec(q{-}{>}x,q{-}{>}y)$$

The first command sets the current point of the plotter to the point previous to the one pointed by q. The second command draws the vector between the two points.

Example 10.10: The following sequence will add a point to the list, with the user indicating both the place of insertion and the location of the new point.

1.   *readp*(x_1,y_1)(User indicates a point on the screen)
2.   Find q such that the pair $(q{-}{>}x,q{-}{>}y)$ is closest to (x_1,y_1).
3. $q_n = q{-}{>}n$ (Save address of old "next point")
4. $q{-}{>}n = L$ (New "next point" will be in first free location)
5.   Prompt user
6.   *readp*(x_2,y_2)(Point to a second location on the screen)
7. $L{-}{>}x = x_2$ $L{-}{>}y = y_2$ (Add point to list)
8. $L{-}{>}p = q$ $L{-}{>}n = q_n$ (Link)
9. $q_n{-}{>}prev = L$ (Update link of old "next point")
10. Increment L (Update address of first free location)

□

For many applications it is important to be able to deal with groups of points, such as arcs. This can be accomplished by the introduction of a hierarchical data structure. A curve could be represented by a pointer to an array of its points, etc.

It is best to write programs implementing point editors in a device independent manner. In particular, the main program should be concerned only with addresses (pairs of x-y coordinates), commands (using a generic name), and, of course, file names. All device dependent procedures should be separate and clearly identified as such. (See the next subsection for more on this topic.) The following list of

---

† The notation $q{-}{>}u$ denotes the object of the structure array u pointed to by the pointer q.

commands is typical. Each command requires either a set of points (their number is shown in parentheses in the list), or a file name (if the letter f appears inside the parentheses). The bold letters denote command abbreviations.

plot(0)   Plot available data from the list.

bezier(0)   Plot a Bezier polynomial using the elements of the list as guiding points.

append(0)   Add points to the end of the list, or create a new list if the current list is empty.

insert(1)   Insert points before the one addressed.

delete(1)   Delete point from the list.

repeat(1)   Insert a new point in the list with coordinates identical to the one addressed. This command can be used to increase the multiplicity of guiding points.

move(2)   Move addressed point to the location of the second address.

write(f)   Write contents of the list on named file.

read(f)   Read contents of file into the list.

The *insert* and *append* commands assume that the user supplies a sequence of points which are added to the list. A special *escape* command is also needed to indicate when the process is finished.

10.8.2 Input and Output for a Point Editor

The *readp*(x,y) function described in Section 1.7 (Table 1.2) can provide the editor with point coordinates. However, there is more to be done before one can select a command or an address. Some pointing devices contain keys (buttons) that allow the user to transmit one or more characters in addition to the point coordinates. If the number of characters is large enough, then they can be used to encode commands. If this is not the case, then one may use a *menu*: an area of the screen is set aside and subdivided into regions that are labeled with the name of a command. When the x-y values received by the program fall within one of these area the corresponding command is selected.

A second problem is to select from the list a point that is nearest to the indicated point. (This is the case when the user wants to select one of the existing points). A naive solution is to search for the minimum of the Euclidean distance between the given point and those of the list. A more efficient way is to maintain an auxiliary data structure where points are sorted according to their locations.

Algorithm 10.3 presents a minimal point editor. It assumes that, in addition to the graphics routines of Table 1.2, the following routines are also available:

command(x,y,c) which returns a string c containing a subroutine name or a null string if (x,y) does not point to any command.

place(x,y,q) which locates the point of the list nearest to (x,y). q is the pointer value for the location found.

Algorithm 10.3 Point Editor

1. **Repeat** (indefinitely!) steps 2 to 5.
   Begin.
2.   *readp* (x,y).
3.   Call *command* (x,y,c).
4.   **If** c is null or if subroutine c requires an address **then** call *place* (x,y,q).
5.   Call c.
   End.
6. **End of Algorithm.**

Algorithm 10.3 assumes that a *quit* command is available in order to exit from the loop. The values of x and y returned in step 2 should be pushed into a stack for possible later use.

10.9 BIBLIOGRAPHICAL NOTES

Most textbooks on numerical analysis describe techniques for polynomial interpolation (e.g. [10.IK]). There are also books devoted entirely to the subject (e.g. [10.DA]). An extensive mathematical treatment is given in [10.RI]. Bezier polynomials are named after a French mathematician who developed them for the Renault car manufacturer [10.BE]. These are discussed in many of the texts dealing with graphics, although little attention is paid (usually) to presenting reasonable algorithms for their computation. Theorem 10.1 was taken from [10.LR], while the more general segmentation property can be found in [10.BE]. The formulas for circular arcs are based on simple analytical geometry and have been included here because of wide interest in their use.

The section on displays could have been much longer because the actual plotting of curves on a discrete grid is a truly challenging problem. The reader is referred to [10.BR] and [10.KU] for additional information on displays of arcs and to [2.GS], [2.KU], [10.CR], and [10.WA] for the use of gray scale to improve the appearance of vector displays in raster graphics.

The questions of numerical stability are treated in most numerical analysis texts. In particular, the problems of divergence caused by discrete approximations can be studied with the methods presented in texts on the numerical solution of differential equations and books on difference equations (e.g.[10.LL]).

The point editor described in this chapter is quite modest and most graphics installations offer far more. A recent review of the question of editing can be found in [10.CG].

10.10 RELEVANT LITERATURE

[10.BE]   Bezier, P. *Numerical Control*, New York: J. Wiley, 1972. (Transl. from the French by A. R. Forrest and A. F. Pankhurst.)

[10.BR]   Bresenham, J. "A Linear Algorithm for Incremental Display of Circular Arcs," *CACM*, **20** (1977), pp. 100-106.

[10.CG]   Coueignoux, P. and Guedj, R. "Computer Generation of Colored Planar Patterns on TV-Like Rasters," *IEEE Proceedings*, **68** (1980), pp. 909-922.

[10.CR]   Crow, F. C. "The Use of Grayscale for Improved Raster Display of Vectors and Characters" *SIGGRAPH'78*, pp. 1-5.

[10.DA]   Davis, P. J. *Interpolation and Approximation*, New York: Random House, Blaisdell, 1963.

[10.IK]   Isaacson, E. and Keller, H. B. *Analysis of Numerical Methods*, New York: J. Wiley, 1966.

[10.KU]   Kulpa, Z. "On the Properties of Discrete Circles, Rings, and Disks" *CGIP*, **10** (1979), pp. 348-365.

[10.LL]   Levy, H. and Lessman, F. *Finite Difference Equations*, New York: Macmillan, 1961.

[10.LR]   Lane, J. M. and Riesenfeld, R. F. "A Theoretical Development for the Computer Generation and Display of Piecewise Polynomial Surfaces," *IEEE Trans. on Pattern Analysis and Machine Intelligence*, **PAMI-2** (1980), pp. 35-46.

[10.RI]   Rice, J. R., *The Approximation of Functions*, vols. 1 and 2, Reading, Mass.: Addison-Wesley, 1965 and 1969.

[10.WA]   Warnock, J. F. "The Display of Characters Using Gray Level Sample Arrays," *SIGGRAPH'80*, pp. 302-307.

10.11 PROBLEMS

10.1. We wish to pass a smooth curve through a set of points $\{x_i, y_i\}$

on the plane. The following solution is proposed. Consider the points as the vertices of a polygon and for each i find the bisectrix of the angle at that vertex. Take the normal to the bisectrix passing through the vertex as the desired tangent of the curve at that point and use Equation (10.5) to define a cubic arc joining each pair of points.

(a) Let Nx_i denote the difference $x_i - x_{i-1}$ divided by the length of the vector from (x_{i-1}, y_{i-1}) to (x_i, y_i), and let Ny_i denote the similar difference for y. Then show that the equation of the normal to the bisectrix at (x_i, y_i) is:

$$(Nx_{i+1} - Nx_i)(x - x_i) + (Ny_{i+1} - Ny_i)(y - y_i) = 0$$

(b) Use the above expression in Equation (10.5) to derive an explicit form for the cubic arc. Do this both for the form $y = f(x)$, and for the parametric representation $x = x(t)$ and $y = y(t)$ where $0 \le t \le 1$.

(c) Examine the advantages and disadvantages of each form and derive a condition on the form of the polygon so that the smooth curve given by the parametric representation does not cross itself.

10.2. Prove Equation (10.10a).

10.3. Write a program implementing Algorithm 10.1.

10.4. Write a program implementing Algorithm 10.2 and compare its running time to that of the program written for the previous exercise. Plot these times as functions of m. How do the observed times compare with the theoretical predictions? To what do you attribute the discrepancy?

10.5. Prove the second part of Theorem 10.1 (for $0.5 \le t \le 1$).

10.6. Write a simple editor incorporating a command for plotting a Bezier polynomial as one of its options. (You can use either of the above implementations for that purpose.) Pick up a set of points that form the contour of some physical object and try to generate a Bezier polynomial that will pass near these points. This requires interactive design since the selection of the guiding points is not at all obvious. Thus the editor is an essential part of the project. (*Note:* Try to arrange the program so that you may add other features to it in the future.)

10.7. Compare the number of bits required for storing the coefficients

of the Bezier polynomial approximating the contour of an object
with the number of bits required for storing the differential chain
code of the same contour. Repeat for a few examples. Can you
draw any general conclusions?

10.8. Given the parametric description of a curve, $X(t)$, $Y(t)$, and a
number N, establish a procedure to choose the density of sample
points on the interval $[0,1]$ so that a display of the curve by vectors joining N sample points is as smooth as possible.

10.9. We wish to display the function ax^n on a raster graphics device.
Because a is not an integer and we want to do the computation
with integer arithmetic only, we decide to plot bx^n where b
denotes the integer closest to a. We assume that both a and b
exceed 1, and so does n. In order to have a continuous plot we
must turn on more than one pixel for each value of x. Can you
find a rule for doing this so that the rounded-off value of ax^n is
always on such a pixel? If you think that this is impossible, provide a formal proof for your assertion.

10.10. Write a program to draw a straight line between a pair of points
without using a graphics command. Repeat for a circle.

10.11. Show that the circle defined by the noncollinear points (x_1,y_1),
(x_2,y_2), and (x_3,y_3) has a center (xc,yc) given by

$$x_c = \frac{C_1(y_2-y_3) - C_2(y_1-y_2)}{(x_1-x_2)(y_2-y_3) - (x_2-x_3)(y_1-y_2)} \qquad (10.48a)$$

$$y_c = \frac{C_2(x_1-x_2) - C_1(x_2-x_3)}{(x_1-x_2)(y_2-y_3) - (x_2-x_3)(y_1-y_2)} \qquad (10.48b)$$

where

$$C_1 = (x_1-x_2)(x_1+x_2) + (y_1-y_2)(y_1+y_2)$$

and

$$C_2 = (x_2-x_3)(x_2+x_3) + (y_2-y_3)(y_2+y_3) \ .$$

Show that the denominator of Equations (10.48) will be zero
unless the three points are not collinear.

Chapter 11

CURVE FITTING WITH SPLINES

11.1 INTRODUCTION

In many applications where curve fitting is used, one would like to modify parts of the curve without affecting other parts. We shall say that a scheme has a local property if local modifications do not propagate. Clearly, the polynomials discussed in Section 10.2 do not have this feature and Bezier polynomials exhibit it only approximately. A change in the location or multiplicity of one of the guiding points requires the recalculation of the whole curve, even though the changes will have little effect far from the changed guiding point. Piecewise polynomial functions offer a direct way of achieving local control. We shall discuss such functions first in the $y = y(x)$ form and later in parametric representations. The following is a general expression for a piecewise polynomial function:

$$p(x) = p_i(x) \qquad x_i \le x \le x_{i+1} \qquad i = 0, 1, \cdots, k-1 \quad (11.1a)$$

$$p_i^{(j)}(x_i) = p_{i-1}^{(j)}(x_i) \quad j = 0, 1, \cdots, r-1; \quad i = 1, \cdots, k-1 \quad (11.1b)$$

The points $x_1, \cdots, x_{k-1}$ that divide an interval $[a,b]$ into k subintervals are usually called breakpoints. The points of the curve at these values of x are usually called knots. The notation $x_0 = a$ and $x_k = b$ is used for convenience. The functions $p_i(x)$ are polynomials of degree m or less. The continuity constraints at the breakpoints are expressed by the second set of equations where $p_i^{(0)}(x)$ stands for $p_i(x)$, and $p_i^{(j)}$ $(j>0)$ for the jth derivative of $p(x)$. Sometimes we shall use the value $r = 0$ to denote the absence of any constraints. When $r = 1$ we have a continuous function but without any constraints on its derivatives. If $r = m+1$, then we have a single polynomial over $[a,b]$ so that $r = m$ is the maximum number of constraints that yields a nontrivial piecewise polynomial function. The case with $m = 3$ and $r = 3$ has a special historical as well as practical significance and the corresponding piecewise polynomial functions are the ones for which the term splines was first used.

Section 11.2 is an introduction to splines and Section 11.3 to B-splines. Sections 11.4 and 11.5 deal with computational problems. Sections 11.6 and 11.7 show how splines can be used to advantage in graphics.

11.2 FUNDAMENTAL DEFINITIONS

The origin of the term spline goes back to the days before computer graphics, when draftsmen used to locate weights at the data points and then place a flexible wooden ruler, called a spline, against the weights, in order to obtain a smooth curve passing through the points. The weights had a protrusion sticking out that fitted into a slot of the spline and held it in place while allowing it to rotate around the fixed point. It is possible to use the theory of mechanical elasticity and prove that the resulting curve is (approximately) a piecewise cubic polynomial that is continuous and has continuous first and second derivatives. These conditions also assure that the curve has continuous curvature and the discontinuities occur only in the third derivative. Since it is very difficult for the human eye to distinguish the latter, the resulting curve appears completely smooth. If we direct a mechanical motion along a spline, a continuous second derivative implies continuous acceleration and therefore no abrupt changes in force. These two properties make such curves very desirable for many practical applications. However, there are cases where one may be satisfied with fewer continuity constraints or lower order polynomials and the term spline has been used to cover these cases as well. Actually, there is little agreement today on the use of the term. In this text we shall use the following terminology:

Definition 11.1: A *simple spline* is a piecewise polynomial function as given by Equations (11.1) with $r = m$. The terms linear spline, quadratic spline, and cubic spline correspond to the values of $m = 1, 2,$ and 3. $\square$

Definition 11.2: A *spline* is a piecewise polynomial function as given by Equations (11.1) with $r < m$. □

We may notice that the functions used in Example 10.2 (Figure 10.1b) and Example 10.3 (Figure 10.2) are quadratic splines while the curve of Problem 10.1 is a cubic spline (see also Problem 11.1). Clearly, one can have interpolating as well as approximating splines. In both cases it is important to evaluate the number of degrees of freedom that the curve has. Equations (11.1) show that we have $k(m+1)$ polynomial coefficients minus $(k-1)r$ constraints for a total of $k(m-r)+k+r$ degrees of freedom for a spline. For a simple spline where $m = r$ we have only $k + m$ degrees of freedom.

Most workers in this area agree that the most important problem in the successful use of splines is the choice of the number and location of the breakpoints. Readers can satisfy themselves of the importance of this question by looking at the examples of Section 10.2. It turns out that this is a far more difficult problem than finding an interpolating or approximating spline after the breakpoints have been defined, and we shall postpone discussing it in detail until the next chapter, while limiting ourselves here to some preliminary remarks. We notice that if we allow breakpoints to coalesce, i.e., have $x_i = x_{i+1}$, then the number of constraints is automatically reduced by one. If we have breakpoints with multiplicity $r+1$, then all constraints are eliminated. The introduction of multiple breakpoints in order to produce nonsimple splines has both theoretical and practical advantages and we shall present some of them later. Many authors also use the terms spline with simple knots and spline with multiple knots to denote simple splines and splines respectively. On the other hand, there exist problems for which it is more convenient to allow r to be different from m, and possibly different at each breakpoint.

Another major problem in the application of splines is the mathematical form used for the curve. Equation (11.1) contains too many parameters, and the use of the constraints to eliminate them results in rather complicated analysis. (It can be shown that the constraints are indeed linearly independent so that all of them are effective.) An alternate form is given by the following equation:

$$p(x) = p_1(x) + \sum_{i=1}^{k-1} q_i \, (x-x_1)_+^m. \tag{11.2}$$

where the function t_+^m stands for t^m when $t > 0$ and 0 when $t \le 0$. We note that t^m and its first $m-1$ derivatives are zero for $t = 0$ so that $p(x)$ and its first $m-1$ derivatives are continuous at all the breakpoints. The term q_i is proportional to the amount of discontinuity of the mth

derivative introduced at x_i and therefore the function defined by Equation (11.2) has the same properties as that given by Equations (11.1). for $r = m$. In particular,

$$p_j(x) = p_1(x) + \sum_{i=1}^{j} q_i \, (x-x_i)_+^m \, . \tag{11.3}$$

Equation (11.2) has only $(m+1) + (k-1) = m+k$ free parameters, the minimum number. Its form resembles that of a polynomial, and this makes it quite convenient for many theoretical studies. Unfortunately, it has certain serious defects. First, Equation (11.3) suggests that if we want to modify the function at a subinterval, i.e., change the value of q_i at its left endpoint, then the representation must be changed at all subsequent subintervals. On the other hand, Equation (11.1) shows that this need not be the case. For example, if $m = 1$, then the form of $p(x)$ must be changed in only two subintervals (see Figure 11.1a). Similarly, if $m = 2$, the number of subintervals need not exceed four. Indeed, in the example of Figure 11.1b, one could decide to keep the location and the tangents at knots A and E fixed so that the rest of the spline is insulated from the change. If the location (but not the tangents) of knots B and D is also kept the same, then the parabolic arcs forming the spline between A and B, and D and E are completely specified. Then for the spline with knots at B, C', and D we have as given the three knots, the two endpoint tangents, and the continuity constraint at C', for a total of six constraints, and there are also six degrees of freedom. Since the representations over each subinterval communicate with each other through the constraints at the breakpoints one expects that, in general, the number of subintervals affected should be proportional to the number of constraints. The following result, dealing with the introduction of a new breakpoint in the subinterval (x_i, x_{i+1}) presents an example of this observation in a rigorous manner.

Proposition 11.1:   If a new breakpoint is introduced in the subinterval (x_i, x_{i+1}), then the spline need be modified only over the subinterval (x_i, x_{i+m}).

Proof: Let u be the number of affected (original) subintervals. Matching the value of the spline and its first $m-1$ derivatives at x_i and x_{i+u} imposes $2m$ constraints. The total number of available subintervals is $u+1$ for a total of $m+u+1$ degrees of freedom. Therefore, $u = m-1$. $\square$

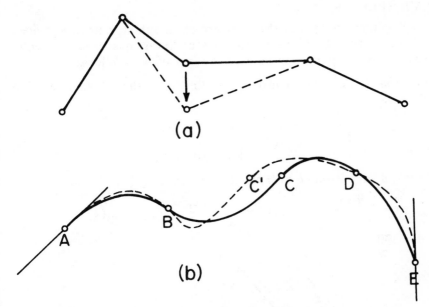

Figure 11.1 Illustration of the local nature of splines: (a) when $m = 1$ the change in the location of a knot requires re-evaluation of the spline only in the two adjacent subintervals. (b) when $m = 2$ there will be four affected subintervals.

For $m = 1$ we do not need to modify any other subinterval while for $m = 3$ the two subsequent subintervals may have to be changed. If the number of the subintervals is not affected but we introduce an additional constraint in one of them, a similar argument can be used to show that $u = m+1$. The reader may be puzzled why we have to modify only the subintervals after the change and not those before it. The answer to the puzzle becomes apparent if we distinguish between the changes in the curve itself and the changes in the representation of the curve. Thus Proposition 11.1 refers to a change in the representation of the curves.

A second disadvantage of Equation (11.2) is that it tends to make certain approximation problems numerically unstable. For these reasons, a third form of spline representation is used in many practical applications. Splines are expressed as sums of other splines, and in particular a special form called B-splines.

11.3 B-SPLINES

B-splines are splines that are zero at all subintervals except $m+1$ of them. Figure 11.2 shows examples of linear, quadratic, and cubic B-splines. Such splines can be defined recursively as follows:

Definition 11.3: The constant B-spline over the ith subinterval is defined as

$$N_{i,0}(x) = \begin{cases} 1 & x_i \le x \le x_{i+1} \\ 0 & \text{otherwise} \end{cases} \qquad (11.4)$$

The mth degree B-spline over the interval $[x_i, x_{i+m+1}]$ is defined as

$$N_{i,m}(x) = \frac{x - x_i}{x_{i+m} - x_i} N_{i,m-1}(x) + \frac{x_{i+m+1} - x}{x_{i+m+1} - x_{i+1}} N_{i+1,m-1}(x) \qquad (11.5)$$

□

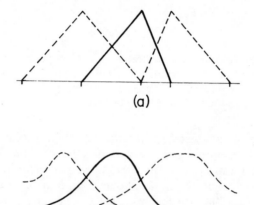

(a)

(b)

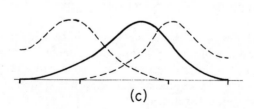

(c)

Figure 11.2 Examples of B-splines: (a) linear, (b) quadratic, (c) cubic

We can use Equations (11.4) and (11.5) to find explicit forms for the lower degree B-splines.

Linear

$$N_{i,1}(x) = \begin{cases} \dfrac{x - x_i}{x_{i+1} - x_i} & x_i \le x \le x_{i+1} \\[2mm] \dfrac{x_{i+2} - x}{x_{i+2} - x_{i+1}} & x_{i+1} \le x \le x_{i+2} \end{cases} \qquad (11.6)$$

Quadratic

$$N_{i,2}(x) = \frac{(x - x_i)^2}{(x_{i+2} - x_i)(x_{i+1} - x_i)} \qquad \text{for } x_i \le x \le x_{i+1} \quad (11.7a)$$

$$N_{i,2}(x) = \frac{(x - x_i)(x_{i+2} - x)}{(x_{i+2} - x_i)(x_{i+2} - x_{i+1})}$$
$$+ \frac{(x_{i+3} - x)(x - x_{i+1})}{(x_{i+3} - x_{i+1})(x_{i+2} - x_{i+1})} \qquad \text{for } x_{i+1} \le x \le x_{i+2} \quad (11.7b)$$

$$N_{i,2}(x) = \frac{(x_{i+3} - x)^2}{(x_{i+3} - x_{i+1})(x_{i+3} - x_{i+2})} \qquad \text{for } x_{i+2} \le x \le x_{i+3} \quad (11.7c)$$

When the breakpoints are equally spaced at intervals of length L, the above expressions are simplified significantly. In this case it is reasonable to assume that $x_i = iL$ and convenient to introduce the normalized variable

$$u = \frac{x - x_i}{L} = \frac{x}{L} - i \qquad (11.8)$$

Then the equations for the B-splines become

Uniform Linear

$$U_{i,1}((i+u)L) = \begin{cases} u & 0 \le u \le 1 \\ 2 - u & 1 \le u \le 2 \end{cases} \qquad (11.9)$$

Uniform Quadratic

$$U_{i,2}((i+u)L) = \frac{1}{2}u^2 \qquad \text{for } 0 \le u \le 1 \qquad (11.10a)$$

$$U_{i,2}((i+u)L) = \frac{3}{4} - (u - \frac{3}{2})^2 \qquad \text{for } 1 \le u \le 2 \qquad (11.10b)$$

$$U_{i,2}((i+u)L) = \frac{1}{2}(3 - u)^2 \qquad \text{for } 2 \le u \le 3 \qquad (11.10c)$$

Equation (11.5) may be used directly for the case of uniform break-point distribution and in this way we can find the expressions for the cubic B-spline from those of the quadratic B-spline.

Uniform Cubic

$$U_{i,3}((i+u)L) = \frac{1}{6}u^3 \qquad \text{for } 0 \le u \le 1 \quad (11.11a)$$

$$U_{i,3}((i+u)L) = \frac{2}{3} - \frac{1}{2}(u-2)^3 - (u-2)^2 \quad \text{for } 1 \le u \le 2 \quad (11.11b)$$

$$U_{i,3}((i+u)L) = \frac{2}{3} + \frac{1}{2}(u-2)^3 - (u-2)^2 \quad \text{for } 2 \le u \le 3 \quad (11.11c)$$

$$U_{i,3}((i+u)L) = \frac{1}{6}(4-u)^3 \qquad \text{for } 3 \le u \le 4 \quad (11.11d)$$

Using the B-splines as a basis, we can express any spline as

$$p(x) = \sum_{i=-m}^{k-1} a_i N_{i,m}(x) \qquad (11.12)$$

This equation contains exactly $k+m$ parameters: a_{-m}, a_{-m+1}, $\cdots a_{k-1}$. On each subinterval, $p(x)$ is given as the sum of at most $m+1$ B-splines, so that it indeed exhibits local behavior. Changing any of the coefficients in Equation (11.12) will change the form of the curve in only $m+1$ intervals. The following example illustrates some of the salient properties of both B-splines and splines in general.

Example 11.1: We wish to find an interpolating quadratic spline for the following data points: (0,0), (1,1), (2,2), (3,P), (4,2), (5,1), (6,0). We shall investigate the effect of the value of P on the approximation while using uniform B-splines with $L = 1$. Substituting the expressions from Equations (11.10) into Equation (11.12) and replacing u by its definition in Equation (11.8) (with $L = 1$) we find

$$p(x) = \frac{1}{2}a_i(x-i)^2 +$$

$$a_{i-1}\{\frac{3}{4} - [x-(i+\frac{1}{2})]^2\} + \frac{1}{2}a_{i-2}(i+1-x)^2 \quad i \le x \le i+1 \quad (11.13a)$$

and for the derivative over the same interval

$$p'(x) = a_i(x-i) - 2a_{i-1}[x-(i+\frac{1}{2})] - a_{i-2}(i+1-x) \qquad (11.13b)$$

Both equations hold for $i = 0, 1, \cdots n-1$, and they yield the following values at the breakpoints.

$$p(i) = \frac{1}{2}[a_{i-1} + a_{i-2}]$$ (11.14a)

$$p'(i) = \ a_{i-1} - a_{i-2}$$ (11.14b)

For the present interpolation problem we have the following set of equations:

$$a_{-1} + a_{-2} = 0 \qquad a_0 + a_{-1} = 2$$
$$a_1 + a_0 \quad = 4 \qquad a_2 + a_1 \ \ = 2P$$
$$a_3 + a_2 \ = 4 \qquad a_4 + a_3 \ = 2$$
$$a_5 + a_4 \ = 0$$

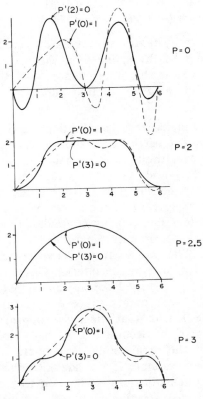

Figure 11.3 Illustration for Example 11.1: Effects of the location of a point (value of P), and the specification of a tangent on the form of a quadratic spline

There are more unknowns than equations and we can choose to specify the tangent at some point. We will study two cases:

Case (a): Choose $p'(3) = 0$, i.e., a horizontal tangent at the middle of the symmetrical set of data points. We find

$$a_{-2} = a_5 = 2-P \qquad a_{-1} = a_4 = -2+P$$

$$a_0 = a_3 = 4-P \qquad a_1 = a_2 = P$$

All the coefficients depend on P so the change in the value of one data point affects the whole spline approximation. Figure 11.3 illustrates four cases: $P = 0, 2, 2.5,$ and 3.

Case (b): Choose $p'(0) = 1$. We find now an asymmetrical interpolant with

$$a_{-2} = -0.5 \qquad a_{-1} = 0.5 \qquad a_0 = 1.5 \qquad a_1 = 2.5$$
$$a_2 = 2P-2.5 \qquad a_3 = 6.5-2P \qquad a_4 = -4.5+2P \qquad a_5 = 4.5-2P$$

It is easy to verify that $p(x)$ equals x over the interval $(0,2)$ and therefore the values of the spline over the first two intervals do not depend on P. However, this improvement has caused the loss of the symmetry. The plots of $p(x)$ for four values of P are also shown on Figure 11.3. □

It should be emphasized that the final results (i.e., the values of $p(x)$) are independent of the choice of representation for the spline and it would have been the same if we had, for example, used Equation (11.2). Example 11.1 and Figure 11.3 illustrate several properties of splines. Although spline interpolations are local, the choice for satisfying the additional degrees of freedom can have a major effect on the final result. This does not actually contradict Proposition 11.1, which simply states that we can modify the curve locally by introducing additional breakpoints. The reader can try, as an exercise, to introduce two breakpoints instead of one in the interval $(2,4)$ in the above example (see Problem 11.4). A second conclusion is that splines can present oscillations between data points as severe as those with polynomial interpolations. The reason that piecewise approximations gave good results in the examples of Section 10.2 is that there was some freedom in the selection of the breakpoints. We could have obtained better results in the above example if we had introduced additional breakpoints. A simple calculation can verify that the locations 2.3 and 3.7 with $p'(x) = 1$ and -1 respectively when $P = 3$ yield linear approximations over $(0,2)$ and $(4,6)$. The same result is obtained with locations 2.5 and 3.5 when $P = 0$. (In this case the proper choice for $p'(x)$ is $p'(2) = 1$ and $p'(4) = -1$.)

We conclude this section with an interesting property of B-splines.

Theorem 11.1: For all values of x and m

$$\sum_i N_{i,m}(x) = 1. \tag{11.15}$$

Note: The limits of summation are not given explicitly because the sum has only $m+1$ terms for each value of x.

Proof: We shall use the recursive Equation (11.5). This can be written for $i-1$ rather than i to yield

$$N_{i-1,m}(x) = \frac{x-x_{i-1}}{x_{i+m-1}-x_{i-1}}N_{i-1,m-1}(x) + \frac{x_{i+m}-x}{x_{i+m}-x_i}N_{i,m-1}(x). \tag{11.16}$$

Adding this equation to Equation (11.5), we find that

$$N_{i-1,m}(x) + N_{i,m}(x) =$$

$$\frac{x-x_{i-1}}{x_{i+m-1}-x_{i-1}}N_{i-1,m-1}(x) + N_{i,m-1}(x) +$$

$$\frac{x_{i+m+1}-x}{x_{i+m+1}-x_{i+1}} N_{i+1,m-1}(x). \tag{11.17}$$

The process that produced Equation (11.17) from Equations (11.5) and (11.16) can be repeated from, say, $i = j$ to $i = k$ to yield

$$\sum_{i=j}^{i=k} N_{i,m}(x) = \frac{x-x_j}{x_{j+m}-x_{j+1}}N_{j,m-1}(x)$$

$$+ \sum_{i=j+1}^{i=k} N_{i,m-1}(x) + \frac{x_{k+m+1}-x}{x_{k+m+1}-x_{k+1}}N_{k+1,m-1}(x). \tag{11.18}$$

By taking j sufficiently small and k sufficiently large, we can ensure that $N_{j,m-1}(x)$ and $N_{k+1,m-1}(x)$ are zero. Then Equation (11.18) can be written as

$$\sum_i N_{i,m}(x) = \sum_i N_{i,m-1}(x). \tag{11.19}$$

In other words, the sum of the B-splines at a point x is independent of the value of m. It can be readily seen from Equation (11.4) that its value for $m = 0$ is 1 and this concludes the proof. $\square$

11.4 COMPUTATION WITH B-SPLINES

Equation (11.5) suggests a simple computational procedure for evaluating a B-spline at some point x. We observe that on any given interval $[x_i, x_{i+1}]$ there are only $m+1$ B-splines of degree m that are nonzero. On that interval, $N_{i,m}(x)$ depends only on $N_{i,m-1}(x)$ because

$N_{i+1,m-1}(x)$ is zero there while $N_{i-l,m}(x)$ $(0<l\leq m)$ depends on both $N_{i-l+1,m-1}(x)$ and $N_{i-l,m-1}(x)$. The interdependence of the B-splines is shown in Figure 11.4. In order to find the splines of degree m, we must find the $m-1$ previous levels in the diagram shown in that figure and at each level we must find the B-splines $N_{i,j}(x)$ to $N_{i-l,j}(x)$, where j is the degree at that level and l ranges from 0 to j. This leads to Algorithm 11.1a.

The number of multiplications and divisions executed by the algorithm is proportional to m^2 at each point x. If the location of the breakpoints is uniform and fixed for a class of problems, then one may calculate the values directly from the explicit formulas of Equations (11.9) to (11.11), or similar ones. This approach also requires an effort proportional to m^2, but the operations used are simpler.

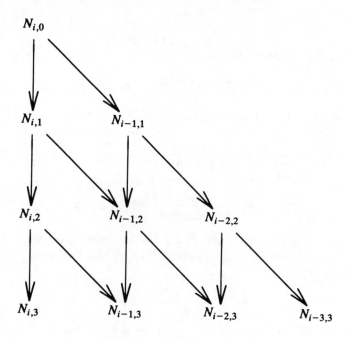

Figure 11.4 Interdependence of the values of the B-splines at a point x. Each term is the weighted sum of one or two terms in the line above it. The lines with arrows indicate the flow of the computation. Vertical lines denote multiplication by the first factor in Equation (11.5) and diagonals by the second factor in that equation.

Algorithm 11.1a Procedure *BSPLINE* (i, x, m)**:** Evaluation of all the B-splines at a point x belonging to the interval $[x_i, x_{i+1}]$.

> *Notation:* m is the degree of the spline. x is the point where the splines are evaluated. The array $N(I, J)$ contains the values $N_{I,J}(x)$. a and b are auxiliary variables.

1. Initialize $N(i, 0)$ to 1.
2. **For** $j = 1$ to m **do:**
   Begin.
3.   **For** $l = 0$ to j **do:**
       Begin.
       {Compute $N(i-l, j)$.}
4. $a = ((x - x_{i-l})/(x_{i-l+j} - x_{i-l})) \times N(i-l, j-1)$.
5. $b = ((x_{i-l+j+1} - x)/(x_{i-l+j+1} - x_{i-l+1})) \times N(i-l+1, j-1)$.
6. $N(i-l, j) = a + b$.
       End.
   End.
7. **End of Algorithm.**

11.5 INTERPOLATING B-SPLINES

Let (t_1, y_1), (t_2, y_2), $\cdots$ (t_n, y_n) be the data points for which an interpolating spline must be found. A number of ways of solving this problem exist. One is to identify each point with a spline knot. Since a spline has $k+m$ degrees of freedom, if m is small (as is usually the case), then one can choose $k = n-1$ and identify the breakpoints with $t_1, t_2, \cdots t_n$. For a linear spline, where $m = 1$, we have exactly n degrees of freedom and the curve is completely specified as the set of lines joining the points (t_i, y_i) to (t_{i+1}, y_{i+1}) for $i = 1, 2, \cdots n-1$. For $m = 3$ the total number of degrees of freedom is $n+2$, which leaves two extra degrees after the curve is constrained to pass through the data points. In practice, these are used to specify the tangents at the end points.

Another approach is to interleave breakpoints and data points, possibly setting $k+m = n$. We shall study this case in detail using B-splines to find the coefficients of the interpolating spline. Suppose that we have $k-1$ breakpoints as defined in Section 11.1. Using the notation of Equation (11.12) we find that if $x_i \leq t_j \leq x_{i+1}$, then the following equation must hold

$$a_i N_{i,m}(t_j) + a_{i-1} N_{i-1,m}(t_j) + \cdots + a_{i-m} N_{i-m,m}(t_j) = y_j$$

$$1 \leq j \leq n \qquad (11.20)$$

There will be n such equations with $k+m$ unknowns. Each one of them has only $m+1$ terms, so that the resulting matrix is banded with at most m lower and m upper diagonals. (Compare also the form of Example 11.1.) The exact form depends on the relative positions of breakpoints and data points. When the breakpoints are uniformly distributed and also coincide with the ordinates of the data points the form is particularly simple. At each point we have only m nonzero B-splines and their values are determined from Equations (11.10) or (11.11). For the quadratic case we have

$$a_i + a_{i-1} = 2y_i \qquad i = 1, 2, \cdots n \ .\tag{11.21a}$$

For the cubic

$$a_i + 4a_{i-1} + a_{i-2} = 6y_i \qquad i = 1, 2, \cdots n \ .\tag{11.21b}$$

The conditions at the endpoints must be added to these systems of equations. Otherwise their solution is straightforward. If the curve is supposed to be periodic then instead of additional endpoint conditions we reduce the number of unknowns by setting a_0 equal to a_n, etc.

The general case is somewhat more complicated. Clearly, there should be no more than $m+1$ data points on each interval, otherwise the system might be overdetermined. If the data points alternate with the breakpoints, then there may be as few as $m+1$ nonzero diagonals. The proper relation between breakpoints and data points is important, and a characterization is given by the following theorem.

Theorem 11.2: The spline interpolation problem has a unique solution if and only if

$$N_{jm}(t_j) \neq 0, \qquad j=1, 2, \cdots n\tag{11.22}$$

We omit the proof of this theorem (see [11.SW]) and point out only its interpretation. On each subinterval between breakpoints there are only $m+1$ nonzero B-splines, and therefore, in order to satisfy the condition of the theorem, the subinterval cannot contain more than $m+1$ data points. This assures that the system of Equations (11.20) will not be overdetermined. We also know that the B-spline N_{jm} is nonzero only over the subinterval (x_j, x_{j+m+1}) and therefore this is the only subinterval where the data point t_j can lie. Because the number of B-splines in Equation (11.12) equals the number of data points $(n = k+m)$ we have some additional constraints. The first of the B-splines is nonzero only over the first subinterval, and therefore that subinterval must contain a data point. The same is true for the last subinterval. If the first subinterval contains two points, the second may not contain any. Otherwise, it must have at least one, and so on.

Algorithm 11.1 Interpolation with B-splines.

Notation: (t_j, y_j), $1 \leq j \leq n$ is the set of data points. x_i, $1 \leq i \leq k+1$ is the set of breakpoints. m is the degree of the spline, and r is an auxiliary variable. $B(j,I)$ is the matrix of the system of Equations (11.20): $B(j,I) = N_{I,m}(t_j)$.

0. **If** there is a positive r such that $x_{m-r-1} \leq t_1 \leq x_{m-r}$, **then** make x_0 a breakpoint of multiplicity $m-r+1$. **If** there is a positive r such that $x_{k-m+r} \leq t_n \leq x_{k-m+r+1}$, **then** make x_k a breakpoint of multiplicity $r+2$.

1. **For** $j=1$ to n verify that $x_{j-m} < t_j < x_j$.

2. **For** $i=1$ to k verify that there are no more than $m+1$ data points on the interval (x_{i-1}, x_i).

3. **For** $j = 1$ to n **do:**
    Begin.

4.   Find the largest i such that $x_i \leq t_j$. {This implies that $t_j \leq x_{i+1}$.}

5.   **For** $I = i$ to $i-m$ by -1 **do:**
        Begin.

6.   Call procedure $BSPLINE(i, t_j, m)$.

7.   Set $B(j,I)$ equal to $N_{I,m}(t_j)$.
        End.
    End.

8. Use a standard procedure for solving linear equations with banded matrices to find $a_{-m}, a_{-m+1}, \cdots a_{k-1}$ from $B(j,I)$ and $y_1, y_2, \cdots y_n$.

9. **End of Algorithm.**

Algorithm 11.1 verifies the conditions of the theorem, sets up the system of Equations (11.20), and then uses a library program to solve them. Step 0 introduces multiple knots at the endpoints. This is necessary in order to have $m+1$ B-splines on each interval where there is a data point. One can always set the multiplicities of x_0 and x_k to $m+1$ without performing the checks. In step 4 of the algorithm some of the array indices may be negative. If the implementation is in a computer language where negative indices are illegal, then one can modify the algorithm by adding m to the values of the array subscripts.

Example 11.2: Find a first order interpolating spline over the interval [0,7] with breakpoints at $x=2$ and $x=5$ for data points (1,1), (3,1), (4,2), and (6,0). In this case both the endpoints must be double. It is easy to verify that the interpolating first order spline consists of the line joining (3,1) and (4,2) over [2,5], the line joining (1,1) and (2,0) over [0,2], and the line joining (5,3) and (6,0) over [5,7] (see Figure 11.5).

The formal derivation of this result is left as an exercise (see Problem 11.6). □

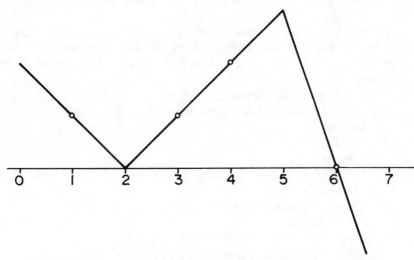

Figure 11.5   A linear interpolating spline with two breakpoints and passing through four points. The relation between data point and breakpoint location illustrates Theorem 11.2.

11.6 B-SPLINES IN GRAPHICS

It is possible to use B-splines to generate curves in a manner similar to Bezier polynomials. If P_i $(i = 0, 1, \cdots k)$ is a set of guiding points, then we define a spline as

$$P(t) = \sum_{i=0}^{k} P_i N_{i,m}(t) \qquad (11.23)$$

The range of t need not be $[0,1]$ any more, but we must define breakpoints $t_1, t_2, \cdots t_{k-1}$, something that was not needed in the case of Bezier polynomials. Note that Equation (11.23) is equivalent to two pairs of Equation (11.12) and the guiding points correspond to the coefficients a_i of that equation. We observe that $P(t)$ is a sum of vectors multiplied by numbers (the B-splines) that themselves add up to one because of Theorem 11.1. Therefore, we have the following result.

Proposition 11.2: $P(t)$ lies in the convex hull of at most $m+1$ of the guiding points P_i. $\square$

For $m = 1$ we obtain the polygon defined by the guiding points. (Each $P(t)$ lies on the line joining two points.) The shaded triangles in Figure 11.6a show the part of the plane where the curve $P(t)$ lies for $m = 3$ in two examples. Multiple points force the curve to pass closer to the guiding points, in much the same way as in the case of Bezier polynomials. Figure 11.6b shows that, for $m = 2$, double points force the curve to pass through them. It is possible to derive even tighter limits for the location of a spline (see Example 11.4 below) but a comparison between the shaded regions in Figure 11.6 and the convex hull of all the points (dotted lines) shows that B-splines offer much tighter control on the shape of the curve than Bezier polynomials do.

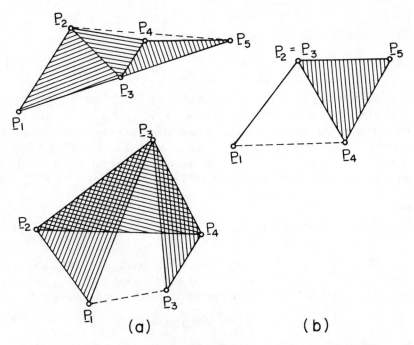

(a)   (b)

Figure 11.6 The parts of the plane where a quadratic spline with the given guiding points must lie are shaded. The dotted lines delimit the part where a Bezier polynomial with the same guiding points must lie.

The formulation of Equation (11.23) has the advantage that P can be a three-dimensional vector, so that one can produce space curves in this way.

Equation (11.23) can be interpreted in one more way if we think of $P(t)$ and the P_is as complex numbers. It is simply a complex spline

$$z(t) = \sum_{i=0}^{k} z_i N_{i,m}(t) \qquad (11.23')$$

Because complex numbers have a geometric interpretation (with x corresponding to the real part and y to the imaginary) the two forms are equivalent. The complex number formalism has been used explicitly by Knuth in font design (see Bibliographical Notes).

We will now look more closely at the behavior of splines expressed through B-splines. Let $B_{i,m,j}(t)$ denote the values of $N_{i,m}(t)$ for $t_{i+j} \le t \le t_{i+j+1}$. The values of j that are of interest are 0, 1, $\cdots m$. Then, Equation (11.23) can be written as

$$P(t) = \sum_{j=0}^{m} P_{i-j} B_{i-j,m,j}(t) \qquad t_i \le t \le t_{i+1}. \qquad (11.24)$$

If there are only $k+1$ points P_0, P_1, $\cdots P_k$, then the spline can be evaluated for $t \ge t_m$ only. In general, $P(t_m) \ne P_0$ and $P(1) \ne P_k$. To ensure that the spline passes through the endpoints, we must make them multiple. It is always true that if a point has multiplicity m, the spline will pass through it. In addition to the geometric argument given earlier, this can also be seen from Equation (11.24). If $P_{i-1} = P_{i-2} = \cdots = P_{i-m}$ we have

$$P(t) = P_{i-1}\left[\sum_{j=1}^{m} B_{i-j,m,j}(t)\right] + P_i B_{i,m,0}(t) \qquad t_i \le t \le t_{i+1}. \quad (11.25)$$

Because of Theorem 11.1 the term in brackets equals $1 - B_{i,m,0}(t)$. From Equation (11.5) we also see that $B_{i,m,0}(t)$ is proportional to $(t - t_i)^m$. If c is an appropriate constant we have

$$P(t) = P_{i-1}\left[1 - c(t-t_i)^m\right] + P_i c(t-t_i)^m. \qquad (11.26)$$

For $t = t_i$ this yields $P(t_i) = P_{i-1}$. Also, for $t_i \le t \le t_{i+1}$, the spline lies on the line joining the vectors P_{i-1} and P_i.

A better understanding of the behavior of the splines can be achieved by considering some simpler cases. If the breakpoints are distributed uniformly, then we may use the expressions of Equations (11.9) to (11.11) and the normalized variable u. We observe from Equation (11.8) that the definition of u depends on i and some care is required when we mix expressions for B-splines on different intervals. However, it is easy to show that if we replace u by $u+J$ in the expressions for $U_{i-J,m}$, then the formulas become consistent with those for $U_{i,m}$. In this way Equation (11.24) takes the following forms

$$m = 1: \quad P(L(i+u)) = uP_i + (1-u)P_{i-1} \tag{11.27a}$$

$$m = 2: \quad P(L(i+u)) + \frac{1}{2}u^2 P_i + \left[\frac{3}{4} - [u - \frac{1}{2}]^2\right]P_{i-1}$$

$$+ \frac{1}{2}(u-1)^2 P_{i-2}. \tag{11.27b}$$

$$m = 3: \quad P(L(i+u)) + \frac{1}{6}u^3 P_i + \left[\frac{2}{3} - \frac{(u-1)^3}{2} - (u-1)^2\right]P_{i-1}$$

$$+ \left[\frac{2}{3} + \frac{u^3}{2} - u^2\right]P_{i-2} + \frac{1}{6}(1-u)^3 P_{i-3} \tag{11.27c}$$

In all cases $0 \le u \le 1$. These expressions can be rewritten as sums of powers of u as follows.

$$m = 1: \quad P(L(i+u)) = (P_i - P_{i-1})u + P_{i-1} \tag{11.28a}$$

$$m = 2: \quad P(L(i+u)) = \left[\frac{P_i + P_{i-2}}{2} - P_{i-1}\right]u^2$$

$$+ \left[P_{i-1} - P_{i-2}\right]u + \frac{1}{2}\left[P_{i-1} + P_{i-2}\right]. \tag{11.28b}$$

$$m = 3: \quad P(L(i+u)) = \frac{1}{2}\left[\frac{1}{3}P_i - P_{i-1} + P_{i-2} - \frac{1}{3}P_{i-3}\right]u^3$$

$$+ \left[\frac{1}{2}P_{i-1} - P_{i-2} + \frac{1}{2}P_{i-3}\right]u^2$$

$$+ \frac{1}{2}\left[P_{i-1} - P_{i-3}\right]u + \frac{1}{3}\left[\frac{1}{2}P_{i-1} + 2P_{i-2} + \frac{1}{2}P_{i-3}\right]. \tag{11.28c}$$

The above expressions are convenient for the study of various spline properties. In particular, we may obtain counterparts of Equation (11.26) for $m = 2$ and $m = 3$. (Equation (11.27a) is its counterpart for $m = 1$.) We obtain

$$m = 2: \quad P(L(i+u)) = \frac{1}{2}\left[P_i - P_{i-1}\right]u + P_{i-1} \tag{11.29a}$$

$$m = 3: \quad P(L(i+u)) = \frac{1}{6}\left[P_i - P_{i-1}\right]u^3 + P_{i-1} \tag{11.29b}$$

In all these cases $P(Li) = P_{i-1}$. On the other hand

$$P((i+1)L) = \frac{1}{2}(P_{i-1}+P_i) \qquad \text{for } m = 2, \qquad (11.30a)$$

and

$$P((i+1)L) = \frac{5}{6}P_{i-1}+\frac{1}{6}P_i \qquad \text{for } m = 3. \qquad (11.30b)$$

If $m+1$ of the guiding points lie on a straight line, then Proposition 11.1 shows that the spline will also lie on the same line. Equation (11.24) says that this will happen for $t_i \leq t \leq t_{i+1}$.

It is possible to produce closed curves by defining $P_{-1} = P_m$, $P_{-2} = P_{m-1}$, etc., and also $t_{-1} = t_m$, $t_{-2} = t_{m-1}$, etc.

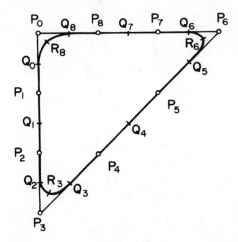

Figure 11.7   Fitting a quadratic spline to a triangle

Example 11.3:   (a) Consider the nine points of Figure 11.7 where (P_0, P_1, P_2, P_3), (P_3, P_4, P_5, P_6), and (P_6, P_7, P_8, P_0) are sets of collinear points. In order to fit a uniform quadratic spline, we use Equation (11.30a) to identify the points $Q_0, Q_1, \cdots Q_8$ where $Q_i = P(iL)$. Setting $u = 1/2$ in Equation (11.27b) we find

$$P((i+\frac{1}{2})L) = \frac{1}{8}P_{i-2} + \frac{3}{4}P_{i-1} + \frac{1}{8}P_i , \qquad (11.31a)$$

or

$$P((i+\frac{1}{2})L) = \frac{1}{2}\left[\frac{1}{4}P_{i-2} + \frac{3}{4}P_{i-1}\right] + \frac{1}{2}\left[\frac{3}{4}P_{i-1} + \frac{1}{4}P_i\right] \qquad (11.31b)$$

The second equation suggests a graphical construction for finding the points R_3, R_6, and R_8 in Figure 11.7. Of course, whenever the three points are collinear, $P((i+1/2)L)$ coincides with P_{i-1}.

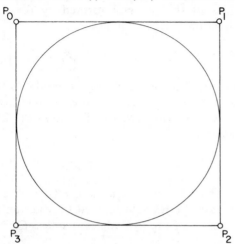

Figure 11.8 Fitting a quadratic spline to a square

(b) Figure 11.8 shows a periodic spline guided by four points, forming a square. Although it looks like a circle, it is not. The ratio of the diagonal radius to the vertical and horizontal radii is $3/(2\sqrt{2}) = 1.06$. □

Equation (11.24) shows that in contrast to the interpolating splines, guided splines indeed show a local dependence on, at most, m points.

11.7 SHAPE DESCRIPTION AND B-SPLINES

There are certain applications where it is important to describe the shape of a curve in a very precise manner. The mathematical design of character fonts for computer-controlled phototypesetters is one such application. In certain commercial machines the characters are defined through a vector encoding of their contours. The contours are then filled by an algorithm of the type discussed in Section 8.2. The use of linear vectors requires that a very large number of them be specified in order to create the impression of smoothness. (This text has been produced by such a system). Curve fitting with splines offers some interesting possibilities because one may have to specify only the guiding points, rather the actual contour points. The following example provides some useful formulas for such an effort.

Example 11.4: We investigate the form of the quadratic spline with uniform breakpoint distribution. Equation (11.28b) shows that $P(iL)$ is always given by Equation (11.30a) i.e., the spline passes through the midpoints of the sides of the polygon formed by the guiding points. Differentiation of Equation (11.27b) yields

$$\frac{\partial}{\partial u}P = \left[P_i+P_{i-2}-2P_{i-1}\right]u + \left[P_{i-1}+P_{i-2}\right] \qquad (11.32)$$

Substituting $u=0$ or $u=1$ in the above equation shows that the spline is tangent to the sides of the polygon of the guiding points for these values of u. If we rearrange the terms of Equation (11.27b) we obtain the following expression:

$$P(u) = \frac{1}{2}\left[P_i+P_{i-1}\right]u^2 + 2(u-u^2)P_{i-1} + \frac{1}{2}\left[P_{i-1}+P_{i-2}\right](u-1)^2 \quad (11.33)$$

One can verify that the sum $u^2 + 2(u-u^2) + (u-1)^2$ equals one, so that the spline lies within the triangle formed by a vertex of the guiding polygon and the midpoints of the two adjacent sides. □

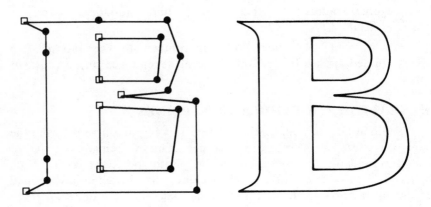

Figure 11.9 The use of guided splines with a B-spline basis for font design: the guiding polygon is shown to the left with solid circles representing the location of the simple guiding points and hollow squares representing the location of the double guiding points. The resulting spline is shown to the right.

The restriction on the location of the spline derived in the example is significantly tighter than that provided by Proposition 11.2. Therefore, quadratic splines with uniform knot distribution are useful in applications where one wants to represent shape accurately, and in particular, to produce smooth outlines using very few data points. Figure 11.9 shows an arrangement of guiding points and the resulting spline forming the outline of a letter. The font is specified by twelve points for the outside contour and four for each of the inside contours. In this respect they are superior to cubic splines where the relation between the guiding polygon and the curve is not as tight. Theoretically a quadratic spline requires more knots than a cubic spline in order to approximate a given curve with the same degree of accuracy. However, the increase in the number of knots appears to be insignificant in many practical problems. Readers may convince themselves on these points by trying to produce the outline of the letter "B" shown in Figure 11.9 (or a similar contour) by a cubic spline. A cubic spline is more convenient to use in applications where a shape is defined by a sequence of points and the tangent to the curve at them. Then the arcs between knots can be found easily by an expression similar to Equation (10.5).

11.8 BIBLIOGRAPHICAL NOTES

Splines are treated, at least briefly, in most modern texts on numerical analysis, and more extensively in most books on approximation theory. The second volume of the book by Rice [10.RI] devotes a chapter to the subject, with major emphasis on the theory. There are also quite a few volumes that deal exclusively with splines. Some of them offer a general mathematical treatment without particular attention to the problems of curve fitting ([11.ANW], [11.SC], [11.SCH]), while others concentrate on the latter subject [11.SP]. [11.LCS] and [11.LS] are collections of relatively recent papers, including many on splines. B-splines have been investigated extensively by de Boor ([11.DB1], [11.DB2]), and his book [11.DB3] is the best reference on splines for anyone interested in using them. The contents of [11.DB3] range from basic theoretical results on splines to listings of computer programs and specific examples. The material of Sections 11.4 and 11.5 of this text is based on [11.DB2]. An interesting special case of splines is discussed in [11.CL].

Riesenfeld was the first to present a systematic study [11.RI] of the use of B-splines in graphics applications and point out their advantages. [11.BR] contains many papers on the use of splines in graphics and related topics. [11.CLR] is an excellent reference describing algorithms for using B-splines for shape description. In particular they present an algorithm for computing a spline using subdivision similar to that discussed for Bezier polynomials in Section 10.5. The paper also contains numerous citations to the literature.

Knuth [11.KN] has used cubic splines for font design. He has specified a *metafont* where each character is defined by a cubic spline with complex coefficients. Actual characters are generated as the unions of circular disks or other simple shapes whose centers are located on the points of such splines.

11.9 RELEVANT LITERATURE

[11.ANW] Ahlberg, J. H.; Nilson, E. N.; and Walsh, J. L. *The Theory of Splines and Their Applications,* New York: Academic Press, 1967.

[11.BR] Barnhill, R. E. and Riesenfeld, R. F. (eds) *Computer Aided Geometric Design,* New York: Academic Press, 1974.

[11.CL] Cline, A. K. "Scalar and Planar Valued Curve Fitting Using Splines Under Tension," *CACM,* **17** (1974) pp. 218-220.

[11.CLR] Cohen, E.; Lyche, T.; and Riesenfeld, R. "Discrete B-Splines and Subdivision Techniques in Computer-Aided Geometric Design and Computer Graphics," *CGIP,* **14** (1980), pp. 87-111.

[11.DB1] de Boor, C. "Splines as Linear Combinations of B-splines," in [11.LCS], pp. 1-47.

[11.DB2] de Boor, C. "Package for Calculating with B-splines," *SIAM J. Numer. Anal.,* **14** (1977) pp. 441-472.

[11.DB3] de Boor, C. *A Practical Guide to Splines,* Heidelberg: Springer Verlag, 1978.

[11.KN] Knuth, D. E. *TEX and METAFONT: New Directions in Typesetting,* Bedford, Mass.: American Mathematical Society and Digital Press, 1979.

[11.LCS] Lorentz, G. G.; Chui, C. K.; and Schumaker, L. L. (eds), *Approximation Theory II,* New York: Academic Press, 1976.

[11.LS] Law, A. G. and Sahney, B. N. (eds), *Theory of Approximation with Applications,* New York: Academic Press, 1976.

[11.RI] Riesenfeld, R. "Applications of B-spline Approximation to Geometric Problems of Computer-Aided Design," *Ph. D. Thesis,* Computer Science Dept., Univ. of Utah, Salt Lake City, March 1973 (Technical Report number UTEC-CSc-73-126.)

[11.SC] Schultz, M. H., *Spline Analysis,* Englewood Cliffs, N.J.: Prentice Hall, 1973.

[11.SCH] Schumaker, L. L. *Spline Functions: Basic Theory,* New York: J. Wiley, 1981.

[11.SP]   Spath, H., *Spline Algorithms for Curves and Surfaces,* Winnipeg: Unitas Mathematica Publ., 1974. (Transl. from the German by W. D. Hoskins and H. W. Sager.)

[11.SW]   Schoenberg, I. J. and Whitney, A. "On Polya frequency functions III," *Trans. Amer. Mathem. Soc.* **74** (1953), pp. 246-259.

11.10 PROBLEMS

11.1. Is the curve produced in Problem 10.1 a simple spline?

11.2. Consider the following linear spline with just one breakpoint
$$p(t) = at - a(t-t_b)_+$$
Compute its value for $a = 10^3$ and $t = 10^{14}$ when $t_b = 2$, using single precision integer arithmetic and assuming that you have a computer with 16-bit words. Does it matter whether you use the above defining expression or the form used in Equation (11.1)?

11.3. Find an expression or a number for the maximum value and the values at the knots for each of the B-splines given in Equations (11.6), (11.7), (11.9), (11.10), and (11.11).

11.4. Repeat the analysis of Example 11.1 by introducing one additional breakpoint in the interval (2,4).

11.5. Write a program implementing Algorithm 11.1. Be careful to select a routine for solving the system of equations that takes advantage of the fact that the system matrix is banded.

11.6. Work out Example 11.2 in detail and prove formally that the curve given in Figure 11.5 is indeed the correct interpolating spline.

11.7. Express Equation (11.23') in polar coordinates. Can you produce a spline that is a circle by the proper choice of coefficients, breakpoints, and degree of the B-splines? If you think that this is impossible, provide a formal proof of your assertion.

11.8. Find an equation of the form $f(x,y) = 0$ equivalent to Equation (11.28b). Use that expression to show that the resulting curve is a parabola. (*Hint:* If a curve is given by an equation of the form $ax^2 + 2bxy + cy^2 + dx + ey + f = 0$, then it is a parabola if $b^2 = ac$.)

11.9. Write a program for computing Equation (11.28b) and use it to obtain displays of smooth curves defined by guiding points.

11.10. Incorporate the previous program in the interactive point editor of Problem 10.6 and compare the difficulty of achieving a desired shape through the use of Bezier polynomials with the difficulty of achieving it through the use of B-splines.

11.11. Use the tight bounding by a triangle of the splines of Example 11.4 to provide a simple rule for the selection of a sampling interval in order to produce displays with a uniform point density.

11.12. Repeat the analysis of Example 11.4 for cubic splines. In particular, use Equation (11.28c) to do the following. (a) Find the location of $P(iL)$. (b) Show that the tangent to the curve at that point is parallel to the line joining P_{i-1} and P_{i-3}. (c) Derive a condition on the location of the four guiding points so that the resulting curve has an inflection point not on a knot.

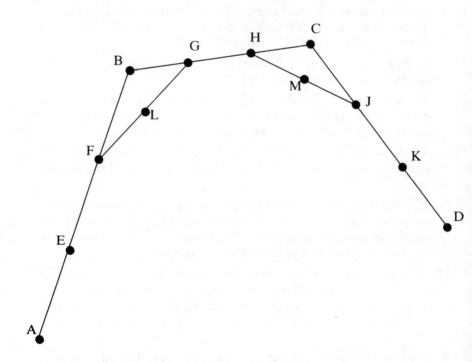

Figure 11.10   Illustration for Problem 11.13

11.13 Figure 11.10 shows four guiding points for an arc of a cubic spline. Let A stand for P_{i-3}, B for P_{i-2}, C for P_{i-1}, and D for P_i. The points E and F divide the segment AB in three equal parts. G and H do the same for BC, and J and K for CD. L is the midpoint of FG and M of HJ. Show the following properties for the spline arc on the interval $[iL,(i+1)L]$. (a) It starts from the point L and is tangent to the line FG there. (b) It ends at the point M and is tangent to the line HJ there. (c) It has an inflection point if the vectors FG and HJ form an angle greater than 90°.

11.14. Modify Equation (10.5) so that it can be used to compute a cubic spline passing through a set of points on the plane and be tangent to given lines through the points.

Chapter 12

APPROXIMATION
OF CURVES

12.1 INTRODUCTION

The last two chapters dealt mostly with interpolation where a curve must pass through all the data points. (Guiding points are part of the design parameters, so that a curve defined by them can still be used for interpolation.) There are many applications where interpolation is not necessary, or even desirable, and one wants the curve to pass only near the data points. This is the approximation problem. If the curve fitting is done in an interactive way the distinction between the two problems is not essential. The user modifies parameters (such as guiding points) until the curve looks right. "Looking right" may mean that the curve passes through all the data points, or through most of them, or near all of them, and so on. If the curve fitting is done automatically, such subjective criteria must be replaced by mathematically precise measures of closeness. The most common such measures are the maximum error and the integral square error (ISE). The error can be measured either along a coordinate or along a normal to the approximating curve. The latter is intuitively more appealing but more difficult to compute. Let e_i denote the pointwise error at the ith point, i.e. the distance between the curve and the point (measured by either of the above techniques). Then we have

$$\text{Maximum error} \equiv E_{\max} = \max_i |e_i| \qquad (12.1a)$$

$$\text{Integral square error} \equiv E_2 \quad = \sum_i e_i^2 \qquad (12.1b)$$

Because ISE approximations are more tractable mathematically than other forms they are more popular. One can find closed formulas that are valid not only for approximations by polynomials but also for approximations by splines and other curves. Sections 12.2 and 12.3 outline the fundamental properties of such approximations when the approximating curves are either polynomials or splines with fixed knots. In order to find the maximum error approximations one must solve a linear programming problem or use some other iterative algorithm. Finding the optimal approximation can thus require significant computation, making heuristic suboptimal algorithms more popular. From a practical viewpoint the most important problem is one that is virtually intractable mathematically: finding an approximation by a spline with variable knots. Sections 12.4 and 12.5 discuss some aspects of this problem but a complete treatment is outside the scope of this text (see Bibliographical Notes). Section 12.6 presents some applications of curve fitting in graphics.

12.2 INTEGRAL SQUARE ERROR APPROXIMATION

Let an approximating curve be defined as

$$g(t) = \sum_{j=0}^m a_j b_j(t) \qquad (12.2)$$

where $b_j(t)$, $j = 0, 1, \cdots m$ is a family of curves that form a basis. In simple terms, this means that all smooth curves of interest can be expressed in a unique way by Equation (12.2). The requirement for uniqueness has the following implication:

Proposition 12.1:   Let $b_0(t), \cdots b_m(t)$ be a basis. If there exist coefficients $a_0 \cdots a_m$, such that

$$\sum_{j=0}^m a_j b_j(t) = 0 \quad \text{for all } t, \qquad (12.3)$$

then $a_0 = a_1 \cdots = a_m = 0$. The converse is also true. Let F be a set of m functions that can satisfy Equation (12.3) only by having all the coefficients a_j zero. Then if another function can be expressed as a sum of the $b_i(t)$'s, that expression is unique.

Proof: Suppose there exist nonzero coefficients for which Equation (12.3) holds. Let

$$h(t) = \sum_{j=0}^{m} a_j' b_j(t) \tag{12.4}$$

where $h(t)$ is some arbitrary function. Adding Equations (12.3) and (12.4) we find that

$$h(t) = \sum_{j=0}^{m} (a_j + a_j') b_j(t) \tag{12.5}$$

i.e., $h(t)$ can be expressed as a sum of the basis functions in more than one way, which is impossible. Thus the proposition is proved by contradiction. Carrying this argument through in the opposite direction proves the converse of the proposition. □

Now let (x_i, y_i) $i = 0, 1, 2, \cdots n$ be the given data points. In order to study the approximation problem, it is convenient to define a parameter t and associate values of t with each point so that we have triplets (t_i, x_i, y_i). Two basic styles for such an assignment are:

(a) *Waveforms:* If the sequence of the x_i's is increasing we may set

$$t_i = \frac{x_i - x_0}{x_n},$$

and consider the data as a waveform in the interval $[0,1]$. Then we have

$$e_i = y_i - g(t_i) = y_i - \sum_{j=0}^{m} a_j b_j(t_i) \tag{12.5a}$$

and

$$E_2 = \sum_{i=0}^{n} e_i^2 = \sum_{i=0}^{n} \left[y_i - \sum_{j=0}^{m} a_j b_j(t_i) \right]^2 \tag{12.5b}$$

(b) *Contours:* Another approach is to set $t_i = iL$, where $L = 1/n$, and then consider approximations in both the x and y directions for values of t in the interval $[0,1]$.

$$e_i^x = x_i - g^x(t_i) = x_i - \sum_{j=0}^{m} a_j^x b_j(t_i) \tag{12.6a}$$

$$e_i^y = y_i - g^y(t_i) = y_i - \sum_{j=0}^{m} a_j^y b_j(t_i) \tag{12.6b}$$

One can then minimize separately

$$E_2^x = \sum_{i=0}^{n} (e_i^x)^2 \text{ and } E_2^y = \sum_{i=0}^{n} (e_i^y)^2 \qquad (12.7)$$

Because of the similarity between Equations (12.6) and Equation (12.5a), we consider only the waveform case. Differentiating Equation (12.5b) with respect to a_k we find

$$\frac{\partial E_2}{\partial a_k} = -2 \sum_{i=0}^{n} \left[y_i - \sum_{j=0}^{m} a_j b_j(t_i) \right] b_k(t_i) \qquad (12.8)$$

$$k = 0, 1, \cdots m.$$

Minimality of E_2 requires that all the righthand sides be zero, which then yields the following system of equations:

$$\sum_{j=0}^{m} \left[\sum_{i=0}^{n} b_k(t_i) b_j(t_i) \right] a_j = \sum_{i=0}^{n} b_k(t_i) y_i \qquad (12.9)$$

$$k = 0, 1, \cdots m.$$

It can be shown that for functions for which Proposition 12.1 holds, the system of Equations (12.9) has a unique solution; and, at least in principle, the ISE approximation problem can be solved by solving Equations (12.9). The contour approximation can be solved in a similar way. Note that in this case we can define vectors

$$P_i = \begin{bmatrix} a_i^x \\ a_i^y \end{bmatrix} \qquad (12.10)$$

and obtain the guiding points of Equation (11.18).

In practice a number of difficulties occur, mainly that the Gram matrix

$$G_{kj} = \sum_{i=0}^{n} b_k(t_i) b_j(t_i) \quad k = 0, 1, \cdots m, \; j = 0, 1, \cdots m \qquad (12.11)$$

is almost singular for some of the most common basis functions. In particular, this is the case when the basis functions are powers of t, and m exceeds 2. This property can be seen easily if we substitute integrals for the sums, i.e., if we assume that $n \rightarrow \infty$. Then we find for the case of powers of t

$$G_{kj} = \int_0^1 t^k t^j dt = \int_0^1 t^{k+j} dt = \left[\frac{t^{k+j+1}}{k+j+1} \right]_0^1 = \frac{1}{k+j+1} \qquad (12.12)$$

The value of the determinant is $1/12$ for $m = 1$, $1/2160$ for $m = 2$, and about $(1/6)10^{-6}$ for $m = 3.$†

12.3 APPROXIMATION USING B-SPLINES

None of the results of the previous section depend on the detailed structure of the functions $b_i(t)$, as long as they form a basis. Consider now the mth degree B-splines defined on an interval with $k-1$ breakpoints. There will be a total of $k + m - 1$ such functions. Suppose that we found a set of coefficients a_i so that

$$\sum_{i=-m+1}^{k} a_i N_{i,m}(t) = 0 \quad \text{for all } t. \tag{12.13}$$

This means that on any interval the sum of the B-splines defined there will also be zero. For $m = 1$ and uniform breakpoint distribution we must have equations of the form

$$a_{i-1}(1-s) + a_i s = 0 \tag{12.14}$$

where

$$s = \frac{x - x_i}{L}$$

Clearly, Equation (12.14) cannot be an identity in s, unless both a_{i-1} and a_i are zero. This type of argument can also be made for the general case ($m > 1$ and nonuniform breakpoint distribution) so that one can show that B-splines indeed form a basis. In this case the Gram matrix will have nonzero elements only along the main diagonal and m diagonals on each side of it. Indeed, $N_{im}(t)$ and $N_{jm}(t)$ are both nonzero over an interval only if $|i-j| \leq m$. If we again use integrals instead of sums in Equation (12.11), then for $m = 1$ and uniformly spaced breakpoints we find that the first and last elements of the main diagonal are $L/3$, the ones in between $2L/3$, and those on the diagonals above and below are $L/6$. For the case of two segments the determinant of the Gram matrix equals $L^3/18$ and for three segments $5L^4/144$, etc. (see Problem 12.1). The inversion of such matrices is much easier than the inversion of the matrix of Equation (12.12).

In practice, it is important to calculate elements of the Gram matrix for arbitrary locations of breakpoints according to Equation (11.5). This can be done easily by the procedure *BSPLINE* of

---

† The small value of the determinant is not by itself an indication that it is difficult to invert the Gram matrix, but a complete discussion of this point is beyond the scope of this text.

Algorithm 11.1a. If sufficient storage space is available, the values of each B-spline may be stored before the scalar products are computed.

The critical problem in the use of the B-splines, or other piece-wise polynomial functions, is the choice of the location of the break-points. We shall discuss this question next.

12.4 APPROXIMATION BY SPLINES WITH VARIABLE BREAKPOINTS

In an interactive system the user may display the data points and then specify the location of the breakpoints through a point editor of the type discussed in Section 10.8. However, there are many applications where it is desirable to have automatic selection of such points. Unfortunately this is a very difficult mathematical problem for the following reasons. Let T be a vector denoting the locations of the breakpoints $t_1, \cdots t_r$. We replace $b_j(t)$ by $b_j(t, T)$ in our equations to make the dependence of the basis on the breakpoints explicit. For example, with a trivial change in notation Equation (11.6) can be written as

$$b_j(t, T) = \begin{cases} \dfrac{t - t_j}{t_{j+1} - t_j} & t_j \leq t \leq t_{j+1} \\[2mm] \dfrac{t_{j+2} - t}{t_{j+2} - t_{j+1}} & t_{j+1} \leq t \leq t_{j+2} \end{cases} \tag{12.15}$$

In order to find the optimal approximation when the breakpoint location is a variable we must estimate the following, in addition to the derivatives given in Equation (12.8):

$$\frac{\partial E_2}{\partial t_k} = -2 \sum_{i=0}^{n} \left[y_i - \sum_{j=0}^{m} a_j b_j(t_i, T) \right] \left[\sum_{j=0}^{m} \frac{\partial b_j}{\partial t_k} \right] \tag{12.16}$$

For the example of Equation (12.15), we find that

$$\frac{\partial b_j(t, T)}{\partial t_i} = \frac{t - t_{j+1}}{(t_{j+1} - t_j)^2} \quad t_j \leq t \leq t_{j+1} \tag{12.17}$$

The last two equations point out that the locations of the breakpoints enter the optimization equations in a nonlinear fashion; there is no explicit solution to this problem. Instead one must use iterative techniques where a set of locations is chosen arbitrarily and then the locations are varied in order to reduce the error E_2. Such a process can be quite time consuming and is impractical for many applications.

As a further illustration of the difficulties, consider the formulation of Equation (11.1) when there are no constraints. In this case, if we use integrals instead of sums in Equation (12.1b), we find the following expression for the error.

$$E_2 = \sum_{k=0}^{r} \int_{t_k}^{t_{k+1}} e_k^2(t)\,dt \qquad (12.18)$$

where e_k is given by

$$e_k(t) = y_i - \sum_{j=0}^{m} a_j^k b_j(t) \qquad (12.19)$$

If we choose a basis that does not depend explicitly on the breakpoint locations (e.g., powers of t), then we find that

$$\frac{\partial E_2}{\partial t_k} = e_{k-1}^2(t_k) - e_k^2(t_k) \; . \qquad (12.20)$$

(We have used the fact that the derivative of an integral with respect to its upper limit equals the integrand at that point:

$$\frac{d}{dx} \int_a^x f(t)\,dt = f(x) \; .$$

Similarly, its derivative with respect to its lower limit is the negative of the integrand at the latter point.) Equation (12.20) has a simple interpretation: at the optimal breakpoint location, the absolute values of the pointwise errors are equal on either side. But this relation cannot be used since the values of these errors depend on the location of the breakpoints. If we introduce them explicitly in Equation (12.20), then we are faced with a nonlinear equation again.

12.5 POLYGONAL APPROXIMATIONS

Strictly speaking, all curves displayed on most graphic systems are polygons, because they are produced by drawing lines between adjacent pixels using a command such as $vec(x,y)$ of Section 1.7 (Table 1.2). (Devices that display only points are the only major exception to this rule.) A well known mathematical result states that any curve can be approximated by a polygon with any desired accuracy, so such representations can have a very smooth appearance†. Given a mathematical description for a curve C

$$f(x,y) = 0 \qquad (12.21)$$

one may be asked to find a polygon that closely approximates C while having as small a number of vertices as possible. Clearly, if the location

---

† Of course, one pays a price for this convenience. See Section 11.7 and Figure 11.9.

of the vertices is a variable, then we can find more efficient representations. A similar problem occurs in pattern recognition, with the difference that C is given by a set of data points rather than by an equation. Fitting a polygon to such points is helpful in determining features that are important for the description of shape. This is shown in Figure 12.1 where some noisy contours are fitted with polygons by an algorithm described later in this section.

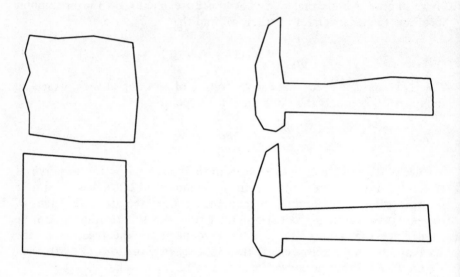

Figure 12.1   Examples of polygonal approximations obtained by Algorithm 12.1. The original contours are shown at the top and the approximations at the bottom.

Interactive graphics are of little help in either case. In the first instance, we must find the polygon in order to display the curve. In the second, we require completely automatic operation. At the same time, we are faced with the intractability of the optimization of the knot location for splines. In order to find at least a suboptimal solution that is easy to compute we simplify both the line fitting procedure and the procedure for locating the breakpoints. In particular, we will not insist on finding the minimum number of knots, but only a number close to it. The basic idea is to examine groups of points and check whether they are approximately collinear. If they are not, then the group is split until the collinearity condition is satisfied. On the other hand, groups are merged if the result will be a group with approximately collinear pixels. Thus we have a split-and-merge process whose result has the following property:

Proposition 12.2: The number of segments found by a split-and-merge procedure is always less than twice the minimum number.

Proof: Let $I_1, I_2, \cdots I_m$ be the intervals of the minimal partition and $J_1, J_2, \cdots J_n$ the intervals found by the split-and-merge process. No interval I_i can contain two intervals J_k and J_{k+1}, otherwise the latter would have been merged. However, each I_i can contain within itself an interval J_k with J_{k-1} and J_{k+1} overlapping with I_{i-1} and I_{i+1} respectively (see Figure 12.2). Thus we can have m intervals entirely within the intervals of the optimal partition, plus as many intervals as dividing points, i.e. a total of $m + m - 1$. Therefore $n \leq 2m - 1$. □

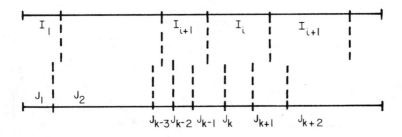

Figure 12.2 Interval arrangement for proving Proposition 12.2

It turns out that this is a very conservative estimate and in practice n is found to be well below $2m - 1$. The example that yields $n = 2m - 1$ requires a rather intricate arrangement between the optimal breakpoints and the endpoints of the groups of pixels to be tested for collinearity. The general idea of a split-and-merge algorithm can be implemented in many ways and we shall present one of the simplest in Section 12.5.2. (See the Bibliographical Notes for more advanced schemes.)

12.5.1 A Suboptimal Line Fitting Algorithm

Any polygonal fitting algorithm requires that the data points be subdivided into groups, each one of them to be approximated by a side of the polygon. The first simplification of the polygon fit problem is to draw a line between the endpoints of each group rather than search for the optimal approximation. The line used to approximate the points (x_j, y_j), (x_{j+1}, y_{j+1}), $\cdots$ (x_k, y_k), is given by

$$x(y_j - y_k) + y(x_k - x_j) + y_k x_j - y_j x_k = 0 \qquad (12.22)$$

This is really Equation (10.2) after multiplication by the denominator, with y standing for $p_2(x)$, j for 1, and k for 2. The following is a useful result.

Proposition 12.3:   If a point (u, v) does not lie on the line given by Equation (12.22), then its distance from the line equals the magnitude of d/L where

$$d = u(y_j - y_k) + v(x_k - x_j) + y_k x_j - y_j x_k \qquad (12.23)$$

and

$$L = \sqrt{(y_j - y_k)^2 + (x_k - x_j)^2} \qquad (12.24)$$

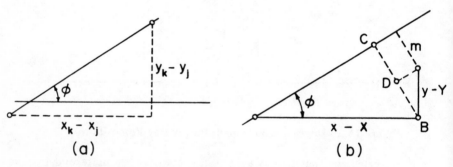

Figure 12.3   Illustration of the definitions used in Proposition 12.3 and its proof

Proof: Dividing Equations (12.23) and (12.24) term by term, we obtain

$$\frac{d}{L} = -u\sin\phi + v\cos\phi + c \qquad (12.25)$$

where the angle ϕ is defined as shown in Figure 12.3a. The constant c can be defined explicitly from Equations (12.23) and (12.24), but it is best to show a simpler interpretation for it. If (X, Y) is any point on the line, then setting $u = X$ and $v = Y$ in Equation (12.25) we find $d = 0$ because (X, Y) must satisfy Equation (12.22). Then we can set $c = X\sin\phi - Y\cos\phi$ and rewrite Equation (12.25) as

$$\frac{d}{L} = -(u-X)\sin\phi + (v-Y)\cos\phi \qquad (12.26)$$

Consider now the configuration of Figure 12.3b. m is the distance of the point from the line. Clearly, $|BC| = (u-X)\sin\phi$ and $|BD| = (v-Y)\cos\phi$. The distance from the line is indeed

$$m = |CD| = |BD| - |BC| = (v-Y)\cos\phi - (u-X)\sin\phi$$

Note that the sign of d/L gives an indication of the side of the line where the point lies. $\square$

A simple collinearity check can be performed by evaluating the expression of the lefthand side of Equation (12.25) for all intermediate points. A maximum distance may be established such that the points of a set are not collinear if some of them are further from the line than that maximum. From a practical viewpoint this is not always desirable. Indeed, one may weight errors that appear to be systematic differently from random errors. A possible measure of randomness is the number of sign changes in d (see Figure 12.4a). If instead of an absolute maximum we prefer one normalized with respect to the line length L, the critical quantity becomes d/L^2.

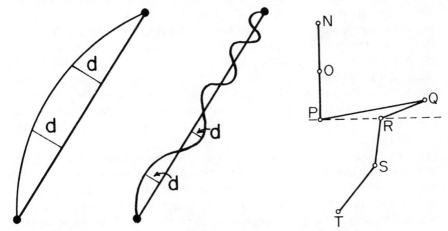

Figure 12.4 (a) The size of the error d is measured along the normal to the line as illustrated in two points in each of the examples. There are no sign changes in the first example, while there are six changes in the second. (b) A singular case where the maximum error is near zero but the points are not collinear if considered as an ordered set.

These tests give wrong results in singular cases such as the one illustrated in Figure 12.4b. There the ordered set of points is P, Q, and

R and it is part of a bigger contour as shown by the other points in the figure. The point Q has a very small distance from the line joining P and R but the three points are not collinear when viewed as an ordered sequence. In order to avoid such singular cases we should check the length of the arc, L_a, along the point sequence and compare it to the length of the line L. If the ratio of L_a to L is too large, then the points cannot be collinear. This is a simple test and it is advisable to apply it before other computation. Practical experience with a variety of data, as well as calculations with simple geometrical models, indicate that if the ratio L_a/L is under 1.1 we may assume collinearity without any other tests while if it exceeds 1.5 we may reject collinearity outright.

The use of the line joining the extreme points instead of the optimal approximating line does not result in major deviations from optimality because the maximum distance of points from the interpolant does not exceed twice the value of the distance from the optimal approximant (see Problem 12.3).

These concepts are implemented in the procedure $COLLINEAR(j,k,m,a,L)$, listed as Algorithm 12.1. Step 1a checks for the singular case and may be omitted if we do not expect such cases in the data. Step 8 contains the formulas for both normalized and unnormalized maximum error T. The algorithm can be simplified by removing steps 6 and 7 and all other references to d_0 and C. Then the check of step 9 will be a comparison of T (maximum distance of a point from the line) and T_0. However, better results are obtained by using a test on the T-C plane as shown in Figure 12.5. A formal justification for the approach can be made if we view the collinearity test as hypothesis testing, but a discussion of this interpretation is outside the scope of this text and we propose the use of the region shown in Figure 12.5 as a heuristic.

Practical experience with such algorithms shows that the criteria that give the best results in one application do not do so in another. For example, if the major source of errors is quantization, then using the maximum error without normalization yields better results than if we normalize with respect to length. On the other hand, if we fit lines to data points obtained from the digitization of a freehand drawing we find better results with the normalization. In this case normalization seems to be justified because people draw long lines less carefully than short ones.

The reader should be aware that any implementation of Algorithm

12.1 must be in floating point rather than integer arithmetic. It also may be a good idea to divide the values of $a(1)$, $a(2)$, and $a(3)$ by L in advance, rather than waiting to divide T by L^2 or L.

Algorithm 12.1 Procedure $COLLINEAR(j,k,m,a,L)$

Notation: Arrays $x()$ and $y()$ are defined globally and are known to the procedure. j is the index of the first point and k the index of the last point of the group of points tested for collinearity. The array a has size three and contains the coefficients of the line joining $x(j),y(j)$ and $x(k),y(k)$. m is the index of the point where the maximum error (in absolute value) occurs, i.e. $x(m),y(m)$ lies the farthest from the line joining the first and last point. L is the length of the line. The procedure returns m, array a, and L. The following local variables are used: T the size of the maximum error (in absolute value), d the size of the error at a point, C the number of sign changes in the error.

1.   Evaluate: $a(1) = y(j) - y(k)$, $a(2) = x(k) - x(j)$,
         $a(3) = y(k)x(j) - y(j)x(k)$, and
         $L = \sqrt{a(1)^2 + a(2)^2}$.

1a. {Optional} Compute the total arc length

$$L_a = \sum_{i=j+1}^{k} \sqrt{[x(i)-x(i-1)]^2+[y(i)-y(i-1)]^2}$$

If the ratio L_a/L exceeds 1.5 **then return** *false*. If it is less than 1.1 **then return** *true*.

2.   Set $m = j$, $T = 0$, $d_0 = 0$, and $C = 0$.
3.   **For** $i = j+1$ to $k-1$ **do:**
         Begin.
4.   Evaluate $d = a(1)x(i) + a(2)y(i) + a(3)$.
5.   **If** $|d|$ is greater than T, **then** set $T = |d|$ and $m = i$.
6.   **If** the sign of d is opposite to the sign of d_0, **then** increment C. {If d_0 is zero no change in C is made.}
7.   Set $d_0 = d$.
         End.
8.   Replace T by T/L^2 (or T/L) and if $k > j+2$ replace C by $C/(k-j-2)$. {Note that if $k = j+2$, then $C = 0$ }.
9.   **If** the point (C,T) lies in the shaded part of the plane in Figure 12.5, **then return** *true*.
10. **Else return** *false*.
11. **End of Algorithm.**

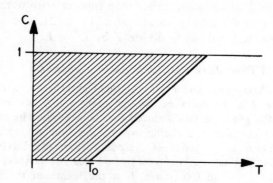

Figure 12.5 The shaded area is the region of acceptable values of C and T.

12.5.2 A Simple Polygon Fitting Algorithm

Algorithm 12.2 does the polygon fitting and proceeds by examining small groups of points of size k_0, so that $k = j + k_0$. (Typical values of k_0 are in the range five to ten.) It keeps track of a current line L_1, and a new line L_2. If the collinearity test succeeds on a group of points (*COLLINEAR* returns a *true* value as tested in step 4), then the block of steps 5 to 10 is executed. Step 5 defines the new line L_2 as the line returned by *COLLINEAR*. If the first point of the group was established as a breakpoint ($p = j$), then the new line becomes the current line (step 6), and steps 7 to 9 are skipped. If p is different from j, then a merge check is performed in step 8 by comparing the lines L_1 and L_2 (Figure 12.6).

If the angle between the two is small, then the two groups are merged and the current line is defined as the one joining $x(p),y(p)$ and $x(k),y(k)$ (step 8). A small angle guarantees that the new approximating line, L_3, will be close to both L_1 and L_2 (see Proposition 12.4 below). If the angle between the lines is large, then step 9 marks the point $x(j),y(j)$ as a breakpoint and sets $p = j$. In all these cases the algorithm advances to a new set of points by setting j equal to k and incrementing k by k_0.

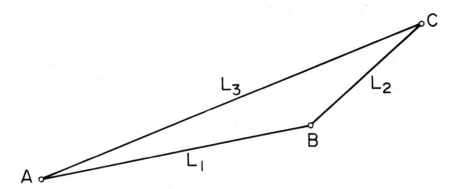

Figure 12.6 Definition of the lines L_1, L_2, and L_3 used by Algorithm 12.2

If the collinearity test of steps 3 and 4 fails, then the collinearity test is performed on the group of points between the first and the point where the maximum error (in absolute value) was observed. This is accomplished in step 11 by simply setting $k = m$ and returning to the top of the loop so that step 3 is performed again. (Note that the loop does not increment j automatically. It only checks whether the last data point has been reached.)

The operations of steps 8 and 9 can be replaced by a repetition of the collinearity test over the union of the intervals by a call to $COLLINEAR(p,k,m,a,L)$. This increases the total amount of computation but it guarantees directly that the test is valid.

Algorithm 12.2 is closely related to a number of algorithms in the literature that "scan along" a set of points. At each point one readjusts the line and checks whether the error is within specified limits. If it is, the algorithm advances to the next data point, otherwise a breakpoint is introduced (see Bibliographical Notes). The algorithm presented here is a "hop along" algorithm. It uses the same line for groups of points and thus avoids the effort of recalculating the line at each point. If an error occurs, though, it must backtrack to the point of maximum error. Thus, it is important to select the group size k_0 small enough to avoid frequent backtracking. For $k_0 = 1$ the algorithm reduces to a "scan along." In this case the collinearity test is always true and the algorithm is reduced to steps 8 and 9.

Algorithm 12.2 Polygonal Fit

Notation: Arrays $x()$ and $y()$ contain the coordinates of the data points. j is the index of the first, and k the index of the last point of the group tested for collinearity. k_0 is the number of data points that such a group normally contains. p is the index of the last polygon vertex and L_1 is the line from $x(p),y(p)$ to $x(j),y(j)$. m is the index of the point where the maximum error was found during a collinearity test.

1.   Set $p = 0$, $j = 0$, and $k = k_0$.
2.   **While** j is less than $n-1$ **do**:
            Begin.
3.   Call *COLLINEAR* (j,k,m,a,L).
4.   **If** the value returned is *true* **then do**:
                  Begin.
5.   Define the line L_2 as the one described by the coefficients a returned by *COLLINEAR*.
6.   **If** p equals j, **then** define the line L_1 as equal to L_2.
7.   **Else do**:
                      Begin.
8.   **If** the angle between L_1 and L_2 is small, **then** define L_1 as the line L_3 joining $x(p),y(p)$ and $x(k),y(k)$.
9.   **Else** set p equal to j and define L_1 as equal to L_2.
                      End.
10.   Set j equal to k and increment k by k_0.
                  End.
11.   **Else** set $k=m$.
            End.
12.   **End of Algorithm.**

12.5.3 Properties of Algorithm 12.2

The following is a summary of the properties of the approximation under certain assumptions about the tolerances used in procedure *COLLINEAR* and step 8 of Algorithm 12.2.

Proposition 12.4:   If in step 9 of procedure *COLLINEAR*, the unnormalized distance from the line is compared only with a fixed threshold T_0 and if the angle ω between the two lines in step 8 of Algorithm 12.2 is less than $\sin^{-1}(T_0/L)$ where L is the maximum of the lengths of L_2 and L_3, then the maximum distance from L_3 will be less than $2T_0$.

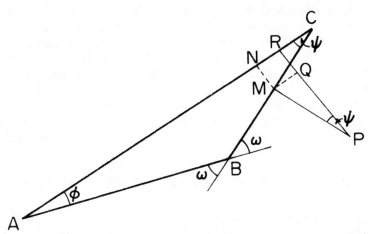

Figure 12.7 Construction used for the proof of Proposition 12.4

Proof: The proof is based on calculating certain trigonometric relations. We use the notation of Figure 12.7 and we notice that both lines L_1 and L_2 can be treated in the same way, i.e. L_2 can be either AB or BC, etc. L_3 is AC. We observe that the new error is $|PR|$ and we have

$$|PR| = |PQ| + |QR| = |PQ| + |MN|$$
$$= |MP|\cos\psi + |CM|\sin\psi .$$

Because ABC is a triangle the angle ψ is less than or equal to the angle ω ($\omega = \psi + \phi$. Equality of ψ and ω occurs when both are zero). Therefore

$$\sin\psi \leq \sin\omega \leq \frac{T_0}{L} .$$

Since $\cos\psi \leq 1$ we have

$$|PR| \leq |MP| + |CM|\frac{T_0}{L}$$

By definition $|MP| \leq T_0$. Also $|CM| \leq L$. Therefore

$$|PR| \leq T_0 + L\frac{T_0}{L} = 2T_0.$$

□

The bound given by Proposition 12.4 is rather conservative

because of the strengthening of inequalities during the proof. Although we have shown that Algorithm 12.2 yields approximations that are close to the data (and are also continuous) we have not shown that it produces a number of segments that is close to the minimum number. If we assume that the data points are quantizations of a convex curve, then the inequalities used in the proof of Proposition 12.4 become tighter and it is possible to show that the number of vertices of the resulting polygon is close to the minimum. However, since applications are rarely restricted to convex curves, we will not describe that analysis here.

12.6   APPLICATIONS   OF   CURVE   APPROXIMATION   IN GRAPHICS

Applications of curve approximation by polygons or splines with variable knots are too numerous to cover completely in this text. Brief surveys of some of them will illustrate the relevance of the subject to pictorial information processing. A potential use of the point editor described in Section 10.8 is to input sketches and then ask the program to display clean versions of them. For example, one could point to a curve, inform the system that it is intended to be a circle, and have the curve replaced by an approximating circle. For this use the editor must be expanded in two ways. One is to allow pointing to groups of points, and the other is to include functional approximation procedures.

12.6.1 Handling of Groups of Points by a Point Editor

This can best be accomplished by a hierarchical data structure. Let us define the structure *curve* as follows:

$$struct \ \ curve \ = \{p,t,s\}$$

where p is a pointer to a structure *point* containing the first point of the arc, t is the type of the structure, and s is a status variable. By type we mean whether the points of the curve should be interpreted as guiding points of a Bezier polynomial, or a spline, or data points approximating one of a set of basic shapes: circle, square, resistor, amplifier, etc. Status indicates whether the object has been erased. One could also expand the structure *point* (Section 10.8.1) to include a pointer to the structure *curve* to which each point belongs, but this is not always necessary. Indeed the procedure *place* (x,y,q) of Section 10.8.2 might be arranged to look as follows:

Algorithm 12.3 Procedure *place* (x,y,q,Q)

   Notation: x and y are given coordinates, q is a pointer to *isapoint*, and Q pointer to the structure *curve* returned by the procedure.

1.   **For** all pointers Z that point to a curve with nonzero *status* **do**:
      Begin.
2.   Set z to $Z{\longrightarrow}p$
3.   Find the pair $z{\longrightarrow}x,z{\longrightarrow}y$ that is nearest to x,y and let d be the distance between the two points. (The sequence of points is searched by replacing z by $z{\longrightarrow}n$ and stopping when z is zero.)
4.   **If** Z points to the first curve set $Q = Z$, $q = z$, and $D = d$. **Else** compare d to D, and if smaller, replace Q by Z, q by z, and D by d.
      End.
5.   **End of Algorithm.**

   If a command with an address is preceded by the word *object* (or its abbreviation **o**), then the operation is applied to the entire curve. The pointer to the curve is the value Q returned by a procedure such as the one listed above. In particular, the first point of the curve is

$$(Q{\longrightarrow}p){\longrightarrow}x,(Q{\longrightarrow}p){\longrightarrow}y.$$

12.6.2 Finding Some Simple Approximating Curves

   We discuss here a few examples of formal shapes.

Example 12.1:   Finding the best circle fitting a set of points by minimizing the integral square error is equivalent to selecting x_c, y_c, and r to minimize

$$E = \sum_{i=1}^{n} \left| (x_i - x_c)^2 + (y_i - y_c)^2 - r^2 \right|. \qquad (12.27)$$

(This assumes that the pointwise error is evaluated along the normal to the curve, and not along some coordinate axis.) The minimization of E is a nonlinear problem and one may try a suboptimal solution by selecting x_c and y_c to be the center of gravity of the data points. (This is justified only when the data points are evenly distributed along the circumference.) Then E can be minimized with respect to r. The best choice is to take r equal to the radius of inertia (see Problem 12.5). Figure 12.8 shows examples of applying this suboptimal scheme. $\square$

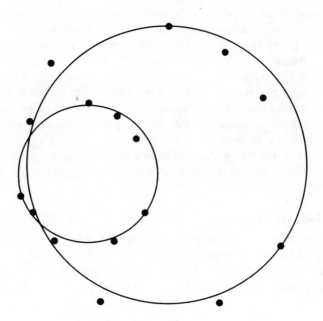

Figure 12.8   Two sets of points approximated by circles. The data points are shown by small filled circles.

Example 12.2:   We are given four points and are told that they are supposed to form an upright square, while they do not actually form one. Each point must be moved to a new location to form a square while keeping the total amount of movement to a minimum. One must choose x, y, and a to minimize the following expression:

$$E = (x_1-x)^2 + (y_1-y)^2 + (x_2-x)^2 + (y_2-y-a)^2 +$$

$$(x_3-x-a)^2 + (y_3-y-a)^2 + (x_4-x-a)^2 + (y_4-y)^2 \quad (12.28)$$

Taking the partial derivatives we find that x, y, and a must satisfy the following system:

$$4x + 2a = \sum_1^4 x_i$$

$$4y + 2a = \sum_1^4 y_i$$

$$2x + 2y + 4a = y_2 + x_3 + y_3 + x_4$$

The solution of this system is

$$a = \frac{1}{4}\left[y_2+y_3-y_1-y_4+x_3+x_4-x_1-x_2\right] \qquad (12.29a)$$

$$x = \frac{3}{8}(x_1+x_2) + \frac{1}{8}(x_3+x_4) - \frac{1}{8}(y_2+y_3) + \frac{1}{8}(y_1+y_4) \quad (12.29b)$$

$$y = \frac{3}{8}(y_1+y_4) + \frac{1}{8}(y_2+y_3) - \frac{1}{8}(x_3+x_4) + \frac{1}{8}(x_1+x_2) \quad (12.29c)$$

Figure 12.9 shows examples of applications of these formulas. $\square$

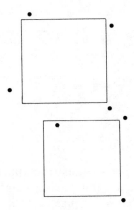

Figure 12.9 Two sets of data points (filled circles) approximated by squares

Example 12.3: We wish to fit an ellipse to a given set of n points. Let a and b be the size of the axes and ϕ the angle formed by one of them with the x-axis. We select again the center of gravity (x_c, y_c) as the center of the ellipse. We calculate the moments of inertia with respect to that center:

$$M_{xx} = \sum_{i=1}^{n} (x_i - x_c)^2, \quad M_{yy} = \sum_{i=1}^{n} (y_i - y_c)^2$$

and

$$M_{xy} = \sum_{i=1}^{n} (x_i - x_c)(y_i - y_c)$$

One can show that if we select ϕ as half of the angle with tangent $M_{xy}/(M_{yy} - M_{xx})$, then the moments M_{xx}^c and M_{yy}^c, with respect to the ellipse axes, will be maximum in one direction and minimum in the other direction. (M_{xy}^c will be zero.) We set as a goal to satisfy the equation of the ellipse on the average, i.e.

$$\sum_i^n \left(\frac{x_i^2}{a^2} + \frac{y_i^2}{b^2} - 1 \right) = 0 \qquad (12.30)$$

where the coordinates x_i and y_i are calculated with respect to a new system of coordinates having its center at the center of the ellipse, and the axes parallel to the ellipse axes. Equation (12.30) is equivalent to

$$\frac{1}{a^2} M_{xx}^c + \frac{1}{b^2} M_{yy}^c - n = 0$$

It can be satisfied by

$$a = \sqrt{M_{xx}^c/pn} \quad b = \sqrt{M_{yy}^c/qn} \ .$$

where

$$p + q = 1 \ .$$

If we choose

$$p = q = \frac{1}{2}$$

then we preserve the shape of the distribution: an ellipse with these axes and uniform mass density along its circumference has moments with respect to both axes that are equal (within a scale factor) of the original moments. □

12.7 BIBLIOGRAPHICAL NOTES

Approximation by polynomials is a standard topic in most texts on numerical analysis, such as [10.DA], [10.IK], and [10.RI]. Approximation by splines with fixed knots can be found in [11.DB3], [11.LCS], etc. Although splines with variable knots are one of the best possible choices for approximating data points with a smooth curve, their use is difficult and the literature is rather limited. [12.MC] describes some of their fundamental properties. A suboptimal solution is presented in [12.DB]. One particular algorithm is described in [12.RI]. That paper is interesting not only for the algorithm presented but also for computational statistics relating polynomial degree, number of knots, and error of approximation. Polygonal approximations where the location and number of corners are variables are simpler and are discussed in [3.PA], [12.PA], and [12.PH]. These references contain extensive descriptions of split-and-merge algorithms. [12.PH] introduces that approach for curve fitting, while [12.PA] uses split-and-merge for initialization of Newton's method. [3.PA] contains description of many of the heuristic methods, including scan along techniques, that have been proposed by various authors. The methods proposed by Tomek [12.TO] and the minimum perimeter polygons [12.SK] are closer to the idea of Algorithm 12.2.

12.8 RELEVANT LITERATURE

[12.DB]   de Boor, C. "Good Approximation by Splines with Variable Knots," *ISNM*, **21** (1973) pp. 57-72.

[12.MC]   McClure, D. E. "Nonlinear Segmented Function Approximation and Analysis of Line Patterns," *Quarterly of Applied Mathematics*, **33** (1975) pp. 1-37.

[12.PA]   Pavlidis, T. "Polygonal Approximations by Newton's method," *IEEE Trans. Computers*, **C-26** (1977), pp. 800-807.

[12.PH]   Pavlidis, T. and Horowitz, S. L. "Segmentation of Plane Curves," *IEEE Trans. Computers*, **C-23** (1974), pp. 860-870.

[12.RI]   Rice, J. R., "On Adaptive Piecewise Polynomial Approximation," *in* [11.LS], pp. 359-386.

[12.SK]   Sklansky, J.; Chazin, R. L.; and Hansen, B. J. "Minimum-Perimeter Polygons of Digitized Silhouettes," *IEEE Trans. Computers*, **C-21** (1972), pp. 260-268.

[12.TO]   Tomek, I. "Piecewise Linear Approximations," *IEEE Trans. Computers*, **C-23** (1974), pp. 445-448.

12.9 PROBLEMS

12.1.   Verify the values of the elements and the determinant of the Gram matrix given in Section 12.3. For example, show that

$$U_{i,1}(x)U_{i,1}(x) \equiv$$

$$\int_{iL}^{iL+L} \left[\frac{x - iL}{L}\right]^2 dx + \int_{iL+L}^{iL+2L} \left[\frac{iL + 2L - x}{L}\right]^2 dx = \frac{2L}{3},$$

etc.

12.2.   Write a program implementing Algorithm 12.2.

12.3.   Prove the claim of Section 12.5.1 about the relation between the maximum error obtained by an interpolant to that of the optimal approximation. (If you have trouble with the proof, check reference [11.DB2].)

12.4. Modify the Point Editor of Problem 10.6 to allow arc addressing and use it to fit polygons by incorporating the results of Problem 12.2.

12.5. Prove that the suboptimal circle fit of Example 12.1 requires that

$$r = \frac{1}{\sqrt{n}}\sqrt{\sum_{i=1}^{n}(x_i - x_c)^2 + \sum_{i=1}^{n}(y_i - y_c)^2}$$

12.6. Derive Equations (12.29) directly by minimizing E in Equation (12.28). Is there an underlying assumption about the order of the data points? Modify the algorithm so that it is not order sensitive. Also, extend it for approximations by rectangles.

12.7. The point editor can be expanded to emulate a draftsperson by incorporating various approximation routines so that sloppy sketches are transformed into neat drawings. Do that by incorporating Algorithm 12.2 into the editor. (This problem is an extension of Problem 12.4.)

12.8. Implement the formulas of Example 12.3 and use them as part of an editor to draw ellipses that fit rough sketches of curves that were intended to be ellipses.

Chapter 13

SURFACE FITTING
AND SURFACE DISPLAYING

13.1 INTRODUCTION

The display of the surface of a three-dimensional object is an important problem in applications of graphics systems where the goal is to provide the user with different views of a group of solid objects. Surface fitting is also necessary when the objects are given initially as sets of points. Surface fitting and displaying are also of interest in other areas. In computerized cartography or geography one deals with models of terrain that are expressed as mathematical surfaces. In picture processing and pattern recognition, surfaces enter into image analysis in at least two ways. First, one can think of a picture as a surface by using the brightness values for the third coordinate. Second, one may wish to consider the surfaces of the objects that appear in a picture. Then the segmentation problem (Chapter 4) is reduced to identifying groups of pixels that are images of a single surface.

In all of these applications the surfaces involved are too complex to be described by a single equation over their domain, and therefore a need for piecewise approximations arises. The simplest approximations are piecewise linear, and in particular polyhedra with triangular faces. Let $\{P\}$ be a set of points located on a surface S. Then each triplet of points defines a plane, and an appropriate choice of triplets constitutes a polyhedral approximation to S. Unfortunately, in many cases the number of triangles necessary for a reasonable approximation is too large, and higher order surfaces must be considered. This leads to the problem of how such piecewise surfaces can be represented.

One solution is to define a set of curves over a surface and then define *interpolating surface patches* over these curves. We discuss such methods in Sections 13.4, 13.5, and 13.6. Another solution is to use *guiding points* or *guiding planes* in the manner done in the plane for Bezier curves and B-splines. These techniques are discussed in Sections 13.7 and 13.8. Sections 13.2 and 13.3 present some basic formulas for the study of all such surfaces. Section 13.9 discusses the problem of display, with emphasis on shading.

An important consideration in selecting a mathematical form for representing surfaces is the ease with which one can solve some important problems in graphics, such as finding the intersection of two surfaces. Clearly, planes are best for this purpose but for large numbers of patches the total amount of computation can be substantial. B-spline surfaces have the convex hull property (Proposition 11.2) that enables one to define planes delimiting the location of the surface. The number of such planes may be significantly smaller than the number needed for a polyhedral approximation, and therefore it is easier to solve for intersections and similar problems in terms of such planes. The additional amount of work to find the exact intersection is often very small. Indeed, most of the convex hulls will not intersect at all, and therefore there is no need to check whether the respective surfaces intersect. In the case of terrain maps for use in computerized cartography, planes seem to be a reasonable choice because the smoothness requirements are not severe.

13.2 SOME SIMPLE PROPERTIES OF SURFACES

In general, a surface is described by one of the following three forms of equations:

$$\text{Explicit:} \quad z = f(x,y) \tag{13.1a}$$
$$\text{Algebraic:} \quad F(x,y,z) = 0 \tag{13.1b}$$
$$\text{Parametric:} \quad x = X(u,v), \, y = Y(u,v), \, z = Z(u,v) \tag{13.1c}$$

The parametric form is the most convenient for graphics applications and it will be the one most frequently used in this text. In many problems it is useful to know the equation of the normal to the surface at a point. This can be found easily from the algebraic form. Since $F(x,y,z)$ is a constant, its total differential will be zero, so that

$$\frac{\partial F}{\partial x}dx + \frac{\partial F}{\partial y}dy + \frac{\partial F}{\partial z}dz = 0 \tag{13.2}$$

The quantities dx, dy, dz denote variations along the surface, so they may be considered as defining a vector tangent to the surface. Equation (13.2) can then be interpreted as the scalar product of a vector whose components are the partial derivatives with a vector tangent to the surface. Since the product is zero, the normal to the surface is parallel to the first vector. (Compare also the discussion of Section 10.7.1.)

Example 13.1: The equation of a plane is given as

$$ax + by + cz = 1 .$$

Normals to it are parallel to (a, b, c). □

Example 13.2: The equation of a sphere centered at the origin is

$$x^2 + y^2 + z^2 = r^2 .$$

The normal at each point (x, y, z) is parallel to the vector (x, y, z). □

In order to study the parametric representation we introduce the following notation

$$X_u = \frac{\partial X}{\partial u} . \tag{13.3}$$

Similar notation is used for the other variables. The vectors (X_u, Y_u, Z_u) and (X_v, Y_v, Z_v) are tangent to the surface so that if (F_x, F_y, F_z) is the normal vector we must have the following two equations:

$$F_x X_u + F_y Y_u + F_z Z_u = 0 \tag{13.4a}$$

$$F_x X_v + F_y Y_v + F_z Z_v = 0 \tag{13.4b}$$

One can show by substitution that the above two equations have the following solution

$$F_x = Y_u Z_v - Z_u Y_v \tag{13.5a}$$

$$F_y = - X_u Z_v + Z_u X_v \tag{13.5b}$$

$$F_z = X_u Y_v - Y_u X_v \tag{13.5c}$$

Because the system of Equations (13.4) has more unknowns than equations the solution is not unique and care should be taken to eliminate all common factors from the righthand side of Equations (13.5). This step is necessary because Equations (13.4) define the direction of the gradient but not its size. This observation is useful for writing an equation connecting the gradient of the parametric and explicit forms. Indeed, the explicit form is a special case of the algebraic, as one can see by writing it as

$$z - f(x,y) = 0 \qquad (13.6)$$

Then we find that

$$F_x = -f_x \qquad F_y = -f_y \qquad F_z = 1 \qquad (13.7)$$

The third equation imposes a constraint so that we end up with the following:

$$f_x = \frac{Z_u Y_v - Z_v Y_u}{X_u Y_v - X_v Y_u} \qquad (13.8a)$$

$$f_y = \frac{X_u Z_v - X_v Z_u}{X_u Y_v - X_v Y_u} \qquad (13.8b)$$

Example 13.3: A parametric definition of a sphere centered at the origin is

$$x = \cos u \cos v \quad y = \sin u \cos v \quad z = \sin v$$

Equations (13.5) yield the following values for the normal after elimination of common factors

$$F_x = \cos u \cos v \quad F_y = \sin u \cos v \quad F_z = \sin v$$

Are these values in agreement with what one expects from Example 13.2? We also find that

$$f_x = -\frac{\cos u}{\tan v} \quad f_y = -\frac{\sin u}{\tan v}$$

□

13.3 SINGULAR POINTS OF A SURFACE

If a surface is given in an explicit form, points where the partial derivatives of z with respect to x and to y vanish are called *singular* or *stationary* points. We shall study the properties of such points through a Taylor expansion of the function f in their neighborhood. We shall use a notation similar to Equation (13.3) for the partial derivatives. If x_0, y_0 are the coordinates of a singular point, we have

$$f(x,y) = f(x_0,y_0) + (x - x_0)f_x + (y - y_0)f_y +$$

$$\frac{1}{2}(x - x_0)^2 f_{xx} + (x - x_0)(y - y_0)f_{xy} + \frac{1}{2}(y - y_0)^2 f_{yy} + \cdots \quad (13.9)$$

f_{xx} is the second partial derivative with respect to x, etc. At a singular point both first partial derivatives are zero. Therefore the form of the function is determined by the second derivatives. We shall investigate the variation of the function along a fixed direction from (x_0, y_0). Denote the ratio $(y - y_0)/(x - x_0)$ by h. Then the above Taylor expansion can be written as

$$f(x, y) = f(x_0, y_0) + 2(x - x_0)^2 \left[f_{xx} + 2hf_{xy} + h^2 f_{yy} \right] + \cdots \quad (13.10)$$

assuming that $x \neq x_0$. We know from elementary algebra that a quadratic polynomial has the sign of the coefficient of its leading term if the discriminant of its coefficients is negative (i.e. it has no real roots). Therefore the sign of the quantity in brackets (regarded as a polynomial in h) will be always the same if

$$f_{xy}^2 - f_{xx} f_{yy} < 0 \quad (13.11)$$

Clearly, this inequality also implies that f_{yy} and f_{xx} have the same sign. When they are positive the quantity in braces will also be positive and the value of the function away from the singularity will be greater than its value at the singular point. Therefore the singular point is a *minimum*. Conversely, if these derivatives are negative the singular point will be a *maximum*. If the inequality of Equation (13.11) does not hold, then we have a *saddle point*. This means that there is a direction along which the singular point appears as a minimum and another direction where it appears as a maximum.

Example 13.4: Consider the function $z = f(x, y) = x^2 + 2axy + y^2$. Clearly, the point $(0,0)$ is singular and the quantity in brackets in Equation (13.10) is now

$$2(1 + 2ah + h^2)$$

If the absolute value of a is less than 1, then the singular point is a minimum. Indeed, for small values of a the surface looks like a cup with nearly circular cross-sections. If a is a large positive number, then the xy term becomes dominant. If x and y have the same sign, the value of the function will be grater than zero for the most part, while the opposite will be true if the x and y have different signs. In particular, let us consider the line $x = y$. Then $z = 2(1 + a)x^2$ and for positive a the intersection of the surface and a plane along the line will show a minimum. If $x = -y$, then we have $z = 2(1 - a)x^2$ and the intersection shows a maximum. Figure 13.1 illustrates the form of the surface for $a = 2$. One can see why the name "saddle point" is used. □

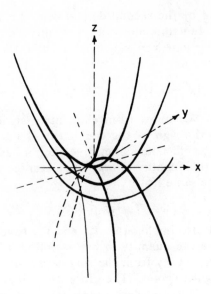

Figure 13.1 A saddle point

13.4 LINEAR AND BILINEAR INTERPOLATING SURFACE PATCHES

The simplest form of interpolant in three dimensions is the plane triangle defined by three points $\{P_j\}_1^3$. Let u and v be scalar variables ranging from 0 to 1. Then the surface of the triangle with vertices at these points is given by

$$T(u,v) = P_1 u + P_2 v + P_3(1-u-v) , \qquad (13.12)$$

provided that $u+v \leq 1$. Clearly, $T(1,0) = P_1$, $T(0,1) = P_2$, and $T(0,0) = P_3$. Furthermore, $T(u,0)$ is the line joining P_1 and P_3, $T(0,v)$ is the line joining P_2 and P_3, and $T(u,1-u)$ is the line joining P_1 and P_2.

A slightly more complex form involves bilinear interpolation over a set of four points (see Figure 13.2). Then an interpolating bilinear surface $S(u,v)$ is defined as

$$S(u,v) = P_1(1-u)(1-v) + P_2(1-u)v + P_3 u(1-v) + P_4 uv , \quad (13.13)$$

where $0 \leq u,v \leq 1$.

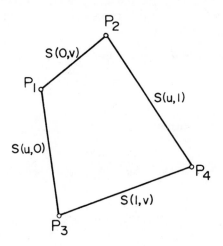

Figure 13.2 Arrangement of the four points defining a bilinear surface

Obviously $S(0,0) = P_1$, $S(0,1) = P_2$, etc. Also $S(0,v)$ is the line segment joining P_1 and P_2, $S(1,v)$ is the line segment joining P_3 and P_4, etc. If the four points are coplanar, then S is the plane quadrilateral interpolating them; otherwise S is a surface of second degree. The gradient of the surface with respect to u and v can be found by simple differentiation of Equation (13.13):

$$\frac{\partial S}{\partial u} = (P_4 - P_2)v + (P_3 - P_1)(1-v) \tag{13.14a}$$

$$\frac{\partial S}{\partial v} = (P_4 - P_3)u + (P_2 - P_1)(1-u) \tag{13.14b}$$

Note that these are vector equations, so that if X_i denotes the x-coordinate of the point P_i, we have

$$X^u = (X_4 - X_2)v + (X_3 - X_1)(1-v) \, ,$$

and similarly for Y^u and Z^u. We have used a superscript to denote the partial derivative rather than a subscript as in Equation 13.3 to avoid confusion with the subscripts identifying the points. The gradient with respect to the x-y coordinates can be found by an application of Equations (13.8).

Example 13.5:   Let $P_1 = (0,0,0)$, $P_2 = (0,1,0)$, $P_3 = (1,0,0)$, and $P_4 = (1,1,1)$. Then the x, y, z coordinates of each point of the bilinear interpolation will be given by

$$x(u,v) = u, \quad y(u,v) = v, \quad z(u,v) = uv \qquad (13.15a)$$

or

$$z = xy \qquad (13.15b)$$

and the gradient of the surface by

$$\frac{\partial S}{\partial u} = \begin{pmatrix} 1 \\ 0 \\ v \end{pmatrix} \qquad (13.16a)$$

$$\frac{\partial S}{\partial v} = \begin{pmatrix} 0 \\ 1 \\ u \end{pmatrix} \qquad (13.16b)$$

The combination of Equations (13.15a), (13.16a), and (13.16b) yields

$$\frac{\partial z}{\partial x} = y \qquad (13.16c)$$

and

$$\frac{\partial z}{\partial y} = x \qquad (13.16d)$$

which also could have been found by a direct differentiation of Equation (13.15b). $\square$

The conclusions of the above example have validity in other cases as well because one can always choose the plane defined by three of the points as $z = 0$ and place one of them at the origin. Then for the surface, $z = z_4 uv$.

13.5 LOFTED SURFACES

Lofted surfaces are produced by linear interpolation not between points, but between curves. Let $P(0,v)$ and $P(1,v)$ be the equations of two space curves. Then a lofted surface is defined as

$$S(u,v) = (1-u)P(0,v) + uP(1,v) . \qquad (13.17)$$

In other words the surface is produced by a line segment sliding between two curves. For example, if the two curves are circles in planes perpendicular to the line joining their centers, then the resulting surface will be a cone cut by two planes.

13.6 COONS SURFACES

These are surfaces that interpolate between four curves. They are named after S. A. Coons, who proposed them around 1960 (see Bibliographical Notes). Let $P(u,v)$ be a function of two variables such that for u or v constant, $P(u,v)$ is reduced to the parametric representation of a space curve. A surface patch is constructed by blending the edge curves $P(u,0)$, $P(u,1)$, $P(0,v)$, and $P(1,v)$ in the following manner:

$$S(u,v) = P(u,0)(1-v) + P(u,1)v + P(0,v)(1-u) + P(1,v)u$$
$$-P(0,0)(1-u)(1-v) - P(0,1)(1-u)v$$
$$-P(1,0)u(1-v) - P(1,1)uv . \qquad (13.18)$$

The last four terms are necessary to avoid counting the pairwise intersections of the four curves twice. In this way we have:

$$S(u,0) = P(u,0) + P(0,0)(1-u) + P(1,0)u$$
$$- P(0,0)(1-u) - P(1,0)u = P(u,0) ,$$

with similar expressions for $S(u,1)$, etc. Equation (13.18) guarantees that the resulting surface will be continuous but not necessarily smooth because of possible gradient discontinuities. Before discussing how to ensure smoothness, we shall introduce a more compact form of Equation (13.18). Let

$$P_1(v) = \begin{bmatrix} P(0,v) \\ P(1,v) \end{bmatrix} , \qquad (13.19a)$$

$$P_2(u) = \begin{bmatrix} P(u,0) \\ P(u,1) \end{bmatrix} , \qquad (13.19b)$$

and

$$b(u) = \begin{bmatrix} 1-u \\ u \end{bmatrix} . \qquad (13.19c)$$

Then Equation (13.18) becomes

$$S(u,v) = b'(u)P_1(v) + P_2'(u)b(v) - b'(u)Mb(v) \qquad (13.20)$$

where M is a matrix with $M_{ij} = P(i,j)$. Up to now we have used linear blending functions, but this can be generalized to allow arbitrary forms. In particular, we define

$$b(u) = \begin{bmatrix} b_0(u) \\ b_1(u) \end{bmatrix} , \qquad (13.21a)$$

for any functions $b_i(u)$ that have the property

$$b_i(u) = \delta_{iu} , \tag{13.21b}$$

for any integer u.

Example 13.6:   The following is a possible choice for blending functions:

$$b_0(u) = \cos^2(\frac{\pi}{2}u) \tag{13.22a}$$

$$b_1(u) = \sin^2(\frac{\pi}{2}u) \tag{13.22b}$$

If the bounding curves are straight lines with corners at the points used in Example 13.5, then we have the following equations for the x, y, and z coordinates:

$$P(u,0) = uP_3, \quad P(u,1) = uP_4 + (1-u)P_2,$$
$$P(0,v) = vP_2, \quad P(1,v) = vP_4 + (1-v)P_3.$$

The equation of the Coons surface defined by these points will be:

$$S(u,v) = \cos^2(\frac{\pi}{2}v)uP_3 + \sin^2(\frac{\pi}{2}v)\left[uP_4 + (1-u)P_2\right] +$$

$$\cos^2(\frac{\pi}{2}u)vP_2 + \sin^2(\frac{\pi}{2}u)\left[vP_4 + (1-v)P_3\right] -$$

$$\cos^2(\frac{\pi}{2}u)\sin^2(\frac{\pi}{2}v)P_2 - \sin^2(\frac{\pi}{2}u)\cos^2(\frac{\pi}{2}v)P_3 -$$

$$\sin^2(\frac{\pi}{2}u)\sin^2(\frac{\pi}{2}v)P_4 .$$

In particular, the coordinates of the surface will be given by

$$x(u,v) = u, \quad y(u,v) = v, \tag{13.23a}$$

and

$$z(u,v) = \sin^2(\frac{\pi}{2}v)u + \sin^2(\frac{\pi}{2}u)v - \sin^2(\frac{\pi}{2}u)\sin^2(\frac{\pi}{2}v) . \tag{13.23b}$$

□

In order to have continuity of the gradient, we may wish to interpolate not only with respect to the curves $P(u,v)$ but also with respect to their derivatives. This can be accomplished by adding two extra components to each of the vectors of Equations (13.19), representing the derivative functions and the blending functions for those derivatives. The matrix M must also be expanded to a 4×4 size. The need to specify these derivatives is a disadvantage of the method and complicates the design process. The usual formalism in this case is to use superscripts to denote a derivative and in particular define for any function $g(u,v)$

$$g^u = \frac{\partial g(u,v)}{\partial u}$$ (13.24a)

and

$$g^{uv} = \frac{\partial^2 g(u,v)}{\partial u\,\partial v}$$ (13.24b)

Then we define

$$\mathbf{P}_1(v) = \begin{bmatrix} P(0,v) \\ P(1,v) \\ P^u(0,v) \\ P^u(1,v) \end{bmatrix}$$ (13.25)

and similarly for $\mathbf{P}_2(u)$. Also

$$\mathbf{b}(u) = \begin{bmatrix} b_{00}(u) \\ b_{01}(u) \\ b_{10}(u) \\ b_{11}(u) \end{bmatrix}$$ (13.26)

with the assumption that

$$b^k_{ji}(u) = \delta_{kj} \cdot \delta_{iu}$$ (13.27)

for integer u, and $k = 0$ if no derivative is taken, and $k = 1$ if there is differentiation. Thus,

$$b_{00}(0) = 1$$ (13.28a)

$$b_{01}(1) = b^u_{00}(0) = b^u_{00}(1) = 0 .$$ (13.28b)

In other words, $b_{0i}(u)$ is the blending function for the curves and $b_{1i}(u)$ the blending function for the slopes. δ_{kj} is one in the following two cases: $k = j = 0$ corresponding to the first two components of the blending vector, and $k = j = 1$ to the derivatives of the last two components. The matrix M is now given by

$$M = \begin{bmatrix} P(0,0) & P(0,1) & P^v(0,0) & P^v(0,1) \\ P(1,0) & P(1,1) & P^v(1,0) & P^v(1,1) \\ P^u(0,0) & P^u(0,1) & P^{uv}(0,0) & P^{uv}(0,1) \\ P^u(1,0) & P^u(1,1) & P^{uv}(1,0) & P^{uv}(1,1) \end{bmatrix}$$ (13.29)

With these notations Equation (13.20) remains valid. Furthermore, one can verify that not only equalities of the type $S(u,0) = P(u,0)$ are valid, but also equalities of the form $S^u(u,0) = P^u(u,0)$, etc. are valid.

13.7 GUIDED SURFACES

It is possible to specify a surface in terms of guiding points by a simple generalization of the Bezier polynomials or the B-splines of the form discussed in Section 11.6.

13.7.1 Bezier Surfaces

If $Q(t)$ and $R(t)$ are two Bezier polynomials, then a surface $S(u,v)$ can be defined as their tensor product $Q(u)R(v)$. This product is evaluated separately for each coordinate of the guiding points. This procedure has no effect on the form in which the variables u and v appear, but it affects the form of the coefficients. If we set $P_{ij}^h = Q_i^h R_j^h$, where h stands for x, y, or z, then we reach the following definition:

$$S(u,v) = \sum_{i=0}^{m} \sum_{j=0}^{n} C_i^m u^i (1-u)^{m-i} C_j^n v^j (1-v)^{n-j} P_{ij} . \qquad (13.30)$$

It is easy to verify that

$$S(u,0) = \sum_{i=0}^{m} C_i^m u^i (1-u)^{m-i} P_{i0} , \qquad (13.31)$$

and to obtain similar expressions for $S(u,1)$, $S(0,v)$, and $S(1,v)$. Thus $S(u,v)$ is bounded by four Bezier polynomials and the four corner points are P_{00}, P_{0n}, P_{m0}, and P_{mn}. One can show that the surface lies in the convex hull of the guiding points by observing that the double sum of the coefficients of P_{ij} equals 1.

It is also possible to describe the surface in terms of its parts in a manner similar to that used in Section 10.5 for Bezier polynomials (Theorem 10.1.) Such a description is useful in graphics applications where one may wish to subdivide a patch into smaller parts to solve visibility problems (see Chapter 17).

13.7.2 B-Spline Surfaces

A B-spline surface is formally defined as

$$P(u,v) = \sum_{i=-m}^{k} \sum_{j=-m}^{l} N_{i,m}(u) N_{j,m}(v) P_{ij} , \qquad (13.32)$$

for $u_0 \le u \le u_{k+1}$ and $v_0 \le v \le v_{l+1}$. Without loss of generality we assume that $u_0 = v_0 = 0$. We recall that $N_{i,m}(u)$ is zero unless $u_i < u < u_{i+m+1}$ and that the sum of all the B-splines at a particular point is 1 (Theorem 11.1). We can then find that

$$P(u,0) = \sum_{i=-m}^{k} N_{i,m}(u) \sum_{j=-m}^{0} N_{j,m}(0)P_{ij}$$

If the guiding points with negative indices are all the same as P_{i0}, then the above equation is simplified into

$$P(u,0) = \sum_{i=-m}^{k} N_{i,m}(u)P_{i0} , \qquad (13.33)$$

i.e., the surface is bounded by a spline for $v = 0$. The same method and assumptions lead to identical results for the other extreme values of u and v. Of course, this result is not as important as in the case of Coons surfaces because Equation (13.32) does not describe a single patch but the whole surface of interest. The patches can be found for each set of values of u and v that are between breakpoints: $u_i \leq u \leq u_{i+1}$, $v_j \leq v \leq v_{j+1}$. It is instructive to study the form of Equation (13.33) for some special cases.

We first consider bilinear interpolation when $m = 1$ and the breakpoints are uniformly distributed, one unit of length apart ($L = 1$ in terms of Equation (11.8)). Then we have

$$P(u,v) = (u-u_i)(v-v_j)P_{ij} + (u-u_i)(v_{j+1}-v)P_{i,j-1}$$
$$+ (u_{i+1}-u)(v-v_j)P_{i-1,j} + (u_{i+1}-u)(v_{j+1}-v)P_{i-1,j-1} . \quad (13.34)$$

This is a bilinear form similar to that given by Equation (13.13). Since $u_{i+1} - u_i = 1$ and $v_{j+1} - v_j = 1$ we find that

$$P(u_i,v) = (v-v_j)P_{i-1,j} + (v_{j+1}-v)P_{i-1,j-1} , \qquad (13.34a)$$

$$P(u_{i+1},v) = (v-v_j)P_{ij} + (v_{j+1}-v)P_{i,j-1} , \qquad (13.34b)$$

etc. Also

$$P(u_i,v_j) = P_{i-1,j-1} , \qquad (13.35a)$$

$$P(u_{i+1},v_{j+1}) = P_{ij} , \qquad (13.35b)$$

etc. Therefore, bilinear interpolation is a special case of Equation (13.32) for $m = 1$.

We next study surfaces obtained through uniform second degree B-splines ($m = 2$) with $L = 1$. We also choose $u_0 = 0$ so that $u_i = i$. We saw in Section 11.7 (Example 11.4) that such splines are particularly suited for shape description. The analysis used to derive Equations (11.30a) and (11.32) can be repeated for the present case to derive similar expressions. In particular, we find that

$$P(u_i,v_j) = \frac{1}{4}\left[P_{i-1,j-1} + P_{i-1,j-2} + P_{i-2,j-1} + P_{i-2,j-2}\right] , (13.36)$$

i.e., the surface passes through the center of the quadrangle formed by four of the guiding points. Also

$$\frac{\partial}{\partial u}P \mid u_i v_j = \frac{1}{2}(P_{i-1,j-1} + P_{i-1,j-2}) - \frac{1}{2}(P_{i-2,j-1} + P_{i-2,j-2}) \ . \quad (13.37)$$

The last two equations mean that if one forms a polyhedron whose sides are quadrangles and whose vertices can be mapped into a square grid, then the spline surface generated with the vertices as guiding points has the property that it passes through the center of each face and is tangent to it at that point.

13.8 THE CHOICE OF A SURFACE PARTITION

If a surface is given by a set of points, one must choose an appropriate partition or define the set of guiding points before applying any of the methods of the previous four sections. This is the generalization of the knot location problem of Section 12.4. Given the difficulty of the latter, it is not surprising that no automatic solutions are available for the current problem. In many graphics applications the curves are drawn on a solid model, and these serve as the input during digitization. In image processing, finding the partition is equivalent to solving the segmentation problem (Chapter 4). Because continuity constraints are not important in that application, the problem is somewhat simplified.

13.9 DISPLAY OF SURFACES AND SHADING

Our major problem in displaying curves was the conversion of the mathematical form into a set of pixel coordinates. This information is all that one needs to display a plane curve. Having the coordinates (x_i, y_i, z_i) of the points of a surface is far from enough for a display. Two basic approaches are possible: encoding the height (z-coordinate) information into color, or shading. Color encoding leads to contour displays that may be useful for some applications but are neither aesthetically appealing nor informative. Shading gives better displays but requires more computation. If all the surfaces are planes one can create the impression of shading by giving a uniform color or gray level to the projection of each visible plane. Sometimes this is sufficient to create the illusion of depth. Some of the problems in the display of nonplanar surfaces occur because we must deal with their projections on a plane, and therefore we must deal with the question of visibility: some of the surface points may hide others. In particular, the outline of the projection of a surface patch is not always the projection of its boundary. A complete treatment of these problems is outside our scope, so we shall limit our discussion to basic principles.

In raster graphics, contours may be displayed in a simple manner by assigning a correspondence between z and color or gray level. If the points have been selected with a high enough density, contours of constant z will show up as curves of constant brightness. The problem is far more difficult in vector graphics because we must trace such curves on the surface.

Shading presumes the existence of a light source as well as knowledge of the reflective properties of the surface. If the light source is very far from the object, then one can assume that the light rays are all parallel and the appearance of a surface will depend on its own properties and the orientation with respect to the light source. The amount of light incident to a surface is proportional to the scalar product of the normal n to the surface and a vector l parallel to the direction of the light source, as shown in Figure 13.3. (In Section 13.2 we saw how to find the normals to mathematically defined surfaces.)

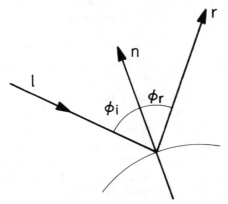

Figure 13.3 Reflection of light from surfaces. n denotes the normal to the surface, l the direction of the light source, and r the direction of reflected light. ϕ_i is the incidence angle and ϕ_r the reflection angle.

If a surface is a perfect mirror, then its brightness at each point can be calculated from the fundamental law of reflection: the reflection angle is equal to the incidence angle. Light will be seen by observers only if they look from the proper direction. Let e be a vector parallel to that direction and let us assume that this vector, as well as l, has been normalized to unit length. Then the bisectrix of their angle will be parallel to their sum $l + e$, so that the amount of light seen varies with the scalar product of that vector and the normal to the surface, n. The surface will appear brightest when the angle is zero, and dark when the angle equals 90°. Such a reflection is called *specular* and it contributes only in part to the total brightness of the surface. *Diffuse* reflection contributes additional brightness. This assumes that light is reflected equally in all directions and differences in brightness are due only to differences in the amount of incident light. Therefore the illumination due to diffuse reflection is proportional to the scalar product of l and n. Clearly, if the scalar product is negative there is no reflected light at all so that in our computation we should consider the scalar product only if it is positive. If I_s denotes the specular reflection and I_d the diffuse reflection we have

$$I_s = \max[0, e \cdot n] \tag{13.38a}$$

$$I_d = \max[0, l \cdot n] \tag{13.38b}$$

In order to calculate the total illumination one must form a weighted sum of these terms. Furthermore, there is empirical evidence that raising I_s to some power k produces more realistic highlights than otherwise (see Bibliographical Notes). Thus we have

$$I = mI_d + gI_s^k \tag{13.39}$$

where m is a coefficient describing how matte the surface is and g a coefficient describing how glossy it is. Clearly, what is important is the relative size of m and g. Some authors select them under the constraint $m + g = 1$. Values of k in the range 5 to 60 have been used to produce some impressive images reported in the literature [13.BN].

The practical application of these formulas requires the calculation of the normal at each point of the surface. Various approximations have been reported that calculate the value only at a few points and interpolate among the rest (see Bibliographical Notes).

Example 13.7:   We shall use the expression for the normal to a sphere, found in Examples 13.2 and 13.3, to construct a shaded display of a sphere. We assume that the surface is illuminated from above so that $l = (0,0,1)$, that an observer is along the x-axis, and that the display is on the y-z plane. Then $e = (1,0,0)$ and the normalized sum of these two vectors will be $(1/\sqrt{2}, 0, 1/\sqrt{2})$. Since $n = (x, y, z)$ we find that

$$I_s = \max\left[0, \frac{x + z}{\sqrt{2}}\right] \quad I_d = \max[0, z]$$

Because of the defining equation for a sphere, we have $x = \pm\sqrt{1 - y^2 + z^2}$, so that Equation (13.39) becomes

$$I = m \max[0,z] + g\left[\max[0,z \pm \sqrt{1 - y^2 + z^2}]\right]^k \quad (13.40)$$

This equation can be evaluated easily for the various values of y and z that satisfy $y^2 + z^2 \leq 1$ (see Problem 13.3). Figure 13.4 (Plate 27) shows two views of the sphere, both for $k = 1$. □

13.10 BIBLIOGRAPHICAL NOTES

Surface display and description is a subject that has received attention in the literature mostly since 1970. Its popularity has coincided with the availability of raster graphics at low cost. Earlier work focused primarily on mathematical descriptions.† For an early survey of Coons surfaces see [13.FO]. [13.LR] is a recent study emphasizing Bezier and B-spline surfaces. [11.BR], [13.LA], and [13.SSS] emphasize the use of surfaces in graphics applications. Because of the highly local nature of the representation, B-spline surfaces seem the most promising for applications where the surface may be designed interactively. [13.BL] is a very good reference on surface display and the discussion of Section 13.7 has relied on it. [13.BN] presents a small part of the material of [13.BN] but contains numerous examples and is easy to find in a library. The model of Equations (13.38) and (13.39) was proposed in [13.PH]. See [13.WH] for a more general model that also includes transmitted light and [13.CT] for a model that takes into account the dependence of the reflectance on the light wavelength. [13.LA] contains a comprehensive treatment of the surface display problem, including strategies for evaluation of the normal, visibility, and shading. [13.HO] is a review of a related subject, the shading of terrain maps. We should point out that the shading rules used by artists are different than the mathematical rules described in Section 13.9. They often assume that the diffuse illumination is due to secondary reflections of the light source and the darkest area is a zone between the highlight of the specular reflection and the maximum of the diffuse reflection (see [13.GU], for example).

13.11 RELEVANT LITERATURE

[13.BL] Blinn, J. F. "Computer Display of Curved Surfaces," *Ph.D. dissertation,* Dept. of Computer Science, University of Utah, 1978.

[13.BN] Blinn, J. F. and Newell, M. E. "Texture and Reflection in Computer Generated Images," *CACM,* **19** (1976), pp. 542-547.

---

† Of course artists have dealt with the problems of surface description and shading for centuries but their methods are not subject to immediate implementation by computers.

[13.CT]   Cook, R. L. and Torrance, K. E. "A Reflectance Model for Computer Graphics," *SIGGRAPH'81*, Dallas, Texas, (August 1981), pp. 307-316.

[13.FO]   Forrest, A. R. "On Coons and Other Methods for the Representation of Curved Surfaces," *CGIP*, **1** (1972), pp. 341-359.

[13.GU]   Guptill, A. L. *Drawing with Pen and Ink*, revised edition, New York: Van Nostrand, 1968.

[13.HO]   Horn, B. K. P. "Hill Shading and the Reflectance Map," *IEEE Proceedings*, **69** (1981), pp. 14-47.

[13.LA]   Lane, J. M.; Carpenter, L. C.; Whitted, T.; and Blinn, J. F. "Scan Line Methods for Displaying Parametrically Defined Surfaces," *CACM*, **23** (1980), pp. 23-34.

[13.LR]   Lane, J. M. and Riesenfeld, R. F. "A Theoretical Development for the Computer Generation and Display of Piecewise Polynomial Surfaces," *IEEE Trans. on Pattern Analysis and Machine Intelligence*, **PAMI-2** (1980), pp. 35-46.

[13.PH]   Phong, B. T. "Illumination for Computer Generated Images," *CACM*, **18** (1975), pp. 311-317.

[13.SSS] Sutherland, I. E.; Sproull, R. F.; and Schumacker, R. A. "A Characterization of Ten Hidden-Surface Algorithms," *ACM Computing Surveys*, **6** (1974), pp. 1-55.

[13.WH]   Whitted, T. "An Improved Illumination Model for Shaded Display," *CACM*, **23** (1980), pp. 343-349.

13.12 PROBLEMS

13.1. Show that the expressions for the normal to a sphere obtained in Examples 13.2 and 13.3 are equivalent.

13.2. Study the form of the surface patch of Example 13.5 by plotting various cross-sections of the $S(u,v)$, such as $S(u,u)$, $S(u,1-u)$, $S(u,1/3)$, $S(u,1/2)$, $S(u,2/3)$, etc.

13.3. (a) Write a program implementing Equation (13.40) and use it to produce a display of a shaded sphere such as the one shown in Figure 13.4 (Plate 27). Study the effect of varying the parameters d, g, and k. (b) Show that the loci of the points that have the same illumination due to specular reflection are ellipses. Show formally that all such ellipses are contained within the circle that is the projection of the sphere.

Chapter 14

THE MATHEMATICS OF TWO-DIMENSIONAL GRAPHICS

14.1 INTRODUCTION

A major goal in computer graphics is to create pictorial displays out of mathematical descriptions of images. This requires the creation (usually by the host computer) of a display file that is then sent to the graphic device. In vector graphics where the device expects commands such as "draw vector," the contents of the display file are for the most part primitive instructions. In raster graphics, instructions such as "draw vector" are not primitive and they are translated by the device into pixel configurations in the refresh memory. Strictly speaking, most raster graphics devices do not have a display file. However, it is useful to think in terms of such a file, regardless of how the display device handles it. The creation of a display file is trivial for very simple displays but becomes quite challenging as the complexity of the desired display increases.

Example 14.1: We can use the following sequence of instructions from the set of Section 1.7 (Table 1.2) to draw a square of intensity L on a display screen, with one corner at (x_0, y_0), side of size s, and sides parallel to the vertical and horizontal axis:

$$fore\,(L)$$
$$setp\,(x_0,y_0)$$
$$vec\,(x_0+s\,,y_0)$$
$$vec\,(x_0+s\,,y_0+s\,)$$
$$vec\,(x_0,y_0+s\,)$$
$$vec\,(x_0,y_0)$$

This group of instructions can be called as a procedure *square* $(x_0,y_0,s\,,L\,)$. The square can be erased by a call to *square* $(x_0,y_0,s\,,0)$. (See below for a discussion of possible side effects of erasing.) Filling a square of an arbitrary orientation with a particular color is a more difficult problem and requires implementation of one of the algorithms discussed in Chapter 8. On the other hand a square with vertical and horizontal sides can be treated as a window and a filled display could be achieved with the following program:

$$back\,(L)$$
$$win\,(x_0,y_0,x_0+s\,,y_0+s\,)$$
$$erase$$

This could be called as a program *fsquare* $(x_0,y_0,s\,,L\,)$. $\Box$

This example also illustrates a common problem with graphic displays. The set of instructions does not specify whether the given corner (x_0,y_0) will be at the upper left, lower left, upper right, or lower right. The answer depends on the device! Some of them assume that the origin (0,0) is at the lower left corner, while others assume it to be at the upper right corner. In some cases it is possible to select the origin by a graphic command, while in others the user must create the files by taking the origin used by the device into account.

Example 14.2: The following simple program can create the illusion of a square moving away from the observer.

Algorithm 14.1 Moving square

1.   **While** s is positive **do:**
           Begin.
2.   *square* $(x\,,y\,,s\,,L\,)$
3.   **sleep(T)**
4.   *square* $(x\,,y\,,s\,,0)$
5.   Decrement s by 2 and L by 1, and increment x and y by 1.
           End.
6.   **End of Algorithm.**

Step 2 causes the display of a square of size s and color L, while step 4 displays a square of similar size and color 0, erasing the one just displayed.† The *sleep*(T) instruction asks the program to suspend execution for T units of time so that the square can be seen before it is erased. In many time-sharing systems the waiting time for service plus the execution time for the instructions are long enough so that no additional delay is needed. One could use *fsquare* instead of *square* to produce the same effect with a filled square. More complicated motions could be programmed by changing step 5. However, if one wants to introduce rotation, the basic routine for displaying the square must be modified, since the sides will not remain parallel to the coordinate axes. Another potential problem is that the square may move outside the limits of the display. One must check for that and modify the commands so that only the part within the display limits is shown. Thus the square must be clipped. (One cannot depend on the device to do the clipping. See Section 15.1 for more on this point.) □

Example 14.3: We want to display a cube with one corner at (x_0, y_0, z_0) and sides of size s. It will be necessary to find a projection of the solid on the plane. If a moving display is going to be created, then many such projections may have to be found. If a line drawing is desired, then a simple program, similar to *square*, can be used for the display. For a filled display we must first decide which three of the six faces of the cube are visible. If more than one cube is involved, then we may have to check whether one of them hides another, so an even more complex visibility problem must be solved. □

These examples illustrate some of the major problems that must be solved in order to create a display. Rotations and projections require the *transformation of coordinates,* which in turn requires one to verify whether objects are still within the field of view and whether they are obscuring each other. Such problems can collectively be called *visibility problems.* In this and the next chapter we shall discuss mostly the display of two-dimensional objects, while three-dimensional graphics will be the subject of Chapters 16 and 17. Two-dimensional coordinate

---

† The implementation of the erase instruction is nontrivial. (Recall the discussion of Sections 1.5 and 1.6.) In a vector graphics system it would be more efficient to manipulate the display list directly. Of course this would make the problem nonportable between vector and raster graphics devices. In raster graphics we may either use an *enable* instruction in order to avoid erasing the background and other objects or to define a window around the object, erase the whole window, and then restore the scene. Clearly, a considerable amount of bookkeeping is required for creating and manipulating complex displays.

transformations will be discussed in Section 14.2. Sections 14.3 and 14.4 present certain mathematical results that are useful for a number of graphics problems. The process of finding whether a line (or polygon) is intersected by another polygon is usually called *clipping* and will be the subject of Chapter 15.

Mathematically, the algorithms of this chapter are very simple and are based on elementary analytical geometry only. However, they provide the foundations for the more complex algorithms that create interesting displays.

14.2 TWO-DIMENSIONAL TRANSFORMATIONS

A very common problem in graphics is to find the location of a pixel (x,y) after it has been rotated by an angle θ around a point (x_0,y_0). Let r be the length of the vector joining (x,y) to (x_0,y_0). This does not change during the rotation and therefore we have the following sets of equations (see Figure 14.1 for the notation).

$$x - x_0 = r\cos\phi \qquad y - y_0 = r\sin\phi \tag{14.1a}$$

$$X - x_0 = r\cos(\phi+\theta) \quad Y - y_0 = r\sin(\phi+\theta) \tag{14.1b}$$

Expanding the cosine and sine functions in Equation (14.1b) and then substituting from Equation (14.1a), we find that the new coordinates (X,Y) are given in terms of the old ones by the following equations:

$$X = x_0 + (x-x_0)\cos\theta - (y-y_0)\sin\theta \tag{14.2a}$$

$$Y = y_0 + (x-x_0)\sin\theta + (y-y_0)\cos\theta \tag{14.2b}$$

It is possible to write these equations in more elegant form by defining the *rotation matrix* around the origin $R(\theta)$ as

$$R(\theta) = \begin{bmatrix} \cos\theta & -\sin\theta \\ \sin\theta & \cos\theta \end{bmatrix} \tag{14.3a}$$

and the vectors

$$X = \begin{bmatrix} X \\ Y \end{bmatrix} \quad x = \begin{bmatrix} x \\ y \end{bmatrix} \quad x_0 = \begin{bmatrix} x_0 \\ y_0 \end{bmatrix}. \tag{14.3b}$$

Then we have

$$X = x_0 + R(\theta)(x-x_0). \tag{14.4}$$

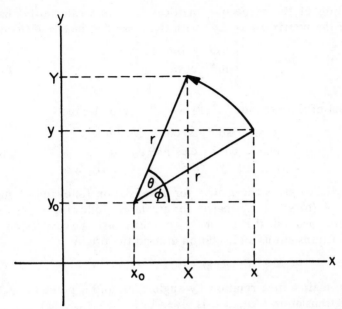

Figure 14.1 Symbols used for the expression of the new coordinates (X,Y) of a point in terms of the old ones (x,y) following a rotation by an angle θ around a point (x_0,y_0)

Translation of a point can be expressed easily by adding to the respective coordinates the amount of the motion. *Scaling* is performed by multiplying the coordinates by a scaling factor, and it can be expressed as a matrix operation by defining the scaling matrix

$$S(S_x,S_y) = \begin{bmatrix} S_x & 0 \\ 0 & S_y \end{bmatrix}. \tag{14.5}$$

There is some uniformity advantage if we express translations through matrices. This can be done by adding a third component equal to 1 to the vector definitions of Equation (14.3b). The rotation and scaling matrices can be modified by adding a third row and a third column whose first two elements are 0 and the third 1, while a translation matrix can now be defined as

$$T(\Delta x,\Delta y) = \begin{bmatrix} 1 & 0 & \Delta x \\ 0 & 1 & \Delta y \\ 0 & 0 & 1 \end{bmatrix}. \tag{14.6}$$

We will now combine these matrices into a single transformation matrix. Indeed, a sequence of transformations corresponds to a multiplication of the respective matrices, and one can verify that the product of the matrix $T(\Delta x, \Delta y)$ with the expanded matrix $R(\theta)$ equals

$$\begin{bmatrix} \cos\theta & -\sin\theta & \Delta x \\ \sin\theta & \cos\theta & \Delta y \\ 0 & 0 & 1 \end{bmatrix}. \tag{14.7a}$$

The product of the expanded $R(\theta)$ with $T(\Delta x, \Delta y)$ equals

$$\begin{bmatrix} \cos\theta & -\sin\theta & \Delta x\cos\theta-\Delta y\sin\theta \\ \sin\theta & \cos\theta & \Delta x\sin\theta+\Delta y\cos\theta \\ 0 & 0 & 1 \end{bmatrix}. \tag{14.7b}$$

Equation (14.7a) gives the matrix for a translation following a rotation. Equation (14.7b) gives the matrix for a rotation following a translation. The rotation around the point (x_0, y_0) can also be expressed as a sequence of translations and rotation around the origin:

$$X = T(x_0, y_0)R(\theta)T(-x_0, -y_0)x \tag{14.8}$$

so that the matrix of a rotation by angle θ around a point (x_0, y_0) followed by a translation $(\Delta x, \Delta y)$, is given by

$$M(x_0, y_0, \theta, \Delta x, \Delta y) = \begin{bmatrix} \cos\theta & -\sin\theta & \Delta x+x_0(1-\cos\theta)-y_0\sin\theta \\ \sin\theta & \cos\theta & \Delta y+y_0(1-\sin\theta)-x_0\cos\theta \\ 0 & 0 & 1 \end{bmatrix} \tag{14.9a}$$

and

$$X = M(x_0, y_0, \theta, \Delta x, \Delta y)x . \tag{14.9b}$$

Equations (14.9) describe the general transformation on the position of a point on the plane. It is worthwhile to point out that the inverse of the matrix $M(x_0, y_0, \theta, \Delta x, \Delta y)$ can be found easily by replacing Δx and Δy with $-\Delta x$ and $-\Delta y$ and θ with $-\theta$, and reversing the order of operations in Equation (14.8).

14.3 HOMOGENEOUS COORDINATES

The representation of a point in the plane by a vector with three components can be used to do some internal scaling during the evaluation of positions. Suppose that we change the unit of measurements for the coordinates x and y. Then the third component will not be 1, but equal to a scale factor h, and we can write

$$x = \begin{bmatrix} hx \\ hy \\ h \end{bmatrix} \tag{14.10}$$

The coordinates (hx, hy, h) are called the *homogeneous coordinates* of a point. It is obvious that none of the transformation matrices needs to be changed since the new representation corresponds to a multiplication by a scalar.† The main advantage of this formulation becomes apparent when we consider equations of straight lines. A common equation of a line with slope μ is

$$y = \mu x + \nu . \tag{14.11a}$$

This form cannot be used to describe lines parallel to the y-axis. On the other hand, the form

$$ax + by + c = 0 \tag{14.11b}$$

allows the description of such lines by setting $b = 0$. Multiplying both sides of Equation (14.11b) by h and setting

$$\xi = xh , \ \eta = yh, \text{ and } \zeta = h$$

we obtain the homogeneous equation for a line

$$a\xi + b\eta + c\zeta = 0 . \tag{14.12a}$$

If we define a to be the column vector with elements a, b, and c, we can express the equation of the line as the scalar product

$$a'x = 0 . \tag{14.12b}$$

If a set of points is transformed by a transformation whose matrix is M, then points that were collinear before the transformation must remain collinear. If A is the column vector where a has been mapped, we must have

$$A'X = 0 , \tag{14.12c}$$

and therefore

$$A = (M')^{-1}a. \tag{14.13}$$

We also note that a point at infinity can be expressed by setting ζ equal to zero. The facility of handling points at infinity in the same way as other points has the practical advantage that points with coordinates outside the range of the available numerical precision (overflow or underflow) can be handled easily. For example, a line may be defined by two points whose coordinates are out of range and at the same time contain other points, within range, that must be displayed.

---

† Note that this multiplication does not introduce a scale change in the display. h will be factored out before the display is created.

If we use homogeneous coordinates, the coordinates of the defining points can be rescaled to reasonable limits. A clipping routine (see Chapter 15) can then be used to find the visible part of the line.

We shall illustrate certain mathematical advantages of homogeneous coordinates while deriving some useful formulas.

14.3.1 Equation of a Line Defined by Two Points

Let the points P_1 and P_2 have coordinates (x_1, y_1, w_1) and (x_2, y_2, w_2) respectively. A point with coordinates (x, y, w) will be collinear with them if its coordinates are linearly dependent on those of P_1 and P_2. This means that the determinant of a matrix whose columns are the coordinates of the three points should be zero, i.e.,

$$\det \begin{bmatrix} x & x_1 & x_2 \\ y & y_1 & y_2 \\ w & w_1 & w_2 \end{bmatrix} = 0 . \tag{14.14}$$

This is the equation of the line through the two points P_1 and P_2. By expanding the determinant, we can rewrite the equation in the more conventional form:

$$x(y_1 w_2 - w_1 y_2) + y(w_1 x_2 - x_1 w_2) + w(x_1 y_2 - y_1 x_2) = 0 \tag{14.14'}$$

(Note that this is equivalent to Equation (10.2).)

14.3.2 Coordinates of a Point Defined as the Intersection of Two Lines

The point at the intersection of two lines L_1 and L_2 with coefficients (a_1, b_1, c_1) and (a_2, b_2, c_2) can be found in a similar way. A third line with coefficients (a, b, c) passing through that point must be linearly dependent on the other two, and therefore a determinant whose columns are the line coefficients must be zero. We have:

$$\det \begin{bmatrix} a & a_1 & a_2 \\ b & b_1 & b_2 \\ c & c_1 & c_2 \end{bmatrix} = 0 . \tag{14.15}$$

The expansion of the determinant yields

$$a(b_1 c_2 - c_1 b_2) + b(c_1 a_2 - a_1 c_2) + c(a_1 b_2 - b_1 a_2) = 0 \tag{14.15'}$$

Since (a, b, c) are the coefficients of any line going through the intersection of L_1 and L_2, the terms in parentheses are the coordinates of their intersection.

14.3.3 Duality

Equations (14.14) and (14.15), or (14.14′) and (14.15′), demonstrate the *duality* between points and lines on the plane when homogeneous coordinates are used. A set of three numbers may represent either a line or point, so equations of a line defined by two points or that of a point defined by two lines are identical. The principle of duality is used extensively in projective geometry because, for each property of points and lines, one can derive another result by interchanging point and line. For example:

Theorem 14.1: If the lines joining the vertices (points) of two triangles pass through a common point, then the points where respective sides (lines) intersect lie on a common line.

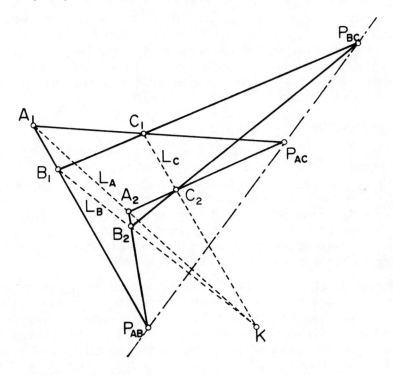

Figure 14.2 Illustration of Theorems 14.1 and 14.2: the points P_{AB}, P_{AC}, and P_{BC} are collinear if and only if the lines L_A, L_B, and L_C pass through a common point.

Figure 14.2 illustrates the theorem. See [14.FI] for a proof. The converse theorem can be expressed immediately in terms of duality.

Theorem 14.2:   (Dual of Theorem 14.1.) If the points where respective sides (lines) of two triangles intersect lie on a common line, then the lines joining respective vertices (points) pass through a common point.

The principle of duality can be used in graphics to economize on software. Thus the same procedure can be used to find either the intersection of two lines or the line joining two points. (In both cases it evaluates the minors of a 3×3 determinant.) The reader should keep in mind that the application of duality is possible only when homogeneous coordinates are used. Furthermore, duality is applicable only to results describing relative position without any distance relations. For example, consider the following simple result: "The points of the bisectrix of the angle formed by two lines are equidistant from the two lines." It is not clear what the dual of the bisectrix should be, but since the bisectrix is a line it must be a point. Let us call it Q so that the dual of the above statement becomes: "The lines passing through the Q defined by two points are equidistant from the two points." Since there is only one line equidistant from two points (the midnormal at the segment defined by them), the last statement in quotes is wrong.†

14.4 LINE SEGMENT PROBLEMS

The solution of many visibility problems, as well as clipping problems, requires computation of the relative position of lines and points. We present here a collection of results that will be used in later sections and in the next chapter. In all cases, we assume that line segments are defined by their endpoints and that such endpoints are ordered. If the segments are part of a closed contour, then the ordering may be in a clockwise or counterclockwise fashion. If no other indication about the ordering is given, then we assume it to be as follows.

Assumption 14.1:   Unless otherwise indicated, all line segments are directed, with the arrows pointing from bottom to top for nonhorizontal segments, and from left to right for horizontal segments. In other words, if (x_1,y_1,w_1) are the coordinates of the endpoint listed first, and (x_2,y_2,w_2) the coordinates of the endpoint listed second, if y_1/w_1 is not equal to y_2/w_2, then y_1/w_1 is less than y_2/w_2. In the case of equality (i.e., a horizontal segment) we have x_1/w_1 less than x_2/w_2 (see Figure

---

† Readers are discouraged from trying to play with the definitions of "bisectrix", "equidistant," etc in order to make duality work in this example. Such time may be spent more profitably by reading a text on projective geometry to understand better why duality does not apply to relations involving metric.

14.3). □

Definition 14.1: We shall say that a point P *lies to the right* of a line segment L if it lies to the right of an observer walking along the line and going from the first endpoint to the second endpoint (see Figure 14.3). □

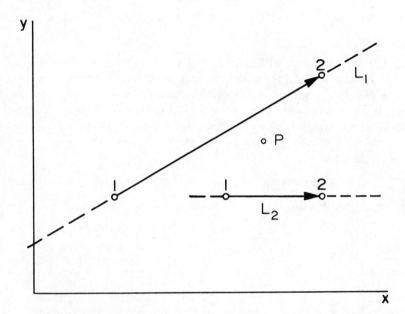

Figure 14.3 Illustration of the notation implied by Assumption 14.1 and Definitions 14.1 and 14.2: point P lies to the right of line L_1 and to the left of line L_2. The point P also obscures the line L_1.

Definition 14.2: We shall say that a point P *obscures* a line L (or a line segment L'), if a horizontal line drawn through P intersects L (or L') at a point whose x coordinate is less than that of P (see Figure 14.3). □

The relation "obscures" does not hold if the point P lies on the line L and it is not defined if the line L is horizontal. In the case of a line segment, the relation is not defined in the following three cases: P lies above the higher endpoint, P lies below the lower endpoint, or P belongs to the segment and the segment is horizontal. When the orientation of a segment is according to Assumption 14.1 and the relation "obscure" is defined, then it is equivalent to the relation "lies to the right of".

14.4.1 Position of a Point with respect to a Line

Proposition 14.1:   Let X, Y, and W be the coordinates of a point P and (x_1,y_1,w_1) and (x_2,y_2,w_2) be the endpoints of a line segment L. If W, w_1, and w_2 are positive, then P lies to the right of the line defined by the segment L if and only if

$$X(y_1w_2-w_1y_2) + Y(w_1x_2-x_1w_2) + W(x_1y_2-y_1x_2) < 0 . \quad (14.16)$$

□

Proof: The lefthand side of Equation (14.16) is the value of the determinant of Equation (14.14), which is zero if P is a point of the line containing the line segment L. Since the determinant is the equation of a line, it has a fixed sign for points on either side of the line. Therefore, in order to complete the proof, we need only verify that Equation (14.16) holds for some point on the right of L. If the line is not horizontal we select the point

$$X = x_1+w_1 \qquad Y = y_1 \qquad W = w_1 .$$

We find that after division by $w_1^2w_2$ the lefthand side becomes

$$(\frac{x_1}{w_1}+1)(\frac{y_1}{w_1} - \frac{y_2}{w_2}) - \frac{y_1}{w_1}(\frac{x_1}{w_1} - \frac{x_2}{w_2}) + (\frac{x_1}{w_1}\frac{y_2}{w_2} - \frac{x_2}{w_2}\frac{y_1}{w_1})$$

which equals

$$\frac{y_1}{w_1} - \frac{y_2}{w_2} .$$

This quantity is negative because of the assumption about the order of endpoints. If the line is horizontal we repeat a similar calculation by selecting a point with $X = x_1$ and $Y = y_1-w_1$. □

If one uses absolute, rather than homogeneous coordinates, then Proposition 14.1 is still valid by setting $W = w_1 = w_2 = 1$. In particular, P will be to the right if

$$X(y_1-y_2) + Y(x_2-x_1) + (x_1y_2-y_1x_2) < 0 \quad (14.16')$$

Equations (14.16) and (14.16') can be written more concisely if we use the vector notation of Equation (14.10). We also define $\det(a,b,c)$ to be the determinant of a 3×3 matrix with columns a, b, and c. This notation has the added advantage that is valid in absolute coordinates if one assumes that the third coordinate of all vectors is equal to 1. Then Equation (14.16) (or Equation (14.16')) becomes

$$\det(P,P_1,P_2) < 0 . \quad (14.16'')$$

The vectors P, P_1, and P_2 have the obvious definitions.

14.4.2 Intersection of Line Segments

We can use the above result to check whether two linear segments intersect, and if they do, to find the intersection. If the two segments are defined by points P_1,P_2 and P_3,P_4, then the two segments will intersect if and only if the coordinates of P_1 yield a different sign from the coordinates of P_2 when they are substituted in the equation of the line joining P_3 and P_4. A similar relation holds when the roles of P_1,P_2 and P_3,P_4 are interchanged (see Figure 14.4). Therefore, one must calculate the signs of the following four quantities:

$$S_1 = x_1(y_3w_4 - w_3y_4) + y_1(w_3x_4 - x_3w_4) + w_1(x_3y_4 - y_3x_4) \quad (14.17a)$$

$$S_2 = x_2(y_3w_4 - w_3y_4) + y_2(w_3x_4 - x_3w_4) + w_2(x_3y_4 - y_3x_4) \quad (14.17b)$$

$$S_3 = x_3(y_1w_2 - w_1y_2) + y_3(w_1x_2 - x_1w_2) + w_3(x_1y_2 - y_1x_2) \quad (14.17c)$$

$$S_4 = x_4(y_1w_2 - w_1y_2) + y_4(w_1x_2 - x_1w_2) + w_4(x_1y_2 - y_1x_2) \quad (14.17d)$$

The condition for intersection is that S_1 and S_2 differ in sign, and the same must also be true for S_3 and S_4. Note that this condition is somewhat less stringent than the one used in Proposition 14.1, since we do not care what the signs are as long as they are different.

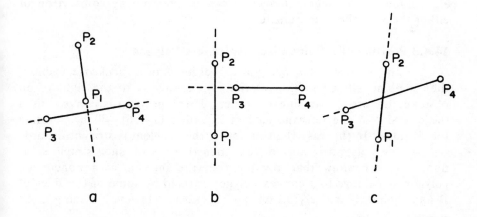

Figure 14.4 Illustration of the signs of Equations (14.17): (a) $S_1S_2 > 0$ and $S_3S_4 < 0$, (b) $S_1S_2 < 0$ and $S_3S_4 > 0$, (c) $S_1S_2 < 0$ and $S_3S_4 < 0$

If the conditions for intersection are satisfied, then the coordinates of the common point can be found by solving the following pair of linear equations:

$$x(y_1w_2-w_1y_2) + y(w_1x_2-x_1w_2) + w(x_1y_2-y_1x_2) = 0 \qquad (14.18a)$$

$$x(y_3w_4-w_3y_4) + y(w_3x_4-x_3w_4) + w(x_3y_4-y_3x_4) = 0 \qquad (14.18b)$$

Note that we have the same number of unknowns and equations because the value of w is arbitrary.

The conditions for intersection may be written under the concise notation as follows.

$$S_1 = \det(P_1,P_3,P_4), \quad S_2 = \det(P_2,P_3,P_4), \quad S_1S_2 < 0. \qquad (14.19a)$$

$$S_3 = \det(P_3,P_1,P_2), \quad S_4 = \det(P_4,P_1,P_2), \quad S_3S_4 < 0. \qquad (14.19b)$$

Equations (14.18) become

$$\det(P,P_1,P_2) = 0 \qquad (14.20a)$$

$$\det(P,P_3,P_4) = 0 \qquad (14.20b)$$

If one or more of the S_i's are zero, then we have a singular case and the sign comparison cannot be carried out.† If S_1 is zero, then we know that P_1 is on the line defined by P_3 and P_4. To find whether it is also on the segment defined by these two points we need check only the signs of S_3 and S_4. If one of them is zero, then we know that two of the points coincide. If both of them are zero, then the four points are collinear. The segment overlap can be checked by comparison of either the x or the y coordinates.

14.4.3 Position of a Point with respect to a Polygon

If the vertices of a polygon are ordered in a clockwise fashion, then a point will be in the interior if it always is to the right of an observer traversing the sides in order. If the polygon is convex, then the quantity of the lefthand side of Equation (14.16) will be negative for all sides. In this case the solution of the problem is straightforward.

If the polygon is not convex, then there is no such simple solution. One can show that any point in the interior of a nonconvex polygon Π belongs to a convex polygon formed by some of the sides of Π and their extensions ([3.PA], pp. 236-241). However, finding these

---

† If one selects four points at random on the Euclidean plane it is highly unlikely that any three of them will be collinear. However, when we move to the discrete plane where coordinates are small integers (e.g. between 0 and 511) the situation is different. Because of the limited precision used in displays such singular cases occur frequently in practice.

polygons is a hard problem. In some applications they may be given in advance, for example, if the nonconvex polygon has been constructed as a union of convex polygons. The effort for finding them may also be justified if we plan to check the position of a large number of points with respect to a fixed nonconvex polygon.

Another solution, valid for any polygon, is to draw a line through P, find its intersection with all the sides of Π, and then apply the parity check discussed in Section 8.1. Solving a set of systems of equations requires far more work than checking the signs of a set of inequalities. In addition we must count the effort required for sorting the points of intersections. Thus the method is useful for nonconvex polygons only. (Of course, the situation is different if we want to find all points in the interior of the polygon.)

Example 14.4: Let the vertices of a convex polygon be $(0,0)$, $(3,3)$, $(6,3)$, $(9,0)$, and $(5,-4)$ (see Figure 14.5). Let X and Y denote the coordinates of P. The five inequalities in this case are:

$$
\begin{array}{lll}
-3X + 3Y < 0 & \text{or} & X > Y \\
3Y - 9 < 0 & \text{or} & Y < 3 \\
3X + 3Y - 27 < 0 & \text{or} & X + Y < 9 \\
4X - 4Y - 36 < 0 & \text{or} & X - Y < 9 \\
-4X - 5Y < 0 & \text{or} & 4X > -5Y
\end{array}
$$

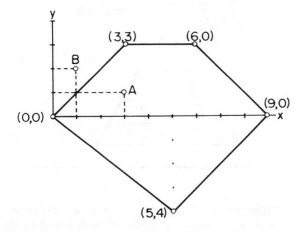

Figure 14.5 Polygon used in Example 14.4. For the point A with coordinates $(3,1)$ the lefthand sides of the first set of inequalities have the following values: -6, -6, -15, -28, and -17. For the point B with coordinates $(1,2)$ the lefthand side of the first inequality equals 3.

14.4.4 Segment Shadow

The solution of certain visibility problems requires the examination of the relative position of linear segments.

Definition 14.3: Segment a is said to shade or obscure segment b if it does not intersect segment b, and if at least one of its points obscures b. $\square$

Figure 14.6 shows a few examples of segments and also lists which segments shade others according to the above definition. Note that the relation "segment a shades segment b" is not transitive, and neither is the negation of the relation "a does not shade b." Therefore the "shading" relation does not introduce a partial ordering, in spite of statements to the opposite effect in the literature (see Bibliographical Notes).

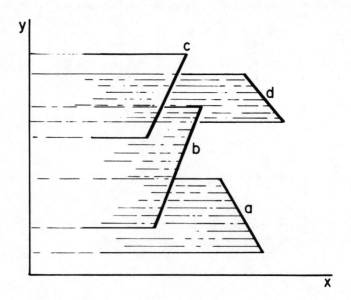

Figure 14.6 Illustration of segment shading: a shades b, b shades c, but a does not shade c. d shades both b and c, but it does not shade a.

The following proposition is a straightforward consequence of the results of the previous sections.

Proposition 14.2: Segment a shades segment b if and only if the following three conditions hold:

$$y_1^a \leq y_2^b \qquad\qquad (14.21a)$$

$$y_1^b \leq y_2^a \qquad\qquad (14.21b)$$

$$x_1^a(y_1^b - y_2^b) - y_1^a(x_1^b - x_2^b) + x_1^b y_2^b - y_1^b x_2^b < 0 \qquad\qquad (14.21c)$$

□

14.5 BIBLIOGRAPHICAL NOTES

Most of the texts on graphics cited earlier discuss the creation of simple two-dimensional displays. Detailed treatment of homogeneous coordinates can be found in all texts on projective geometry, such as [14.FI], [14.MA], [14.PE], [14.RO], and [14.TO]. The formulas for coordinate transformation after rotation can be found in most texts on analytical geometry, such as [14.LE]. Theorems 14.1 and 14.2 are due to Desargues (1593-1661). Projective geometry is the study of geometrical properties that are invariant under linear transformations, such as multiplication by the matrices of Section 14.2. Its origins go back to the fourth century A.D. (Pappus of Alexandria) but it became a mature subject only during the nineteenth century. Clearly, it deserves some attention by anyone who is seriously interested in graphics. For a discussion of the properties of the shadow relation and similar topics see [14.GY].

A challenging problem in graphics is to implement some of the geometrical transformations on the discrete rather than the analog plane. This could save both computation and communication between processors. It seems, though, that there are certain insurmountable difficulties with such an approach. Readers can persuade themselves that this is indeed so by attempting to write a program for rotations on the discrete plane.

14.6 RELEVANT LITERATURE

[14.FI]   Fishback, W. T. *Projective and Euclidean Geometry,* New York: J. Wiley, 1969.

[14.GY]   Guibas, L. J. and Yao, F. F. "On Translating a Set of Rectangles," *Proc. Twelfth ACM Symp. on Theory of Computing,* Los Angeles, Calif., (April 1980), pp. 154-160.

[14.LE]   Lehmann, C. H. *Analytic Geometry,* New York: J. Wiley, 1942. (12th printing, 1961.)

[14.MA]   Maxwell, E. A. *Plane Projective Geometry Based on the use of General Homogeneous Coordinates,* Cambridge: University Press, 1957 (reprint of first edition of 1946).

[14.PE]   Pedoe, D. *An Introduction to Projective Geometry,* New York: Mac-Millan, 1963.

[14.RO]   Rosenbaum, R. A. *Introduction to Projective Geometry and Modern Algebra,* Reading, Mass: Addison-Wesley, 1963.

[14.TO]   Todd, J. A. *Projective and Analytic Geometry,* New York: Pitman, 1948.

14.7 PROBLEMS

14.1.   Write a program that displays a hexagon in successively smaller sizes until it shrinks to a single pixel.

14.2.   Let C be a curve defined by a sequence of points $\{x_i, y_i\}_1^N$. It is possible to display C by a sequence of *vec* instructions, but in order to produce the effect of thickness we may want to use a "pen." We consider here the case of a square tipped pen: the curve will be displayed by a sequence of squares, each centered at one of the points x_i, y_i with a pair of sides of the square being parallel to the line defined by the points x_{i-1}, y_{i-1} and x_i, y_i. Write a program implementing such a display.

14.3.   (Extension of the previous problem.) The square tip is not very aesthetic. It is best to use an ellipse for a tip. Write a program performing this task with the constraint that the minor axis of the ellipse is always parallel to the vector joining two successive points.

14.4.   Add to the editor of Problem 10.6 a feature for rotating, enlarging, and/or translating a curve.

14.5.   Write a program that displays the planets moving around the sun. You may wish to use a distorted distance scale and choose one earth week as the time between display renewal. Simplify the problem by having the trajectories of the planets be circles that all lie on the same plane, so that you may use the equations of Section 14.2. You may choose different polygons for each planet (e.g., square for Earth, hexagon for Mars, etc.), or similar polygons, but of different color, or any other combination, depending on what kind of display you have access to.

14.6.   Write a procedure for finding the intersection of two lines in homogeneous coordinates and use the duality principle to have the same procedure find the line defined by two points.

14.7. Write a program that executes an infinite loop with the following
       steps:

   (1) Prompt the user for a color code and four coordinates.
        (You may wish to reserve a color code as a flag for a grace-
        ful exit.)

   (2) Display the segment between the two points defined by the
        given coordinates.

   (3) Change the color of all segments displayed so that if seg-
        ment *a* obscures *b*, *b* should be displayed in the color of
        a.

   (If you do not have access to a color graphics display, have a
   letter displayed next to each segment, and use those letters
   instead of the color code.)

Chapter 15

POLYGON CLIPPING

15.1 INTRODUCTION

The term clipping is used to describe the process of finding whether a line (or polygon) is intersected by another polygon. A major application of clipping is to decide whether certain constructs fall within the display window. We should point out here that one cannot rely on the display device to achieve clipping for two reasons. First, the display area may be only a subset of the display screen (for example, a part of the screen may be reserved for the display of text). Second, there is no uniform way by which points with invalid coordinates are displayed. Quite often a display device ignores the high order bits, so that the constructs wrap around the screen. Therefore, there is a need for algorithms to solve this problem explicitly.

Another use of clipping is in the solution of visibility problems. Deciding whether one object obscures another requires that one first find whether two objects intersect each other. A third use that has been explored very little is the decomposition of a nonconvex polygon into convex subpolygons. This may be useful not only in graphics (see Section 14.4.3) but also in pattern recognition. There the convex subsets of a polygon may be used as primitive elements for describing the shape of the original polygon (see Bibliographical Notes).

We shall use the results of Section 14.4 to design various clipping algorithms. Section 15.2 describes the clipping of a line segment by a convex polygon while Section 15.3 solves the same problem for the practically important case when the polygon is a rectangle with sides parallel to the coordinate axes. Section 15.4 deals with the clipping of an arbitrary polygon by a line, and Section 15.5 with the clipping of a polygon by another polygon. Finally, Section 15.6 examines the question of computational efficiency for some geometrical problems.

15.2 CLIPPING A LINE SEGMENT BY A CONVEX POLYGON

This problem is of intermediate generality between the extremes of clipping a line by a regular rectangle (see next section) and clipping a line by a nonconvex polygon.

Problem: If A_1, A_2, $\cdots A_n$ are the vertices of a convex polygon Π on the plane, find the part of a line segment L (defined by its endpoints P_1 and P_2) that lies within the interior of the polygon. $\square$

Note that the naive solution, checking whether both points P_1 and P_2 are inside the polygon, is incorrect because a line segment may intersect a convex polygon even if both endpoints are outside the polygon. The following solution, based on the material of Section 14.4, is possible. First evaluate the n quantities

$$S_i = \det(A_i, P_1, P_2) = X_i(y_1 w_2 - w_1 y_2)$$

$$+ Y_i(w_1 x_2 - x_1 w_2) + W_i(x_1 y_2 - y_1 x_2) \qquad i = 1, 2, \cdots n \quad (15.1)$$

where A_i denotes the coordinate vector (X_i, Y_i) of the vertex A_i of the polygon and P_j $(j = 1, 2)$ the coordinate vector (x_j, y_j) of the endpoints of the line P_j. The results of the computation will fall in one of the following cases.

(1) All S_i's are nonzero and have the same sign. Then all vertices of the polygon lie on the same side of L and no part of the line is in the interior of the polygon.

(2) One of them is zero and all others have the same sign. Then the line passes through one of the vertices but all other vertices are on the same side of the line. This case is equivalent to (1).

(3) Two of them are zero and all others have the same sign. Because Π is convex this can happen only when two successive vertices lie on L. Then we have the singular case discussed in Section 14.4.2: one side of the polygon lies along the same line as the segment L.

(4) One or two of them are zero and the others have different signs. This means that L intersects Π while passing through one or two of its vertices. Because Π is convex there will be only two changes in signs and we shall consider this case together with the next.

(5) All of the S_i's are nonzero but they have different signs. Then there will be two changes of sign as one goes along the perimeter of the polygon. We shall use A_j, A_{j+1} and A_k, A_{k+1} to denote the pairs where the change occurs. S_i may be zero in one of the vertices of one or both pairs if case (4) occurs. L_1 will denote the line segment joining the first pair and L_2 the line segment joining the second pair. Note that which pair will be called first and which second is arbitrary and the particular notation is unimportant as long as we are consistent.

Once we find out that the line containing L intersects the polygon (last two cases) we must check the position of the points P_1 and P_2 with respect to the lines L_1 and L_2, i.e., find the sign of the four quantities

$$U_1 = \det(P_1,A_j,A_{j+1}) = x_1(Y_j W_{j+1} - W_j Y_{j+1})$$
$$+ y_1(W_j X_{j+1} - X_j W_{j+1}) + w_1(X_j Y_{j+1} - Y_j X_{j+1}) \quad (15.2a)$$

(location of P_1 with respect to the segment L_1)

$$U_2 = \det(P_2,A_j,A_{J+1}) = x_2(Y_j W_{j+1} - W_j Y_{j+1})$$
$$+ y_2(W_j X_{j+1} - X_j W_{j+1}) + w_2(X_j Y_{j+1} - Y_j X_{j+1}) \quad (15.2b)$$

(location of P_2 with respect to the segment L_1)

$$U_3 = \det(P_1,A_k,A_{k+1}) = x_1(Y_k W_{k+1} - W_k Y_{k+1})$$
$$+ y_1(W_k X_{k+1} - X_k W_{k+1}) + w_1(X_k Y_{k+1} - Y_k X_{k+1}) \quad (15.2c)$$

(location of P_1 with respect to the segment L_2)

$$U_4 = \det(P_2,A_k,A_{k+1}) = x_2(Y_k W_{k+1} - W_k Y_{k+1})$$
$$+ y_2(W_k X_{k+1} - X_k W_{k+1}) + w_2(X_k Y_{k+1} - Y_k X_{k+1}) \quad (15.2d)$$

(location of P_2 with respect to the segment L_2)

If the directions of the sides of the polygon are set up in a clockwise manner, the sign of U_i in Equations (15.2) is negative when a point lies in the interior of the polygon. U_i will be zero if a side contains one of the points P_1 or P_2. We omit the discussion of such singular cases and leave the needed modification of Algorithm 15.1 as an exercise (Problem 15.1). Figure 15.1 shows various relative positions of the points P_1 and P_2 with respect to the two lines, and Table 15.1 lists the signs of U_i's, and the calculation of the endpoints of the displayed segment. This table and the algorithm use the following notation: Q_1 and Q_2 are the endpoints of the line segment to be drawn. $L \cap L_i$ ($i = 1, 2$) denotes the point where the segments L and L_i intersect.

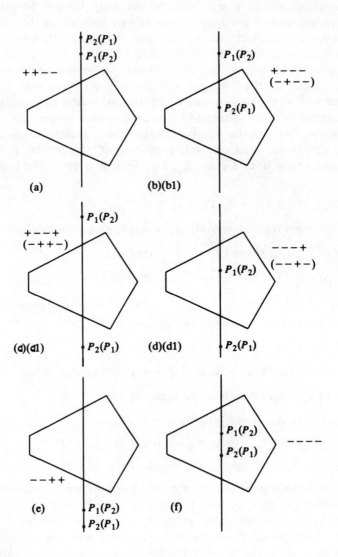

Figure 15.1 Clipping of a line segment by a polygon. The six possible positions of a segment with respect to a polygon are shown. Three of them have a double labeling, so that we have a total of nine cases as shown in Table 15.1.

Theoretically we have sixteen nonsingular possibilities (the signs of four variables), but because of geometrical constraints we have only nine cases. Indeed, it is impossible to have all the U_i's positive because positive half-planes of the two sides are outside the polygon. Similarly, it is impossible to have three positive signs. This leaves eleven cases. The configuration $-+-+$ means that P_1 is inside the polygon while P_2 is above the line $A_j A_{j+1}$ and below the line $A_k A_{k+1}$, an impossibility. A symmetric argument can be made for the configuration $+-+-$, so that leaves the nine cases shown in Table 15.1. Note that in terms of actual geometric configurations we have only six cases, those shown in Figure 15.1. Three of the cases can have one of two possible labelings. These are cases b, c, and d in Figure 15.1 where the second labeling is shown in parentheses. If we assume that P_1 is below P_2 we can limit our attention to only six cases but we want to avoid that assumption in case $P_1 P_2$ is a side of a polygon where the ordering of the endpoints is not determined by their y coordinates.

Table 15.1
Position of a line segment with respect to a polygon

Figure	U_1	U_2	U_3	U_4	Q_1	Q_2
(a)	$+$	$+$	$-$	-	invisible	
(b)	$+$	$-$	-	$-$	$L \cap L_1$	P_2
(b´)	$-$	$+$	$-$	-	P_1	$L \cap L_1$
(c)	$+$	$-$	-	$+$	$L \cap L_1$	$L \cap L_2$
(c´)	$-$	$+$	$+$	$-$	$L \cap L_2$	$L \cap L_1$
(d)	$-$	-	$-$	$+$	P_1	$L \cap L_2$
(d´)	$-$	-	$+$	$-$	$L \cap L_2$	P_2
(e)	$-$	-	$+$	$+$	invisible	
(f)	$-$	-	$-$	-	P_1	P_2

Algorithm 15.1 checks the signs of the quantities in Equation (15.1) and Equations (15.2) and implements the decisions listed in Table 15.1. The first part examines the location of the line with respect to the vertices of the polygon, while the second examines the position of the endpoints of the line. The variables v and u are set equal to the signs of S_i, as computed from Equation (15.1), for successive vertices of the polygon. If u and v differ, it means that the two vertices lie on opposite sides of the line containing L. The coordinates of such vertices are saved in step 5. K counts the number of such intersections. Since the polygon is assumed to be convex, its value must be either zero or two. If it is found to be zero at the end of the loop of steps 3-

6, then we know that the line containing L does not intersect the polygon and we are finished (step 7). Otherwise we proceed with steps 8-17.

Step 9 evaluates Equations (15.2) and the remaining steps carry out the checks of Table 15.1. Cases (a) and (e) where the segment is outside the polygon are checked in step 10. If the check of step 10 fails, then an inspection of Figure 15.1 and Table 15.1 reveals that if U_1 and U_3 have opposite signs the line L will intersect one of L_1 or L_2. Similarly for U_2 and U_4. These checks are done in steps 14 and 15, first for U_1 and U_3, and then for U_2 and U_4.

Because of duality, this clipping algorithm can also be used to solve the following problem:

Problem: Given n lines which are the sides of a convex polygon, find whether a point given as the intersection of two lines lies within that polygon. $\square$

Solution: Apply the dual of Algorithm 15.1. $\square$

Algorithm 15.1 Clipping a Line Segment by a Convex Polygon

Notation: Array A has dimension $n{\times}3$ and contains the triplets of homogeneous coordinates of the n vertices of the polygon. The coordinates of the endpoints of the line segment L are stored in the $2{\times}2$ array P. Arrays B and C have dimension $2{\times}3$. B is used to store the first of a pair of vertices lying on either side of the line containing L; C contains the second member of such pairs. S_i and U_i are defined in Equation (15.1) and Equations (15.2). The algorithm finds Q_1 and Q_2, the endpoints of the segment contained within the polygon.

1. Set the counter K to zero.
2. Set v equal to the sign of S_1 in Equation (15.1) which is evaluated using $A(1,1)$ for X_1, $A(1,2)$ for Y_1, etc.
3. **For** $i = 2$ to n **do**:
    Begin.
4.   Set u equal to the sign of S_i in Equation (15.1) which is evaluated using $A(i,1)$ for X_i, $A(i,2)$ for Y_i, etc.
5.   **If** v is not equal to u, **then** increment K, set $B(K,j)$ to $A(i-1,j)$, $C(K,j)$ to $A(i,j)$ and $v = u$.
6.   **If** K equals 2, **then break** from the loop.
    End.
7. **If** K equals zero, **then** exit.

8. **Else do**:
   Begin.
9. Set up Equations (15.2) using the array $B(1,*)$ for the point A_j, the array $C(1,*)$ for A_{j+1}, the array $B(2,*)$ for A_k, and the array $C(2,*)$ for A_{k+1}. Then evaluate the expressions for U_1 to U_4.
10. **If** U_1 and U_3 have the same sign and this sign is opposite to that of U_2 and U_4, **then exit.**
11. **Else do**:
    Begin.
12.   **For** $m = 1$ to 2 **do**:
        Begin.
13.   **If** U_m and U_{m+2} have opposite signs, **then do**:
            Begin.
14.   **If** the sign of U_m is *minus*, **then** set Q_m to the intersection of the line segments L and L_2.
15.   **Else** set Q_m to the intersection of L and L_1.
            End.
16.   **Else** set Q_m equal to P_m.
            End.
        End.
    End.
17. Display segment between points Q_1 and Q_2.
18. **End of Algorithm.**

15.3 CLIPPING A LINE SEGMENT BY A REGULAR RECTANGLE

A special case of the clipping algorithm occurs when $n = 4$ and the polygon is a rectangle with sides parallel to the coordinate axes. We shall call such a rectangle *regular*. It is possible to perform some simple checks for the locations of P_1 and P_2 with respect to the vertical and horizontal lines bounding the rectangle. In Figure 15.2, region 5 is the viewing window. If both points lie in a single region except 5, or if both lie in one of the groups (1,4,7), (1,2,3), (3,6,9), or (7,8,9), the segment is not visible. It is visible when both points lie in 5. We must examine the question of visibility in detail for all other locations of endpoints.

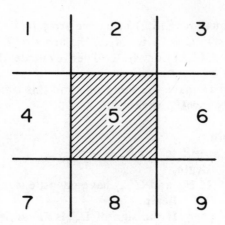

Figure 15.2 Clipping with a rectangular window

This special case is of sufficient practical importance to justify a special clipping algorithm. It is listed as Algorithm 15.2. Step 1 checks whether the segment lies entirely in one of the four groups of three blocks, each shown in Figure 15.2: (1,4,7), (3,6,9), (7,8,9), or (1,2,3). Then the whole segment lies outside the window and there is no need for further processing. Step 2 makes sure that the labeling of the end-points agrees with Assumption 14.1. Step 3 (including 3a-3c) deals with a horizontal line and step 4 (including 4a and 4b) with a vertical line. Steps 5-11 deal with the general case. We could have omitted steps 1, 3, and 4 without causing any errors, but at the expense of increased computation. These steps dispose quickly of cases where it is not necessary to apply the general line intersection criterion. This is an example where an increase in the length of the algorithm decreases the average execution time.

Step 5 evaluates the signs of the four corners with respect to the line. In particular, U_1 corresponds to the lower left corner (X_{MIN}, Y_{MIN}), U_2 to (X_{MIN}, Y_{MAX}), U_3 to the upper right corner (X_{MAX}, Y_{MAX}), and U_4 to (X_{MAX}, Y_{MIN}). The condition of step 7 is true when the line intersects the left boundary of the window. Steps 7b and 7c find the coordinates of the intersection and use those as an endpoint of the line for all subsequent calculations. Note that it is impossible to have the condition of both steps valid. If that were the case (i.e. both x_1 and x_2 less than X_{MIN}), the algorithm would not have proceeded past step 1. The condition of step 8 is true when the line intersects the top boundary of the window. Step 8b calculates the intersection. Note that because of Assumption 14.1 we need to check for the location of only one endpoint. The condition of step 9 is true when the line intersects the right boundary of the window and that of step 10 is true when the line intersects the bottom boundary of the window. Steps 9b, 9c, and 10b calculate intersections and use those to replace endpoints.

Note that only two of the four conditions of steps 7, 8, 9, and 10 can be true. Therefore it is possible to speed up the algorithm by skipping the remaining sign checks as soon as j reaches the value 2. Another observation is that if the line segment is contained entirely within the window, none of the checks 7b, 7c, 8b, 9b, 9c, or 10b will be true and the only nontrivial computation will be that of step 5.

Algorithm 15.2 Clipping a Line Segment by a Regular Rectangle

Notation: Line endpoints are (x_1, y_1) and (x_2, y_2). Rectangle is from X_{MIN} to X_{MAX} and Y_{MIN} to Y_{MAX}. *draw* is procedure that displays the line. dy, dx, dxy, qx, qX, qy, and qY are auxiliary quantities defined in step 5.

1. **If** (x_1 and x_2 are both less than X_{MIN}) or (x_1 and x_2 are both greater than X_{MAX}) or (y_1 and y_2 are both less than Y_{MIN}) or (y_1 and y_2 are both greater than Y_{MAX}), **then return.**

2. **If** y_1 exceeds y_2, **then** interchange endpoints.

3. **If** y_1 equals y_2, **then**
   Begin.
3a.   **If** x_1 exceeds x_2, **then** interchange endpoints.
3b.   **If** x_1 is less than X_{MIN}, **then** set $x_1 = X_{MIN}$. **If** x_2 is greater than X_{MAX}, **then** set $x_2 = X_{MAX}$.
3c.   *draw* (x_1, y_1, x_2, y_2) and **return.**
   End.

4. **If** x_1 equals x_2, **then**
   Begin.
4a.   **If** y_1 is less than Y_{MIN}, **then** set $y_1 = Y_{MIN}$. **If** y_2 is greater than Y_{MAX}, **then** set $y_2 = Y_{MAX}$.
4b.   *draw* (x_1, y_1, x_2, y_2) and **return.**
   End.

5. Set
   $dy = y_1 - y_2$; $dx = x_1 - x_2$; $dxy = x_1 y_2 - y_1 x_2$.
   $qx = X_{MIN} \cdot dy$; $qX = X_{MAX} \cdot dy$; $qy = Y_{MIN} \cdot dx$; $qY = Y_{MAX} \cdot dx$.
   $U_1 = qx - qy + dxy$, $U_2 = qx - qY + dxy$, $U_3 = qX - qY + dxy$,
   $U_4 = qX - qy + dxy$.

6. Set j to zero.

7.   **If** U_1 and U_2 differ in sign, **then**
      Begin.
7a.   Increment j.
7b.   **If** x_1 is less than X_{MIN}, **then** set
          $y_1 = (X_{MIN} \cdot dy + dxy)/dx$; $x_1 = X_{MIN}$. Update dx, dy, and
          dxy.
7c.   **If** x_2 is less than X_{MIN}, **then** set
          $y_2 = (X_{MIN} \cdot dy + dxy)/dx$; $x_2 = X_{MIN}$. Update dx, dy, and
          dxy.
          End.
8.   **If** U_2 and U_3 differ in sign, **then**
      Begin.
8a.   Increment j.
8b.   **If** y_2 is greater than Y_{MAX}, **then**
          $x_2 = (Y_{MAX} \cdot dx - dxy)/dy$; $y_2 = Y_{MAX}$. Update dx, dy, and
          dxy.
          End.
9.   **If** U_3 and U_4 differ in sign, **then**
      Begin.
9a.   Increment j.
9b.   **If** x_1 is greater than X_{MAX}, **then** set
          $y_1 = (X_{MAX} \cdot dy + dxy)/dx$; $x_1 = X_{MAX}$. Update dx, dy, and
          dxy.
9c.   **If** x_2 is greater than X_{MAX}, **then** set
          $y_2 = (X_{MAX} \cdot dy + dxy)/dx$; $x_2 = X_{MAX}$. Update dx, dy, and
          dxy.
          End.
10.   **If** U_4 and U_1 differ in sign, **then**
      Begin.
10a.   Increment j.
10b.   **If** y_1 is less than Y_{MIN}, **then** set
          $x_1 = (Y_{MIN} \cdot dx - dxy)/dy$; $y_1 = Y_{MIN}$. Update dx, dy, and
          dxy.
          End.
11.   **If** j is greater than zero, **then** $draw(x_1, y_1, x_2, y_2)$.
12.   **Return**
13.   **End of Algorithm.**

15.4 CLIPPING AN ARBITRARY POLYGON BY A LINE

In order to display a polygon that is not necessarily convex over a window that is a regular rectangle, we may either clip each one of its sides with respect to the window (Algorithm 15.2), or clip the whole polygon with respect to each of the sides of the window. Algorithm 15.3 solves the latter problem. It can also be used as a basic algorithm for finding the intersection of two arbitrary polygons.

The algorithm computes U_1 and U_2 as given by Equations (15.2) for all vertices. (Note that as we advance from one pair to the next the new U_2 equals the old U_1 so that the computation has to be made only once at each vertex.) It assumes that the line is oriented according to Assumption 14.1 and that visible points are those that do not obscure the line (see Definition 14.2). Thus if U_i is positive, the vertex is visible. Step 3 compares the signs of U_1 and U_2 and if at least one of them is positive, then the algorithm proceeds with steps 4-7. Step 5 finds the intersection of the side of the polygon with the line.

Theoretically, it is impossible to have w_a equal to zero in step 5 because this would imply that the segment is parallel to the line, and therefore U_1 and U_2 have the same sign, a contradiction. Table 15.2 summarizes the actions taken by the algorithm depending on the signs of U_1 and U_2.

Table 15.2 Position of a polygon with respect to a line

U_1	U_2	Status	Step of Algorithm
+	+	all visible	4
+	0	all visible	4
+	−	partly visible	7
0	+	all visible	4
0	0	invisible	3
0	−	partly visible	7
−	+	partly visible	6
−	0	invisible	3
−	−	invisible	3

When both points are on the line, the algorithm treats the segment as invisible. In fact the polygon drawn will be open where the line intersects it, as shown in Figure 15.3. This may be undesirable in certain applications but it is not difficult to modify the algorithm so that the intersections are joined by lines (see Problem 15.4).

Algorithm 15.3 Clipping a Polygon by a Line

Notation: The input to the algorithm is the coefficients dY, dX, and D of the equation of the line:

$$dY \cdot x - dX \cdot y + D = 0$$

and the coordinates of the polygon vertices x_i, y_i, $i = 1, 2, \cdots N$. The result is the display of the clipped polygon that is not obscured by the line. dy, dx, and dd are the coefficients of the line defined by a polygon side and are computed in step 5. The homogeneous coordinates of the intersection are found according to the method of Section 14.3.2.

1.   Set $U_1 = dY \cdot x_1 - dX \cdot y_1 + D$.

2.   **For** i from 2 to N **do** steps 3-8.
      Begin.

3.   Set $U_2 = dY \cdot x_i - dX \cdot y_i + D$. If both U_1 and U_2 are non-positive, **then do** nothing.
          Else
              Begin.

4.   If both U_1 and U_2 are nonnegative, **then** *draw* the vector from (x_{i-1}, y_{i-1}) to (x_i, y_i).
              Else
                  Begin.

5.   Set $dy = y_{i-1} - y_i$, $dx = x_{i-1} - x_i$, and $dd = x_{i-1} \cdot y_i - y_{i-1} \cdot x_i$, and then compute
                  $x_a = -(dx \cdot D - dX \cdot D)$,
                  $y_a = -(dy \cdot D - dY \cdot D)$, and
                  $w_a = -(dy \cdot dX - dY \cdot dx)$.
                  If w_a is not zero, **then** set $x_{intr} = x_a/w_a$, and $y_{intr} = y_a/w_a$.
                  Else raise error flag and exit.

6.   If U_1 is negative, **then** *draw* the vector from (x_{intr}, y_{intr}) to (x_i, y_i).
                  Else
                      Begin.

7.   {U_1 is nonnegative and U_2 is positive}
                      Draw the vector from x_{i-1}, y_{i-1} to x_{intr}, y_{intr}.
                      End.

                  End.

              End.

8.   Set $U_1 = U_2$.
      End.

9.   **End of Algorithm.**

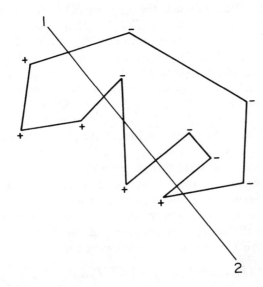

Figure 15.3   Illustration of a polygon clipped by a line. Each vertex is marked with the sign of U_i computed there.

15.5 INTERSECTION OF TWO POLYGONS

Finding the intersection of two polygons is of great interest in the solution of visibility problems and represents the most general formulation of the clipping problem. The problem can be solved by repeated applications of Algorithm 15.3. Let the two polygons be Π_1 and Π_2 and let us also assume that Π_2 is convex. Then the following solution is possible. If q_1, q_2, $\cdots q_n$ are the sides of Π_2, and P_i, $i = 1$, 2, $\cdots m$ are the vertices of Π_1, which may or may not be convex, then we may apply Algorithm 15.3 for each one of the sides q_i for the polygon Π_1. The result of clipping Π_1 by q_1 will be any number of polygons, from zero to one over the number of concave vertices of Π_1. Because of the possible increase in the number of polygons some careful bookkeeping is required.†

It is best to use a linked list for describing Π_1, and any other polygons that may be found. In particular, with each vertex we associate a pointer to the next vertex when the polygon is traversed in a

---

† The careful reader may object to this method by pointing out that Algorithm 15.3 clips a polygon by a line rather than a line segment. However, our assumption that Π_2 is convex makes such a substitution legal.

clockwise fashion. We shall use the symbol $NXT(P_i)$ to denote that pointer. Initially we have $NXT(P_i) = P_{i+1}$ for $i < m$ and $NXT(P_m) = P_1$. We proceed now to modify Algorithm 15.3. Instead of drawing the sides we will simply update the respective pointers. In particular, in step 6 we add the point of intersection to the list and we set $NXT(P_{m+j}) = P_i$, where j is some number denoting the position of the new point at the end of a list. In step 7 we set $NXT(P_{i-1}) = P_{m+j}$ and $NXT(P_{m+j}) = 0$, since we do not know the next point as yet. If a vertex is not visible we also set the value of its pointer to zero. Figure 15.4 illustrates part of this process by using heavy arrows to denote the effect of the pointers. In order to complete the process we must establish pointers between the points of intersection. To this end we sort the points P_{m+j} in order of increasing y, or increasing x if the clipping line is horizontal. Then we take them by pairs and change whichever of the pointers is zero to the address of the other element of the pair. Thus, in the case of Figure 15.4 we add the following two links:

$$NXT(P_{m+1}) = P_{m+4} \qquad NXT(P_{m+3}) = P_{m+2}$$

It is now a simple process to traverse the list of vertices and find the new polygons. Actually this does not have to be done until the end because Algorithm 15.3 does not really care how many separate polygons there are. Probably the best way to traverse the vertex list is to use a second set of pointers containing the address on the list of a single point from each polygon. This set can be scanned sequentially and the next pointers used for going around the contour of each polygon.

The above process finds the intersection of the two polygons by finding the intersection of Π_1 with the halfplanes H_i defined by the sides of Π_2. (The straight line containing the side q_i divides the plane in two parts. H_i is the part containing points of the interior of the polygon near q_i.) If Π_2 is not convex, then the result of the application of this method is the intersection of Π_1, not with Π_2, but with the intersection of the halfplanes: $N = \bigcap H_i$. N is called the *nucleus* or *kernel* of Π_2. It is a convex polygon that has the property that from any one of its points one can draw a line to any one of the vertices of Π_2 and have the line entirely within Π_2. (Of course the nucleus may be an empty set.) A discussion of the nucleus and its properties is beyond the scope of this text (see Bibliographical Notes).

On the other hand Algorithm 15.3 may be used to decompose a nonconvex polygon into convex components. In particular, let q_j and q_{j+1} be the sides of one of the concave angles of a polygon Π. Clipping Π_2 first with q_j and then with q_{j+1} produces two polygons: $\Pi \cap H_j$ and

$\Pi \cap H_{j+1}$. Each one of them has at least one fewer concave angles than Π. If we repeat that process for all sides with concave angles we obtain a collection of polygons whose union is Π. These polygons may be clipped with the sides of their concave angles, and so forth, until all resulting polygons are convex (see Problems 15.6 and 15.7).

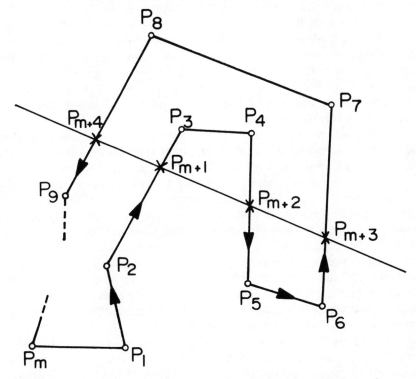

Figure 15.4 Illustration of pointer setting for clipping of a polygon with a line

Instead of attempting a convex decomposition of Π_2 we may try to modify the application of Algorithm 15.3 as follows. Each of the sides of Π_2 is used to clip the original polygon Π_1, rather than the polygons resulting from the previous intersections. At the end the intersection points along the sides of Π_2 are sorted to form the intersection of the polygons. A complete treatment of this subject is outside our scope, not only because of its complexity, but also because in most graphics applications the polygon Π_2 either corresponds to the display window (a regular rectangle), or is the projection of a triangle or quadrangle (see Chapter 17).

15.6 EFFICIENT POLYGON INTERSECTION

Finding the intersection of two polygons by repeated applications of Algorithm 15.3 as described in the previous section is not always efficient. For example, we do not transmit any information about the location of the vertices of Π_1 from one application of the algorithm to another. There are various ways for improving the efficiency of the process and we shall outline some of them here. We recall that n and m were used to denote the number of vertices (or sides) of Π_2 and Π_1 respectively. In the worst case steps 3-8 of Algorithm 15.3 will be executed mn times. At a minimum, the effort for finding the intersection will be $m + n$, because one must check all the vertices at least once. The gap between mn and $m + n$ may be substantial and this invites an investigation for efficient procedures.

However, we should note that if m is a small number (e.g. three or four), as is often the case in graphics applications, an increase in efficiency may not be possible. Whatever is saved in reducing the number of times a vertex is visited may be lost in the increased book-keeping effort. Thus the discussion in the rest of this section is relevant to the problem of finding the intersection of two polygons only when both of them have a large number of vertices. What is important in graphics is algorithms for finding efficiently the pairwise intersections of a large number of polygons. This is the case with solutions of the visibility problem and with checking circuit layouts, especially when large scale integration is used. The principles used for the efficient polygon intersection algorithms are also applicable there. For this reason we outline some of the major methods used.

One possible speedup in finding intersections is to use simpler shapes than the original polygons. Let M_1 and M_2 be the circumscribed regular rectangles of the polygons Π_1 and Π_2. (These can be found easily from the extrema values of the coordinates of the polygon vertices.) Instead of solving the intersection problem for the polygons one can solve it instead for M_1 and M_2, a much easier task. If the rectangles do not intersect, then we know that the polygons would not either. If one of the rectangles is contained within another, say M_2 is within M_1, then we may consider the intersection of M_2 and Π_1, and then the intersection of the latter polygon and Π_2 (Figure 15.5a). If M_1 and M_2 have a nonempty intersection M_{12}, we may consider the intersection of each polygon with the rectangle M_{12}, then define two new polygons and apply the entire procedure to them (Figure 15.5b). This approach has the advantage that it quickly eliminates from consideration vertices of the polygons that are far from each other.

Other approaches depend on presorting the vertices and most of the savings occur when at least one of the polygons remains fixed.

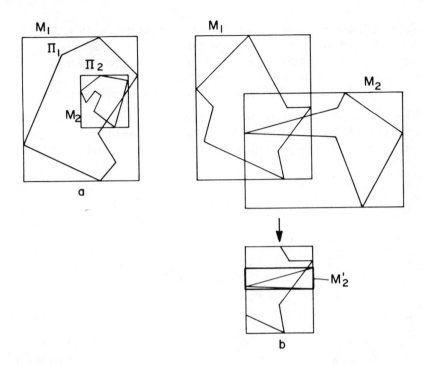

Figure 15.5 (a) Definition of new polygons for checking the intersection of Π_1 and Π_2. (b) Use of recursive subdivision for clipping.

The first method, proposed in [15.DL], is quite general and can be applied to various geometrical problems. Let L_1, L_2, $\cdots L_k$ be a set of lines on the plane and P_1, P_2, $\cdots P_h$ the distinct points of their pairwise intersections. Clearly, $h \leq k(k+1)/2$. Let x_i, y_i be the coordinates of P_i. We may assume without loss of generality that the points of intersection have been labeled in such a way as to have $x_i \leq x_{i+1}$. The vertical lines $x = x_i$ divide the plane into $h + 1$ slabs with the property that there are no line intersections within each slab. It is possible now to order the line segments within each slab according to, say, the y coordinate of their midpoint. This ordering is well defined because there are no intersections. The cost of ordering K objects is of order $K \log_2 K$ and in this case will be of order $h \log_2 h$ plus $hk \log_2 k$.

Suppose now that we are a given a new point (x,y) and we wish to find whether it belongs to any of the k lines, or lies inside a region defined by those lines. We can solve this problem by first finding the slab to which the point belongs on the basis of its x coordinate, and then place it with respect to the lines on the basis of its y coordinate.

Both of these placings are equivalent to insertion in an ordered list, a problem that requires time proportional to the logarithm of the list size.† In our case this equals $\log_2 h$ plus $\log_2 k$. Since $\log_2 h \leq 2\log_2 k$ we may say that the effort is proportional to $\log_2 k$. (The naive algorithm requires effort of order of k.) Therefore we can state formally:

Theorem 15.1: It is possible to check the position of a point with respect to k lines in time of order $\log_2 k$, provided that the lines have been presorted. The presorting effort is of order $k^3 \log_2 k$. [15.DL] □

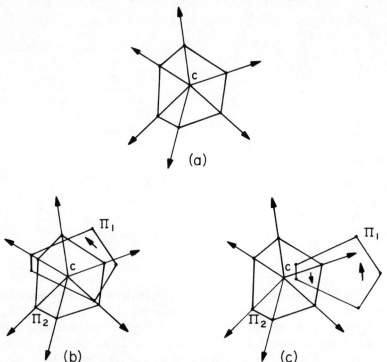

(a)

(b)   (c)

Figure 15.6 (a) Definition of the sectors for finding the intersection of two convex polygons. (b) Finding the intersection when C is inside both polygons. A common direction of sequential traversal can be established for both polygons. (c) Finding the intersection when C is outside Π_1. Two directions of sequential traversal for Π_1 must be used, but only some of the sectors of Π_2 need be visited.

---

† This assumes that the list is maintained in an appropriate data structure such as a balanced tree. See [6.AHU], Chapter 3 for more on this topic.

Another method, proposed in [15.SH], does a similar presorting, but in polar coordinates. It has the severe restriction that both polygons must be convex. It proceeds by selecting a point C in the interior of one of the polygons, say Π_2, and finds the halflines L_1, L_2, $\cdots L_m$ joining C with the m vertices of Π_2. The effort for finding the point and the lines is proportional to m. If the lines are directed from the center to the vertex so that points to the right give a positive sign in Equation (15.1), then it is simple to check whether a point belongs to a sector. It will be in the sector of the lines L_i and L_{i+1} if it is positive with respect to the first and negative with respect to the second (Figure 15.6a). The sectors can be ordered in, say, a clockwise fashion so that one can find the sector where a point belongs in time proportional to $\log_2 m$. Once the sector for one vertex of the second polygon, say Π_1, has been found, the sectors for the remaining vertices can be found by considering the sectors sequentially to see whether they contain any vertices. If Π_1 contains the center (Figure 15.6b) the sectors and the vertices of Π_1 are traversed together without ever having to back up. If the center is outside Π_1 (Figure 15.6c), then one can find a new sector containing Π_1 and centered at C. The vertices of Π_1 fall now in two groups and can be examined sequentially to find their sectors. In either case the process requires time proportional to n, where n is the number of vertices of Π_1. After this process is finished, one examines the position of the vertices in each sector with respect to the side of Π_2 there.

15.7 BIBLIOGRAPHICAL NOTES

[1.NS] describes a line clipping algorithm with respect to a regular rectangle that uses recursive subdivisions. [15.SUH] has a detailed treatment of Algorithm 15.3 and some other related problems. [15.WE] discusses the general problem of operations between polygons: splitting a polygon into parts, joining two intersecting polygons, etc. Clearly, such problems can be solved easily by variations of the clipping algorithms, but one may perform excessive computations without the proper strategy to avoid multiple examination of parts of the polygons.

The use of the decomposition of polygons into convex components for pattern recognition is described in [3.PA].

Theorem 15.1 is a paraphrase of one by Dobkin and Lipton [15.DL]. The second efficient intersection algorithm is due to Shamos [15.SH]. Even though this algorithm and others similar to it are asymptotically (as the number of polygon vertices tends to infinity) faster than those described in this text, their direct applicability in graphics and pattern recognition is questionable for the reasons discussed in

Section 15.6. Also polygons with many vertices (in excess of, say, ten) that are encountered in graphics are likely not to be convex. Therefore asymptotically efficient algorithms for the intersection problem are of interest there only if they are applicable to nonconvex polygons. On the other hand the principle of presorting and the use of circumscribed rectangles can be useful when dealing with very large numbers of polygons. There we may use a simple method such as Algorithm 15.3 to find the actual intersection but apply an asymptotically efficient algorithm for narrowing down the number of polygons that must be examined. See [15.CD] for methods for detecting intersections rather than for computing them.

15.8 RELEVANT LITERATURE

[15.CD]   Chazelle, B. and Dobkin, D. P. "Detection is Easier than Computation," *Proc. Twelfth Annual ACM Symposium on Theory of Computing,* Los Angeles, Calif., April 28-30, 1980, pp. 146-153.

[15.DL]   Dobkin, D. and Lipton, R. J. "Multidimensional Searching Problems," *SIAM J. Computing,* 5 (1976), pp. 181-186.

[15.SH]   Shamos, M. I. "Geometric Complexity" *Proc. Seventh Annual ACM Symposium on Theory of Computing,* 1975, pp. 224-233.

[15.SUH]   Sutherland, I. E. and Hodgman, G. W. "Reentrant Polygon Clipping," *CACM,* 17 (1974), pp. 32-42.

[15.WE]   Weiler, K. "Polygon Comparison using a Graph Representation," *Computer Graphics,* 14 (July 1980), pp. 10-18. (Proceedings of SIGGRAPH 80, published by ACM.)

15.9 PROBLEMS

15.1. Investigate the clipping algorithm for the special case when the line L passes through one of the vertices of the polygon. Are there any changes necessary?

15.2. What changes should be made in Algorithm 15.1 if the line segment is replaced by an (infinite) line given by its coefficients?

15.3. Write a program implementing Algorithm 15.2.

15.4. Modify Algorithm 15.3 so that it draws a vector between successive intersections of the polygon with the line. Then the resulting figure will be closed and could be filled by using one of the algorithms of Chapter 8. (*Hints:* It is necessary to keep a flag indicating on what side of the polygon we are. When the flag is changed the point of intersection is saved. The next time the flag is changed a vector is drawn between the saved point and the new intersection. Care should be taken to handle properly situations such as a polygon vertex lying on the line, and proper initialization. Establishing a clockwise order of traversal of the vertices is helpful.)

15.5. Design and implement an algorithm for finding the intersection and the union of two polygons. The results should be expressed as a set of polygons. (The set may be empty for the intersection.)

15.6. Design and implement an algorithm for decomposing a (nonconvex) polygon into convex subsets. Follow the suggestion given in Section 15.5 and prove that the union of the resulting polygons is indeed the original polygon. Give an estimate of the computational complexity of the algorithm.

15.7. Design and implement an algorithm for decomposing a (nonconvex) polygon into convex subsets with the added constraint that the convex components are nonintersecting. Compare the computational complexity of this algorithm and that of the previous problem.

15.8. Make an exact count of the times that the expressions of Equation (15.1) or Equations (15.2) must be evaluated in order to find the intersection of two pentagons, first using the method of Section 15.5, and then one of the methods of Section 15.6.

Chapter 16

THE MATHEMATICS OF THREE-DIMENSIONAL GRAPHICS

16.1 INTRODUCTION

Computer graphics offers an interesting example of revival of some almost forgotten methodologies and branches of mathematics. The rendering of three-dimensional scenes on a plane surface preoccupied painters for many centuries and the study of perspective projections occupied a prominent position in art schools. Around the beginning of the nineteenth century the study of *descriptive geometry* became a central subject in engineering and dealt with problems such as finding the intersection of cylinders by graphical means, etc. The invention of photography reduced the significance of realistic art, and the advent of abstract art placed studies of projections in the background. Similarly, descriptive geometry lost its prominence in engineering and by 1960 few engineering students in the United States were studying the subject.†

Computer graphics that creates two-dimensional representations

---

† In a sense, I was fortunate to complete my undergraduate studies in a country where the curriculum changed little with time. Descriptive geometry was emphasized in the Technical University of Athens well into the fifties.

for three-dimensional scenes has revived the interest in these subjects. The major mathematical tools necessary for creating displays that appear three-dimensional include methods for the solution of geometrical problems (discussed in Section 16.2), positional transformations (Section 16.3), and projections (Sections 16.4 and 16.5).

The mathematical knowledge is only a necessary tool, and by no means sufficient for designing good displays. Good engineering judgment, as well as some skill in the visual arts, are other essential prerequisites. During the last ten or fifteen years there has been a substantial interest in what is called computer art. For the most part such creations were two-dimensional. Perhaps the greatest technical challenge is in the use of the computer to create scenes that appear three-dimensional. The large amount of computing required is an impediment to such efforts; more emphasis on the study of the mathematical tools used may result in more efficient implementations.

16.2 HOMOGENEOUS COORDINATES

The analysis of Section 14.3 can be extended to three dimensions. A point P can be described by homogeneous coordinates x, y, z, w and a plane A by coefficients a, b, c, d, so that the equation of the plane is

$$ax + by + cz + dw = 0 \tag{16.1}$$

In three dimensions the duality is between point and plane. Thus three points define a plane by an equation of the form

$$\det \begin{vmatrix} x & x_1 & x_2 & x_3 \\ y & y_1 & y_2 & y_3 \\ z & z_1 & z_2 & z_3 \\ w & w_1 & w_2 & w_3 \end{vmatrix} = 0 \tag{16.2}$$

and three planes intersect at a point with coordinates that are minors of the following determinant.

$$\det \begin{vmatrix} a & a_1 & a_2 & a_3 \\ b & b_1 & b_2 & b_3 \\ c & c_1 & c_2 & c_3 \\ w & w_1 & w_2 & w_3 \end{vmatrix} = 0 \tag{16.3}$$

These definitions fail in singular cases: if the three points lie on a line, if the three planes have a common line, or if the two points or planes defining a line coincide. In terms of Equation (16.2) the singularity conditions manifest themselves by the fact that one of the columns 2 to

4 is a linear combination of the other two, and therefore the determinant is zero for all values of (x,y,z,w).

Lines now require a pair of equations, either as intersections of two planes, or as joining two points. To express the equation of a line joining two points in homogeneous coordinates, we observe that such a line should belong to all the planes defined by (x_1,y_1,z_1,w_1), (x_2,y_2,z_2,w_2), and any third point. Therefore Equation (16.2) should be an identity with respect to the values of the elements of the fourth column. This in turn means that the minor determinants with respect to the elements of that column should be zero. However, the resulting four equations are not all independent. Indeed, considering the minor with respect to x_3 we conclude that the row (w,w_1,w_2) is linearly dependent on the rows (y,y_1,y_2) and (z,z_1,z_2) in order for the determinant to be zero. Similarly, we find that (w,w_1,w_2) is linearly dependent on (x,x_1,x_2) and (z,z_1,z_2). These two linear dependencies imply the linear dependence of (x,x_1,x_2), (y,y_1,y_2), and (z,z_1,z_2). Therefore the minor with respect to w_3 is zero, if the minors with respect to x_3 and y_3 are zero. The proof can be repeated for the minor with respect to z_3 so that we are left with two independent equations:

$$\det\begin{vmatrix} x & x_1 & x_2 \\ y & y_1 & y_2 \\ w & w_1 & w_2 \end{vmatrix} = \det\begin{vmatrix} x & x_1 & x_2 \\ z & z_1 & z_2 \\ w & w_1 & w_2 \end{vmatrix} = 0 \qquad (16.4)$$

If we set $w = w_1 = w_2 = 1$ in the above equations we obtain the ordinary expressions for a line joining two points:

$$\frac{x - x_1}{x_2 - x_1} = \frac{y - y_1}{y_2 - y_1} = \frac{z - z_1}{z_2 - z_1} \qquad (16.5)$$

16.2.1 Position of a Point with respect to a Plane

In order to check the position of a point with respect to a plane we must evaluate the sign of the determinant of Equation (16.1) for the coordinates of the point. The problem in three dimensions is more complicated than in two and we need certain preliminaries first.

Definition 16.1:   Let v_1, v_2, and v_3 be three vectors, all starting from a common point and not lying on the same plane. We shall say that these vectors form a *righthanded system* if they have the following property. Let P be the plane defined by v_1 and v_2, and H the halfspace defined by P where v_3 lies. Then, for an observer located in H, and standing at the common point of the three vectors, the vector v_1 can be brought to v_2 by a counterclockwise rotation. $\square$

The usual choice of x-y-z axes results in such a system. A common illustration of a righthanded system is offered by the thumb, index, and middle finger of a right hand, if assigned to v_1, v_2, and v_3 respectively. When the fingers are held in such a way as to be mutually perpendicular they form a righthanded system. A simple analytical way of checking this property is offered by the following lemma.

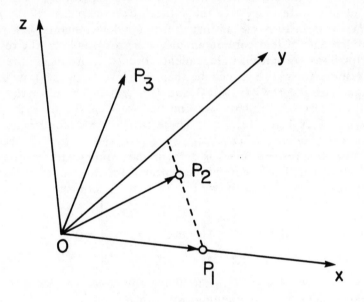

Figure 16.1 Arrangement of vectors forming a right system

Lemma 16.1: The value d of the determinant

$$d = \det \begin{vmatrix} x_1 & x_2 & x_3 \\ y_1 & y_2 & y_3 \\ z_1 & z_2 & z_3 \end{vmatrix} \qquad (16.6)$$

is positive if the three points form a *righthanded system* with respect to the origin. □

Proof: Without any loss of generality we can take the x-axis along the line joining the origin with the first point, the y-axis on the plane defined by the first two points and forming an angle less than 90 degrees with the line joining the origin with the second point, and the z-axis normal to that plane and forming a righthanded system with the other two axes (see Figure 16.1). Then Equation (16.6) becomes

$$d = \det \begin{vmatrix} x_1 & x_2 & x_3 \\ 0 & y_2 & y_3 \\ 0 & 0 & z_3 \end{vmatrix} = x_1 y_2 z_3 \qquad (16.6')$$

Because of our selection of the axes, all three coordinates of the right-hand side of the above equation are positive, and therefore the same is true for their product. $\square$

It can be shown (see [16.SA], p.21) that d equals six times the volume of a pyramid whose base is the triangle formed by the three points, and whose vertex is the origin.

The following is a counterpart of Assumption 14.1.

Assumption 16.1: If a plane is specified by three of its points, then these points are ordered so that they form a righthanded system with respect to the origin. $\square$

Proposition 16.1: Let X, Y, Z, and W be the coordinates of a point P and (x_i, y_i, z_i, w_i), $i = 1, 2, 3$ three points that define a plane. If W and all the w_is are positive, then P lies at the same side of the plane as the origin if the value of the determinant given by Equation (16.7) is positive.

$$D = \begin{vmatrix} X & x_1 & x_2 & x_3 \\ Y & y_1 & y_2 & y_3 \\ Z & z_1 & z_2 & z_3 \\ W & w_1 & w_2 & w_3 \end{vmatrix} \qquad (16.7)$$

$\square$

Proof: The righthand side of Equation (16.7) is a linear function of x, y, z, and w, and therefore its sign will be fixed on either side of the plane defined by $D = 0$. Substituting $X = Y = Z = 0$ into this equation we find

$$D = Wd \qquad (16.8)$$

where d is the determinant given by Equation (16.6). Because of Assumption 16.1, Lemma 16.1, and the assumption about the sign of W, both factors of the product are positive. $\square$

The above result can be extended so that it can be used to define the position of a point with respect to nonplanar surfaces. Indeed, almost any surface may be subdivided into triangles whose vertices can be marked in a consistent way so they form a righthanded system with respect to the origin. The only exceptions are surfaces such as the

Moebius strip, which are not common in graphic applications (see [16.PF], p.214 for more on surface orientation).

16.2.2 Intersection of Triangles

We introduce the following notation for a determinant:

$$
S_{ijkn} = \begin{vmatrix} x_i & x_j & x_k & x_n \\ y_i & y_j & y_k & y_n \\ z_i & z_j & z_k & z_n \\ w_i & w_j & w_k & w_n \end{vmatrix} \tag{16.9}
$$

Proposition 16.2: Consider two triangles given by three points each: P_1, P_2, P_3 the first triangle, and P_4, P_5, P_6 the second. Let x_i, y_i, z_i, and w_i be the homogeneous coordinates of P_i ($1 \leq i \leq 6$). Then the two triangles intersect if the three quantities S_{1456}, S_{2456}, and S_{3456} do not all have the same sign, and the same condition is true for the three quantities S_{4123}, S_{5123}, and S_{6123}. □

Proof: A direct consequence of Proposition 16.1. □

This result is a generalization of the discussion of Section 14.4.2 from two to three dimensions.

16.3 THREE-DIMENSIONAL TRANSFORMATIONS

Translation and scaling transformations in three dimensions can be expressed in the same manner as in two dimensions, but for rotations, we must now choose an axis. The formulas for transforming the coordinates after a rotation around an arbitrary axis are rather cumbersome but it is possible to give them in concise form with rather simple proofs if we introduce certain concepts of vector algebra.

16.3.1 Mathematical Preliminaries

We have assumed throughout this text that readers are familiar with elementary linear algebra and we have already used the concepts of scalar product and product of a matrix and vectors in earlier sections (Section 2.2, Section 10.3, etc.). We introduce here some additional vector operations, which although widely used in mechanics and electromagnetic theory, may not be very familiar to students in computer science or signal processing.

Definition 16.2: The cross-product of two three-dimensional vectors u and v, denoted $u \times v$, is defined as a vector with components

$$
u_y v_z - u_z v_y,\ u_z v_x - u_x v_z,\ u_x v_z - u_z v_x . \tag{16.10}
$$

The following proposition summarizes certain properties of the cross-product. The proofs are straightforward.

Proposition 16.3: (a) If u and v are collinear, i.e., $u = cv$ for some constant c, then $u \times v = 0$.
(b) If u and v are not collinear, then $u \times v$ is normal to the plane defined by them.
(c) $u \times v = -v \times u$.
(d) The size of the cross-product equals $|u| \cdot |v| \sin\theta$, where θ is the angle between the two vectors. $\square$

Definition 16.3: The cross-product of a vector v and a matrix A is a matrix whose columns equal the cross-product of the columns of A with v. $\square$

We also observe that the product of an n-dimensional vector v with the transpose u' of another n-dimensional vector is a matrix W whose elements are given by the equation

$$W_{ij} = v_i u_j \tag{16.11}$$

Since the column vector is a $n \times 1$ matrix and the row vector a $1 \times n$ matrix, the above product will be a $n \times n$ matrix. (If the order of the operation is reversed we have a 1×1 matrix, i.e. a scalar.) This vector operation has a special name:

Definition 16.4: A *dyad* is the product of a column vector u with a row vector v': uv'. The *dyadic* representation of a matrix A is the form

$$A = a_1 a_1' + a_2 a_2' + \cdots + a_k a_k'$$

for some vectors $a_1, a_2, \cdots a_k$. $\square$

We shall use the concept of a dyad to derive the expression for coordinate transformation caused by a rotation around an axis through the origin. A discussion of dyadic representations is outside the scope of the text and we limit ourselves to giving only an example. Note that not all matrices have dyadic representations.

Example 16.1: The matrix

$$A = \begin{bmatrix} 2 & 0 \\ 1 & 3 \end{bmatrix}$$

has the dyadic representation

$$A = \begin{pmatrix} 1 \\ 0 \end{pmatrix}(2 \; -2) + \begin{pmatrix} 3 \\ 3 \end{pmatrix}(0 \; 1)$$

On the other hand there is no way to express the matrix

$$A = \begin{bmatrix} 2 & 1 \\ 0 & 2 \end{bmatrix}$$

in a dyadic form. $\square$

16.3.2 Rotation around an Axis through the Origin

We shall study this problem first in x, y, z coordinates. Let an axis through the origin be defined by the angles ϕ_1, ϕ_2, and ϕ_3 that it forms with the three coordinate axes x, y, and z. Note that these angles are not independent since the following equation holds for their cosines:

$$\cos^2\phi_1 + \cos^2\phi_2 + \cos^2\phi_3 = 1 \tag{16.12}$$

For the given axis we define a vector a that is parallel to the axis, and which has unit length. Then $a_i = \cos\phi_i$, $i = 1, 2, 3$.

Theorem 16.1: The matrix of the coordinate transformation imposed by the rotation by an angle θ around an axis through the origin parallel to the unit length vector a is given by

$$R(\theta) = aa' + \cos\theta(I - aa') + \sin\theta(I \times a) \tag{16.13}$$

where I is the 3×3 identity matrix. $\square$

Proof: Let b be a vector from the origin that is going to be rotated around the axis. It is always possible to decompose b into two components, one parallel to the axis and another, d, normal to it, so that b can be written as the sum

$$b = \lambda a + d \tag{16.14}$$

for some constant λ. We compute the product Rb using the expressions of Equations 16.13 and 16.14.

$$Rb = \lambda aa'a + \lambda\cos\theta(a - aa'a) + \lambda\sin\theta(I \times a)a$$
$$+ aa'd + \cos\theta(d - aa'd) + \sin\theta(I \times a)d \tag{16.15}$$

All the operations on the vectors are associative and the product of a dyad ef' with a vector g equals e times the scalar product of $f'g$. If we apply this term rearrangement to all the terms of Equation (16.15) we can simplify that equation significantly. Because a was assumed to be of unit length we observe that $a'a = 1$, and because d was chosen as orthogonal to a we have $a'd = 0$. Also $(I \times a)a$ must be zero because all the columns of $I \times a$ are orthogonal to a. Then the above equation becomes

$$Rb = \lambda a + \cos\theta d + \sin\theta(I\times a)d \qquad (16.16)$$

To complete the proof of the theorem we need only show that the last two terms represent a rotation of d by an angle θ on the plane perpendicular to the axis. First, we observe that $(I\times a)d = d\times a$. We can show that formally by computing explicitly the matrix $I\times a$:

$$I\times a = \begin{bmatrix} 0 & a_3 & -a_2 \\ -a_3 & 0 & a_1 \\ a_2 & -a_1 & 0 \end{bmatrix}$$

and then taking the product with d. Therefore the last two terms can be written as

$$\cos\theta d + \sin\theta d\times a \qquad (16.17)$$

The vector $d\times a$ is perpendicular to both d and a and has length equal to the length of d because of Proposition 16.3d. If we introduce a local coordinate system on the plane perpendicular to the axis, then we may choose one axis parallel to d and the other parallel to $d\times a$ so that Equation (16.17) is indeed a rotation by an angle θ on that plane. This completes the proof. $\square$

Equation (16.16) can be expanded so the rotation matrix is expressed in terms of the angles θ and ϕ_i. We may also add an extra row and column so that it can be applied to homogeneous coordinates. Then a rotation by an angle θ is given by a 4×4 matrix whose elements are defined by Equations (16.18). There k is the number from the set $\{1,2,3\}$ which is different from i and j.

(a) For $1\leq i, j\leq 3$

$$R_{ij} = \cos\phi_i\cos\phi_j(1-\cos\theta)-\cos\phi_k\sin\theta(-1)^{i+j} \text{ if } i<j \quad (16.18a)$$

$$R_{ij} = \cos\phi_i\cos\phi_j(1-\cos\theta)+\cos\phi_k\sin\theta(-1)^{i+j} \text{ if } i>j \quad (16.18b)$$

$$R_{ii} = \cos^2\phi_i(1-\cos\theta)+\cos\theta \qquad (16.18c)$$

(b) For $i = 4$ or $j = 4$

$$R_{i4} = 0 \quad 1\leq i\leq 3 \qquad (16.18d)$$

$$R_{4j} = 0 \quad 1\leq j\leq 3 \qquad (16.18e)$$

$$R_{44} = 1 \qquad (16.18f)$$

If the axis of rotation coincides with one of the coordinate axes, then the above expressions are simplified considerably and are reduced, in effect, to the formula for the rotation on the plane.

16.4 ORTHOGONAL PROJECTIONS

Projections are probably the most important class of transformations in graphics because they produce the two-dimensional views of three-dimensional objects. The simplest kind of projection is the *orthogonal projection* where the image of a point is found as the foot of the normal from the point to the plane of projection. If the plane of projection is the x-y plane, then one simply sets z equal to zero (or some other constant).

Example 16.2:   A cube is defined by eight vertices: $A(0,0,0)$, $B(2,0,0)$, $C(2,2,0)$, $D(0,2,0)$, $E(0,0,2)$, $F(2,0,2)$, $G(2,2,2)$ and $H(0,2,2)$. Find its orthogonal projection after it is rotated by 60° around the axis joining the points $(0,0,0)$ and $(2,2,2)$.

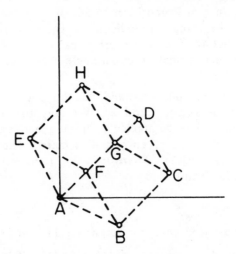

Figure 16.2   Location of the cube vertices used in Example 16.2

In this case $\cos\phi_1 = \cos\phi_2 = \cos\phi_3 = 1/\sqrt{3}$ and the first group of elements of the rotation matrix is given by

$$R_{ij} = \frac{1}{3}(1-\cos\theta) - \frac{1}{\sqrt{3}}\sin\theta(-1)^{i+j} \quad \text{if } i<j$$

$$R_{ij} = \frac{1}{3}(1-\cos\theta) + \frac{1}{\sqrt{3}}\sin\theta(-1)^{i+j} \quad \text{if } i>j$$

$$R_{ii} = \frac{1}{3}(1-\cos\theta) + \cos\theta$$

for any θ. For $\theta=60°$ we have the following matrix

$$R = \begin{bmatrix} \dfrac{2}{3} & \dfrac{2}{3} & -\dfrac{1}{3} \\ -\dfrac{1}{3} & \dfrac{2}{3} & \dfrac{2}{3} \\ \dfrac{2}{3} & -\dfrac{1}{3} & \dfrac{2}{3} \end{bmatrix} \qquad (16.19)$$

We do not list the last column and last row of R because they will still be given by Equation (16.18d-f), and, in this example, we will not use homogeneous coordinates. The vertices of the cube will now be at the following locations:

$A(0,0,0)$, $B(\dfrac{4}{3},-\dfrac{2}{3},\dfrac{4}{3})$, $C(\dfrac{8}{3},\dfrac{2}{3},\dfrac{2}{3})$, $D(\dfrac{4}{3},\dfrac{4}{3},-\dfrac{2}{3})$, $E(-\dfrac{2}{3},\dfrac{4}{3},\dfrac{4}{3})$, $F(\dfrac{2}{3},\dfrac{2}{3},\dfrac{8}{3})$, $G(2,2,2)$, and $H(\dfrac{2}{3},\dfrac{8}{3},\dfrac{2}{3})$.

The projection at $z = 0$ will consist of the following eight points:

$A(0,0)$, $B(\dfrac{4}{3},-\dfrac{2}{3})$, $C(\dfrac{8}{3},\dfrac{2}{3})$, $D(\dfrac{4}{3},\dfrac{4}{3})$, $E(-\dfrac{2}{3},\dfrac{4}{3})$, $F(\dfrac{2}{3},\dfrac{2}{3})$, $G(2,2)$, and $H(\dfrac{2}{3},\dfrac{8}{3})$. These are shown in Figure 16.2. In order to produce a proper projection, we must decide which one of the points $D(\dfrac{4}{3},\dfrac{4}{3})$ and $F(\dfrac{2}{3},\dfrac{2}{3})$ will be visible. The first has $z = -\dfrac{2}{3}$ and the second $z = \dfrac{8}{3}$. If we view the cube from above, the one with the greater z will be visible, producing Figure 16.3a. Otherwise, we will have Figure 16.3b. $\square$

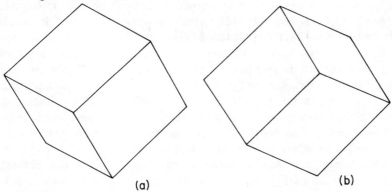

(a)   (b)

Figure 16.3 Possible views of the cube of Example 16.2

Although orthogonal projections are easy to obtain, they do not provide realistic scenes unless observers are assumed to be very far from the objects. When their distance from the scene is comparable to its dimensions, we must use perspective projections.

16.5 PERSPECTIVE PROJECTIONS

Perspective projection attempts to imitate the way an observer forms an impression of a scene. Objects are projected onto a plane of vision from a central point, the eye of the observer (Figure 16.4).

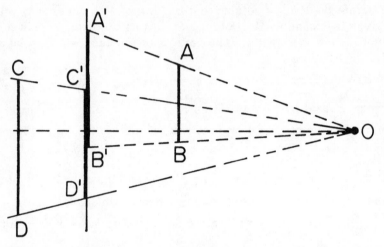

Figure 16.4 Illustration of perspective projections. Segment *AB* is projected as *A'B'*, and CD as *C'D'*

Such a projected image can be constructed easily from the description of the solids and has been an artistic tool for many centuries. It should be pointed out that very few artists adhere strictly to the rules of perspective because the images created by the rules do not always look right. Unfortunately, in computer graphics, one must follow some precise rule because computer programs can only implement mathematical formulas. If we are not pleased with the results of the application of the strict perspective rules, we must amend them in some mathematically explicit way. The location of the center of projection is usually taken to be the position of a viewer of the screen at a distance d from the center, which can also be taken as the origin of the coordinates. Using the notation of Figure 16.5 we find that a point P with coordinates (x,y,z) will be mapped into P' with coordinates

$$\frac{xd}{d+z}, \ \frac{yd}{d+z}, \ 0 \ .$$

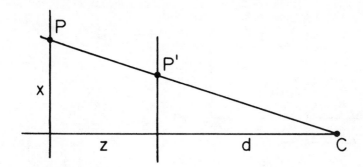

Figure 16.5 Relation between the coordinates of a point and those of its perspective projection

In order to display the result, though, one must consider which objects obscure others, and therefore it is necessary to preserve information about the z-coordinate. For reasons to be explained later, we choose to apply a similar scaling on z as on x and y. This does not affect the relative distances of the objects from the screen because if $z_1 > z_2 > 0$ it is also true that

$$\frac{dz_1}{d + z_1} > \frac{dz_2}{d + z_2} > 0$$

The perspective transformation can be expressed in an elegant way in homogeneous coordinates because we need to modify only the last component. In particular, we can write

$$P = \begin{bmatrix} 1 & 0 & 0 & 0 \\ 0 & 1 & 0 & 0 \\ 0 & 0 & 1 & 0 \\ 0 & 0 & \dfrac{1}{d} & 1 \end{bmatrix} \tag{16.20}$$

If (ξ, η, ζ, w) are the homogeneous coordinates, we find that after the projection

$$w_p = w + \frac{\zeta}{d} = w\left(1 + \frac{z}{d}\right) = w\left(\frac{d + z}{d}\right)$$

since $\zeta = wz$. This provides the correct scaling factor. In order to display a scene, one must first multiply all points by P, then decide which ones are visible, and finally illuminate the points of the screen whose x, y coordinates correspond to those of the visible objects.

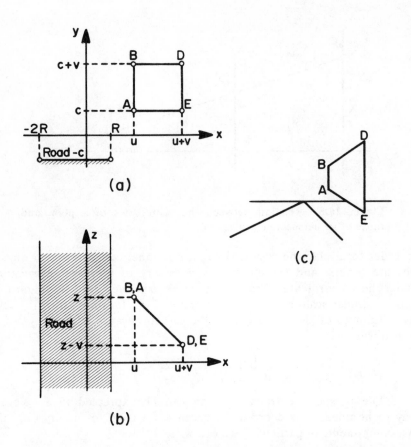

Figure 16.6 Arrangement of objects for Example 16.3. (a) shows the location of the x and y coordinates while (b) shows x and z. (c) is a projection.

Example 16.3: Create a display simulating the view of a person driving along a straight road. We place the observer at the origin of the coordinates and we assume that the observer moves along a direction perpendicular to the screen. Since the system of the coordinates moves also in that direction we may create various views by changing the z coordinate of the objects in the scene. For simplicity, we assume that besides the road and the horizon there is only one other object in the scene, a square billboard situated as shown in Figures 16.6a and 16.6b. It forms an angle of 45° with the road axis, its leftmost side is at distance u from the line along which the observer drives, it has height v, width $\sqrt{2}v$, and the distance between its lower corner and the observer is c. Then the coordinates of its corners will be:

$$A = \begin{pmatrix} u \\ c \\ z \end{pmatrix} \quad B = \begin{pmatrix} u \\ c+v \\ z \end{pmatrix} \quad D = \begin{pmatrix} u+v \\ c+v \\ z-v \end{pmatrix} \quad E = \begin{pmatrix} u+v \\ c \\ z-v \end{pmatrix} \quad (16.21)$$

The distance between the road surface and the observer is c, the right edge is at a distance R, and the left edge at a distance $2R$ from the observer. Therefore the two parallel lines delineating the road will be given by the following pairs of equations:

$$x = +R \quad y = -c \quad \text{(right edge)} \tag{16.22a}$$

$$x = -2R \quad y = -c \quad \text{(left edge)} \tag{16.22b}$$

We observe that some parts of the display will remain unchanged. A point of the right edge at a distance z from the observer will be shown at

$$x = \frac{Rd}{d+z} \quad y = -\frac{cd}{d+z} \tag{16.23}$$

For $z \rightarrow \infty$ we find $x = y = 0$ and for $z = 0$, $x = R$, $Y = -c$. Therefore, the right edge will always appear as a line segment from the point $(R,-c)$ to the point $(0,0)$. Similarly, the left line will be a point connecting the points $(-2R,-c)$ and $(0,0)$. This is shown in Figure 16.6c. The perspective projections of the billboard corners will have coordinates

$$A_p = \begin{pmatrix} \dfrac{ud}{d+z} \\[2mm] \dfrac{cd}{d+z} \end{pmatrix} \quad B_p = \begin{pmatrix} \dfrac{ud}{d+z} \\[2mm] \dfrac{(c+v)d}{d+z} \end{pmatrix} \tag{16.24a}$$

$$D_p = \begin{pmatrix} \dfrac{(u+v)d}{d+z-v} \\[2mm] \dfrac{(c+v)d}{d+z-v} \end{pmatrix} \quad E_p = \begin{pmatrix} \dfrac{(u+v)d}{d+z-v} \\[2mm] \dfrac{cd}{d+z-v} \end{pmatrix} \tag{16.24b}$$

For $z \rightarrow \infty$ all points collapse to the origin. If the display has a resolution of N pixels, then the smallest discernible value is $1/N$ so that if $c < u$ the largest value of z giving nonzero coordinates will be $d(Nc-1)$. The program will consist of a loop starting from $z = d(Nc-1)$ and going down to $z = 0$. Care should be taken to clip the display because points E and D will be first to disappear from view. If an appropriate bit selection can be made in the words of the refresh memory (see Sections 1.6 and 1.7), then one can erase the area off the screen and redisplay it without affecting the background. The display of the board can be done using a simplified filling algorithm for the whole area. □

The example shows that perspective projections are straightforward when there are no interactions among objects. If T is the matrix of motion between frames and P the projection matrix, one proceeds by multiplying all (homogeneous) vectors u by $P \cdot T$, clipping the scene with respect to the viewing window, and finally displaying the results. The problem becomes more difficult when objects interfere with each other and the hidden line problem must be solved.

16.6 BIBLIOGRAPHICAL NOTES

The proof for the formulas of the rotation around an axis is based on [16.WI], admittedly a rather early reference. Because of its complexity, the formula seems to have become extinct in most of the modern treatises, and even books on graphics seem to ignore it (e.g. [1.NS]). Even when it is presented, the proof is given by laborious formula manipulation rather than the elegant dyadic representation of Wilson and Gibbs [16.WI]. Not surprisingly, projective geometry offers many tools for the study of projections. The reader should be aware though that the relation between an object and its perspective projection is called simply a *perspective* in that literature [14.FI], [14.MA], [14.PE], [14.RO], and [14.TO]. The results of perspective projections are often counterintuitive (see Problem 16.8), because they distort metric relations. See [16.ER] for some ingenious applications of perspective that produce "impossible" scenes.

16.7 RELEVANT LITERATURE

[16.ER]   Ernst, B. *The Magic Mirror of M.C.Escher*, New York: Ballantine Books, 1976.

[16.PF]   Pach, K. and Frey, T. *Vector and Tensor Analysis*, Budapest: Terra, 1964.

[16.SA]   Salmon, G. *Analytic Geometry of Three Dimensions*, vol. I, 7th edition, New York: Chelsea, 1927.

[16.WI]   Wilson, E. B. *Vector Analysis*, (founded upon the lectures of J. W. Gibbs), New Haven: Yale University Press, 1901. *(Fourth Printing, 1922.)*

16.8 PROBLEMS

16.1. Prove Equation (16.2) and Equation (16.3).

16.2. (a) Show that the area of a triangle with vertices at (x_1, y_1, z), (x_2, y_2, z), and (x_3, y_3, z) is given by the formula

$$area = \frac{1}{2}\left[x_1(y_2 - y_3) + x_2(y_3 - y_1) + x_3(y_1 - y_2) \right]$$

(b) Find the expression for the area when the z coordinates of the vertices are not all the same.

16.3. Provide a detailed proof of Proposition 16.2.

16.4. Prove the four parts of Proposition 16.3.

16.5. Find the rotation matrix for a rotation around the y-axis.

16.6. Find the transformation for the orthogonal projection on the plane defined by the three points $(1,0,0)$, $(0,1,0)$, and $(0,0,1)$. *Hint:* You should find the expression for the matrix in Equation (16.19) helpful.

16.7. Show that each of the four points A_p, B_p, D_p, and E_p of Example 16.3 moves along a line passing through $(0,0)$ while z is changing.

16.8. Show that the orthogonal projection of a sphere is always a circle while the perspective projection may be either a circle or an ellipse. (The latter result is counterintuitive for most people. It is one of the deviations of artistic perspective from mathematical perspective. The following experiment may persuade you about its truth. Hold a flashlight next to a basketball in an otherwise dark room. The shadow on the wall will be an ellipse unless the line joining the light source and the center of the sphere is perpendicular to the wall.)

16.9. Expand the point editor introduced in Chapter 10 to allow the handling of three-dimensional constructions. To this end you must introduce the capacity for three-dimensional transformations.

Chapter 17

CREATING THREE-DIMENSIONAL GRAPHIC DISPLAYS

17.1 INTRODUCTION

We use the term *three-dimensional display* for displays that are projections of three-dimensional scenes rather than for displays in three dimensions.† However, the use of proper projection operations, elimination of surfaces that are not supposed to be visible, and shading can create a realistic impression of depth, as one can see from Figures 17.1 (Plate 28) and 17.2 (Plate 29). Visibility problems are central in the creation of such displays, as are shading algorithms (Section 13.9) and randomization techniques for introducing the appearance of texture, as shown in Figure 17.2. The efficient solution of visibility problems is probably one of the major steps in creating such a display. These are often referred to as the *hidden line* or *hidden surface* problems. Section 17.2 is a general discussion of the subject. Section 17.3 deals with a

---

† Truly three-dimensional displays can be created by holographic means, a technology that is outside the scope of this text. Stereographic displays require the creation of two views, each of which can be generated with the techniques described in this chapter, although we will not go into methods for the precise coordination between the two. See [17.JH] for an example.

visibility algorithm using a quad tree and Section 17.4 with an algorithm particularly appropriate for raster graphics. Section 17.5 discusses the subject of *coherence*: how to take advantage of the interdependence of different parts of a scene to speed up the solution of the visibility problem. Even though there exist a large number of visibility algorithms in the literature, we present here only two of the simplest. The reason is that the choice of a particular method is strongly application dependent. It is primarily a question of putting together some of the techniques we discussed earlier, in particular clipping and filling algorithms. Section 17.6 discusses the necessary modifications for applying such algorithms to nonlinear object descriptions. Finally, Section 17.7 reviews briefly the use of randomization and multiple reflections.

In general, visibility problems can be attacked either in the object space or in the image space. A solution in the object space focuses on geometric relations among the parts of the objects in order to decide what is visible and what is not. A solution in the image space traverses the area of the picture and examines the projections as they occur. Both algorithms described in Sections 17.3 and 17.4 operate in the image space. Section 17.5 discusses an example in the object space.

In order to display complex objects, it is necessary to have appropriate mathematical descriptions for them. Two solutions are commonly employed. In one, a set of curves is drawn on a real solid (see Figure 17.3a), and the mathematical description of these curves is used to generate the display. Such a method is particularly appropriate for vector graphics, but the resulting displays have a wire frame appearance.

The second solution requires the division of the surface of the solid into a set of patches. A simple mathematical approximation can be found over each patch, and the object display is produced as the aggregate of the displays of these surface patches. Figure 17.3b shows an example. Often, the surface patches are plane triangles because triangulation of a surface is a rather simple process since three points define a plane. Also, the display of triangles, their filling, and the finding of pairwise intersections are straightforward. The major disadvantage of this representation is that one may need a very large number of triangles to produce the impression of a smooth surface. Surface patches of the types discussed in Sections 13.4 to 13.7 offer an alternative and most modern displays use them for object description.

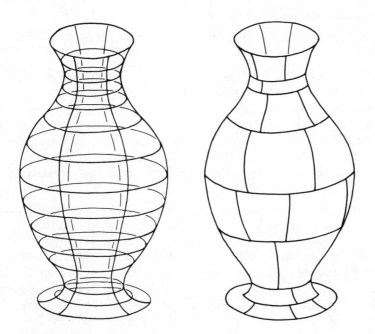

Figure 17.3 (a) Representation of a solid object by a set of curves. (b) Representation of a solid object by a set of surface patches.

17.2 THE HIDDEN LINE AND HIDDEN SURFACE PROBLEMS

The display of the cube in Example 16.2 illustrates a simple instance of the hidden line problem. Although there are twelve lines on the object, only nine of them should be displayed to create the impression of a solid display. The problem can also be expressed in terms of hidden surfaces, by considering the faces of the cube. In vector graphics, one usually deals with hidden lines, while in raster graphics, the problem is expressed in terms of hidden surfaces. The importance of the problem is not because of its inherent difficulty, but because of the requirement that the solution be computed quickly, for instance, while an object is being rotated. The first step in solving this problem is a generalization of the material of Section 14.4.4 to three dimensions, using the results of Section 16.2.

17.2.1 Surface Shadow

Let $S_1, S_2, \cdots S_n$ be the faces (surface patches) of all objects in the display.

Definition 17.1:   Face S_i is said to shadow or obscure face S_j along the direction v, if the following three conditions hold:

(a) S_i does not intersect S_j;

(b) the orthogonal projections T_i and T_j of the faces on a plane perpendicular to v have a nonempty intersection T_{ij};

(c) at least one of the points of S_i which is projected into T_{ij} lies farther from the origin along the direction v than the respective point of S_j. $\square$

Usually, we assume that the direction v is the z-axis and that the faces are plane polygons. Without the second assumption the verification of the conditions of Definition 17.1 is very difficult, if not completely intractable. A comparison of the above definition with Proposition 14.2 shows the increased difficulty of the problem in three dimensions: instead of checking Equation (14.21a) or Equation (14.21b) one must solve the clipping problem on the x-y plane. The verification of nonintersection is also rather complicated. In the plane a line segment is uniquely defined by its two endpoints, and the analysis of Section 14.4.2 is directly applicable. In the three-dimensional space a face need not be a triangle, so the selection of three points for checking the signs of the determinants of Proposition 16.2 is not sufficient. One must check them for all the vertices of both faces. The location with respect to the origin may be checked by substituting one of the points of one of the planes into the equation for the other, after the selection of a righthand system on the latter. The following definition is a modification of Definition 17.1 for perspective projections.

Definition 17.2:   Face S_i is said to shadow or obscure face S_j, when viewed from point C, if the following three conditions hold:

(a) S_i does not intersect S_j;

(b) the perspective projections T_i and T_j of the faces on a plane not containing C have a nonempty intersection T_{ij};

(c) at least one of the points of S_i which is projected into T_{ij} lies farther along the line from C than the respective point of S_j. $\square$

It is possible to avoid the distinction between projections if we use the expressions of Section 16.5 for perspective projections. To do this, we construct scenes resulting from perspective projections in two steps. First we apply the three-dimensional transformation given by matrix P of Equation (16.20) on all objects. A point with coordinates x, y, z will map into

$$x' = \frac{dx}{z+d}, \quad y' = \frac{dy}{z+d}, \quad z' = \frac{dz}{z+d}. \tag{17.1}$$

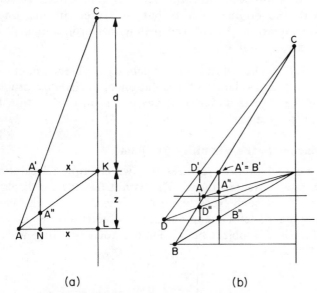

$$(a) \qquad\qquad\qquad (b)$$

Figure 17.4 (a) Geometric construction of the transformation given by Equation (16.20). A'' is the image of A. (b) The same transformation applied to a group of points.

Figure 17.4a illustrates a geometrical interpretation of these expressions on the x-z plane. According to elementary geometry we have

$$\frac{A'K}{AL} = \frac{CK}{CL} = \frac{d}{d+z},$$

since $AL = x$ and $A'K = x'$. Also

$$\frac{A'A''}{A'N} = \frac{CK}{CL} = \frac{d}{d+z},$$

since $A'N = KL = z$ and $A'A'' = z'$. Therefore A'' is the image of A

under this transformation. Figure 17.4b shows the transformation applied to a group of points. We can see from Equation (17.1) as well as from Figure 17.4 that the images of points lying on the same line from the projection center C (such as A and B) line up along a vertical line to the projection plane (such as A'' and B''). Points that are on different lines from C (such as A and D) have images that do not line up vertically (such as A'' and D'').

We can now proceed with the second step. Check surface shadows, not with the original objects but with their images under the transformation Equation (16.20) and orthogonal projections. We summarize our results as follows:

Proposition 17.1: The solution of a visibility problem under perspective projections is equivalent to the solution of a visibility problem for the images of the objects under the transformation of Equation (16.20) and orthogonal projections. □

17.2.2 Approaches to the Visibility Problem

Definition 17.1 or 17.2 requires that we examine all pairs of faces to find which ones obscure others. This is not feasible for displays containing thousands of such faces but it could be done for the faces of a single object. Indeed, let a scene contain k objects and let the number of surfaces for the ith object be s_i. Then a total ordering will require effort proportional to

$$\left[\sum_{i=1}^{k} s_i \right]^2 \tag{17.2}$$

while comparing only the surfaces within each object would require effort proportional to

$$\sum_{i=1}^{k} s_i^2 \tag{17.3}$$

Usually, objects do not intersect so that one may consider the solution of the surface shadow problem for their outlines, requiring effort proportional to k^2. This approach requires some careful bookkeeping. Many visibility algorithms resolve the difficulty by transforming the three-dimensional problem into a two-dimensional problem in one of the following ways:

(a) Consider the polygonal projections of the faces and, by using a clipping algorithm, find all intersecting pairs (including polygons where one surrounds the other completely). Then the application of Proposition 16.1 will show which one obscures the other. Instead of checking pairs directly one may consider their intersection with windows that are regular rectangles. Two polygons can obscure each other only if they intersect the same window. Algorithm 17.1 is based on this idea.

(b) Intersect all faces by a horizontal plane and solve the visibility problem for the resulting segments. This approach is implemented by Algorithm 17.2.

17.2.3 Single Convex Object Visibility

If we deal with only one object, and that object is convex, then we may solve the visibility problem by examining the directions of the normals to the faces of the object. These can be found with the methods of Section 13.2. If the normal points away from the screen then we have a back face that is invisible. If the normal points toward the screen the face is visible. (The direction of the normal can be found easily from the sign of F_z defined in Equation (13.5c).) See the discussion of Section 17.5 on geometric coherence for some related techniques.

17.3 A QUAD TREE VISIBILITY ALGORITHM

This algorithm considers windows of the display that correspond to nodes of the quad tree (see Section 6.4). If there are no edges within a window, then its color can be decided by a simple ordering in the z direction. This is the case with windows 11, 22, 24, 42, 44, and 33 in Figure 17.5. (They are part of the background.) If there are edges, then the window is subdivided by descending the quad tree. Figure 17.5 shows the subdivisions for two more levels after the initial partition. Homogeneous windows now include 1413, 1431, etc. Eventually, the partition proceeds down to the single pixel level. Pixel contour edges can be given a value (brightness or color) depending on that of their neighbors. Clearly, the method greatly resembles a segmentation process, using "no edge present in region" as a uniformity predicate. (Historically, things came the other way around. See Bibliographical Notes.) Edges that are not visible will disappear automatically because regions on either side of them will have the same color, that of the obscuring surface.

The main effort in this algorithm occurs in deciding on whether a face intersects a window. There are three possibilities: (a) the face surrounds the window, (b) it intersects or lies within the window, or (c) it is completely disjoint from the window (Figure 17.6). The decision can

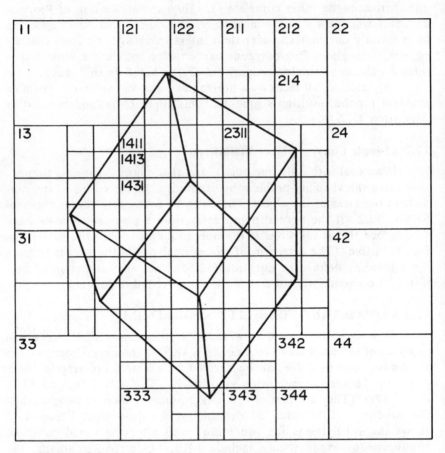

Figure 17.5 Use of a quad tree hidden line algorithm. The projections of the edges of the object are shown in heavy lines and the thin lines delimit the squares corresponding to the first three levels of the quad tree.

be made by solving the clipping problem for the face F and the window W by using Algorithm 15.2 for all sides of the face. The process may be simplified because the algorithm does not need to know the actual intersection of the polygons, only whether they intersect or not (see Problem 17.3). Let us call $LOC(W,F)$ a procedure that implements such a method and returns the following values: two for case (a) when face F surrounds the window W, as illustrated in Figure 17.6a; one for either of two configurations of case (b) when the face F is either inside W or intersects W (Figure 17.6b); and zero for case (c) when F and W are disjoint (Figure 17.6c).

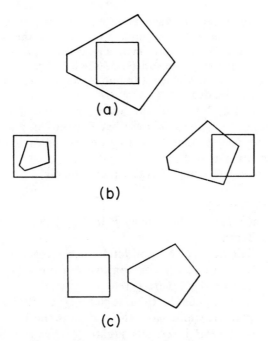

Figure 17.6 Possible relations between a face and a window. The values of K returned by procedure LOC are two for (a), one for both of the cases shown in (b), and zero for (c).

The algorithm starts with a partition of the display area into windows corresponding to the leaves of a quad tree. It maintains two lists for each window: L contains all faces in the display that may intersect the node; and M contains those faces that surround the node. In the beginning M is empty, and L has all the faces; but at the end L is empty and M contains those faces that surround the node. For each window the algorithm calls procedure LOC for all faces in L (step 4 in Algorithm 17.1). Initially the number of such faces will be very large but most of them will be eliminated because they are outside the window. This elimination is done in step 5. If LOC returns the value zero for all the faces for a given window this means that the window has the color of the background, and it will not be examined again (flag F is left equal to zero). When the returned value is two, the face is transferred from L to M (step 7). If zero or two are the only values returned for a window, this window may also be set aside. It is surrounded completely by one or more faces and its color will be that of the face nearest to the observer. This can be found by searching the

Algorithm 17.1 Quad Tree Hidden Line Algorithm

Notation: Q is a square corresponding to a leaf of the quad tree. For each such square the algorithm maintains two lists, L and M. L is the list of all faces that may intersect Q, M the list of faces that were found to surround Q. The flag F is set to one for all squares where the visibility has not been decided yet.

0.   Select a starting level of the quad tree and for each square corresponding to a node create a list L containing all faces of the solids in the display. List M will be empty for each square. Initialize the flag array F to 1.

1.   **For** each square Q where $F(Q)$ equals one **do**:
     Begin.

2.   Set $F(Q)$ to zero.

3.   **For** each face of the display P in $L(Q)$ **do**:
          Begin.

4.   Call $LOC(Q,P)$ and let K be the returned value.

5.   If K equals 0, **then** remove P from $L(Q)$ {face P lies outside the square Q}.

6.   If K equals 1, **then** replace Q by its children in the quad tree and have them inherit the lists L and M of Q {face P intersects square Q}. Set F to one for each one of the children and **break** from the loop.

7.   If K equals 2, **then** place P in $M(Q)$ and remove it from $L(Q)$. {face P surrounds square Q}.
               End.
          End.

8.   **For** each square Q **do**:
     Begin.

9.   If M is empty **then** display the color of the background.

10.   **Else** search the contents of M for the face nearest to the observer and display its color.
          End.

11. **End of Algorithm.**

contents of M in step 8. If the returned value is one for some face, then we must subdivide the window (step 6.) Clearly, any faces that were disjoint from the original window will also be disjoint from its children in the quad tree. Also, faces surrounding the window will also surround its children. Since a subdivision occurs the first time that LOC returns the value 1, we know that any changes in the lists L and M were due to disjoint or containing faces. Therefore the lists may be inherited by the children of the window.† The face that causes the return of 1 must remain in L for all the children.

See Section 17.5 for some possible modifications of the initialization step. It is also possible to speed up the operation by modifying step 4 so that a face that intersects a square is compared to the elements of M. If it is behind one of them, it is ignored.

17.4 A RASTER LINE SCAN VISIBILITY ALGORITHM

A raster line scan algorithm solves the visibility problem while generating the display line by line. If all the objects are planar regions and if there are no overlaps among them, the algorithm reduces to the edge filling of Algorithm 8.1. (Section 8.2.) In that case the edges of the contours to be filled were sorted in the y direction.* Here we consider the intersections of the objects with planes whose equation is $y = $ constant. For polyhedral objects such intersections will be polygons in the x-z plane and the line segments to be filled are projections of these polygons on the x-axis.

Figure 17.7a shows a cube (projected on the x-y plane) and a $y = $ constant plane (projected as a line) that intersects the cube edges ab at B, ae at C, and ad at D. Figure 17.7b is a projection of the intersection on the x-z plane, also showing the projection of the vertices on the screen along the line $A'E'$. These are the points B', C', and D'. For that example the visibility problem reduces to deciding whether the filling algorithm will fill the interval $B'D'$ with the color of the face $abcd$, or, instead, will fill intervals $B'C'$ and $C'D'$ with the color of faces $abfe$ and $aehd$ respectively.

Algorithm 17.2 implements these ideas. The main part consists of steps 3 to 6 and the brevity of the listing is because some of the steps are expressed in terms of operations described in detail in other parts of the text. If the scene to be displayed varies with time, then one must find for each y the intersections of all faces with planes $y = $ constant. This is done in step 4. It requires the application of a clipping algorithm such as Algorithm 15.1 (or Algorithm 15.3 if the faces are not convex). The polygon is the projection of the face on the x-y plane and the line is the intersection of a $y = $ constant plane with the projection plane. The result will be a set of line segments on the x-y plane.

---

† We should be careful in implementations of the algorithm to have the lists copied rather than shared, because the lists may be modified later in different ways for each one of the children of the node.

* We assume that z is the coordinate perpendicular to the screen and y the coordinate perpendicular to the direction of the scan on the screen.

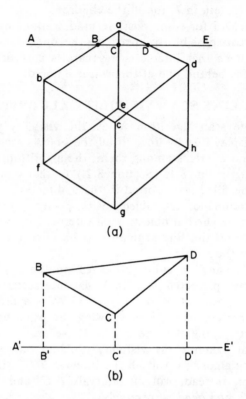

(a)

(b)

Figure 17.7 Operation of the scan line visibility algorithm. (a) Projection of a cube to be displayed and a $y =$ constant plane on the x-y plane. (b) Projection of the intersection on the x-z plane and along a scan line.

On the other hand, if the same scene is to be displayed repeatedly, then we may improve the efficiency of the algorithm by providing the description of objects in terms of polygons that are their intersections with $y =$ constant planes. Furthermore, such intersections may be sorted according to the value of y. (This is similar to storing contours sorted according to the y value in Algorithm 8.1.) Then step 4 will simply traverse the list of such polygons.

After step 4 we must consider which segments shadow others, as discussed in Section 14.4.4. One could choose to apply that approach

Algorithm 17.2 Scan Line Hidden Surface Algorithm

Notation: Array *COLOR* is a buffer where the color of a pixel to be displayed is stored. Array *DEPTH* contains the value of z for the point nearest to the observer at each x of the scan line. P is an intersection of a face with the scan line R, a line segment. x_p and z_p are the coordinates of the points p of P.

1. **For** each scan line R of the screen **do**:
      Begin.
2.   Initialize the array *COLOR* to the background color and the array *DEPTH* to the largest possible z.
3.   **For** each face F of the objects of the scene **do**:
               Begin.
4.   **If** F intersects the horizontal plane with equation $y = R$, **then** find the intersection P and **do**:
                    Begin.
5.   **For** each point p of the intersection P **do**:
                         Begin.
6.   **If** z_p is less than $D[x_p]$, **then** set $C[x_p]$ equal to the color of P and set $D[x_p]$ equal to z_p.
                         End.
                    End.
               End.
7.   Display *COLOR*.
      End.
8. **End of Algorithm.**

directly and come up with a list of intervals that are visible. Algorithm 17.2 follows a different path. It maintains two arrays *COLOR* and *DEPTH* whose entries correspond to the pixels along the scan line. *COLOR* contains the color of a particular pixel and *DEPTH* the z coordinate of the segment closest to the observer. For each scan line *COLOR* is initialized to the background color and *DEPTH* to the largest possible value of z. When the algorithm examines a segment on the x-z plane (e.g., *BC* in Figure 17.7) it compares the z values of its points with the value in *DEPTH* for the same x. If a point has a value of z smaller than that in *DEPTH*, then the value in *DEPTH* is updated and the color of the point goes into the respective point of *COLOR*. Clearly, after all the segments have been examined, *COLOR* contains a correct copy of the scene and can be displayed.

17.5 COHERENCE

Algorithm 17.1 and Algorithm 17.2 are inefficient because they do not make any assumptions about the size or the relative positions of faces. They are applicable to a scene containing a number of polygonal faces at random positions. This is rarely the case in practice where there exist many relations among the various parts of the image. Such inter-dependencies are referred to as *coherence*. We shall discuss briefly how the algorithms can be improved, while listing the various types of coherence used in graphics. Coherence can be specified in a number of ways and may be expressed in terms of either the object space or the image space. The following is a list of possibilities:

Edge coherence: The visibility of an edge changes only when it crosses another edge. One can take advantage of this property by creating a list of edge segments without intersections. Then we need to check only one point of each segment. Finding the intersection involves a certain amount of work so that one can take advantage of the property only for repeated displays of the same scene.

Face coherence: Because of the small size of polyhedral faces as compared to the total image, it is often true that if one part of the face is visible, the whole face is visible.

Object coherence: The visibility of an object can often be decided by examining a circumscribing solid, which may be of a simple form: a sphere or a polyhedron with faces parallel to the coordinate planes. This is an extension of the idea used for finding the intersection of the polygons in Section 15.6 and may be applied in a number of ways. For example, step 4 of Algorithm 17.2 may be simplified by maintaining the range of y values (maximum and minimum) for each object in a separate list. Or we may use object coherence in Algorithm 17.1 to reduce the initial size of the list L. Finally, it can make the detection of the surface shadow relations easier, as discussed in Section 17.2.2.

Scanline coherence: Segments that are visible in one line are also likely to be visible in the next line. If we have some estimate of the minimum object size then we may choose a number K and modify Algorithm 17.2 as follows. After we examine and display a scan line l_i, we skip $K-1$ lines and examine the next line, l_{i+K}. If the same segments are visible on both lines, let F be the set of faces where they belong. Then for the skipped lines we calculate the array C using only the faces in F and display the K lines together. (We may avoid the solution of the visibility problem for the intermediate lines altogether by interpolating the partitions between those of l_i and l_{i+K}.) If the segments visible in l_{i+K} are different from those visible in l_i, then we may backtrack to an intermediate line, say $l_{i+K/2}$, and repeat the same analysis. The process may be organized in a manner similar to the algorithm for fitting polygons discussed in Section 12.5. This approach will give correct results if no object is small enough to be contained entirely in K scan lines.

Frame coherence: The image does not change much from frame to frame. To use this type of coherence effectively one must keep a list of moving and background objects. Then the display algorithm need reexamine only the area near the moving objects from frame to frame. Recall also the discussion of Section 1.6 about the treatment of moving objects.

Geometric coherence: The number of possible visible/invisible configurations on any vertex is limited.

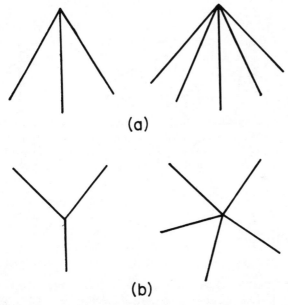

Figure 17.8   (a) If the edges shown belong to a convex object, then the two extreme ones must be visible. (b) For a convex object all edges surrounding a vertex have the same visibility.

The last case is one that has received little attention in graphics but has been widely discussed in pictorial pattern recognition (scene analysis). It leads to very simple rules if we know that all the solids are convex. In particular, if the maximum angle between convergent edges is under 180° (Figure 17.8a), then the two extreme edges are visible and the visibility of the other edges depends on their relative location to the plane defined by the first two. If the angle exceeds 180°, then all the edges have the same visibility (Figure 17.8b). The best way to use geometric coherence is to solve the visibility problem for each object first and label its edges or faces accordingly. When the display is generated, one need be concerned only with the visible faces of each object and this reduces the number of items to be sorted. If the vertices or edges of the contour of the projection (*ABCGHE* in Figure 17.9) are given a special label and the object is convex, then it is easy to establish object or frame coherence. For the given example suppose that we determined that *D* is visible in the first frame. As long as *D* stays within the polygon *ABCGHE* there will be no change in the visibility of faces. See the Bibliographical Notes for some of the more recent approaches to the problem.

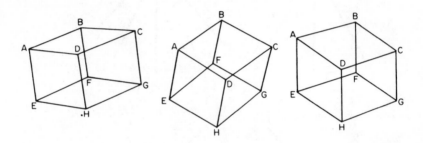

Figure 17.9 Establishment of object frame coherence. Faces *ABCD*, *ADHE*, and *DHGC* have the same visibility in all three frames.

We should point out that many simple techniques for solving visibility problems fail in nontrivial situations. Figure 17.10a shows that the extrema in the *z* direction are not sufficient. If *P* is a point of the intersection of the projections of the two segments, then visibility may be decided by comparing only the points P_A and P_B that project into *P*. This technique is also valid when both faces are convex planar regions. If the surfaces are planar regions, but not convex, then more detailed examination is needed to consider cases of the type shown in Figure 17.10b. Calculations for nonplanar surfaces are still more extensive than calculations for planes. Subdivision of surface patches into smaller patches can simplify the problem.

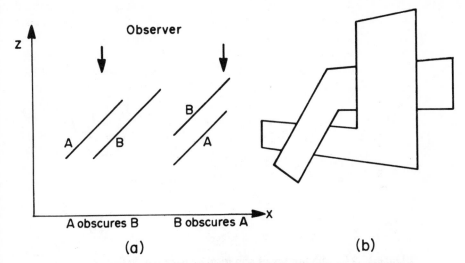

Figure 17.10 (a) Example where the extrema in the *z* direction are not enough to determine visibility. On the other hand visibility can be determined by comparing the points P_A and P_B. (b) Example of two plane surfaces that are mutually obscuring.

17.6 NONLINEAR OBJECT DESCRIPTIONS

Algorithm 17.2 is quite general and does not depend at all on the form of the surfaces used for the faces, as long as one ignores the details of the computation. The algorithm requires that the following operations be performed. (a) Find whether a plane y = constant intersects a face. (b) If the plane intersects the face, then find the intersection. (c) Search for the nearest curve in the *z* direction. These operations are very simple when the faces are plane convex polygons. Indeed, for (a) we need only check the extreme values of y for the boundary of the face. Operations (b) and (c) deal only with line segments. If the display is to be shaded one also needs the normal to the surface at each segment (see Section 13.9). For a plane polygon the normal is fixed for all points. If we use nonlinear patches we lose these simplifications. In order to find whether a patch intersects a plane we must consider not only the boundary of the patch but also the *silhouette* of its projection because of the possibility of a bulge. Figure 17.11 shows two such silhouettes for a spherical patch. Since the normal to the surface is not fixed any more, all the interior points must be examined.

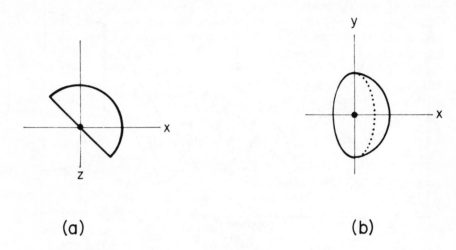

(a)   (b)

Figure 17.11 Silhouettes of spherical surface patches

Let $S(u,v)$ be the parametric equation of the surface and assume that the curves $S(u,0)$, $S(u,1)$, $S(0,v)$, and $S(1,v)$ bound the patch. Such a representation is possible for the Coons surfaces (Section 13.6), Bezier surfaces (Section 13.7.1), or B-spline surfaces (Section 13.7.2). Recall that $S(u,0)$ is a given curve for Coons surfaces, as shown in Equation (13.18′), and a Bezier polynomial (see Equation 13.31) or a B-spline (see Equation 13.33) for the other two cases. The same is true for the other bounding curves. Let $X(u,v)$, $Y(u,v)$, and $Z(u,v)$ be the coordinates of the point $S(u,v)$. In order to find the intersection with a particular plane $y = c$ we must solve the equation

$$Y(u,v) = c \qquad\qquad (17.4)$$

In general such an equation imposes a dependence between u and v and if $v(u)$ is an expression of v in terms of u, then $S(u,v(u))$ is a curve on the plane $y = c$. Such a general approach is impractical and instead one may try to find a numerical solution of each of the following four equations

$$Y(u,0) = c \qquad\qquad (17.5a)$$

$$Y(u,1) = c \qquad\qquad (17.5b)$$

$$Y(0,v) = c \qquad\qquad (17.5c)$$

$$Y(1,v) = c \qquad\qquad (17.5d)$$

The results will specify the four points where the boundaries of the patch intersect the plane $y = c$. If there are no solutions to these equations, this does not mean that the plane does not intersect the patch because it may do so in the interior. The silhouette of the surface that is projected on a plane perpendicular to the z-axis consists of those points where the plane tangent to the surface is parallel to the z-axis. Therefore the normal to the surface must have no component parallel to that axis. According to Equation (13.5c), such points must satisfy the equation

$$X_u Y_v - Y_u X_v = 0 \qquad (17.6)$$

where the subscripts denote partial derivatives. In addition, the points must satisfy Equation (17.4). If we want to find the range of y values occupied by the patch we must find the extrema in the y direction. These are either boundary points or places where the variation of $S(u,v)$ in the y direction is zero, namely

$$\frac{\partial Y}{\partial u}(u,v) = 0 , \quad \frac{\partial Y}{\partial v}(u,v) = 0 \qquad (17.7)$$

For shading we must find the exact coordinates for a particular x, i.e., we must solve a system consisting of Equation (17.6) and

$$X(u,v) = x \qquad (17.8)$$

All these equations are nonlinear and are typically solved by numerical techniques that proceed by guessing a solution and then correcting it by iterations.† In such a case scanline coherence becomes very important because the solutions from one line may be used as guesses for the solutions in the next line. Analytical solutions are possible only in very simple cases. We present one of them as an example to illustrate the relevant concepts, although not the methods of solution.

Example 17.1: We consider the case of a spherical sector given by the following equations

$$X(u,v) = \cos u \cos v , \ Y(u,v) = \sin v , \ Z(u,v) = \sin u \cos v , \qquad (17.9a)$$

and

$$x + z \geq 0 . \qquad (17.9b)$$

In nonparametric form Equation (17.9a) is equivalent to

$$x^2 + y^2 + z^2 = 1 . \qquad (17.9a')$$

---

† This approach has been proposed by Blinn [13.BL], who has used Newton's method for finding the solution. See [17.LA] for a summary.

The projection on the x-z plane has the form shown in Figure 17.10a and consists of points satisfying Equation (17.9b) as well as the inequality

$$x^2 + z^2 \le 1 .\tag{17.10}$$

Finding the projection on the x-y plane is more difficult. In this case the edge of the patch is not described by the values of u and v given above but is defined as the intersection of the sphere and the plane

$$x + z = 0 .\tag{17.10'}$$

Eliminating z between this equation and Equation (17.9a') we find the projection of the edge to be the ellipse

$$2x^2 + y^2 = 1 .\tag{17.11}$$

If we work in the parametric form, we observe that

$$x + z = \sqrt{2}\sin(u + \frac{\pi}{4})\cos v .$$

This will be zero if either $v = \dfrac{\pi}{2}$ or if $u = -\dfrac{\pi}{4}$. The first value yields

$$x = z = 0 \quad \text{and} \quad y = 1$$

and the second

$$x = \frac{1}{\sqrt{2}}\cos v , \ z = -\frac{1}{\sqrt{2}}\cos v , \ y = \sin v$$

which is the parametric equation of an ellipse in three dimensions. The projection on the x-y plane is found by ignoring the value of z. The reader can verify that this is indeed the same as Equation (17.11). For any fixed value of y we find a pair of values of x of the form

$$\pm\sqrt{\frac{1 - y^2}{2}}$$

However, only one of them is a delimiter of the projection. In order to examine the silhouette we compute the expression of Equation (17.7) which yields the value $-\sin u \cos^2 v$. This becomes zero for either $u = 0$ or $v = \pi/2$. We can also find from the nonparametric form that $z = 0$. The silhouette is then the circle

$$x^2 + y^2 = 1$$

and the complete projection consists of one elliptical and one circular arc, as shown in Figure 17.10b. □

An alternative to the solution of the nonlinear equations is to subdivide patches until they become small enough to be approximated by polygons. This approach is based on Theorem 10.1, which states that the domain of a Bezier polynomial can be divided in two, and each subset of the curve is again a Bezier polynomial. Similar results can be found for other curves.

17.7 MAKING A NATURAL LOOKING DISPLAY

Texture, randomization, and multiple light reflections have all been used to give displays the appearance of a natural scene. Another set of efforts, directed toward the same goal, has dealt with the elimination of the "staircase" or "jagged" appearance of the piecewise constant reconstructions (see Section 2.4). We shall briefly review the techniques that have been used to produce the impression of texture.

As we discussed in Section 3.3, texture corresponds to the second order statistics of the brightness distribution over an image. In order to produce such an impression in a synthesized image we must assign the color or brightness of a pixel on the basis of the color or brightness of its neighbors. There are two ways of doing so. In one we assume that the geometry of the surface remains fixed, given by $S(u,v)$, but the color changes according to some function $C(u,v)$. The values of $C(u,v)$ could be given by a formula or in tabular form, but one could also generate them through a random process. A more realistic approach is to allow variations in the surface, such as wrinkles and bumps, and produce the effect of texture by changes in the reflected light. One way to simulate such surface roughness is to perturb the surface along the direction of its normal by a given (scalar) function $P(u,v)$. If X^p, Y^p, Z^p denote the perturbed values we have

$$X^p(u,v) = X(u,v) + P(u,v)\frac{F_x}{||F||} \qquad (17.12a)$$

$$Y^p(u,v) = Y(u,v) + P(u,v)\frac{F_y}{||F||} \qquad (17.12b)$$

$$Z^p(u,v) = Z(u,v) + P(u,v)\frac{F_z}{||F||} \qquad (17.12c)$$

where (F_x,F_y,F_z) are the components of the normal to the surface given by Equations (13.5) and $||F||$ is its norm. In order to calculate the apparent brightness we must find the values of the normal to the surface under the perturbation. Let X_u^p denote the partial derivative of X^p with respect to u. We shall use similar notation for the other derivatives. Then we find that

$$X_u^p = X_u + P_u\frac{F_x}{||F||} + P\frac{\partial}{\partial u}\left[\frac{F_x}{||F||}\right] \qquad (17.13)$$

We assume now that $P(u,v)$ takes very small values but that it has large derivatives. Then it is possible to neglect the third term of the righthand side of Equation (17.13). We may find similar expressions for Y_u^p, Z_u^p, etc. and thus find the equation for the perturbed normal to be

$$F_x^p = Y_u^p Z_v^p - Z_u^p Y_v^p =$$

$$\left[Y_u + P_u \frac{F_y}{||F||} \right]\left[Z_v + P_v \frac{F_z}{||F||} \right] -$$

$$\left[Z_u + P_u \frac{F_z}{||F||} \right]\left[Y_v + P_v \frac{F_y}{||F||} \right] \qquad (17.14)$$

Carrying out the multiplications and using Equation (13.5a) we find after some cancellations

$$F_x^p = F_x + (P_u Z_v - Z_u P_v)\frac{F_y}{||F||} + (Y_u P_v - P_u Y_v)\frac{F_z}{||F||} \qquad (17.15)$$

If we repeat the calculations for the other two components of the normal we find similar expressions and conclude that the perturbed normal can be found from the unperturbed normal through multiplication with a 3×3 symmetric matrix. The matrix has ones on its main diagonal and the form of its other elements can be derived from Equation (17.15).

The function $P(u,v)$ may be given either in tabular form or explicitly, or it may chosen to be a random variable. See [13.BL] for more on this topic.

If the perturbation to the surface or its color at a point is to be independent from that at other points, then the problem is very simple. All one has to do is call a (pseudo) random number generator at each point. Such independent perturbations are not a realistic model of physical textured surfaces. The introduction of correlation from point to point is not too complicated if one is willing to form a large table of the perturbing function $P(u,v)$. It cannot be done "on the fly", though, because points that are seen close during the creation of the display may be very far apart on surface. See the Bibliographical Notes for more on this subject and on related techniques.

17.8 BIBLIOGRAPHICAL NOTES

An early survey of visibility algorithms can be found in [17.SSS]. The quad tree algorithm listed here is based on one developed by War-nock (see [1.NS] or [17.SSS] for a complete reference), and it is the first published use of this data structure in image processing. The scan line algorithm is based on one by Watkins (see [1.NS] or [17.SSS]). A collection of more recent methods can be found in [13.LA], which includes the solution of visibility problems with nonlinear surface patches. [17.WH] presents a combination of visibility and shading problems, including multiple reflections. [13.BL] gives a comprehensive analysis of a raster scan algorithm when the objects are described through surface patches. It also includes an extensive discussion of methods for producing a textured appearance and Sections 17.6 and 17.7 are based to a large extent on this work. (A summary of part of this thesis can be found in [13.LA].) [17.FF] describes a randomization technique that has been used successfully to produce images of terrain.

[17.KC] describes a visibility algorithm in the object space when the objects are spheres or cylinders. It uses a function similar to *LOC* of Section 17.3 but instead of comparing faces and windows compares faces with each other. [17.MA] is an extension of this work with the introduction of shading (including highlights). It avoids some of the difficulties of nonlinear patches by taking advantage of the simple geometry of the sphere. The techniques described in these papers have been used to produce images of molecular models. Another use of spheres in graphics is described in [17.BOT]. A model of a physical object is produced not through surface patches, but as the envelope of intersecting spheres. The authors present a model of the human body made out of about 300 spheres and claim that comparable descriptions would require as many as 3000 surface patches. [17.ON] describes related work and [17.KN] presents further elaborations of the technique.

Recent studies of the visibility problem have placed emphasis on the proper order of face and window comparison. [17.CL] is a theoretical discussion of the object space approach. [17.FR] presents an algorithm of the same type as Algorithm 17.1 but with a careful strategy for examining window and face overlaps. The result is linear rather than quadratic time complexity. [17.HZ] deals with a combination of frame and object coherence.

[17.HA] is collection of papers on perception that people designing displays may find useful.

17.9 RELEVANT LITERATURE

[17.BOT] Badler, N. I.; O'Rourke, J.; and Toltzis, H. "A Spherical Representation of a Human Body for Visualizing Movement," *IEEE Proceedings,* **67** (October 1979), pp. 1397-1403.

[17.CL] Clark, J. H. "Hierarchical Geometric Models for Visible Surface Algorithms," *CACM,* **19** (1976), pp. 547-554.

[17.FF] Fournier, A.; Fussel, D.; and Carpenter, L. "Computer Rendering of Stochastic Models," *CACM,* **25** (1982), pp. 371-384.

[17.FR]   Franklin, W. R. "A Linear Exact Hidden Surface Algorithm," *SIG-GRAPH'80*, Seattle, Wash., July 1980, pp. 117-123.

[17.HA]   Hagen, M. (ed.) *The Perception of Pictures*, New York: Academic Press, 1980.

[17.HZ]   Hubschman, H. and Zucker, S. W. "Frame-to-Frame Coherence and the Hidden Surface Computation: Constraints for a Convex World," *SIGGRAPH'81*, Dallas, Texas, August 1981, pp. 45-54.

[17.JH]   desJardins, M. and Hasler, A. F. "Stereoscopic Displays of Atmospheric Model Data" *SIGGRAPH'80*, Seattle, Wash., July 1980, pp. 134-146.

[17.KC]   Knowlton, K. and Cherry, L. "Atoms — A Three-D Opaque Molecular System for Color Pictures of Space-Filling or Ball-and-Stick Models," *Computers & Chemistry*, **1** (1977), pp. 161-166.

[17.KN]   Knowlton, K. "Computer-Aided Definition, Manipulation and Description of Objects Composed of Spheres," *ACM Computer Graphics*, **15** (1981), pp. 48-71.

[17.MA]   Max, N. L. "ATOMLLL - ATOMS with Shading and Highlights" *SIGGRAPH'79*, Chicago, August 1979, pp. 165-173.

[17.ON]   O'Rourke, J. and Badler, N. "Decomposition of Three-Dimensional Objects into Spheres," *IEEE Trans. on Pattern Analysis and Machine Intelligence*, **PAMI-1** (1979), pp. 295-305.

[17.SSS] Sutherland, I. E.; Sproull, R. F.; and Schumacker, R. A. "A Characterization of Ten Hidden-Surface Algorithms," *ACM Computing Surveys*, **6** (March 1974), pp. 1-56.

[17.WH]   Whitted, T. "An Improved Illumination Model for Shaded Display" *CACM*, **23** (1980), pp. 343-349.

17.10 PROBLEMS

17.1. Investigate the form of the solid that is the image of the sphere under the transformation of Equation (16.20).

17.2. Write a program implementing Algorithm 17.1. In order to simplify the solution of the clipping problem assume that all the faces are regular rectangles parallel to the x-y plane.

17.3. Implement the procedure $LOC(W,F)$ described in Section 17.3. Note that you may omit those parts of the clipping algorithms that calculate the intersection of lines and also shorten the checks by returning to the calling procedure as soon as a pair of intersecting sides is found. On the other hand, some care is required to distinguish the cases when F surrounds W, W surrounds F, and F and W are mutually disjoint.

17.4. Implement Algorithm 17.2 under the conditions stated in

Problem 17.2.

17.5. Let's make a movie! For the simplest version we shall use two objects, a cube and a regular tetrahedron. The latter should have sides that are about half as long as the sides of the cube. The cube should be positioned with one of its diagonals vertical and should be rotating around it. (Careful choice of a coordinate system will greatly simplify the formulas for the rotation transformation.) The tetrahedron should also rotate about the same axis at a distance of about three times the side of the cube. Its angular velocity should be about one tenth that of the cube. Write a program to compute a sequence of views of the scene. The whole arrangement should resemble that of a planet going around the sun. The project can be expanded by adding more objects as well as by increasing the number of the faces of the polyhedra.

Hints: This is an example where it makes sense to use object coherence for solving the visibility problem.† Most of the pixels will belong to the background and most of the time their projections will be disjoint.

17.5. Repeat the previous problem by replacing the polyhedra with spheres. Since this simplifies the solution of the visibility problem, introduce the following complications. Add more planets whose planes of rotation are nearly normal to the display plane, assume that the stationary object is a source of light, and appropriately shade the surfaces of the other objects.

---

† When this assignment was given to students at Princeton about half of them used object coherence and the others implemented a general algorithm in the image space. They had about three weeks to complete the project.

AUTHOR INDEX

Index refers only to full citations. Entries with the prefix P- refer to plates.

SUBJECT INDEX

---

bold numbers refer to pages with the definition of the term. *italic* numbers refer to pages where the term is used in a problem. *ff* following a number denotes reference to footnote.

ALGORITHM INDEX